Lecture Notes in Computer Science 13223

More information about this series at https://link.springer.com/bookseries/558

Eric Medvet · Gisele Pappa · Bing Xue (Eds.)

Genetic Programming

25th European Conference, EuroGP 2022
Held as Part of EvoStar 2022
Madrid, Spain, April 20–22, 2022
Proceedings

Editors
Eric Medvet ⓘ
University of Trieste
Trieste, Italy

Gisele Pappa ⓘ
Universidade Federal de Minas Gerais
Belo Horizonte, Minas Gerais, Brazil

Bing Xue ⓘ
Victoria University of Wellington
Wellington, New Zealand

ISSN 0302-9743   ISSN 1611-3349 (electronic)
Lecture Notes in Computer Science
ISBN 978-3-031-02055-1   ISBN 978-3-031-02056-8 (eBook)
https://doi.org/10.1007/978-3-031-02056-8

This Springer imprint is published by the registered company Springer Nature Switzerland AG
The registered company address is: Gewerbestrasse 11, 6330 Cham, Switzerland

Preface

The 25th European Conference on Genetic Programming (EuroGP 2022) took place at the Complutense University of Madrid, Madrid, Spain, during April 20–22, 2022. Due to the travel restrictions caused by the COVID-19 pandemic, the conference was held in a hybrid mode to allow both in-person and online attendance.

Genetic programming (GP) is a unique branch of evolutionary computation that has been developed to automatically solve design problems, in particular the computer program design, without requiring the user to know or specify the form or structure of the solution in advance. It uses the principles of Darwinian evolution to approach problems in the synthesis, improvement, and repair of computer programs. The universality of computer programs, and their importance in so many areas of our lives, means that the automation of these tasks is an exceptionally ambitious challenge with far-reaching implications. GP has attracted a significant number of researchers and a vast amount of theoretical and practical contributions are available, as shown by consulting the GP bibliography.[1]

Since the first EuroGP event in Paris in 1998, EuroGP has been the only conference exclusively devoted to the evolutionary design of computer programs and other computational structures. In fact, EuroGP represents the single largest venue at which GP results are published. It plays an important role in the success of the field, by serving as a forum for expressing new ideas, meeting fellow researchers, and initiating collaborations. It attracts scholars from all over the world. In a friendly and welcoming atmosphere authors present the latest advances in the field and GP-based solutions to complex real-world problems.

EuroGP 2022 received 35 submissions from around the world. The papers underwent a rigorous double-blind peer review process, each being reviewed by multiple members of an international Program Committee.

Among the papers presented in this volume, 12 were accepted for full-length oral presentation (34% acceptance rate) and seven as short talks. In 2022, papers submitted to EuroGP could also be assigned to the "Evolutionary Machine Learning Track". Among the 35 submissions, the authors of eight papers indicated their papers fit the track, with two accepted for full-length oral presentation and four as short talks. Authors of both categories of papers also had the opportunity to present their work in poster sessions to promote the exchange of ideas in a carefree manner.

The wide range of topics in this volume reflects the current state of research in the field. The collection of papers covers interesting topics including developing new variants of GP algorithms, synthesizing computer programs with GP, and evolving neural networks using GP, as well as exploring GP-based explainable or interpretable methods and applying GP to address complex real-world problems.

Together with three other co-located evolutionary computation conferences (Evo-COP 2022, EvoMUSART 2022, and EvoApplications 2022), EuroGP 2022 was part of

---

[1] http://liinwww.ira.uka.de/bibliography/Ai/genetic.programming.html.

the Evo* 2022 event. This meeting could not have taken place without the help of many people. The EuroGP Organizing Committee is particularly grateful to the following:

- SPECIES, the Society for the Promotion of Evolutionary Computation in Europe and its Surroundings, which aims to promote evolutionary algorithmic thinking within Europe and wider, and more generally to promote inspiration of parallel algorithms derived from natural processes.
- The high-quality and diverse EuroGP 2022 Program Committee. Each year the members give freely of their time and expertise in order to maintain high standards in EuroGP, providing constructive feedback to help the authors to improve their papers.
- Nuno Lourenço (University of Coimbra, Portugal) for his dedicated work with the submission system.
- João Correia (University of Coimbra, Portugal), Ignacio Hidalgo (Universidad Complutense de Madrid, Spain), and Francisco Chicano (University of Málaga, Spain) for their great work on the Evo* publicity, social media service, and website.
- Sérgio Rebelo (University of Coimbra, Portugal), João Correia (University of Coimbra, Portugal), and Tiago Martins (University of Coimbra, Portugal) for their important graphic design work.
- The local organizing team, in particular Iñaki Hidalgo (Universidad Complutense Madrid, Spain) for his proactivity in getting us a new venue for the conference. We also thank Federico Divina (Universidad Pablo de Olavide, Spain) as the original local organizing chair for Seville, Spain, but unfortunately the conference had to be moved due to the COVID-19 pandemic.
- Our invited speakers, Gabriela Ochoa and Pedro Larrañaga, who gave inspiring and enlightening keynote talks.
- Finally, we express our continued appreciation to Anna I. Esparcia-Alcázar (Universitat Politècnica de València, Spain), from SPECIES, whose considerable efforts in managing and coordinating Evo* helped towards building a unique, vibrant, and friendly atmosphere.

April 2022

Eric Medvet
Gisele Pappa
Bing Xue

Organization

Program Co-chairs

Eric Medvet   University Degli Studi di Trieste, Italy
Gisele Pappa   Universidade Federal de Minas Gerais, Brazil

Publication Chair

Bing Xue   Victoria University of Wellington, New Zealand

Local Chair

Iñaki Hidalgo   Universidad Complutense Madrid, Spain

Publicity Chair

João Correia   Victoria University of Wellington, New Zealand

Conference Administration

Anna I. Esparcia-Alcazar   Evostar Coordinator

Program Committee

Ignacio Arnaldo   Massachusetts Institute of Technology, USA
R. Muhammad Atif Azad   Birmingham City University, UK
Wolfgang Banzhaf   Michigan State University, USA
Heder Bernardino   Federal University of Juiz de Fora, Brazil
Anthony Brabazon   University College Dublin, Ireland
Stefano Cagnoni   University of Parma, Italy
Mauro Castelli   Universidade Nova de Lisboa, Portugal
Ernesto Costa   University of Coimbra, Portugal
Antonio Della Cioppa   University of Salerno, Italy
Francisco Fernandez de Vega   Universidad de Extremadura, Spain
James Foster   University of Idaho, USA
Jin-Kao Hao   University of Angers, France
Erik Hemberg   Massachusetts Institute of Technology, USA
Malcolm Heywood   Dalhousie University, Canada
Ting Hu   Memorial University, Canada

Contents

Short Presentations

Long Presentations

Evolving Adaptive Neural Network Optimizers for Image Classification

Pedro Carvalho[✉], Nuno Lourenço, and Penousal Machado

CISUC, Department of Informatics Engineering, University of Coimbra,
Polo II - Pinhal de Marrocos, 3030 Coimbra, Portugal
{pfcarvalho,naml,penousal}@dei.uc.pt

Abstract. The evolution of hardware has enabled Artificial Neural Networks to become a staple solution to many modern Artificial Intelligence problems such as natural language processing and computer vision. The neural network's effectiveness is highly dependent on the optimizer used during training, which motivated significant research into the design of neural network optimizers. Current research focuses on creating optimizers that perform well across different topologies and network types. While there is evidence that it is desirable to fine-tune optimizer parameters for specific networks, the benefits of designing optimizers specialized for single networks remain mostly unexplored.

In this paper, we propose an evolutionary framework called Adaptive AutoLR (ALR) to evolve adaptive optimizers for specific neural networks in an image classification task. The evolved optimizers are then compared with state-of-the-art, human-made optimizers on two popular image classification problems. The results show that some evolved optimizers perform competitively in both tasks, even achieving the best average test accuracy in one dataset. An analysis of the best evolved optimizer also reveals that it functions differently from human-made approaches. The results suggest ALR can evolve novel, high-quality optimizers motivating further research and applications of the framework.

Keywords: Neuroevolution · Adaptive Optimizers · Structured Grammatical Evolution

1 Introduction

Artificial Neural Networks (ANN) are an essential part of modern Artificial Intelligence (AI) and Machine Learning (ML). These systems are popular as solutions in a variety of different tasks such as computer vision [5,11], and natural language processing [8,12].

ANN's design is loosely inspired by the workings of the biological brain. Like their biological counterpart, ANNs are comprised of several inter-connected units called neurons. Each connection has an associated value called *weight* which determines the strength of the connections between neurons. When using an ANN for a specific task, a suitable set of weights is necessary to solve the problem.

E. Medvet et al. (Eds.): EuroGP 2022, LNCS 13223, pp. 3–18, 2022.
https://doi.org/10.1007/978-3-031-02056-8_1

The process through which these weight are found is called *training*. Proper training is vital for ANN performance, motivating extensive research into how ANNs should be trained [1, 6, 9, 10, 14, 20]. As a result, several methodologies and hyper-parameters were developed to tune the training process.

One vital hyper-parameter is the *Learning Rate* (LR), a numeric value that scales changes made to the weights during training. The choice of LR value has a profound impact on the effectiveness of training, motivating the researchers to create various solutions (known as optimizers) to optimize the size of the changes made during training. While optimizers vary in their complexity and effectiveness [1, 6, 10, 14], one aspect most optimizers share is their generality. Since training is ubiquitous across most applications of ANNs, optimizers are designed to be effective on a wide variety of problems and ANN architectures. This general approach has led to the creation of optimizers that are effective and easy to apply, but it also raises the question: Can optimizers be pushed further if we specialize them for specific problems?

To answer this question, we must first establish a way to specialize optimizers for a specific problem. It is challenging for humans to understand all the dimensions required for manual specialization because ANNs comprise many inter-dependent components and parameters. However, it is possible to use a search algorithm to perform this specialization automatically. Evolutionary algorithms (EA) are strong candidates for this task; these heuristic algorithms can navigate complicated problem spaces efficiently through biologically inspired procedures (e.g., crossover, mutation, selection). Using an EA, it is possible to test several different optimizers and combine the best performing ones to achieve progressively better results. The benefits of specialization can then be assessed by comparing the evolved optimizers with standard, human-made optimizers.

This work uses an evolutionary framework to create optimizers for specific ML problems. The resulting evolved optimizers are benchmarked against state-of-the-art hand-made optimizers. Finally, the applicability of evolved optimizers to different problems is also tested. The results suggest that the evolved optimizers can compete with the human-made optimizers developed over decades of research. Additionally, one of the evolved optimizers, ADES, remains competitive even when applied to tasks that were not addressed during evolution, suggesting EAs may be used to create generally applicable optimizers. Finally, ADES does not function like human-made optimizers; hinting that the evolutionary approach can find creative solutions undiscovered by humans.

The structure of this paper is the following: In Sect. 2 we give historical background on the human-made optimizers created over the years. In Sect. 3 we describe how Adaptive AutoLR, the evolutionary framework, is used to evolve ANN optimizers. The components developed for this work are also presented and discussed. In Sect. 4 we present the experiments performed and discuss the results. The evolutionary parameters used are presented as well as the resulting optimizers. In this we section also compare the evolved optimizers with human-made solutions in performance and ability to generalize. In Sect. 5 we review the work presented in this article and summarizes our contributions.

2   Background

In a typical training procedure, after each training epoch, the system compares the ANN's output with the expected output and calculates the error. Based on this error, back-propagation [19] is used to calculate the changes that should be made to each weight (known as the gradient). The gradient, often scaled by the LR, is frequently use to dictate the direction and size of weight changes.

The original LR optimizer, SGD [1], simply sets the new weight (w_t) to be the difference between the old weight (w_{t-1}) and the product of the learning rate (lr) with the gradient (∇l), shown in Eq. 1.

$$w_t \leftarrow w_{t-1} - \text{lr} * \nabla l(w_{t-1}) \tag{1}$$

Traditionally, a single LR value is used for the entirety of the training. In this case, all the tuning must be done before the training starts. The problem with this approach is that one is often forced to rely on experience and trial-and-error to find an adequate static LR. Research also suggests that different LR values may be preferable at different points in training [20], meaning a single, static LR is rarely ideal.

These limitations led to the creation of dynamic LRs which vary the LR value as training progresses. Dynamic approaches are frequently used [7,22] because they are easy to implement and usually outperform static LRs [20]. However, these approaches are limited because they only change the size of changes based on the training epoch. This is shortcoming motivated the development of the more sophisticated adaptive optimizers.

Adaptive optimizers are variations of SGD that use long-term gradient information to adjust the changes made. In adaptive optimizers, the LR is a static value combined with weight-specific auxiliary variables. While it is possible to utilize gradient information to adjust a single LR value, most adaptive optimizers use different rates for each weight. The result is an ANN optimizer that allows each weight to be updated at a different rate. The most straightforward adaptive optimizer is the momentum optimizer [9], shown in Eq. 2. The auxiliary variable is a momentum term (x_t) that increases the size of adjustments made to weights that keep changing in the same direction. Two constants accompany this term: the learning rate (lr) is responsible for directly scaling the gradient, the momentum constant (mom) dictates how strong the effect of the momentum is.

$$\begin{aligned} x_t &\leftarrow mom * x_{t-1} - lr * \nabla l(w_{t-1}) \\ w_t &\leftarrow w_{t-1} + x_t \end{aligned} \tag{2}$$

A variation of the momentum optimizer, known as Nesterov's momentum [14] is presented in Eq. 3. Nesterov's momentum varies from the original because the gradient is calculated for the weight plus the momentum term. As a result, the optimizer can look-ahead and make corrections to the direction suggested by the momentum. The look-ahead is beneficial because the momentum term is slow to change which may hinder the training process.

$$x_t \leftarrow mom * x_{t-1} - lr * \nabla l(w_{t-1} + mom * x_{t-1})$$
$$w_t \leftarrow w_{t-1} + x_t \tag{3}$$

RMSprop [6] is an unpublished optimizer that divides the LR by a moving discounted average of the weights' changes. This optimizer will decrease the LR when the weight changes rapidly and increase it when the weight stagnates. This LR annealing simultaneously helps the weights converge and prevents them from stagnating. In Eq. 4, x_t is the moving average term, and ρ is the exponential decay rate used for this same average. The root moving average is then used in w_t to scale the LR and gradient.

$$x_t \leftarrow \rho x_{t-1} + (1 - \rho)\nabla l(w_{t-1})^2$$
$$w_t \leftarrow w_{t-1} - \frac{lr * \nabla l(w_{t-1})}{\sqrt{x_t} + \epsilon} \tag{4}$$

The final optimizer we will be discussing is Adam [10]. Adam is similar to RMSprop, but it attempts to correct the bias of starting the moving average at 0 using a new term (z_t). Adam also calculates a range where it expects the gradient to remain consistent ($\frac{x_{t-1}}{\sqrt{y_{t-1}}}$). In Eq. 5 x_t and y_t are both moving averages; β_1 and β_2 are exponential decay rates for the averages (similar to ρ in Eq. 4).

$$x_t \leftarrow \beta_1 x_{t-1} + (1 - \beta_1)\nabla l(w_{t-1})$$
$$y_t \leftarrow \beta_2 y_{t-1} + (1 - \beta_2)\nabla l(w_{t-1})^2$$
$$z_t \leftarrow lr * \frac{\sqrt{1 - \beta_2^t}}{(1 - \beta_1^t)}$$
$$w_t \leftarrow w_{t-1} - z_t * \frac{x_t}{\sqrt{y_t} + \epsilon} \tag{5}$$

3   Adaptive AutoLR

AutoLR is an open-source [16] framework developed to evolve ANN optimizers. This framework has previously been used to evolve dynamic LR policies [2]. In this work, we propose **Adaptive AutoLR** (ALR), an implementation of the framework capable of evolving the more complex adaptive ANN optimizers. This framework is used to create optimizers specialized for specific tasks to assess the benefits of optimizer specialization and the potential of evolved optimizers.

For this work, ALR is used to create, evaluate, and improve optimizers during the **evolutionary phase**. A separate **benchmark phase** is performed, where the evolved optimizers are fairly compared with the human-made solutions. In the following sections, we will describe the grammar used to determine the structure of the optimizers and the fitness function utilized to quantify the quality of the evolved solutions.

3.1 Grammar

Adaptive optimizers are comprised of a few functions that calculate a set of auxiliary variables and adjust the weights of the ANN. This definition is expansive, creating a complex problem space that demands many evaluations during evolution. The grammar must account for the problem's difficulty, enabling diversity while promoting a smooth evolutionary process.

A consequence of the adaptive optimizer's broad definition is that the majority of possible solutions cannot train the ANN. It is possible to counteract this issue through a restrictive grammar that limits the types of functions that can be evolved. However, we are interested in promoting novel optimizers as much as possible and will avoid such restrictions as a result. The complete grammar used for ALR cannot be included due to space restrictions, but an abridged version is presented in Fig. 1 (full version is available in [15]).

$$
\begin{aligned}
\text{<start>} ::=\ & \text{x\_func, y\_func, z\_func, weight\_func} = \\
& \text{<x\_expr>, <y\_expr>, <z\_expr>, <weight\_expr>} \\
\text{<x\_expr>} ::=\ & \text{add(x, <x\_update>) | <x\_update>} \\
\text{<x\_update>} ::=\ & \text{<x\_func> | <x\_terminal>} \\
\text{<x\_func>} ::=\ & \text{negative(<x\_expr>)} \\
& \text{| subtract(<x\_expr>, <x\_expr>)} \\
& \text{| multiply(<x\_expr>, <x\_expr>)} \\
& \text{| pow(<x\_expr>, <x\_expr>)} \\
& \text{| square(<x\_expr>)} \\
& \text{| divide\_no\_nan(<x\_expr>, <x\_expr>)} \\
& \text{| add(<x\_expr>, <x\_expr>) | sqrt(<x\_expr>)} \\
\text{<x\_terminal>} ::=\ & \text{<x\_const> | x | grad | grad} \\
\text{<x\_const>} ::=\ & \text{4.53978687e-05 | ... | 9.99954602e-01} \\
& \quad\quad ... \\
\text{<weight\_expr>} ::=\ & \text{<weight\_func> | <weight\_terminal>} \\
\text{<weight\_func>} ::=\ & \text{negative(<weight\_expr>) | ...} \\
\text{<weight\_terminal>} ::=\ & \text{<weight\_const> | x | y | z} \\
\text{<weight\_const>} ::=\ & \text{4.53978687e-05 | ... | 9.99954602e-01}
\end{aligned}
$$

Fig. 1. CFG for the evolution of ANN optimizers.

Individuals in ALR are made up of 4 functions, named: x_func, y_func, z_func and $weight\_func$. Functions x through z work as the auxiliary functions found in human-made adaptive optimizers; these functions have an associated result stored between epochs (e.g., x_t). By default, the previous iteration result is included in the function, as shown in Eq. 6, but this behavior can be unlearned using the grammar provided. These stored values are a staple of adaptive optimizers as they are essential to implement mechanisms such as momentum.

$$
\begin{aligned}
x_t &\leftarrow x_{t-1} - \ldots \\
y_t &\leftarrow y_{t-1} - \ldots \\
z_t &\leftarrow z_{t-1} - \ldots \\
w_t &\leftarrow w_{t-1} - \ldots
\end{aligned}
\tag{6}
$$

When the training algorithm calls the optimizer, the individual utilizes its functions to calculate the new weight values. The auxiliary functions are called first; the role of these functions is to calculate and store relevant information based on the gradient changes. These functions are executed sequentially, starting with x and ending with z. The order is essential because each auxiliary function has access to the result of those that precede it. After all auxiliary functions have been executed, the *weight* function is called with access to all the results. The result of the weight update function, *weight_func*, is then used as the weight for the next epoch.

There are some aspects of the grammar design that must be discussed. It should be noted that several productions in the grammar used are identical, but they are not combined in order to keep the genotype of each function isolated. The operations and constants were chosen for their presence in human-made adaptive optimizers. The grammar also includes some bias to facilitate evolution. The weight function is not allowed to use the gradient; this encourages the use of auxiliary functions. Auxiliary functions' terminals are biased in favor of the gradient, so it is picked more often. Additionally, the *expr* productions are biased to facilitate the removal of the function's previous iteration from the calculations.

3.2   Fitness Function

ALR is usable in any ML application that employs gradient-based training. In this work, we focus on applying ALR to image classification as there is a vast backlog of research on the topic that provides proven models and datasets. Specifically, we chose Fashion-MNIST as it is a good balance between an easy dataset (e.g., regular MNIST) and a harder one (e.g., CIFAR-10). The ANN used in ALR can be found in [18]. This ANN is compatible with the Fashion-MNIST dataset and trains quickly as it has a small number of weights.

The objective of ALR is to create solutions that maximize the accuracy of the ANN's predictions. As a result, the fitness function (shown in Algorithm 1) will utilize the evolved optimizer to train an ANN and use its accuracy after training and fitness.

However, additional measures are implemented to ensure the fitness value accurately measures the solution's actual quality. Specifically, the data used by the fitness function is split into three sets. The **evolutionary training set** is used to train the ANN; this is the only data that interacts with the optimizers directly. The **evolutionary validation set** is used to calculate validation metrics to track training progress. An early stop mechanism also monitors the validation loss, aborting the training when the validation loss stagnates. The early

---

Algorithm 1: Simplified version of the fitness function used to evaluate optimizers in ALR

---

   params: network, optimizer, evolutionary_training_data,
             evolutionary_validation_data, fitness_assignment_data,
             evaluation_number

1 minimum_acceptable_accuracy ← 0.8;
2 fitness ← 1.0;
3 evaluation_count ← 0;
4 **while** *evaluation_count < evaluation_number* **do**
5   trained_network ← train(network, optimizer, evolutionary_training_data, evolutionary_validation_data);
6   evaluation_accuracy ← get_accuracy(trained_network, fitness_assignment_data);
7   **if** *evaluation_accuracy < fitness* **then**
8   fitness ← evaluation_accuracy;
9   **if** *evaluation_accuracy < minimum_acceptable_accuracy* **then**
10   **return** fitness_score;
11   evaluation_count ++;
12 **return** fitness;

---

stop mechanism helps prevent over-fitting and saves computational resources. After training is complete, the ANN is used to classify the third set of data, the **fitness assignment set**. We consider that the accuracy of the ANN in this final dataset is an accurate measure of the optimizer's fitness. We refer to this process of training and calculating the accuracy of the ANN as an **evaluation**. It is worth noting that there are other desirable optimizer features that this fitness function does not account for, such as convergence speed and hyper-parameter sensitivity.

We found that some solutions were inconsistent, producing very different fitness values when repeating the same evaluation. Consequently, we consider that multiple evaluations should be used to calculate the fitness. Specifically, the optimizers are trained and evaluated up to five times. While five evaluations is insufficient to perform any statistical analysis, we found that it was enough to nurture the evolution of stable solution. The evolutionary training data is split among the evaluations, forcing the solutions to train using different data each time. Since each evaluation is computationally expensive and it is desirable to minimize the number of evaluations. As a result, we define a *minimum acceptable accuracy*. If the accuracy achieved in the fitness assignment set is below this threshold, the optimizer is not considered a viable solution, and the rest of the evaluations are canceled. This mechanism significantly reduces the resources used to evaluate low-quality solutions. We consolidate all the results into a single fitness value using the *worst accuracy across all evaluations* as this further incentivizes the system to produce consistently good solutions.

4   Experimental Study

This section documents the experiments performed to validate ALR. In Sect. 4.1 we detail the configuration used for the evolutionary process, going over the parameters used to configure ALR and train the ANN. In Sect. 4.2 we present and analyze the results of evolution. The typical progress of an evolutionary run is discussed, and the most notable evolved optimizers are showcased. In order to properly compare the quality of the evolved optimizers to human-made solutions, additional experiments are performed to benchmark their quality; this procedure is documented in Sect. 4.3. Benchmarks are performed on two different problems. In Sect. 4.4 we present and discuss the performance of the optimizers in the problem used in evolution, Fashion-MNIST. In Sect. 4.5 we conduct the same analysis in a different image classification task, CIFAR-10.

4.1   Evolutionary Runs

ALR has a set of evolutionary parameters that must be configured for experimentation. The parameters used in our experiments are presented in Table 1. The search space posed in this problem is vast; as a result, we found it adequate to use a high number of generations and a small population. This combination of parameters is likely to stagnate the population, so a large tournament size is used to reduce selective pressure.

Fashion-MNIST is the dataset used to evolve the optimizers, and it is comprised of training (refer to as Fashion-MNIST-Training) and test (Fashion-MNIST-Test) data. We will only use Fashion-MNIST-Training (60000 examples) in the evolutionary runs, splitting it into the evolutionary training set, evolutionary validation set, and fitness assignment set with 53000, 3500, and 3500 examples, respectively. The 53000 evolutionary training examples are split evenly among the evaluations (resulting in 10600 training examples per evaluation). The Fashion-MNIST-Test is deliberately excluded from the evolutionary process; it is essential to reserve a set of data that the evolved solutions never interact with to draw fair comparisons with human-made optimizers later. Additionally, the early stop mechanism interrupts training when the validation loss does not improve for 5 consecutive epochs (controlled by the *Patience* parameter). Each evaluation trains the ANN for a maximum of 100 epochs using a batch size of 1000. We empirically found that using these parameters with a human-made optimizer was sufficient to train competent networks.

4.2   Evolutionary Results

Figure 2 shows the averages of the best solution and average population quality across all runs throughout the evolutionary process. The typical behavior of the runs can be described as follows. In an early stage, the population is dominated by individuals that utilize the gradient directly to adjust the weights, without an LR or any type of adaptive components. While these individuals can train ANNs adequately occasionally, they fail to replicate their success across different

Table 1. Experimental parameters.

SGE Parameters	Value
Number of runs	9
Number of generations	1500
Number of individuals	20
Tournament size	5
Crossover rate	0.90
Mutation rate	0.15
Dataset Parameters	**Value**
Dataset	Fashion-MNIST-Training (60000 instances)
Evolutionary Training set	53000 instances, 10600 instances per evaluation
Evolutionary Validation set	3500 instances
Fitness set	3500 instances
Early Stop	**Value**
Patience	5
Metric	Validation Loss
Condition	Stop if Validation Loss does not improve in 5 consecutive epochs
ANN Training Parameters	**Value**
Batch Size	1000
Epochs	100
Metrics	Accuracy

evaluations. Nevertheless, these individuals play a vital role in the evolutionary process as they identify the importance of including the gradient. In most runs, this genetic material is used in more robust optimizers that can consistently train competent ANNs leading to an increase in solution quality.

The best and most robust evolved optimizers employ simple, familiar mechanisms like a static LR or a simple momentum term. However, two evolved optimizers stood out as worthy of a focused study and further experimentation. Since evolved optimizers have a considerable amount of unused genetic material that hurts readability (e.g., complex auxiliary functions that are not used in calculating the weights), we will be presenting simplified versions of the optimizers to improve clarity.

The first notable individual was the best performing optimizer across all runs; a simplified version of this optimizer is shown in Eq. 7; in the instance produced in evolution $lr = 0.0009$. This optimizer is unusual in a few ways. The gradient is never used directly, only its sign. As a result, this optimizer always changes the weights by a fixed amount. We named this optimizer the *Sign Optimizer*. The size of the changes proposed in the evolved instance of this optimizer is small, likely leading to successive small changes that steadily improve the ANN until a local optimum is reached. This strategy allows for a lengthy training procedure even with the early stop mechanism. Early stop only

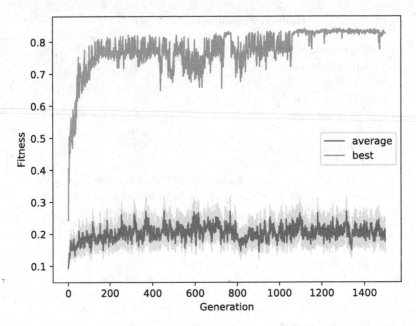

Fig. 2. Progression of average fitness and best fitness throughout evolution. Plot shows the average and standard deviation across all runs.

interrupts training if the validation loss does not improve. The magnitude of improvements is not considered, favoring optimizers that improve the ANN by a small margin many times. Additionally, the use of the sign operation adjusts the direction of the gradient before it is applied to the weights. As far as we know, this strategy is not used in any human-made optimizers, and it is challenging to understand its implications completely. While changing the direction of the gradient seems undesirable, this approach may make the optimizer more resistant to the common vanishing/exploding gradient problems that can occur during training. The Sign optimizer does not exhibit any adaptive components; since adaptive optimizers were the main object of this system, we also selected the best optimizer with adaptive features for benchmark.

$$w_t = w_{t-1} - lr * sign(\nabla l(w_{t-1})) \tag{7}$$

The best adaptive evolved optimizer is presented in Eq. 8. As far as we know, this individual is a novel adaptive optimizer. Specifically, this solution's unique aspect is the presence of a squared auxiliary variable that was not found in human-made approaches. This optimizer is named Adaptive Evolutionary Squared (ADES) after its defining characteristic; in the instance produced in evolution $\beta_1 = 0.08922, \beta_2 = 0.0891$. ADES is considerably more complex than the Sign optimizer, so assessing how and why it functions is challenging. Since ADES does not operate similarly to human-made optimizers, we cannot relate its operations to familiar components. Nevertheless, we empirically observed that this optimizer employs a momentum-like mechanism that increases the magnitude of changes when moving in the same direction. However, we consider that thoroughly dissecting ADES and understanding the role of all its components is outside the scope of this work as it requires significant study outside the field of evolutionary computation.

$$
\begin{aligned}
y_t &= y_{t-1} - (\beta_1 * y_{t-1}^2 + \beta_2 * (y_{t-1} * \nabla l(w_{t-1})) + \beta_2 * \nabla l(w_{t-1})) \\
w_t &= w_{t-1} + y_t
\end{aligned}
\tag{8}
$$

4.3 Benchmark

The evolved optimizers performed well during evolution, but this may not be representative of their actual quality. During evolution, optimizers were evaluated using a limited set of data and an early stop mechanism. Furthermore, training was restricted to 100 epochs at most, possibly limiting the quality of ANNs created. In order to determine the actual quality of evolved solutions, it is essential to benchmark them with human-made optimizers.

Benchmarks use three sets of data with distinct roles: training, validation, and test. Training data, as the name suggests, is used to train the ANN. The validation data is used to monitor the ANN's ability to generalize as training progresses. The test data is used to make a final assessment of the ANN's performance. Furthermore, every benchmark is comprised of two phases. In the first phase (**tuning phase**), Bayesian optimization [13] tunes the hyper-parameters of all optimizers. While Bayesian optimization is often used to search for optimizer and network parameters [21], we believe it remains an adequate solution when applied in this smaller scope. Bayesian optimization tunes all parameters between 0 and 1. Specifically, the algorithm performs 100 function evaluations with 10 restarts and each optimizer's default parameters are used as a probe to help guide the search. During the tuning phase, ANNs are trained using the selected optimizer and parameters during 100 epochs. The Bayesian optimization procedure is guided by the best validation accuracy obtained during training. In the second phase (**trial phase**), the best set of hyper-parameters (i.e., the values that achieved the highest validation accuracy) found for each optimizer through the tuning process are used to train the ANN. In this phase, training is performed for 1000 epochs. After training, the best weights (i.e., the weights that achieved the highest validation accuracy during training) are used to test the ANN on the test data for a final accuracy assessment. Trials are repeated 30 times, and all results presented show the average and standard deviation of these trials. No early stop is used at any point during benchmarks.

The evolved optimizers are compared with three human-made optimizers previously presented: Nesterov's momentum, RMSprop and Adam on two different benchmarks. The first benchmark compares the evolved optimizers with the human-made adaptive optimizers in Fashion-MNIST (the task used in evolution). The second benchmark performs the comparison on CIFAR-10, a different dataset and network architecture (Keras-CIFAR [3], available in [17])), but the task is still image classification.

4.4   Fashion-MNIST

In this benchmark, we test the optimizers in the network architecture (Keras-MNIST [4], available in [18]) and dataset (Fashion-MNIST) used in evolution. Additional measures are necessary to ensure fair comparisons in this environment, since evolved optimizers have an unfair advantage if evaluated on the data used during evolution. As previously mentioned, the Fashion-MNIST-Test was deliberately excluded from evolution to enable just comparisons in this phase. Consequently, it is possible to make fair comparisons between evolved and human-made optimizers as long as the Fashion-MNIST-Test data is used to evaluate the final accuracy. As a result, Fashion-MNIST-Training is used for training (53000 instances) and validation (7000 instances), and Fashion-MNIST-Test is only used for the final accuracy assessment (10000 instances).

The results of the tuning phase (best hyper-parameter values) and the trial phase (validation and test accuracy) are presented in Table 2. All optimizers performed similarly in this benchmark. The exception is the Sign optimizer that performed about 1.5% worse than its peers. We believe the odd way the Sign optimizer changes weights is particularly effective at avoiding the early stop mechanism used during evolution. While the Sign optimizer thrives in the evolutionary system's specific evaluation conditions, when moved into a more traditional training environment, it cannot compete with the other optimizers. Despite weaker results, the Sign optimizer exhibits the smallest accuracy drop between the validation and test sets.

Table 2. Trial results of all optimizers in Fashion-MNIST. The parameters tuned for each optimizer, as well as the best values found through Bayesian optimization are also presented.

Optimizer	Parameter			Validation Accuracy	Test Accuracy
ADES	beta_1	beta_2		$93.53 \pm 0.11\%$	$92.87 \pm 0.16\%$
	0.87621	0.76132			
Sign	lr			$92.08 \pm 0.13\%$	$91.29 \pm 0.25\%$
	0.0009				
Adam	lr	beta_1	beta_2	$93.46 \pm 0.10\%$	$92.69 \pm 0.20\%$
	0.00127	0.07355	0.78162		
RMSprop	lr	rho		$93.61 \pm 0.08\%$	$92.80 \pm 0.17\%$
	0.00097	0.85779			
Nesterov	lr	momentum		$93.41 \pm 0.14\%$	$92.82 \pm 0.15\%$
	0.09999	0.86715			

Notably, ADES has the best test accuracy in Fashion-MNIST, suggesting ALR succeed in its objective of specialization. While it is expected that the evolved optimizer would perform well in its native task, it is still remarkable that this automatically generated solution can empirically outperform human-made optimizers. It must be noted that the human-made optimizers are the culmination of many years of research into this subject and ADES competes with these methods despite being automatically generated. Nevertheless, it must be acknowledged that the differences in performance between the four best optimizers are minimal. Performing a Mann-Whitney U test for the null hypothesis comparing the two best solutions: "ADES and Nesterov are equal" with a significance level of 0.05, we are unable to reject the null hypothesis ($p = 0.267$).

4.5   CIFAR-10

This benchmark was designed to test the ability of the evolved optimizers to generalize to a different problem within the same domain. The dataset chosen was CIFAR-10, a common problem used to evaluate image classification approaches. CIFAR-10 also has training (CIFAR-10-Training) and test (CIFAR-10-Test) sets, similar to Fashion-MNIST. Following the procedure outlined in the previous section, CIFAR-10-Training is used for training (43000 instances) and validation (7000 instances), while CIFAR-10-Test (10000 instances) is used to make the final test accuracy assessment. The architecture used was the Keras CIFAR-10 architecture [3] (available in [17]).

The best parameter values found using Bayesian optimization, and the trial phase results are presented in Table 3. Once again, despite its weak performance overall, the Sign optimizer is the most resistant to the dataset change, even slightly improving its performance when moved to the test set. While this may seem unusual, consider that the validation accuracy is only used to select the best weights for testing. Additionally, note that the Sign optimizer does not strictly follow the direction of the gradient when adjusting weights, possibly making Sign resistant to overfitting.

However, the most notable result in this benchmark is that ADES remains one of the best solutions, outperforming Adam and RMSProp in both validation and test accuracy. While the difference in accuracy is not massive, it is essential to acknowledge that an evolved optimized can compete with state-of-the-art solutions even outside its native task. Considering that the supposed advantage of an evolved optimizer is that it is fine-tuned for the task it is evolved in, this result is remarkable.

Additionally, the fact that ADES can be successfully used in other image classification tasks motivates research into other applications of the optimizer. What other datasets, architectures and ML problems can ADES succeed in? Further research is necessary to fully understand the contribution of ADES to ML.

However, the success of ADES in this benchmark also highlights the value of ALR. A vital characteristic of ADES it is competitive with human-made optimizers using a novel way of changing weights. Even if future work reveals that ADES is not widely applicable, understanding its unique features and why it succeeds in specific tasks may provide helpful insights for creating better human-made optimizers. Specially because adaptive optimizers historically retool or

Table 3. Trial results of all optimizers in CIFAR-10. The parameters tuned for each optimizer, as well as the best values found through Bayesian optimization are also presented.

Optimizer	Parameter			Validation Accuracy	Test Accuracy
ADES	beta_1	beta_2		82.04 ± 0.20%	81.85 ± 0.29%
	0.92226	0.69285			
Sign	lr			74.97 ± 0.40%	75.09 ± 0.50%
	0.0009				
Adam	lr	beta_1	beta_2	81.93 ± 0.21%	81.56 ± 0.26%
	0.00163	0.81344	0.71023		
RMSprop	lr	rho		80.97 ± 0.27%	80.65 ± 0.45%
	0.00085	0.64813			
Nesterov	lr	momentum		82.45 ± 0.25%	82.03 ± 0.25%
	0.00907	0.98433			

adjust ideas from older solutions to create new, better optimizers. ALR's ability to create unique, competitive, evolved optimizers may help researchers improve human-made optimizers.

It is also worth highlighting that the evolutionary conditions did not incentivize the creation of an optimizer that performed well outside its native task. ALR created ADES while evaluating optimizers strictly based on their performance in the Fashion-MNIST dataset but the optimizer still operates successfully in a different task. We consider that this result motivates research into other applications of ALR. Specifically, it may be interesting to use ALR with a fitness function that evaluates optimizers based on their performance on several tasks, promoting general applicability. The evolutionary setup used also enforced minimal limitations on the solutions created. While this led to the creation of a novel solution, it is relevant to investigate the potential of ALR when using additional rules that guarantee evolved optimizers are closer to strong, established human-made optimizers. In fact, it could be interesting to utilize ALR starting from the population of human-made optimizers. Evolving solutions closer to human-made optimizers may work as an alternative to hyper-parameter optimization, where the entire optimizer is tuned for a specific task.

5   Conclusion

This work presents an adaptive implementation of the AutoLR framework. This framework is capable of producing novel, specialized ANN optimizers through an EA. Specifically, the framework [2] is used to evolve optimizers for an image classification task. The setup used included no incentive to imitate traditional optimizers as solution were rated solely based on their performance.

Some of the optimizers evolved under these circumstances can compete with the established human-made optimizers. This optimizer, called ADES, showed other exciting properties. Despite being evolved in a specific task, this optimizer could compete with human-made optimizers even in a different task. As such, the results obtained with ADES indicate that the AutoLR framework could create new general ANN optimizers that can be employed on a breadth of problems. To summarize, the contributions of this paper are as follows:

- The proposal of ALR, an implementation of AutoLR capable of producing adaptive ANN optimizers.
- The evolution, benchmark, and analysis of two new ANN optimizers.
- The discovery of ADES, an automatically-generated adaptive ANN optimizer capable of competing with state-of-the-art human-made optimizers in two relevant image classification tasks.

The results obtained in this work also warrant further study into a few topics. The evolved optimizer ADES remained competitive with human-made solutions when moved outside of its native task. However, all tasks considered are image classification problems. It is vital to understand whether ADES retains its utility when applied to different problems. Furthermore, in this work we only compared optimizers based on their final test accuracy. However, there are other properties that are desirable in optimizers such as convergence speed and sensitivity to hyper-parameters. Studying evolved optimizers in this lens may reveal additional advantages and disadvantages to this approach. Finally, the success of ADES outside its native task suggests ALR may serve as a tool for the creation of optimizers in other applications. In this work, the experiments were designed to explore the benefits of specializing optimizers, however we found that the applicability of the solutions produced were also interesting. It would be relevant to study the benefits of using ALR to create generally applicable optimizers (e.g., by assigning optimizer fitness based of their performance in several different tasks).

Acknowledgments. This work is partially funded by: Fundação para a Ciência e Tecnologia (FCT), Portugal, under the grant UI/BD/151053/2021, and by national funds through the FCT - Foundation for Science and Technology, I.P., within the scope of the project CISUC - UID/CEC/00326/2020 and by European Social Fund, through the Regional Operational Program Centro 2020.

References

1. Bottou, L.: On-Line Learning and Stochastic Approximations, pp. 9–42. Cambridge University Press, Cambridge (1999)
2. Carvalho, P., Lourenço, N., Assunção, F., Machado, P.: AutoLR: an evolutionary approach to learning rate policies. In: Proceedings of the 2020 Genetic and Evolutionary Computation Conference, GECCO 2020, pp. 672–680. Association for Computing Machinery, New York (2020). https://doi.org/10.1145/3377930.3390158
3. Chollet, F., et al.: Keras CIFAR10 architecture (2015). https://keras.io/examples/cifar10_cnn_tfaugment2d/

4. Chollet, F., et al.: Keras MNIST architecture (2015). https://keras.io/examples/mnist_cnn/

5. Farabet, C., Couprie, C., Najman, L., LeCun, Y.: Learning hierarchical features for scene labeling. IEEE Trans. Pattern Anal. Mach. Intell. **35**(8), 1915–1929 (2012)

6. Hinton, G., Srivastava, N., Swersky, K.: Overview of mini-batch gradient descent. University Lecture (2015). https://www.cs.toronto.edu/~tijmen/csc321/slides/lecture_slides_lec6.pdf

7. He, K., Zhang, X., Ren, S., Sun, J.: Deep residual learning for image recognition. In: Proceedings of the IEEE Conference on Computer Vision and Pattern Recognition, pp. 770–778 (2016)

8. Hochreiter, S., Schmidhuber, J.: Long short-term memory. Neural Comput. **9**(8), 1735–1780 (1997)

9. Jacobs, R.A.: Increased rates of convergence through learning rate adaptation. Neural Netw. **1**(4), 295–307 (1988)

10. Kingma, D.P., Ba, J.: Adam: a method for stochastic optimization. arXiv preprint arXiv:1412.6980 (2014)

11. Krizhevsky, A., Sutskever, I., Hinton, G.E.: Imagenet classification with deep convolutional neural networks. Commun. ACM **60**(6), 84–90 (2017)

12. Lopez, M.M., Kalita, J.: Deep learning applied to NLP. arXiv preprint arXiv:1703.03091 (2017)

13. Mockus, J., Tiesis, V., Zilinskas, A.: The application of Bayesian methods for seeking the extremum, vol. 2, pp. 117–129 (2014)

14. Nesterov, Y.: A method for unconstrained convex minimization problem with the rate of convergence o $(1/k^2)$. In: Doklady an USSR, vol. 269, pp. 543–547 (1983)

15. Pedro, C.: Adaptive AutoLR grammar (2020). https://github.com/soren5/autolr/blob/master/grammars/adaptive_autolr_grammar.txt

16. Pedro, C.: AutoLR (2020). https://github.com/soren5/autolr

17. Pedro, C.: Keras CIFAR model (2020). https://github.com/soren5/autolr/blob/benchmarks/models/json/cifar_model.json

18. Pedro, C.: Keras MNIST model (2020). https://github.com/soren5/autolr/blob/benchmarks/models/json/mnist_model.json

19. Rumelhart, D.E., Hinton, G.E., Williams, R.J.: Learning representations by back-propagating errors. Nature **323**(6088), 533–536 (1986)

20. Senior, A., Heigold, G., Ranzato, M., Yang, K.: An empirical study of learning rates in deep neural networks for speech recognition. In: 2013 IEEE International Conference on Acoustics, Speech and Signal Processing, pp. 6724–6728. IEEE (2013)

21. Snoek, J., Larochelle, H., Adams, R.P.: Practical Bayesian optimization of machine learning algorithms. In: Proceedings of the 25th International Conference on Neural Information Processing Systems, NIPS 2012, vol. 2, pp. 2951–2959. Curran Associates Inc., Red Hook (2012)

22. Suganuma, M., Shirakawa, S., Nagao, T.: A genetic programming approach to designing convolutional neural network architectures. In: Proceedings of the Genetic and Evolutionary Computation Conference, GECCO 2017, pp. 497–504. Association for Computing Machinery, New York (2017). https://doi.org/10.1145/3071178.3071229

Combining Geometric Semantic GP with Gradient-Descent Optimization

Gloria Pietropolli[1], Luca Manzoni[1(✉)], Alessia Paoletti[1], and Mauro Castelli[2]

[1] Dipartimento di Matematica e Geoscienze, Università degli Studi di Trieste,
Via Alfonso Valerio 12/1, 34127 Trieste, Italy
gloria.pietropolli@phd.units.it, lmanzoni@units.it
[2] Nova Information Management School (NOVA IMS), Universidade Nova de Lisboa,
Campus de Campolide, 1070-312 Lisboa, Portugal
mcastelli@novaims.unl.pt

Abstract. Geometric semantic genetic programming (GSGP) is a well-known variant of genetic programming (GP) where recombination and mutation operators have a clear semantic effect. Both kind of operators have randomly selected parameters that are not optimized by the search process. In this paper we combine GSGP with a well-known gradient-based optimizer, *Adam*, in order to leverage the ability of GP to operate structural changes of the individuals with the ability of gradient-based methods to optimize the parameters of a given structure.

Two methods, named HYB-GSGP and HeH-GSGP, are defined and compared with GSGP on a large set of regression problems, showing that the use of Adam can improve the performance on the test set. The idea of merging evolutionary computation and gradient-based optimization is a promising way of combining two methods with very different – and complementary – strengths.

1 Introduction

Genetic Programming (GP) [13] is one of the most prominent evolutionary computation techniques, with the ability to evolve programs, usually represented as trees, to solve specific problems given a collection of input and output pairs. Traditionally, operators in GP have focused on manipulating the syntax of GP individuals, like swapping subtrees for crossover or replacing subtrees for mutation. While simple to describe, these operations produce an effect on the *semantics* [25] of the individuals that can be complex to describe, with small variations in the syntax that may significantly affect the semantics. To address this problem, semantic operators were introduced. In particular, geometric semantic operators, first introduced in [15], have been used for defining Geometric Semantic GP (GSGP), a new kind of GP where crossover and mutation operators have a clear effect on the semantics. While in the original formulation GSGP was only of theoretical interest, due to the size of the generated individuals, the algorithm introduced in [24] provided a way for implementing GSGP efficiently.

E. Medvet et al. (Eds.): EuroGP 2022, LNCS 13223, pp. 19–33, 2022.
https://doi.org/10.1007/978-3-031-02056-8_2

While the introduction of GSGP helped in establishing a clear effect of recombination and mutation operators, also improving the quality of the generated solutions, there is still a largely untapped opportunity of combining GSGP with local search methods. In particular, we can observe that, give two GP trees T_1 and T_2, their recombination is given by $\alpha T_1 + (1 - \alpha)T_2$, and the mutation of one of them is given by $T_1 + ms(R_1 - R_2)$, where R_1 and R_2 are two random trees. As we can observe, there are three parameters, α, $\beta = 1 - \alpha$, and ms that are either fixed or randomly selected during the evolution process. As long as each function used in the generation of the individuals is derivable, we can compute the *gradient* of the error with respect to the parameters used in crossover and mutation. Thus, we can employ a gradient-based optimizer to update the parameters of each crossover and mutation.

In this paper, we propose a way to combine GSGP and Adam, a well-known gradient-based optimizer. In some sense, by combining GSGP with a gradient-based optimizer, we are leveraging the strengths of each of the two methods: GSGP (and GP in general) is good at providing structural changes in the shape of the individuals, while gradient-based methods are perfect for optimizing a series of parameters of the individuals that the evolutionary process has difficulty in optimizing.

We experimentally show that the proposed method can provide better performance with respect to plain GSGP, thus suggesting that a combination of local search (via Adam) with GSGP is a new promising way to leverage knowledge from other areas of artificial intelligence: Adam and the gradient-based optimizers are well-studied in the area of neural networks, representing the main tool to perform the learning process in a neural network.

This paper is structured as follows: Sect. 2 provides an overview of the applications of local search to evolutionary methods and GP in particular. Section 3 recalls the reliant notions of GSGP (Sect. 3.1) and the Adam algorithm (Sect. 3.2). Section 3.3 introduces the proposed hybridized algorithms combining GSGP and the Adam algorithm. The experimental settings and the dataset used in the experimental validation are described in Sect. 4 and the results of the experimental campaign are presented in Sect. 5. Section 6 summarizes the main contributions of the paper and provides directions for further research.

2   Related Works

The combination of Evolutionary Algorithms (EAs) and local search strategies received greater attention in recent years [5,6,17]. While EAs can explore large areas of the search space, the evolutionary search process improves the programs in a discontinuous way [20]. On the other hand, when considering local optimizers, the solutions can be improved gradually and steadily in a continuous way. Thus, as stated by Z-Flores *et al.* [7], a hybrid approach that combines EAs with a local optimizer can result in a well-performing search strategy. Such approaches are a simple type of memetic search [5], and the basic idea is to include within the optimization process an additional search operator that, given an individual, searches for the local optima around it. Thanks to the possibility of fully exploiting the local region around each individual, memetic algorithms obtained excellent results over different domains [5,17], and they outperform evolutionary algorithms in multimodal optimisation [18]. Despite these results, the literature presents a poor number of contributions dealing with GP [23], thus indicating that the GP community may have not addressed the topic adequately. Some examples are the works of Eskridge [8] and Wang [26] that are domain-specific memetic techniques not addressing the task of symbolic regression considered in this work. Muñoz et al. [16], proposed a memetic algorithm that, given a regression (or classification) problem, creates a new feature space that is subsequently considered for addressing the underlying optimization problem. The algorithm, by maximizing the mutual information [12] in the new feature space, shows superior results with respect to other state-of-the-art techniques.

Focusing on the use of gradient descent in GP, the existing contributions are focused on particular tasks or particular components of the solutions. For instance, Topcyy et al. [22] analyzed the effectiveness of gradient search optimization of numeric leaf values in GP. In particular, they tuned conventional random constants utilizing gradient descent, and they considered several symbolic regression problems to demonstrate the approach's effectiveness. Zhang et al. [27] applied a similar strategy to address object classification problems and, also in this case, better results were obtained compared to the ones achieved with standard GP. Graff et al. [9] employed resilient backpropagation with GP to address a complex real-world problem concerning wind speed forecasting, showing improved results. In [21], the authors used gradient-descent search to make partial changes of certain parts of genetic programs during evolution. To do that, they introduced weight parameters for each function node, what the authors call inclusion factors. These weights modulate the importance that each node has within the tree. The proposed method, which uses standard genetic operators and gradient descent applied to the inclusion factors, outperformed the basic GP approach that only uses standard genetic operators (i.e., without gradient descent and inclusion factors).

The aforementioned contributions are related to syntax-based GP. In the context of semantics-based GP [25], the integration of a local search strategy into GP was proposed by Castelli et al. [4] with the definition of a specific semantic mutation operator. Experimental results showed excellent performance on the training set, but with a severe overfitting [3]. To the best of our knowledge, this is the only attempt to integrate a local optimizer within semantic GP.

In this paper, we follow a different strategy, and, to create a hybrid semantic GP framework, we rely on gradient descent optimization.

3   Gradient Descent GSGP

This section will discuss the two tools that will be combined later in this work. First, Geometric Semantic GP is described. Later, Adam, one of the most powerful gradient descent optimizers, is introduced and discussed. Afterward, the main contribution of this paper, i.e., the first integration of a gradient descent optimizer within GSGP, is presented.

3.1   Geometric Semantic GP

Traditional genetic programming investigates the space of programs exploiting search operators that analyze their syntactic representation. To improve the performance of GP, recent years have witnessed the integration of semantic awareness in the evolutionary process [25]. The semantic of a solution can be identified by the vector of its output values calculated on the training data. Thus, we can represent a GP individual as a point in a real finite-dimensional vector space, the so-called semantic space. Geometric Semantic Genetic Programming (GSGP) is an evolutionary technique originating from GP that directly searches the semantic space of the programs. GSGP has been introduced by Moraglio and coauthors [15], together with the definition of the correspondent Geometric Semantic Operators (GSOs). These operators replace traditional (syntax-based) crossover and mutation, inducing geometric properties on the semantic space. GSOs induce on the training data a unimodal error surface for any supervised learning problem where input data has to match with known targets. More precisely: given two parents functions T_1, $T_2 : \mathbb{R}^n \rightarrow \mathbb{R}$, *Geometric Semantic Crossover* (GSC) generates the real function $T_{XO} = (T_1 \cdot T_R) + ((1 - T_R) \cdot T_2)$, where T_R is a random real functions whose output range in the interval $[0, 1]$. Similarly, given a parent function $T : \mathbb{R}^n \rightarrow \mathbb{R}$, *Geometric Semantic Mutation* (GSM) generates the real functions $T_M = T + ms \cdot (T_{R1} - T_{R2})$ where T_{R1} and T_{R2} are random real functions whose output range in the interval $[0, 1]$ and ms is a parameter called mutation step. This means that GSC generates one offspring whose semantics stands on the line joining the semantics of the two parents in the semantic space, while GSM generates an individual contained in the hyper-sphere of radius ms centred in the semantics of the parent in the semantic space. An intrinsic GSGP's problem is that this technique leads to larger offsprings with respect to their parents. Due to this issue, the algorithm becomes excessively unbearably slow generation after generation, making it unsuitable for real-world applications. In [2,24], Vanneschi and coauthors introduced a GSGP implementation that solves this problem and consists in storing only the semantic vectors of newly created individuals, besides storing all the individuals belonging to the initial population and all the random trees generated during the generations. This improvement turn the cost of evolving g generations of n individuals from $\mathbf{O}(ng)$ to $\mathbf{O}(g)$. The same idea was subsequently adopted to reconstruct the best individual found by GSGP, thus allowing for its usage in a production environment [1].

3.2   Adam Algorithm

Adam (Adaptive Moment Estimation) [11] is an algorithm for first-order gradient-based optimization of stochastic objective functions, based on adaptive estimates of lower-order models. Adam optimizer is efficient, easy to implement, requires little memory usage for its execution, and is well suited for problems dealing with a vast amount of data and/or parameters. The steps performed by the Adam optimizer are summarized in Algorithm 1. The inputs required for this method are the parametric function $f(\theta)$, the initial parameter vector θ_0, the number of steps N, the learning rate α, the exponential decay rate of the first momentum β_1, the one for the second momentum β_2, and ϵ, set by default at 10^{-8}. At every iteration, the algorithm updates first and second moment estimates using the gradient computed with respect to the stochastic function f. These estimates are then corrected to contrast the presence of an intrinsic initialization bias through the divisions described in line 7 and 8, where β_1^{i+1} stands for the element-wise exponentiation. For further details about the implementation of the Adam optimizer and the demonstration of its properties, the reader can refer to [11].

Algorithm 1. Pseudocode of the *Adam* algorithm.

Require: $f(\theta)$, θ_0, N, α, $\beta_1 \in [0,1)$, $\beta_2 \in [0,1)$, ϵ

 1: $m_0 \leftarrow 0$
 2: $v_0 \leftarrow 0$
 3: **for** $i = 0 \cdots N$ **do**
 4: $\quad d_{i+1} \leftarrow \nabla_\theta f_{i+1}(\theta_i)$
 5: $\quad m_{i+1} \leftarrow \beta_1 \cdot m_i + (1 - \beta_2) \cdot d_{i+1}$
 6: $\quad v_{i+1} \leftarrow \beta_2 \cdot v_i + (1 - \beta_2) \cdot d_{i+1}^2$
 7: $\quad \bar{m}_{i+1} \leftarrow m_{i+1}/(1 - \beta_1^{i+1})$
 8: $\quad \bar{v}_{i+1} \leftarrow v_{i+1}/(1 - \beta_2^{i+1})$
 9: $\quad \theta_{i+1} \leftarrow \theta_i - \alpha \cdot \bar{m}_{i+1}/(\bar{v}_{i+1})$
10: **end for**

3.3 GSGP Hybridized with Gradient Descent

The idea introduced in this work is to combine the strength of the two methods presented above, i.e., GSGP and the Adam optimizer. Geometric semantic GP, thanks to the geometric semantic operators, allows big jumps in the solution space. Thus, new areas of the solution space can be explored, with GSOs also preventing the algorithm to get stuck in a local optimum. Adam optimizer, on the other hand, is a gradient-based optimization technique. Thus, it performs small shifts in the local area of the solution space. A combination of these techniques should guarantee a jump in promising areas (i.e., where good-quality solutions lie) of the solution space, thanks to the evolutionary search of GSGP and subsequent refinement of the solution obtained with the Adam algorithm. Let's describe in more detail how to implement this combination. Let us consider an input vector x of n features, and the respective expected scalar value output y. By applying GSGP, an initial random population of functions in n variables is created. After performing the evolutionary steps involving GSM and GSC, a new population $T = (T_1, T_2, \cdots, T_N)$ of N individuals is obtained. The resulting vector T is composed of derivable functions, as they are obtained through additions, multiplications, and compositions of derivable functions. At this point, to understand for which parameter we should differentiate T, it is necessary to introduce an equivalent definition of the geometric semantic operators presented in Sect. 3.1. In particular let us redefine the *Geometric Semantic Crossover* as $T_{XO} = (T_1 \cdot \alpha) + ((1 - \alpha) \cdot T_2)$, where $0 \leq \alpha \leq 1$, and the *Geometric Semantic Mutation* as $T_M = T + ms \cdot (R_1 - R_2)$, where $0 \leq m \leq 1$. As the values of α and m are randomly initialised, we can derive T with respect to α, $\beta = (1 - \alpha)$ and m. Therefore, the Adam optimizer algorithm can be applied, considering as objective function $f(\theta)$ the generation considered, while the parameter vector becomes $\theta = (\alpha, \beta, m)$. Thus, GSGP and Adam optimizer can be applied together to find the best solution for the problem at hand. We propose and investigate two ways to combine them:

- HYB-GSGP: the abbreviation stands for *Hybrid Geometric Semantic Genetic Programming*. Here, one step of GSGP is alternated to one step of the Adam optimizer.
- HeH-GSGP: the abbreviation stands for *Half et Half Geometric Semantic Genetic Programming*. Here, initially, all the GSGP genetic steps are performed, followed by an equal number of Adam optimizer steps.

In the continuation of the paper, we will refer to these two methods using the abbreviations just introduced.

4 Experimental Settings

This section describes the datasets considered for validating our technique (Sect. 4.1) and provides all the experimental settings (Sect. 4.2) to make the experiments completely reproducible. The code, for the complete reproducibility of the proposed experiments, is available at https://github.com/gpietrop/GSGP-GD [19].

4.1 Dataset

To assess the validity of the technique proposed in Sect. 3.3, real-world, complex datasets, ranging from different areas, have been considered and tested. All of them have been widely used as benchmarks for GP, and their properties have been discussed in [14]. Table 1 summarizes the characteristics of the different datasets, such as the number of instances and the number of variables. The objective of the first group of datasets is the prediction of pharmacokinetic parameters of potential new drugs. *Human oral bioavailability* (**%F**) measures the percentage of initial drug dose that effectively reaches the system blood circulation; *Median lethal dose* (**LD50**) measures the lethal dose of a toxin, radiation, or pathogen required to kill half the members of a tested population after a specified test duration; *Protein-plasma binding level* (**%PPB**) corresponds to the percentage of the initial drug dose that reaches the blood circulation and binds the proteins of plasma. Also, datasets originating from physical problems are considered: *Yacht hydrodynamics* (**yac**) measures the hydrodynamic performance of sailing yachts starting from its dimension and velocity; *Concrete slump* (**slump**) measures the value about the slump flow of the concrete; *Concrete* *compressive strength* (**conc**) measures values about the compressive strength of concrete; *Airfoil self-noise* (**air**) is a NASA dataset obtained from a series of aerodynamic and acoustic test of airfoil blade sections.

Table 1. Principal characteristics of the considered datasets: the number of variables, the number of instances, the domain, and the task request.

Dataset	Variables	Instances	Area	Task
%F	242	359	Pharmacokinetic	Regression
LD50	627	234	Pharmacokinetic	Regression
%PPB	627	131	Pharmacokinetic	Regression
yac	7	308	Physics	Regression
slump	10	102	Physics	Regression
conc	9	1030	Physics	Regression
air	6	1503	Physics	Regression

4.2   Experimental Study

For all the datasets described in Sect. 4.1, samples have been split among train and test sets: 70% of randomly selected data has been used as a training set, while the remaining 30% has been used as a test set. For each dataset, 100 runs have been performed, each time with a random train/test split.

To assess the performance of HYB-GSGP and HeH-GSGP, the results obtained within these methods are compared to the ones achieved with classical GSGP. The comparison with the performance achieved by standard GP is not reported, because after some preliminary tests it has been observed that standard GP is non competitive against GSGP. We considered two hyperparameters settings to evaluate our methods' performance with different values assigned to the learning rate of the Adam algorithm. Both of them are compared against 200 generations of standard GSGP. To make the comparison fair, the total number of fitness evaluations must be equal for every method considered: 200 generations in the standard GSGP routine correspond to a combination of 100 generations of GSGP plus 100 steps of Adam optimizer, both for HYB-GSGP and HeH-GSGP.

The first learning rate value we considered is 0.1 and we will refer to HYB-GSGP and HeH-GSGP where Adam optimizer used this hyperparameter as, respectively, HYB-0.1 and HeH-0.1. The second learning rate value we considered is 0.01 and we will refer to HYB-GSGP and HeH-GSGP where Adam optimizer used this hyperparameter as, respectively, HYB-0.01 and HeH-0.01. The population size for all the considered systems is set to 50, and the trees of the first generation are initialized with the ramped half and half technique. Further details concerning the implementation of the semantic system and the Adam optimization algorithm are reported in Table 2. The considered fitness function is the Root Mean Squared Error (RMSE).

Table 2. Experimental settings. A horizontal line separates the parameters belonging to GSGP algorithm and the ones belonging to the Adam technique.

Parameter	Value
Function Set	$+, -, *, //$
Max. Initial Depth	6
Crossover Rate	0.9
Mutation Rate	0.3
Mutation step	0.1
Selection Method	Tournament of size 4
Elitism	Best individuals survive
Learing Rate - A (α)	0.1
Learing Rate - B (α)	0.01
Exponential Decay Rate - First Momentum (β_1)	0.9
Exponential Decay Rate - Second Momentum (β_2)	0.99
ϵ	10^{-8}

5   Experimental Results

Table 3. Training and testing fitness (RMSE) for the considered benchmark problems. Bold font indicates the best results.

		GSGP	HYB-0.1	HYB-0.01	HeH-0.1	HeH-0.01
%F	Train	38.08	37.74	**36.80**	39.61	40.60
	Test	40.15	40.48	**39.61**	40.85	41.23
LD50	Train	2118.00	**2086.56**	2128.22	2144.27	2161.00
	Test	2214.78	**2203.25**	2229.87	2221.72	2215.09
%PPB	Train	30.15	27.00	**24.32**	34.79	33.26
	Test	328.1	401.43	263.81	**213.86**	235.53
yac	Train	**11.83**	11.92	12.48	12.28	12.31
	Test	11.92	**11.83**	12.52	12.38	12.48
slump	Train	4.56	3.47	**2.92**	5.19	4.41
	Test	5.08	3.63	**3.32**	5.77	4.76
conc	Train	9.62	8.86	**8.50**	10.59	10.05
	Test	9.65	8.88	**8.69**	10.47	10.07
air	Train	27.76	31.54	**21.98**	30.37	30.46
	Test	27.94	31.71	**21.97**	30.15	30.53

As stated in Sect. 3.3, the goal of this study is to compare the performance of GSGP against the one obtained by the proposed methods.

For each problem, the median of the fitness (calculated over the 100 runs performed), for both the training and the validation sets, is displayed in Table 3. The corresponding statistical analysis is reported Fig. 1 (for the test set), thorough

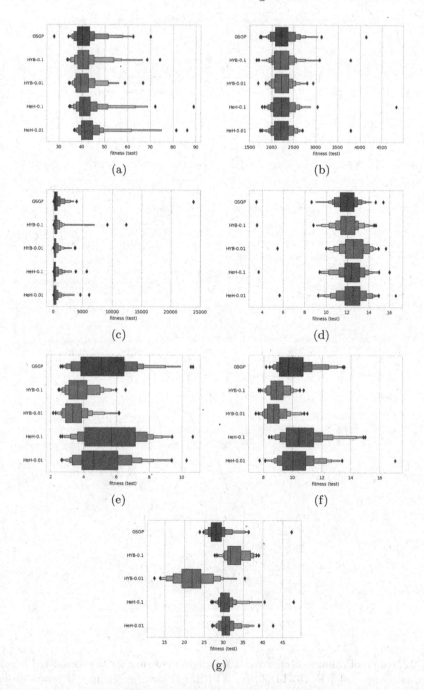

Fig. 1. Boxplots of Testing RMSE obtained over 100 independent runs of the considered benchmark problems. (a) %F, (b) LD50, (c) %PPB, (d) yac, (e) slump, (f) conc, (g) air.

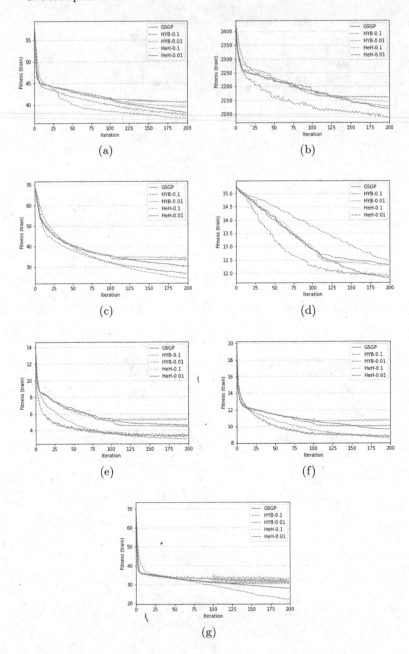

Fig. 2. Median of training fitness over 100 independent runs for the considered benchmark problems. (a) %F, (b) LD50, (c) %PPB, (d) yac, (e) slump, (f) conc, (g) air.

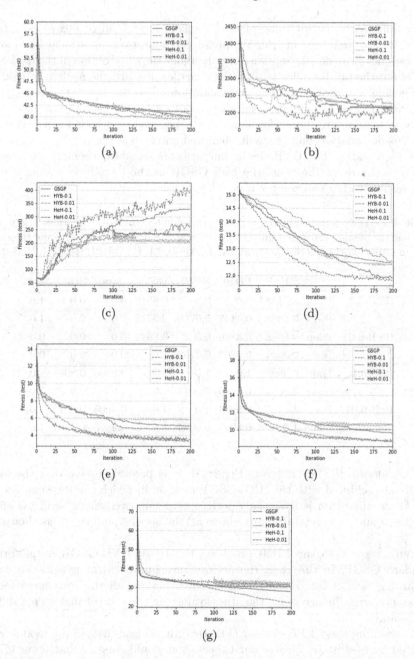

Fig. 3. Median of testing fitness over 100 independent runs for the considered benchmark problems. (a) %F, (b) LD50, (c) %PPB, (d) yac, (e) slump, (f) conc, (g) air.

letter-value plots. Letter-value plots are a particular kind of box-plots, introduced for the first time in [10]. We preferred them, over traditional box-plots, because they provide information not only about the distribution of the data but also about the tail behavior beyond the quartiles. Finally, the median fitness, at each generation, for the training and validation set, is displayed, respectively, in Fig. 2 and in Fig. 3. Training results are reported for the sake of completeness. Anyway, to compare the performance of the proposed methods against GSGP, we focus our analysis on the results achieved on the test set.

Table 3 shows that HYB-GSGP outperforms standard geometric semantic GP, while, most of the time, the HeH-GSGP method produces higher errors with respect to the two competitors.

Table 4. P-values returned by the Wilcoxon ran-sum test under the alternative hypothesis that the median errors obtained from classical GSGP are smaller or equal than the median errors of other methods considered, i.e. HYB-0.1, HYB-0.01, HeH-0.1, HeH-0.01

		%F	LD50	%PPB	*yac*	*slump*	*conc*	*air*
HYB-0.1	Train	0.01484	0.0	0.0	0.9512	0.0	0.0	1.0
	Test	0.5978	0.4143	0.6716	0.9512	0.0	0.0	1.0
HYB-0.01	Train	0.5978	0.3820	0.0	0.8948	0.0	0.0	0.0
	Test	0.0631	0.6862	0.2158	1.0	0.0	0.0	0.0
HeH-0.1	Train	0.9998	1.0	1.0	1.0	0.9998	0.9998	1.0
	Test	0.8384	0.5445	0.0018	1.0	0.9989	0.9992	1.0
HeH-0.01	Train	1.0	0.9984	1.0	1.0	0.4805	0.9573	1.0
	Test	1.0	0.6923	0.0074	1.0	0.4805	0.9652	1.0

Considering the %F dataset (Fig. 1(a)), it is possible to see that the best results are achieved with the HYB-GSGP method in which the learning rate of the Adam algorithm is 0.01. This performance improvement is achieved after 25 epochs and is maintained throughout all the epochs performed, as shown in Fig. 3(a).

With respect to the LD50 problem (Fig. 1(b)), HYB-GSGP outperforms standard GSGP. In this case, the performance improvement is achieved with a learning rate of 0.1. However, on this benchmark, all the considered techniques perform similarly, with the fitness values on the test set that do not differ significantly.

Concerning the %PPB dataset (Fig. 1(c)), it is clear that all the models are affected by overfitting. Hence, our expectation would suggest that lower error on the training set should lead to higher error on the test set. However, the HYB-GSGP method is able to perform better than GSGP, both in the training and validation set. Thus, HYB-GSGP seems to be capable of (slightly) reducing overfitting.

Taking into account the *yac* problem (Fig. 1(d)), the best results on the test set are obtained with HYB-0.1 and, again, this method reaches such a performance improvement in approximately 25 epochs. As shown in Fig. 3(d), the test fitness of GSGP decreases linearly, while for HYB-0.1 fitness decreases more rapidly, leading the hybrid method to a faster converge.

For the *slump* dataset (Fig. 1(e)), the combination of GSGP and Adam optimizer is successful, as HYB-GSGP outperforms standard GSGP for both the considered learning rate values. Moreover, also HeH-0.01 achieved better fitness values with respect to GSGP. Also in this case, it is interesting to highlight that the performance improvement provided by HYB-GSGP is achieved in a few epochs (Fig. 3(e)). A similar behaviour can be observed for the *conc* dataset (Fig. 1(f)): HYB-GSGP outperforms classical GSGP after a few epochs. Concerning the *air* problem (Fig. 1(g)), the HYB-GSGP method with the Adam's learning rate of 0.01 leads to a significant improvement in terms of test fitness. On the other hand, the other hybrid methods introduced in this work are characterized by some instability.

Table 4 reports a statistical significance assessment of the result achieved. In particular, Table 4 displays the p-values obtained from the Wilcoxon rank-sum test for pairwise data comparison, with $\alpha = 0.05$, applied under the alternative hypothesis that the median errors resulting from the considered techniques are smaller or equal than the median errors obtained with classical GSGP. The statistical tests show that, on the test set, the HYB method, in particular HYB-0.01, obtains better results than GSGP on three benchmark problems.

While there is no clear superiority of one method with respect to the others, it is interesting to note, especially in Fig. 1, how the distribution of the results obtained by the hybrid methods is usually as tight or tighter than the distribution produced by GSGP, showing consistent results that are, in some cases, better than GSGP. Thus, it appears that using half of the "evolutionary" iterations coupled with local search via gradient-descent optimization can actually improve the results.

6   Conclusions

This paper investigates the possibility of integrating a gradient-based optimization method, the Adam algorithm, within a genetic programming system, GSGP. The idea behind this work relies on the possibilities of exploiting and combining the advantages of these two methods to achieve faster convergence of the evolutionary search process.

Two different ways of combining these methods have been investigated. In the former, denoted as HYB-GSGP, a step of GSGP is alternated to a step of Adam. In the latter, denoted as HeH-GSGP, first, all the GSGP steps are performed, and, subsequently, the refinement with Adam is executed. The results achieved with these two methods were compared against classical GSGP on eight real-world complex benchmark problems belonging to different applicative domains. The experiments were performed considering two different values of the learning rate, which is the most relevant parameter of the Adam algorithm.

Experimental results show that, in each of the considered benchmarks, HYB-GSGP outperforms classic GSGP in both training and test sets (with a statistically significant difference on the test set on three problems). These results corroborate our hypothesis: the combination of GSGP with the Adam optimizer can improve the performance of GSGP. Moreover, HYB-GSGP converges to good-quality solutions faster than classical GSGP. In more detail, HYB-GSGP requires fewer epochs to converge, and the performance achieved by GSGP at the end of the evolutionary process is worse than the one achieved by the proposed hybrid method after a few fitness evaluations. On the contrary, the HeH-GSGP does not outperform GSGP even if it generally ensures good quality results on the test set. Thus, the results suggest that a combination of one step of GSGP and one step of Adam is the best way to mix these techniques.

This work represents the first attempt to create a hybrid framework between GSGP and a gradient descent-based optimizer. Considering the promising results obtained in this first analysis, this work paves the way to multiple possible future developments focused on improving the benefits provided by this kind of combination.

References

1. Castelli, M., Manzoni, L.: GSGP-C++ 2.0: a geometric semantic genetic programming framework. SoftwareX **10**, 100313 (2019)
2. Castelli, M., Silva, S., Vanneschi, L.: A C++ framework for geometric semantic genetic programming. Genet. Program Evolvable Mach. **16**(1), 73–81 (2015)
3. Castelli, M., Trujillo, L., Vanneschi, L.: Energy consumption forecasting using semantic-based genetic programming with local search optimizer. Comput. Intell. Neurosci. **2015** (2015)
4. Castelli, M., Trujillo, L., Vanneschi, L., Silva, S., Z-Flores, E., Legrand, P.: Geometric semantic genetic programming with local search. In: Proceedings of the 2015 Annual Conference on Genetic and Evolutionary Computation, pp. 999–1006 (2015)
5. Chen, X., Ong, Y.S., Lim, M.H., Tan, K.C.: A multi-facet survey on memetic computation. IEEE Trans. Evol. Comput. **15**(5), 591–607 (2011)
6. Črepinšek, M., Liu, S.H., Mernik, M.: Exploration and exploitation in evolutionary algorithms: a survey. ACM Comput. Surv. (CSUR) **45**(3), 1–33 (2013)
7. Z-Flores, E., Trujillo, L., Schütze, O., Legrand, P.: Evaluating the effects of local search in genetic programming. In: Tantar, A.-A., et al. (eds.) EVOLVE - A Bridge between Probability, Set Oriented Numerics, and Evolutionary Computation V. AISC, vol. 288, pp. 213–228. Springer, Cham (2014). https://doi.org/10.1007/978-3-319-07494-8_15
8. Eskridge, B.E., Hougen, D.F.: Imitating success: a memetic crossover operator for genetic programming. In: Proceedings of the 2004 Congress on Evolutionary Computation (IEEE Cat. No. 04TH8753), vol. 1, pp. 809–815. IEEE (2004)
9. Graff, M., Pena, R., Medina, A.: Wind speed forecasting using genetic programming. In: 2013 IEEE Congress on Evolutionary Computation, pp. 408–415. IEEE (2013)
10. Hofmann, H., Kafadar, K., Wickham, H.: Letter-value plots: boxplots for large data. Technical report, had.co.nz (2011)

11. Kingma, D.P., Ba, J.: Adam: a method for stochastic optimization (2017)
12. Kojadinovic, I.: On the use of mutual information in data analysis: an overview. In: Proceedings International Symposium Applied Stochastic Models and Data Analysis, pp. 738–47 (2005)
13. Koza, J.R., Koza, J.R.: Genetic Programming: on the Programming of Computers by Means of Natural Selection, vol. 1. MIT Press, Cambridge (1992)
14. McDermott, J., et al.: Genetic programming needs better benchmarks. In: Proceedings of the 14th Annual Conference on Genetic and Evolutionary Computation, pp. 791–798 (2012)
15. Moraglio, A., Krawiec, K., Johnson, C.G.: Geometric semantic genetic programming. In: Coello, C.A.C., Cutello, V., Deb, K., Forrest, S., Nicosia, G., Pavone, M. (eds.) PPSN 2012. LNCS, vol. 7491, pp. 21–31. Springer, Heidelberg (2012). https://doi.org/10.1007/978-3-642-32937-1_3
16. Muñoz, L., Trujillo, L., Silva, S., Castelli, M., Vanneschi, L.: Evolving multidimensional transformations for symbolic regression with M3GP. Memetic Comput. **11**(2), 111–126 (2019)
17. Neri, F., Cotta, C.: Memetic algorithms and memetic computing optimization: a literature review. Swarm Evol. Comput. **2**, 1–14 (2012)
18. Nguyen, P.T.H., Sudholt, D.: Memetic algorithms outperform evolutionary algorithms in multimodal optimisation. Artif. Intell. **287**, 103345 (2020)
19. Pietropolli, G.: GSGP-GD (2022). https://github.com/gpietrop/GSGP-GD
20. Smart, W., Zhang, M.: Continuously evolving programs in genetic programming using gradient descent. Technical report, CS-TR-04-10, Computer Science, Victoria University of Wellington, New Zealand (2004)
21. Smart, W., Zhang, M.: Continuously evolving programs in genetic programming using gradient descent. In: Proceedings of The Second Asian-Pacific Workshop on Genetic Programming, Cairns, Australia, p. 16pp (2004)
22. Topchy, A., Punch, W.F., et al.: Faster genetic programming based on local gradient search of numeric leaf values. In: Proceedings of the Genetic and Evolutionary Computation Conference (GECCO-2001), vol. 155162. Morgan Kaufmann (2001)
23. Trujillo, L., et al.: Local search is underused in genetic programming. In: Riolo, R., Worzel, B., Goldman, B., Tozier, B. (eds.) Genetic Programming Theory and Practice XIV. GEC, pp. 119–137. Springer, Cham (2018). https://doi.org/10.1007/978-3-319-97088-2_8
24. Vanneschi, L., Castelli, M., Manzoni, L., Silva, S.: A new implementation of geometric semantic GP and its application to problems in pharmacokinetics. In: Krawiec, K., Moraglio, A., Hu, T., Etaner-Uyar, A.Ş, Hu, B. (eds.) EuroGP 2013. LNCS, vol. 7831, pp. 205–216. Springer, Heidelberg (2013). https://doi.org/10.1007/978-3-642-37207-0_18
25. Vanneschi, L., Castelli, M., Silva, S.: A survey of semantic methods in genetic programming. Genet. Program Evolvable Mach. **15**(2), 195–214 (2014)
26. Wang, P., Tang, K., Tsang, E.P., Yao, X.: A memetic genetic programming with decision tree-based local search for classification problems. In: 2011 IEEE Congress of Evolutionary Computation (CEC), pp. 917–924. IEEE (2011)
27. Zhang, M., Smart, W.: Genetic programming with gradient descent search for multiclass object classification. In: Keijzer, M., O'Reilly, U.-M., Lucas, S., Costa, E., Soule, T. (eds.) EuroGP 2004. LNCS, vol. 3003, pp. 399–408. Springer, Heidelberg (2004). https://doi.org/10.1007/978-3-540-24650-3_38

One-Shot Learning of Ensembles
of Temporal Logic Formulas for Anomaly
Detection in Cyber-Physical Systems

Patrick Indri[1,3], Alberto Bartoli[2], Eric Medvet[2(✉)], and Laura Nenzi[1,2,3]

[1] Department of Mathematics and Geosciences, University of Trieste, Trieste, Italy
[2] Department of Engineering and Architecture, University of Trieste, Trieste, Italy
emedvet@units.it
[3] TU Wien Informatics, Vienna, Austria

Abstract. Cyber-Physical Systems (CPS) are prevalent in critical infrastructures and a prime target for cyber-attacks. Multivariate time series data generated by sensors and actuators of a CPS can be monitored for detecting cyber-attacks that introduce anomalies in those data. We use Signal Temporal Logic (STL) formulas to tightly describe the normal behavior of a CPS, identifying data instances that do not satisfy the formulas as anomalies. We learn an ensemble of STL formulas based on observed data, without any specific knowledge of the CPS being monitored. We propose an algorithm based on Grammar-Guided Genetic Programming (G3P) that learns the ensemble automatically in a single evolutionary run. We test the effectiveness of our data-driven proposal on two real-world datasets, finding that the proposed one-shot algorithm provides good detection performance.

Keywords: Ensemble learning · Grammar Guided Genetic Programming · Specification mining

1 Introduction

Cyber-Physical Systems (CPS) consist of large collections of mechanical components controlled by software modules. Interactions between software modules and physical world occur through the numerous sensors and actuators that compose the CPS. Such systems are prevalent in critical infrastructures and, consequently, have to be considered as a prime target for cyber-attacks. A cyber-attack usually introduces anomalies in the multivariate time-series data generated by sensors and actuators, i.e., deviations from the data generated when the CPS operates normally. Defining which data instances have to be considered normal and which ones anomalous is very complex, though, because such a classification requires a significant amount of CPS-specific knowledge.

Signal Temporal Logic (STL) [10, 16] is a formal language for describing properties of signals and, as such, can be used for specifying and monitoring the

© The Author(s), under exclusive license to Springer Nature Switzerland AG 2022
E. Medvet et al. (Eds.): EuroGP 2022, LNCS 13223, pp. 34–50, 2022.
https://doi.org/10.1007/978-3-031-02056-8_3

behavior of a CPS. In this work we address the problem of modeling the correct behavior of a CPS by means of STL formulas learned automatically from data collected while the CPS is working and not annotated in any way—CPS data is only assumed to be attack-free and fault-free. Violations of the formulas can then be used to identify anomalous behavior when it occurs. Our approach requires no specific domain knowledge and is *template-free*, i.e., we learn both structure and parameters of STL formulas.

We frame the learning task as an optimization problem, employing Grammar Guided Genetic Programming (G3P) [28]. We propose a one-shot evolutionary algorithm that learns an ensemble of STL formulas in a single evolution. Each formula tightly models the available data based on a subset of the observed signals—in a sense, each formula defines a CPS property discovered automatically. The voting scheme used for the ensemble defines a data instance as an anomaly when that instance violates an excessive amount of properties. We apply our technique on two real-world case studies—the SWaT water treatment plant [8] and the N-BaIoT set of Internet-of-Things (IoT) devices [20]—and assess the learned formulas on testing data that include real attacks.

2   Related Work

Specification mining is the research field dealing with methods for determining and formalizing the requirements of a target system based on its observed behavior. An important line of research in specification mining for CPSs focuses on STL, in particular, on finding STL formulas satisfied by the observed executions as much as possible. *Template-based* methodologies [12,13] rely on a specific, user-defined template formula, and limit the learning process to determining good parameters for the template. Such methodologies usually assume that the available data do not contain any anomalies and introduce a *tightness* metric to favor STL formulas that satisfy the data as tightly as possible [12]. The more challenging *template-free* approaches, on the other hand, learn both the structure and the parameters of the STL formulas. Unlike our proposal, template-free approaches usually require training data with both normal and anomalous examples annotated as such [2,6,21]. Template-free STL mining with normal data only was proposed in [24], that also exploited evolutionary computation (as [21] did): differently than this work, the cited papers do not produce ensembles of STL formulas, and are hence less suitable for CPSs where more properties should be monitored at once for an effective anomaly detection.

Other kinds of artifacts, different from STL specification, have been used for anomaly detection in CPSs. A powerful method on the SWaT testbed has been proposed in [7], based on data-driven mining of invariants (i.e., relations between data instances) expressed with an ad-hoc formalism. Anomaly detection on the same testbed has been developed with Generative Adversarial Networks (GAN) [14,15] and Deep Neural Networks (DNN) [9,11]. The anomaly criteria embedded in the neural networks trained on the observed data, however, are intrinsically much less interpretable than those resulting from an ensemble of STL formulas.

Ensemble learning has been proposed as way for learning models from data that collectively capture several properties of the underlying system, hence improving the models effectiveness. There are several cases in which ensemble learning has been combined with evolutionary computation and, in particular, with GP. The author of [27] proposed a simple variant of standard GP that allows to learn an ensemble of formulas for symbolic regression in a single evolutionary run, similarly to our case. Forms of ensemble learning with GP have been proposed also as the learning of different formulas on different partitions of the training data—*sequential covering* [23] and *separate-and-conquer* [3,19]. However, those approaches learn the formulas constituting the ensemble sequentially and are thus intrinsically unable for a one-shot framework.

3   Background: Signal Temporal Logic

Syntax and Semantics. We assume that the system under analysis can be described by a set of n real-valued variables $V = \{x_1, \ldots, x_n\}$. We define a *signal* (or trace or trajectory) w a function $w : \mathbb{T} \to \mathbb{R}^n$, where $\mathbb{T} = \mathbb{R}_{\geq 0}$ is the time domain, and denote by $x_i(t)$ the value of the i-th variable of w at time $t \in \mathbb{T}$. A signal describes the evolution of the system over time.

The logical statements of STL consist of a combination of temporal operators, Boolean connectives, and propositions, according to the following syntax. Formally, an *STL formula* φ is a string defined as:

$$\varphi := \top \mid \mu \mid \neg\varphi \mid \varphi \wedge \varphi \mid \varphi \vee \varphi \mid \varphi \to \varphi \mid \varphi \mathcal{S}_I \varphi \mid \mathcal{O}_I \varphi \mid \mathcal{H}_I \varphi \qquad (1)$$

where $\top$ is the true value, $\neg$, $\wedge$, $\vee$, and $\to$ are the negation, conjunction, disjunction, and implication logical operators, $\mu : \mathbb{R}^n \to \{\top, \bot\}$ is an *atomic proposition* (an inequality of the form $y(x_1, \ldots, x_n) \lessgtr c$, with $y : \mathbb{R}^n \to \mathbb{R}$ and $c \in \mathbb{R}$), $\mathcal{S}_I$, $\mathcal{O}_I$, and $\mathcal{H}_I$ are the *Since*, *Once*, and *Historically* temporal operators, and $I \subseteq \mathbb{T}$ is an interval of the form $I = [a, b]$, with $0 \leq a < b$ and $a, b \in \mathbb{T}$.

For a given signal w, the satisfaction of an STL formula φ with respect to the signal at a time t can be evaluated according to either qualitative (Boolean) or quantitative (real-valued) semantics [16]. The former states if a signal satisfies a formula at time t; the latter outputs the degree of satisfaction defined in a continuous range. Here, we report only quantitative semantics; the reader may refer to [5,16,17] for more details. The *quantitative satisfaction function ρ* returns a value $\rho(\varphi, w, t) \in \mathbb{R} \cup \{-\infty, +\infty\}$ that quantifies the *robustness* (or satisfaction) degree of an STL formula φ with respect to a signal w at time t, and is defined inductively as:

$$\rho(\top, \boldsymbol{w}, t) = +\infty$$

$$\rho(\mu, \boldsymbol{w}, t) = \begin{cases} y(x_1(t), \ldots, x_n(t)) - c & \text{if } \mu \equiv y(x_1(t), \ldots, x_n(t)) \geq c \\ -y(x_1(t), \ldots, x_n(t)) + c & \text{otherwise} \end{cases}$$

$$\rho(\neg\varphi, \boldsymbol{w}, t) = -\rho(\varphi, \boldsymbol{w}, t)$$

$$\rho(\varphi_1 \wedge \varphi_2, \boldsymbol{w}, t) = \min(\rho(\varphi_1, \boldsymbol{w}, t), \rho(\varphi_2, \boldsymbol{w}, t))$$

$$\rho(\varphi_1 \vee \varphi_2, \boldsymbol{w}, t) = \rho(\neg(\neg\varphi_1 \wedge \neg\varphi_2), \boldsymbol{w}, t)$$

$$\rho(\varphi_1 \rightarrow \varphi_2, \boldsymbol{w}, t) = \rho(\neg\varphi_1 \vee (\varphi_1 \wedge \varphi_2), \boldsymbol{w}, t)$$

$$\rho(\varphi_1 \mathcal{S}_{[a,b]} \varphi_2, \boldsymbol{w}, t) = \sup_{t' \in t - [a,b]} \left(\min \left(\rho(\varphi_2, \boldsymbol{w}, t') \right), \inf_{t'' \in [t',t[} \left(\rho(\varphi_1, \boldsymbol{w}, t'') \right) \right)$$

$$\rho(\mathcal{O}_{[a,b]}\varphi, \boldsymbol{w}, t) = \rho(\top \mathcal{S}_{[a,b]}\varphi, \boldsymbol{w}, t)$$

$$\rho(\mathcal{H}_{[a,b]}\varphi, \boldsymbol{w}, t) = \rho(\neg\mathcal{O}_{[a,b]}\neg\varphi, \boldsymbol{w}, t)$$

The sign of the robustness $\rho(\varphi, \boldsymbol{w}, t)$ provides a link to Boolean semantics [4]. If $\rho(\varphi, \boldsymbol{w}, t) \geq 0$, then $\boldsymbol{w}$ satisfies φ at t, denoted by $(\boldsymbol{w}, t) \models \varphi$; otherwise $\boldsymbol{w}$ does not satisfies φ at t, denoted by $(\boldsymbol{w}, t) \not\models \varphi$.

Tightness. Given two signals $\boldsymbol{w}$, $\boldsymbol{w}'$ over the same time domain and a time t in that domain, the *correctness property* holds, stating that if $(\boldsymbol{w}, t) \models \varphi$ and $\|\boldsymbol{w} - \boldsymbol{w}'\|_\infty < \rho(\varphi, \boldsymbol{w}, t)$ then $(\boldsymbol{w}', t) \models \varphi$, where $\|\boldsymbol{v}\|_\infty = \max_i |v_i|$ is the infinity norm. Intuitively, the correctness property suggests that the value of ρ is an upper bound for perturbations in a signal $\boldsymbol{w}$ for ensuring its satisfaction of φ.

Based on the correctness property, we define the *tightness* of a formula φ with respect to a signal $\boldsymbol{w}$ as $\|\rho(\varphi, \boldsymbol{w}, \cdot)\|_\infty = \max_{t \in \mathbb{T}} |\rho(\varphi, \boldsymbol{w}, t)|$, where $\rho(\varphi, \boldsymbol{w}, \cdot)$: $\mathbb{T} \rightarrow \mathbb{R} \cup \{-\infty, +\infty\}$ is the *robustness signal* that describes how $\rho(\varphi, \boldsymbol{w}, t)$ varies over time. Moreover, we say that a formula φ *tightly models* a signal $\boldsymbol{w}$ if its tightness is $\|\rho(\varphi, \boldsymbol{w}, \cdot)\|_\infty = 0$. Intuitively, this means that φ is satisfied by the signal $\boldsymbol{w}$, but it is not satisfied by any other signal that is slightly different than $\boldsymbol{w}$.

Finite Length Signals. Signals related to real systems are defined on a limited time domain, i.e., $\mathbb{T} = [0, t_{max}]$ instead of $\mathbb{T} = \mathbb{R}_{\geq 0}$. It follows that it is not possible to compute the robustness for certain STL formulas on signals that are defined over a too short time domain. For instance, the operator $\mathcal{H}_{[0,b]}$ cannot be evaluated on signals defined on $[0, t_{max}]$ with $t_{max} < b$.

For formalizing this requirement, we introduce the *necessary length* [16] of a formula. The necessary length $\|\varphi\| \in \mathbb{R}_{\geq 0}$ of a formula φ, is defined inductively as:

$$\|\top\| = 0$$
$$\|\mu\| = 0$$
$$\|\neg\varphi\| = \|\varphi\|$$
$$\|\varphi_1 \vee \varphi_2\| = \max(\|\varphi_1\|, \|\varphi_2\|)$$
$$\|\varphi_1 \wedge \varphi_2\| = \max(\|\varphi_1\|, \|\varphi_2\|)$$

$$\|\varphi_1 \to \varphi_2\| = \max(\|\varphi_1\|, \|\varphi_2\|)$$
$$\|\varphi_1 \mathcal{S}_{[a,b]}\varphi_2\| = \max(\|\varphi_1\|, \|\varphi_2\|) + b$$
$$\|\mathcal{O}_{[a,b]}\varphi\| = \|\varphi\| + b$$
$$\|\mathcal{H}_{[a,b]}\varphi\| = \|\varphi\| + b$$

Given a signal w, we denote by $|w| = t_{\max}$ the *signal length*. The robustness $\rho(\varphi, w, t)$ of a formula φ can be evaluated only for $\|\varphi\| \le t \le |w|$. As a consequence, if $|w| < \|\varphi\|$, the robustness cannot be computed for any t and the degree of satisfaction is undecidable.

In an ideal experimental setting, $|w| \gg \|\varphi\|$ holds and no indecision arises; this condition is satisfied by all our experimental settings.

On Discrete Signals. In many practical cases, as, e.g., for CPSs, the signal describing the evolution of the system is a multivariate time series generated by querying, at regular intervals, the sensors and actuators that constitute the system.

Particularly, we assume that the system is observed every Δt seconds, and that interval bounds are expressed in units of Δt. It follows that the time domain is $\mathbb{T} \subseteq \mathbb{N}$ and that the length of a time interval corresponds to its cardinality— e.g., for $I = [1, 4]$, $|I| = 4$. Accordingly, the *length* of a signal is redefined as the cardinality of its time domain.

The necessary length for formulas remains as above, with the exceptions of $\|\top\|$ and $\|\mu\|$, that are defined as $\|\top\| = \|\mu\| = 1$.

4   Problem Statement

Let w_{train} be a signal describing the evolution of a discrete-time system that operates normally—i.e., as intended, in absence of anomalies—in the time interval $I_{\text{train}} = [t_0, t_1]$. Let w_{test} be a signal describing the behavior of the same system in a later time interval $I_{\text{test}} = [t_2, t_3]$, with $t_1 < t_2$, for which it is not known whether the system is operating normally or not normally. We are interested in finding a way for generating, based on w_{train}, a collection Φ of one or more STL formulas that can be used for finding anomalies in w_{test}, i.e., determining the (possibly empty) subset I' of I_{test} containing all and only the time instants in which the system is not operating normally.

We assume that, given a collection $\Phi = \{\varphi_1, \varphi_2, \ldots\}$ of STL formulas and a threshold $\tau \in [0, 1]$, the subset of time instants in which the system is not operating normally is obtained as:

$$I_{\text{anomalous}} = \left\{ t \in I_{\text{test}} : \frac{1}{|\Phi|} |\{\varphi \in \Phi : (w_{\text{test}}, t) \not\models \varphi\}| > \tau \right\}$$

Intuitively, at each time instant t, we consider the proportion of formulas not satisfied by w_{test} at t and compare it against τ: if the proportion is greater than the threshold, we say that the system is not operating normally at t. The normality of the behavior at t is hence based on a voting scheme based on Φ formulas. It should be noted that, due to the constraints related to the necessary length of formulas, an initial part of w_{test} cannot be evaluated.

We remark that we are stating the problem as an anomaly detection problem, no observations are present in w_{train} that describe how the system operates not normally; examples of anomalies are hence not available for generating Φ. Moreover, we remark that we implicitly assume that, when anomalies occur, the system output, captured by w_{test}, differs from the output of the system under normal operation. If this is not the case, detection of anomalous behavior is not possible.

5   Methodology

To address the challenging task of detecting anomalies, learning from normal behavior only, we propose an evolutionary optimization approach based on two key ideas. First, we learn ensembles of STL formulas, instead of single formulas: the aggregation of the predictions of many low-bias, high variance models can favor generalization [27]. Second, we look for STL formulas that tightly model the training signal w_{train}, instead of just modeling it: since we have only observations of the system operating normally, we are hence assuming that small deviations from the observed behavior are anomalous. The combination of these two key ideas and the voting scheme employed when looking for anomalies corresponds to learning an ensemble of STL formulas, each one tightly describing a specific property of the system, and to saying that an anomaly occurs when the behavior of the system is not consistent with at least a given proportion of these properties.

We use a grammar-based version of Genetic Programming (Grammar-Guided GP, G3P) for performing the search in the space of (ensemble of) STL formulas. G3P is naturally suited to our scenario, since the language of formulas is defined by means of a context-free grammar (see Eq. (1)). Moreover, GP has been recently shown to be naturally suited for learning ensembles of models in an efficient and effective way [27]. In fact, we propose a *Complex Simultaneous Ensemble Learning Algorithm* (CESL-Alg) [27], that is, an algorithm that obtains an ensemble of estimators in a single GP evolution, where we exploit the fact that GP itself is a population-based technique and naturally deals with ensembles of individuals. When doing our evolutionary search each individual is a single STL formula, but the overall outcome is an ensemble and the ensemble is learned in a single evolution—i.e., we do *one-shot learning* of ensembles. In the next sections, we describe the key components of our approach.

Solution Representation. During the evolutionary search, each individual is a string of the language defined by the context-free grammar of Fig. 1. The grammar encodes numbers with a precision of two decimals in the $[0.00, 0.99]$ range and interval bounds with a single digit precision in the $[0, 9]$ range. Intervals are interpreted as $I = [d_1, d_1 + \max(1, d_2)]$. The grammar also defines the temporal operators $\mathcal{S}_{[a,b]}$, $\mathcal{O}_{[a,b]}$, and $\mathcal{H}_{[a,b]}$, and the logical operators $\land$, $\lor$, $\neg$, and $\rightarrow$. For simplicity, and for the kind of problems we deal with in this study, the grammar specify propositions that are in the form $x_i \lessgtr c$.

The grammar of Fig. 1 poses no explicit limit on the complexity of a formula, allowing for formulas with very large necessary length resulting from the nesting of many temporal operators. However, during the evolution, we enforce a maximum depth to the derivation trees of the formulas, which limits the nesting. Moreover, the range of temporal operators is limited to $[0, 9]$. Other means could be used to impact on the complexity of evolved formulas as, e.g., using a different grammar for the same language with repeated production rules [22]—as shown in [18], this could result in better evolvability.

$$
\begin{aligned}
\langle\text{formula}\rangle &:= \langle\text{proposition}\rangle \mid \langle\text{operator}\rangle \\
\langle\text{operator}\rangle &:= \neg\langle\text{formula}\rangle \mid \langle\text{formula}\rangle \land \langle\text{formula}\rangle \mid \langle\text{formula}\rangle \lor \langle\text{formula}\rangle \mid \\
&\quad \langle\text{formula}\rangle \rightarrow \langle\text{formula}\rangle \mid \langle\text{formula}\rangle \mathcal{S}_{[\langle\text{ibound}\rangle,\langle\text{ibound}\rangle]}\langle\text{formula}\rangle \mid \\
&\quad \mathcal{O}_{[\langle\text{ibound}\rangle,\langle\text{ibound}\rangle]}\langle\text{formula}\rangle \mid \mathcal{H}_{[\langle\text{ibound}\rangle,\langle\text{ibound}\rangle]}\langle\text{formula}\rangle \\
\langle\text{proposition}\rangle &:= \langle\text{variable}\rangle\langle\text{comparison}\rangle\langle\text{number}\rangle \;\cdot \\
\langle\text{ibound}\rangle &:= \langle\text{digit}\rangle \\
\langle\text{variable}\rangle &:= x_1 \mid \dots \mid x_n \\
\langle\text{comparison}\rangle &:= \geq \mid < \\
\langle\text{number}\rangle &:= 0.\langle\text{digit}\rangle\langle\text{digit}\rangle \\
\langle\text{digit}\rangle &:= 0 \mid 1 \mid 2 \mid 3 \mid 4 \mid 5 \mid 6 \mid 7 \mid 8 \mid 9
\end{aligned}
$$

Fig. 1. Our context-free grammar for a system with variables $x_1, \dots, x_n$.

Fitness Function. We aim at defining a fitness function that measures, for a given signal, (i) the tightness of a formula and (ii) the overall length of time intervals when the formula is not satisfied. For both, the lower, the better. Thus, we measure the fitness $f(\varphi, \boldsymbol{w})$ of a candidate STL formula on a signal $\boldsymbol{w}$ as:

$$
f(\varphi, \boldsymbol{w}) = \frac{1}{|\boldsymbol{w}| - \|\varphi\|} \sum_{\|\varphi\| \leq t \leq |\boldsymbol{w}|} \begin{cases} \rho(\varphi, \boldsymbol{w}, t) & \text{if} \quad \rho(\varphi, \boldsymbol{w}, t) \geq 0 \\ k & \text{if} \quad \rho(\varphi, \boldsymbol{w}, t) < 0 \end{cases} \tag{2}
$$

where $k \in \mathbb{R}_{>0}$ is a parameter corresponding to a penalty for instants when the signal does not satisfy the formula.

The proposed function reaches its minimum (zero) for formulas that tightly model the signal $\boldsymbol{w}$, i.e., those having a robustness always equals to 0. Additionally, the fitness function favors formulas with positive robustness: by means of the parameter k, formulas with robustness signal that assumes many negative values will be penalized. A higher value of k will penalize formulas with negative robustness more. This, in turn, favors solutions that better agree with the training data, leading to fewer false positives: since we learn STL formulas from normal data only and we consider instants with negative robustness as anomalous, the parameter k can be interpreted as a penalty for false positives on the training data, on the assumption that a *positive* instant is an anomaly.

One-Shot Evolutionary Algorithm. Inspired by [27], we propose a variant of G3P that produces an ensemble of STL formulas in a single evolutionary run.

A key requirement for ensemble learning to be effective is that models of the ensemble should be independent. While G3P, being a population-based optimization algorithm, can very efficiently learn many models at the same time, it might fall short in ensuring their independency, due to the lack of diversity and premature convergence that frequently afflict GP [25]. In our proposal, we attempt to minimize the risk of premature convergence as detailed below.

Our proposal employs iteratively a form of *extinction* to remove individuals from the population once it has converged to a solution, substituting them with *random immigrants*, randomly generated individuals that introduce fresh genetic material and favor diversity. Particularly, at each iteration we perform three phases.

- *Population update.* For each variable defined by the grammar, a *group* including all the individuals (STL formulas) that contain said variable is built. Individuals with multiple distinct variables will thus belong to multiple groups. The best individual of each group is copied into the next generation, as a form of *elitism*. The offspring for the next generation is completed by reproducing individuals from the current generation—including elites and with no consideration for grouping—using tournament selection with enforced-diversity (i.e., genetic operators are applied on parents until the child is not present in the population) and a non-overlapping generational model.

  Since all groups propagate their best individual, the population update promotes the presence of all variables at each iteration, avoiding the utter predominance of a small percentage of variables that may appear in fit individuals.
- *Solutions update.* If some individuals *solve the problem* (e.g., they have $f = 0$), consider the groups these solutions belong to. All the individuals belonging to these groups are removed from the population (extinction) and added to the solutions ensemble. The population is then refilled with newly generated individuals (random immigrants).

  The solution update exploits individuals homogenisation to find near-optimal solutions: once a solution is found, individuals belonging to its groups are expected to have good—although sub-optimal—performance whilst retaining some diversity. They can thus be added to the solution ensemble and be replaced with new, randomly generated individuals, to encourage exploration of other areas of the search space.

  Usually, not every individual of the population has variables in common with individuals that currently solve the problem, and the population is not entirely replaced with new individuals (which would essentially be equivalent to restarting the evolutionary process). This is especially true if many variables are involved. A computational advantage over repeated standard G3P evolutions is therefore expected.

- *Stop condition*. When n_{target} distinct variables have been solved (i.e., n_{target} distinct variables appear in formulas that *solve the problem*), the stop condition is met.

The stop condition can be used to explore a greater amount of the search space and act against premature convergence. It controls the trade-off between performance and efficiency.

We remark that in the context of anomaly detection for CPSs, it is not "hard" to find a formula with a perfect fitness: a trivial case is the one of a proposition $x_i \geq c$ for a signal whose $x_i(t) = c$ for any t. On one hand, this makes the solution update phase actually triggerable. On the other hand, it makes the ability of the ensemble to discover anomalies dependent on the number of variables occurring in the formulas: for this reason, we use n_{target} as stopping criterion. Moreover, since no pruning is performed on the ensemble, the ensemble size is (indirectly) controlled by n_{target}.

Algorithm 1 presents our one-shot G3P algorithm in detail. The *population update* step (lines 6–14) builds the variable *groups*, propagates the best individual for each group and fills the population of n_{pop} individuals. In line 12, a single child individual is generated by the `selectAndReproduceWithEnfDiv` procedure, using tournament selection with enforced-diversity. In the *solutions update* step (lines 15–25), the variables of the individuals that satisfies the `isSolution` condition are considered and added to the set of solved variables V_{solved}; all individuals that contain at least one of these variables are extracted from the population and added to the solutions ensemble S. If necessary, the population is refilled with newly generated individuals (lines 26–28). The stop condition (line 5) counts the number of distinct variables in V_{solved} and, stops the iterative algorithm if $V_{solved} \geq n_{target}$. The algorithm returns the ensemble of solutions S.

6   Experimental Evaluation

6.1   Datasets and Preprocessing

We considered two real-world case studies to evaluate our proposal, to investigate its performance in the anomaly detection task and its efficiency in learning the ensemble of STL formulas.

The Secure Water Treatment (SWaT) [8] testbed is a scaled down water treatment plant for research in the area of cyber security. Data log is collected every $\Delta t = 1\,s$ for $495\,000\,s$ under normal operation ($|\boldsymbol{w}_{train}| = 495\,000$) and for $449\,920\,s$ with attack scenarios ($|\boldsymbol{w}_{test}| = 449\,920$). The dataset consists of 24 sensors and 26 actuators readings, for a total of 50 attributes. Sensor readings are numerical variables, whilst actuator readings are ternary non-ordinal variables. In $\boldsymbol{w}_{test}$ the dataset contains 36 attacks: attacks can affect a single component of the testbed, or span across different components and different stages of the water treatment procedure. A detailed description of the attacks can be found in [8]. Actuators assume the binary values on/off, and a third value corresponding to a short-lasting transition state [26]; we convert actuator variables to binary variables, replacing the transition state with the state towards which the transition is headed.

N-BaIoT is a suite of nine datasets originally proposed in [20] obtained by monitoring nine commercial IoT devices, operating both under normal and anomalous conditions. Benign data and attack data under several attack conditions is collected; particularly, the devices are infected with Mirai and BASH-LITE, two well known IoT malware that can be used to perform botnet attacks. Botnet attacks aim at the creation of a network of infected devices, to perform distributed attacks. The attacks are described in greater detail in [20]. Separately for each device, the datasets collect 115 traffic statistics every, extracted

```
1  function evolve():
2      P ← initialise(n_pop)
3      S ← ∅
4      V_solved = ∅
5      while countDistinct(V_solved) < n_target do
6          P' ← ∅
7          {P_1, ..., P_n} ← buildGroups(P)
8          foreach i ∈ {1, ..., n} do
9              P' ← P' ∪ best(P_i)
10         end
11         while |P'| < n_pop do
12             P' ← P' ∪ selectAndReproduceWithEnfDiv(P)
13         end
14         P ← P'
15         foreach p ∈ P do
16             if isSolution(p) then
17                 {v_1, ..., v_k} ← getVariables(p)
18                 V_solved = V_solved ∪ {v_1, ..., v_k}
19                 foreach v ∈ {v_1, ..., v_k} do
20                     S' ← getIndividualsWithVariable(P, v)
21                     S ← S ∪ S'
22                     P ← P \ S'
23                 end
24             end
25         end
26         if |P| < n_pop then
27             P ← P ∪ initialise(n_pop − |P|)
28         end
29     end
30     return S;
31 end
```

Algorithm 1: One-shot algorithm.

from raw network traffic, $\Delta t = 1\,$s; all attributes are numerical. Considering all datasets, a total of 555 937 benign and 7 329 517 malign observations is collected. Similarly to [20], we used 2/3 of the benign observations as the training set, and concatenated the remaining benign observations and the attack observations to build the test set. Considering median values across the nine datasets, $|w_{\text{train}}| = 33\,032$ and $|w_{\text{test}}| = 844\,327$.

In accordance with the grammar of Fig. 1, we rescaled numerical features to $[0.00, 0.99]$, using min-max normalization, and converted binary states $\{\text{off}, \text{on}\}$ to numerical variables $\{0.00, 0.99\}$. It should be noted that we perform rescaling on the training set only. Consequently, test observations can assume values outside $[0.00, 0.99]$ on numerical variables. This is consistent with the proposal of modeling normal behavior, where values outside the normal ranges may suggest anomalous behavior. Additionally, this choice makes online anomaly detection feasible, since the rescaling of a test observation does not require the entirety of the test set.

6.2 Procedure and Evaluation Metrics

We investigated both the efficiency of our one-shot G3P and the effectiveness in detecting anomalies of the evolved STL. In particular, we were interested in verifying that (i) our one-shot G3P learns STL ensembles faster than a set of executions of plain G3P and (ii) the evolved ensembles are better in detecting anomalies than single STL formulas.

For putting the results of one-shot G3P in perspective, we considered a baseline consisting in a serial execution of 30 runs, with different random seeds, of a plain version of G3P with the same representation, genetic operators, and fitness function (along with other key parameters) of our one-shot G3P. By taking the ensemble composed of the best individuals (all those with perfect fitness) at the last generation of n of the 30 runs, we were able to compare our one-shot G3P against a baseline that evolves few STL formulas (with $n = 1$) or with a G3P-based ensemble learning technique that is not one-shot (with $n > 1$). In other words, in this baseline n allows to control the efficiency-effectiveness trade-off, on the assumption that the larger the ensemble, the better the detection effectiveness and the longer the learning. We call this baseline *multi-run G3P*.

In our one-shot G3P, we used $n_{\text{target}} = 20$, Eq. (2) with $c = 1$ as the fitness function, and $f = 0$ as the isSolution() condition. In both our proposal and the baseline we used the ramped half-and-half initialization with derivation trees depth in $[3, 20]$, a population size of 200 individuals, a maximum tree depth of 20 when applying genetic operators, a tournament size of 5. We used standard G3P mutation and crossover for producing, respectively, 20% and 80% of the offspring. When enforcing diversity, we did a maximum of 100 applications of the genetic operators.

Concerning the thresholds τ, we set it in such a way that 20 and 1 not satisfied formulas, respectively for SWaT and N-BaIoT, suffice for raising an anomaly. We set these values after exploratory analysis.

We implemented[1] our proposal in the Java programming language, building on the tool of [24] which in turns employ the STL monitoring tool Moonlight [1].

For both one-shot G3P and the baseline, we used the trailing 20% of w_{train} as a validation signal. We computed the fitness on the leading 80% and, at the end of the evolution, we discarded STL formulas that resulted in FPR > 0 on the validation set.

Effectiveness and Efficiency Metrics. We evaluated the anomaly detection effectiveness by means of the True Positive Rate (TPR), the False Positive Rate (FPR), and the Area Under the Curve (AUC), obtained by varying τ at prediction time. We adopt the convention that *positive* denotes anomalous instants and *negative* denotes normal (i.e., not anomalous) instants.

Concerning learning efficiency, since in G3P the largest proportion of the computational effort lies in determining the fitness of a solution, we use the number of fitness evaluations f_{evals} to measure efficiency.

6.3   Results

Table 1 presents a comparison of the multi-run G3P and our one-shot G3P over the 10 problems. For the multi-run approach, a single ensemble was produced out of 30 runs for each dataset. For the one-shot algorithm, instead, median values across 10 runs are reported.

The one-shot approach compares favorably with the multi-run one, reaching higher AUC in 6 out of 10 datasets. The one-shot algorithm performs markedly better in N-BaIoT-4 and N-BaIoT-8, where the multi-run baseline ensemble detects no anomaly. Moreover, the one-shot G3P requires significantly fewer f_{evals}, resulting in a substantial efficiency improvement. It should however be noted that the one-shot G3P results in larger ensembles: on SWaT, the median ensemble size is 934 with one-shot and 82 with multi-run—for both, no ensemble pruning was performed.

If we consider an attack scenario as detected when at least one instant during anomalous behavior is labeled as anomalous, then the one-shot approach detects a median of 9 on 36 attacks on SWaT and all attacks on N-BaIoT.

Figure 2 presents an alternative comparison between the baseline and the one-shot approach. The results are displayed in terms of f_{evals} vs. AUC, with the optimum being located in the top left corner (i.e., few fitness evaluations—denoting high efficiency—and high AUC). The results show that reducing the number of runs for building ensembles in multi-run G3P monotonically increases efficiency, but reduces effectiveness as well. Single run ensembles learned with G3P have a tendency to produce solutions with AUC ≈ 0.5 which, in this case, usually denotes STL solutions that are always satisfied by the test set and that identify no anomalies. This, in retrospective, motivates the ensemble learning

---

[1] The code is publicly available at https://github.com/pindri/OneShot-ensemble-learning-anomaly-detection-MTS.

Table 1. Comparison of multi-run and one-shot G3P. For each dataset, the highest AUC and the lowest f_{evals} between the two approaches are highlighted.

Dataset	Multi-run G3P (30 runs)				One-shot G3P ($n_{target} = 20$)			
	TPR	FPR	AUC	f_{evals}	TPR	FPR	AUC	f_{evals}
SWaT	0.6648	0.0005	0.8321	43243	0.6571	0.0007	**0.8401**	**11767**
N-BaIoT-1	0.9981	0.0000	**0.9990**	47152	0.8952	0.0011	0.9475	**3297**
N-BaIoT-2	0.9996	0.0016	0.9989	355696	1.0000	0.0422	**0.9998**	**5732**
N-BaIoT-3	0.9949	0.0000	**0.9974**	51979	0.9596	0.0076	0.9739	**5965**
N-BaIoT-4	0.0000	0.0002	0.4998	298158	0.9272	0.0025	**0.9632**	**35811**
N-BaIoT-5	0.6152	0.0012	0.7681	156033	0.7492	0.0010	**0.8742**	**7898**
N-BaIoT-6	0.7192	0.0011	**0.8594**	371358	0.6807	0.0023	0.8387	**12235**
N-BaIoT-7	0.7070	0.0000	0.8534	269708	0.6896	0.0009	**0.9072**	**16736**
N-BaIoT-8	0.0000	0.0000	0.5000	1015286	0.4166	0.0027	**0.7050**	**88921**
N-BaIoT-9	0.7812	0.0005	**0.8905**	260259	0.7440	0.0011	0.8702	**13696**

approach, since the results show that a single standard G3P run does not reliably produce useful formulas.

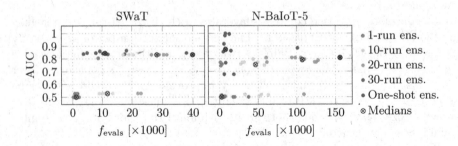

Fig. 2. Comparison of multi-run and one-shot ensembles, efficiency (f_{evals}) vs. performance (AUC).

Formulas Complexity. Figure 3 considers all the STL formulas generated with either the standard G3P approach or our one-shot algorithm. Limiting the analysis to SWaT, we investigate the complexity of the formulas—in isolation, regardless of the ensemble they belong to—in terms of the number of distinct variables, and the necessary length. The latter can be used as a measure of temporal complexity.

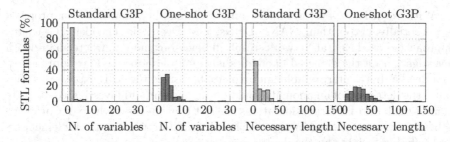

Fig. 3. Complexity of STL formulas obtained with standard G3P and one-shot algorithm on SWaT, in terms of number of variables and necessary length.

With regards to the number of variables, the standard G3P runs produce significantly simpler formulas, with more than 60% of the formulas containing a single variable. The one-shot algorithm, instead, produces a larger percentage of solutions with more variables, with some STL formulas containing more than 20 variables. With regards to the necessary length, the one-shot algorithm produces, once more, formulas that are significantly more complex. In fact, approximately 35% of standard G3P formulas have unitary necessary length: this indicates that they do not contain temporal operators, but rather consist of (combinations of) atomic propositions.

For the standard G3P approach, the large percentage of formulas with small number of variables and small necessary length suggests that premature convergence may indeed be a problem: the evolutions typically converge to *temporally simple* formulas that consider only few variables. Each of these solutions perfectly model the training set in terms of fitness, but is not able to capture actual anomalous behaviors, since it considers only few aspects of the CPS.

Comparison with Literature. We can perform a qualitative[2] comparison of our results and the existing literature. [14] and [15] perform anomaly detection on the SWaT testbed using Generative Adversarial Networks (GAN), whilst [11] uses Deep Neural Networks (DNN). These approaches reach comparable TPR but, when specified, suffer from higher FPR: TPR = 0.6464 and FPR = 0.0046 for [14], TPR = 0.6734 and precision = 0.9897 for [15], and TPR = 0.6785 and precision = 0.9830 for [11]. [7], instead, performs significantly better than our proposal, reaching TPR = 0.7087 with comparable FPR, using invariant-based anomaly detection. The N-BaIoT dataset is used in [20] employing Deep Autoencoders, where all anomalies are detected with low FPR.

Thus, our proposal is competitive on SWaT, whilst it compares unfavourably on N-BaIoT, where it reaches a perfect detection rate only on N-BaIoT-2. However, as mentioned, on N-BaIoT at least one anomalous instant for each attack is correctly identified, and all attacks might thus be considered as identified.

---

[2] For the SWaT testbed, different versions of the dataset exist. Thus, no direct quantitative comparison can be made.

With regards to interpretability and explainability, however, our proposal is potentially better than GANs, DNNs, and Deep Autoencoders. Crucially, approaches based Neural Networks result in black-box models, where an in-depth investigation on the detected anomalies is usually impossible. Our approach is, to a degree, both interpretable and explainable, since the STL expressions that cause the detection of an anomaly could be singled out and investigated, and are human-readable. These considerations suggest that, in cases where our proposal is bested by more performing approaches, it could be used as a complementary tool, offering insights on the detection process.

7   Conclusions

We proposed a one-shot GP algorithm for ensemble learning, evaluating its performance on an anomaly detection task. We compared our proposal with ensembles obtained by repeated evolutions of a standard GP implementation. We deem our results satisfactory and we can summarize the merits of our proposal as follows: (i) it obtains an ensemble of STL formulas more efficiently than repeated independent GP runs, whilst reaching comparable detection performance, (ii) it competes with some of the results available in literature and, when surpassed by more performing but less interpretable methods, can still be useful to gain insights on the detection procedure.

In the future, this work could possibly be extended by an analysis of the role of n_{target} in the trade-off between performance and efficiency, and, additionally, by the implementation of techniques to reduce the size of the one-shot ensembles, to improve explainability and interpretability.

References

1. Bartocci, E., Bortolussi, L., Loreti, M., Nenzi, L., Silvetti, S.: MoonLight: a lightweight tool for monitoring spatio-temporal properties. In: Deshmukh, J., Ničković, D. (eds.) RV 2020. LNCS, vol. 12399, pp. 417–428. Springer, Cham (2020). https://doi.org/10.1007/978-3-030-60508-7_23
2. Bartocci, E., Bortolussi, L., Sanguinetti, G.: Data-driven statistical learning of temporal logic properties. In: Legay, A., Bozga, M. (eds.) FORMATS 2014. LNCS, vol. 8711, pp. 23–37. Springer, Cham (2014). https://doi.org/10.1007/978-3-319-10512-3_3
3. Bartoli, A., De Lorenzo, A., Medvet, E., Tarlao, F.: Learning text patterns using separate-and-conquer genetic programming. In: Machado, P., et al. (eds.) EuroGP 2015. LNCS, vol. 9025, pp. 16–27. Springer, Cham (2015). https://doi.org/10.1007/978-3-319-16501-1_2
4. Deshmukh, J.V., Donzé, A., Ghosh, S., Jin, X., Juniwal, G., Seshia, S.A.: Robust online monitoring of signal temporal logic. Form. Methods Syst. Des. 51(1), 5–30 (2017). https://doi.org/10.1007/s10703-017-0286-7
5. Donzé, A., Ferrère, T., Maler, O.: Efficient robust monitoring for STL. In: Sharygina, N., Veith, H. (eds.) CAV 2013. LNCS, vol. 8044, pp. 264–279. Springer, Heidelberg (2013). https://doi.org/10.1007/978-3-642-39799-8_19

6. Ergurtuna, M., Gol, E.A.: An efficient formula synthesis method with past signal temporal logic. IFAC-PapersOnLine **52**(11), 43–48 (2019)
7. Feng, C., Palleti, V.R., Mathur, A., Chana, D.: A systematic framework to generate invariants for anomaly detection in industrial control systems. In: NDSS (2019)
8. Goh, J., Adepu, S., Junejo, K.N., Mathur, A.: A dataset to support research in the design of secure water treatment systems. In: Havarneanu, G., Setola, R., Nassopoulos, H., Wolthusen, S. (eds.) CRITIS 2016. LNCS, vol. 10242, pp. 88–99. Springer, Cham (2017). https://doi.org/10.1007/978-3-319-71368-7_8
9. Goh, J., Adepu, S., Tan, M., Lee, Z.S.: Anomaly detection in cyber physical systems using recurrent neural networks. In: 2017 IEEE 18th International Symposium on High Assurance Systems Engineering (HASE), pp. 140–145. IEEE (2017)
10. Wayne, H.: Temporal logic. In: Practical TLA+, pp. 97–110. Apress, Berkeley (2018). https://doi.org/10.1007/978-1-4842-3829-5_6
11. Inoue, J., Yamagata, Y., Chen, Y., Poskitt, C.M., Sun, J.: Anomaly detection for a water treatment system using unsupervised machine learning. In: 2017 IEEE International Conference on Data Mining Workshops (ICDMW), pp. 1058–1065. IEEE (2017)
12. Jha, S., Tiwari, A., Seshia, S.A., Sahai, T., Shankar, N.: TeLEx: learning signal temporal logic from positive examples using tightness metric. Form. Methods Syst. Des. **54**(3), 364–387 (2019). https://doi.org/10.1007/s10703-019-00332-1
13. Jin, X., Donzé, A., Deshmukh, J.V., Seshia, S.A.: Mining requirements from closed-loop control models. IEEE Trans. Comput. Aided Des. Integr. Circuits Syst. **34**(11), 1704–1717 (2015)
14. Li, D., Chen, D., Goh, J., Ng, S.K.: Anomaly detection with generative adversarial networks for multivariate time series. arXiv preprint arXiv:1809.04758 (2018)
15. Li, D., Chen, D., Jin, B., Shi, L., Goh, J., Ng, S.-K.: MAD-GAN: multivariate anomaly detection for time series data with generative adversarial networks. In: Tetko, I.V., Kůrková, V., Karpov, P., Theis, F. (eds.) ICANN 2019. LNCS, vol. 11730, pp. 703–716. Springer, Cham (2019). https://doi.org/10.1007/978-3-030-30490-4_56
16. Maler, O., Nickovic, D.: Monitoring temporal properties of continuous signals. In: Lakhnech, Y., Yovine, S. (eds.) FORMATS/FTRTFT -2004. LNCS, vol. 3253, pp. 152–166. Springer, Heidelberg (2004). https://doi.org/10.1007/978-3-540-30206-3_12
17. Maler, O., Ničković, D.: Monitoring properties of analog and mixed-signal circuits. Int. J. Softw. Tools Technol. Transfer **15**(3), 247–268 (2013)
18. Manzoni, L., Bartoli, A., Castelli, M., Gonçalves, I., Medvet, E.: Specializing context-free grammars with a (1+1)-EA. IEEE Trans. Evol. Comput. **24**(5), 960–973 (2020)
19. Medvet, E., Bartoli, A., Carminati, B., Ferrari, E.: Evolutionary inference of attribute-based access control policies. In: Gaspar-Cunha, A., Henggeler Antunes, C., Coello, C.C. (eds.) EMO 2015. LNCS, vol. 9018, pp. 351–365. Springer, Cham (2015). https://doi.org/10.1007/978-3-319-15934-8_24
20. Meidan, Y., et al.: N-BaIoT-network-based detection of IoT botnet attacks using deep autoencoders. IEEE Pervasive Comput. **17**(3), 12–22 (2018)
21. Nenzi, L., Silvetti, S., Bartocci, E., Bortolussi, L.: A robust genetic algorithm for learning temporal specifications from data. In: McIver, A., Horvath, A. (eds.) QEST 2018. LNCS, vol. 11024, pp. 323–338. Springer, Cham (2018). https://doi.org/10.1007/978-3-319-99154-2_20

22. Nicolau, M.: Understanding grammatical evolution: initialisation. Genet. Program Evolvable Mach. **18**(4), 467–507 (2017). https://doi.org/10.1007/s10710-017-9309-9

23. Pappa, G.L., Freitas, A.A.: Evolving rule induction algorithms with multi-objective grammar-based genetic programming. Knowl. Inf. Syst. **19**(3), 283–309 (2009)

24. Pigozzi, F., Medvet, E., Nenzi, L.: Mining road traffic rules with signal temporal logic and grammar-based genetic programming. Appl. Sci. **11**(22), 10573 (2021)

25. Squillero, G., Tonda, A.: Divergence of character and premature convergence: a survey of methodologies for promoting diversity in evolutionary optimization. Inf. Sci. **329**, 782–799 (2016)

26. Umer, M.A., Mathur, A., Junejo, K.N., Adepu, S.: Generating invariants using design and data-centric approaches for distributed attack detection. Int. J. Crit. Infrastruct. Prot. **28**, 100341 (2020)

27. Virgolin, M.: Genetic programming is naturally suited to evolve bagging ensembles. In: Proceedings of the Genetic and Evolutionary Computation Conference, pp. 830–839 (2021)

28. Whigham, P.A., et al.: Grammatically-based genetic programming. In: Proceedings of the Workshop on Genetic Programming: From Theory to Real-World Applications, vol. 16, pp. 33–41. Citeseer (1995)

Multi-objective Genetic Programming with the Adaptive Weighted Splines Representation for Symbolic Regression

Christian Raymond[ID], Qi Chen[✉][ID], Bing Xue[ID], and Mengjie Zhang[ID]

School of Engineering and Computer Science, Victoria University of Wellington,
Wellington, New Zealand
{Christian.Raymond,Qi.Chen,Bing.Xue,Mengjie.Zhang}@ecs.vuw.ac.nz

Abstract. Genetic Programming (GP) based symbolic regression is prone to generating complex models which often overfit the training data and generalise poorly onto unseen data. To address this issue, many pieces of research have been devoted to controlling the model complexity of GP. One recent work aims to control model complexity using a new representation called Adaptive Weighted Splines. With its semi-structured characteristic, the Adaptive Weighted Splines representation can control the model complexity explicitly, which was demonstrated to be significantly better than its tree-based counterpart at generalising to unseen data. This work seeks to significantly extend the previous work by proposing a multi-objective GP algorithm with the Adaptive Weighted Splines representation, which utilises parsimony pressure to further control the model complexity, as well as improve the interpretability of the learnt models. Experimental results show that, compared with single-objective GP with the Adaptive Weighted Splines and multi-objective tree-based GP with parsimony pressure, the new multi-objective GP method generally obtains superior fronts and produces better generalising models. These models are also significantly smaller and more interpretable.

Keywords: Genetic Programming · Symbolic Regression · Multi-objective Optimization · Generalisation

1 Introduction

As a regression technique, Genetic Programming (GP) for symbolic regression (GPSR) [14] aims to learn a mathematical function that best represents the underlying relationship between the given input features X and an output target y, where X and y are drawn on the assumption of a joint probability distribution $P(X, y)$. Different from traditional and numerical regression methods [15], GPSR has the capability to learn both the model structure and the model parameters simultaneously with few assumptions on the model structure or the data distribution. Due to the symbolic nature of its solutions and the flexible representation ability, GPSR is typically good at learning complex underlying

© The Author(s), under exclusive license to Springer Nature Switzerland AG 2022
E. Medvet et al. (Eds.): EuroGP 2022, LNCS 13223, pp. 51–67, 2022.
https://doi.org/10.1007/978-3-031-02056-8_4

relationship in the data. However, it also has the downside of leading to over-complex models which not only bring unnecessary computational costs but also have poor interpretability. Moreover, these over-complex models often overfit the training data thus have poor generalisation ability.

The model evaluation measure is also another component in GPSR which often leads to over-complex models. The GP individual in the population that best min-imises/maximises an objective function, *i.e.* the fitness function, is selected as the final model. Traditionally selecting individuals is guided through the Empirical Risk Minimisation (ERM) principle, giving propagation rights to individuals that have the lowest training error. However, chasing a lower training error without suf-ficient regularization often leads GPSR to generate over-complex models which learn spurious patterns from the training data; consequently, poorly generalising to the unseen data. This is particularly the case when learning from noisy data or in the low data regime when there are few instances available to train on.

Recent work presented in [21,23] attempted to regulate the problem of poor generalisation by introducing a new representation for GPSR called Adaptive Weighted Splines (AWS). The AWS representation is a semi-structured represen-tation that has some of the symbolic properties of traditional tree-based GP. It has the additional benefit of more explicit control over the model complexity through the use of splines. Preliminary experimental results into GP with the AWS repre-sentation has shown promising generalisation performance, consistently outper-forming its tree-based counterpart on a diverse set of regression tasks. However, the limitation of ERM, which is a key driving force behind over complex GPSR models, has not been considered in GPSR with the AWS representation [23].

1.1   Research Objectives

Multi-objective optimisation in traditional tree-based GP [16], which minimises both the training error and the model complexity has been shown to result in better generalization and more interpretable models [8,9], while there has been no such similar work yet in regard to using the proposed AWS representation in GP [23]. Therefore, the overall goal of this work is to develop a new multi-objective GP method with the AWS representation which will fill this void and further enhance the generalisation ability and model interpretability of GPSR. Explicitly, this work aims to achieve the following four research objectives:

1. Develop a multi-objective GP-AWS method to minimise both the training error and the number of features used in the model.
2. Evaluate the performance of the proposed method by comparing its perfor-mance against both single-objective and multi-objective GP methods.
3. Investigate whether the new multiobjective GP method can lead to the devel-opment of more parsimonious and better generalising symbolic regression models.
4. Perform a visual interpretation of the models generated by the multi-objective GP-AWS method, as well as providing feature importance analysis regard-ing the number of mutually shared features and their corresponding feature weights.

2   Background

2.1   Model Complexity and Generalisation

Many papers have been devoted to improving the generalisation of the GPSR models via regulating the model complexity [1, 6, 16, 22]. These contributions can broadly be partitioned into two distinct categories, *i.e.* regulating the structural complexity and the functional model complexity.

Structural Complexity of GP Models – Research into regulating the structural complexity of GP models usually involves examining the size and/or the structure of the trees. Typical examples include counting the number of structural elements such as the number of nodes, layers/depth, then applying the Minimum Description Length (MDL) *i.e.* Occam's razor principle [4], to prefer simpler models. Other structure-based approaches include Operator Equalization [24] which controls the distribution of individual sizes in the population and explicit feature selection [5] to avoid incorporating less informative features to thus reduce the unnecessary structural complexity.

Regulating the structural complexity tends to be easy to implement and applicable to many different domains. However, many of these approaches are relatively ineffective at eliminating overfitting since the structural complexity has limited correlation with the generalisation ability of the models. GP individuals can be simplified numerically [13] and/or algebraically [27], such that the structural complexity is decreased significantly, but the functional complexity and generalisation performance remains the same.

Functional Complexity of GP Models – The functional complexity of a GP model is measured by the behavior of model over a possible input space. Some examples of regulating functional complexity for improving generalisation in GPSR are summarized as follows: Vladislavleva et al. [26] use the Order of Nonlinearity of a Chebyshev polynomial approximation of GP individuals to perform multi-objective optimisation on the error and the model complexity. Chen et al. [7] develop GP with Structural Risk Minimisation methods which measure the behavioral complexity of GP models via their Vapnik-Chervonenkis dimensions. Raymond et al. [9, 22] introduce the Rademacher Complexity, which is a data dependent complexity measure and considers the distribution of the training data, into GPSR to approximate the complexity of GP individual and penalise individuals which fit the Rademacher variable.

Regulating functional complexity tends to be more effective at enhancing generalisation due to being more closely related to overfitting. However, measuring the functional complexity of an unstructured function is not trivial, as getting a reliable approximation of the model complexity is often very computational expensive [7].

2.2   Genetic Programming with Adaptive Weighted Splines

Seeking new more well behaved representations is an alternative choice for controlling model complexity. Previous work in [23] proposed a new representation for GP named Adaptive Weighted Splines (AWS), which is a semi-structured representation that concedes some of the symbolic properties of GP in order to offer more explicit control over the complexity of the models through the use of splines. The AWS representation and the relevant components are introduced in the following sections.

Individual Representation – When using the AWS representation, given the inputs space X which has p features, a GP model f is represented by an aggregation of p *feature splines* as shown in Eq. (1). Each feature spline models one feature in the input space X. Each spline consists of three components: a *smoothing spline* S, a *primary coefficient* θ and a *secondary coefficient* β. The smoothing spline S_i has a degree k, and it is composed of m smoothing spline knots. The two coefficients θ and β simulate the processes of embedded feature selection and feature weighting. This has the benefit of making the influence of each feature on the final predictions of f quantitative and explicit. The p splines are linearly combined using the weighted summation operation to predict y.

$$f(X; m, k, \lambda) = \frac{\sum_{i=1}^{p} \Big(round(\theta_i) \cdot \beta_i \cdot S_i(x; \mathcal{T}_i, k, \lambda) \Big)}{\sum_{i=1}^{p} \Big(round(\theta_i) \cdot \beta_i \Big)} \tag{1}$$

With AWS, a GP individual is conveniently represented using a continuous vector which consists of the two coefficients and a knot vector of the smoothing spline knots points for each of the feature spline components. Figure 1 shows an example of GP-AWS model with two features splines which are both modelled by a cubic *i.e.* $k = 3$ smoothing spline, defined by six smoothing spline knots *i.e.* $m = 6$, and with no smoothing penalty applied *i.e.* $\lambda = 0$.

Smoothing Splines – A smoothing spline is defined by a *smoothing spline knot vector*. It consists of a sequence of m points $\mathcal{T}_i = \{(x_1, y_1), (x_2, y_2), \cdots, (x_m, y_m)\}$, a degree k and a smoothing penalty λ. To reduce the number of parameters, all knots in $\mathcal{T}_i$ are placed equispaced along x_i. Larger values of m will lead to models with higher variance and lower bias, while a smaller m leads to higher bias and lower variance of the model. The smoothing penalty λ controls the trade-off between closeness and smoothness of fit. The larger λ, the more smoothing of the model. Moreover, to simplify implementation of the representation, min-max scaling is applied to all the training features X and targets y. The scaling process allows the feature splines to be represented using continuous vectors with values sitting between the interval of $(0, 1)$.

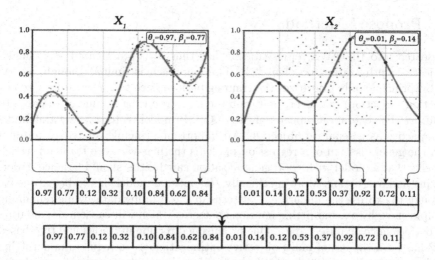

Fig. 1. A GP-AWS model to the bi-variate regression problem: $f(x_1, x_2) = \sin(x_1) + 0.25 \cdot x_1 + 2 + N(0, 0.2)$, where x_2 is random noise.

Primary Coefficient for Feature Selection – The primary coefficient θ takes a discrete value of either 0 or 1, which controls whether or not the respective feature spline is used in the model. The value is represented as a continuous value between 0 and 1, but is rounded to the nearest integer when the model is evaluated. Incorporating the coefficient θ in AWS emulates embedded feature selection, as only a subset of the original features are used in constructing the final model.

Secondary Coefficient for Feature Weighting – The secondary coefficient β in the feature spline of AWS takes on a continuous value between 0 and 1. β controls the amount of influence made by the respective feature splines to the prediction of the model. This simulates a feature weighting process, whereby more important features are associated with larger weights, compared to less important features which are associated with smaller weights.

Learning Process – The learning process in GP with the AWS representation follows a very prototypical implementation of a genetic algorithm, using the standard genetic operators of crossover, mutation and elitism as well as selection. For the selection operator, the commonly used tournament selection samples a predefined number (*i.e.* tournament size) of individuals and selects the best individual which best minimises some typical regression loss function, such as the Mean Squared Error (MSE) or Root Mean Squared Error (RMSE). For termination criteria, either a predefined number of maximum generations can be set or termination can occur when there is a stagnation in the performance.

3   Proposed Method

Research into the AWS representation has thus far been treated as a single-objective optimization problem [23]. This approach is limited though, as the ERM principle only prioritizes the training performance when performing reproduction (selection, crossover, mutation etc.). A promising avenue of research to improve the generalisation capabilities of GPSR models is to consider the model complexity as a separate objective. An important principle related to improving the generalisation of a regression model is the bias-variance trade-off, which asserts that a model with good generalisation capabilities should balance underfitting and overfitting. More specifically, the optimal model should be expressive enough to express the underlying patterns in the training data, while remaining simple enough to avoid fitting spurious patterns which will cause a degradation in performance on unseen data. One promising direction in traditional tree-based GP has been the use of multi-objective optimization [1] to regulate underfitting and overfitting by minimizing both the training error and some model complexity penalty simultaneously.

3.1   Multi-objective Fitness Function

In this section a new multi-objective method for GPSR is developed, which is called *Genetic Programming with Adaptive Weighted Splines and Parsimony Pressure* (GP-AWS-PP). Similar to the baseline single-objective GP-AWS method [23], the new GP method will continue to learn the parameters of the AWS representation, which is conveniently internally encoded as a $p \cdot (2 + m)$ length continuous vector. However, instead of only minimizing a single objective f_1 in GP-AWS, such as the Mean Squared Error (MSE), where y and $\hat{y}$ are the true and predicted output values respectively, and n is the number of instances.

$$f_1 = \frac{1}{n} \sum_{i=1}^{n} \left(y_i - \hat{y}_i \right)^2 \tag{2}$$

An additional objective is also minimised simultaneously which is the total number of active features f_2 used by the model, made explicit by the primary coefficients θ.

$$f_2 = \sum_{i=1}^{p} \theta_i \begin{cases} 1, & \text{if } \theta_i \geq 0.5 \\ 0, & \text{if } \theta_i < 0.5 \end{cases} \tag{3}$$

This is also equivalent to minimizing the number of active parameters in the AWS representation (*i.e.* L_0 regularization), as a θ_i value of 0 will turn the corresponding i^{th} feature spline into an inactive component, *i.e.* an intron, which can be discarded when presenting the final model at inference time.

Incorporating this additional objective f_2 is expected to improve both the generalisation and interpretability of the solutions generated by GP. With respect to generalisation, minimizing the number of active/selected features can reduce the tendencies of a regression model to learn spurious patterns in features that are not relevant to the target y, or are redundant if the signal is captured by another related feature. In regard to interpretability, a model that uses fewer features is easier to communicate and understand, as the set of features that composes the model is smaller [5].

3.2 Non-dominated Sorting Genetic Algorithm II

To optimise the multiple objectives in this work, the popular algorithm non-dominated Sorting Genetic Algorithm (NSGA-II) [10] is used instead. NSGA-II is a computationally fast and elitist algorithm based on the key ideas of non-dominated sorting, which involves sorting individuals into ordered fronts based on their fitness. Additionally, in NSGA-II a unique selection operator is used that generates the next generation of individuals by taking the union of the parent and offspring populations and selecting only the best individuals with respect to their fitness and crowding distance, which ensures that the population is composed from a high performing set of diverse solutions.

Compared with the single objective GP-AWS method which requires tuning of a weighting parameter to balance the training performance with the model complexity, the newly proposed multi-objective GP-AWS-PP method utilizes the advantage of the population-based mechanism in GP to attain a wide set of pareto non-dominated solutions with strong performance in each objective with only a single execution of the entire algorithm.

3.3 Combining Multi-objective Optimization with the Adaptive Weighted Splines

In traditional tree-based GPSR, many papers have been devoted to improving the generalisation performance as well as the interpretability of models through the use of multi-objective optimization on both the error and the structural complexity, which are often referred to as GP with Parsimony Pressure [17–19]. These methods have shown some limited success, often making the models noticeably smaller (fewer parameters). However, they have been shown to be relatively ineffective at improving generalisation, as the performance is greatly restricted by the tree-based representation which can be both algebraically [27] and numerically [13, 28] simplified. This makes the structural complexity in tree-based GP necessarily only a loose proxy for how the model will behave.

Fortunately, one of the key benefits of the new AWS representation is its semi-structured fixed-length representation, which avoids the use of overly verbose sub-components by enforcing structure into the representation. Therefore, by minimising the number of active features in multi-objective AWS, which by association will also minimise the number of effective parameters in the model, and by upfront defining the desired flexibility of the splines through the number of smoothing spline knots m, it is possible to explicitly control the bias-variance trade-off in AWS as well as increase the interpretability. This is quantified by the number of active feature used by the learnt models.

4   Experiment Settings

4.1   Benchmark Methods

To examine the generalisation capabilities and interpretability of the proposed method GP-AWS-PP, comparisons are performed against a multi-objective parsimony pressure GP method using the traditional tree-based representation which also treats the model complexity as an independent objective. This is intended to highlight the benefits of the AWS representation over the traditional tree-based representation for GPSR. In addition, experiments are also conducted to compare against two baseline single-objective GP methods, which are utilized to demonstrate the benefits of considering both the training error and the model complexity as two separate objectives. More specifically, the three benchmark methods are as follows:

- **Genetic Programming with Parsimony Pressure (GP-PP)**: a multi-objective GP method, which introduces parsimony pressure into GP by simultaneously minimizing both the training MSE as well as the the number of nodes, *i.e.* the model size, via NSGA-II.
- **Genetic Programming (GP)**: a standard implementation of GPSR, which uses the traditional tree based representation to minimise the single-objective of the training MSE.
- **Genetic Programming with Adaptive Weighted Splines (GP-AWS)**: a single-objective GPSR method which uses the AWS representation to minimise the training MSE [23].

4.2   Benchmark Problems

In this work, the newly proposed method as well as the three benchmark methods are evaluated on a number of regression datasets of varying characteristics and sizes. The datasets selected are summarized in Table 1. There are eight real-world datasets which have been selected from previous GPSR research [20, 22–24]. The following datasets *Concrete Compressive Strength*, *Diabetes*, *Red Wine*, *Boston Housing*, *Automobile* and *Communities and Crime* were taken from the University of California Irvine's (UCI) Machine Learning Repository [11]. The remaining real-world dataset *Pollution* and *Tecator* can be found in the Carnegie Mellon University (CMU) StatLib dataset archive [25].

Table 1. Benchmark Datasets

Dataset	Number of Features	Number of Instances		
		Total	Training	Testing
Concrete Strength	8	1030	309	721
Diabetes	10	442	132	310
Red Wine	11	1599	480	1119
Boston House	13	506	152	354
Pollution	15	60	18	42
Automobile	75	205	61	144
Communities Crime	122	1994	199	1795
Tecator	124	240	72	168

In regard to the partitioning of the datasets, for pre-partitioned datasets, the original partitioning was preserved, while for those that did not come pre-partitioned, following previous research [22], they were split into training and testing sets using a 30:70 partitioning. The number of training instances was deliberately made small to simulate the real-world situations where there are often very few instances available, resulting in supervised learning methods being highly prone to overfitting, which is one of the primary areas of interest in this work.

4.3   Parameter Settings

To ensure a fair comparison is made between the four tested methods, identical parameters have been used where possible. For all the methods, the population size has been set to 512 and has been evolved over 100 generations to optimise for the MSE. To evolve the individuals, the following genetic operator rates were used: *crossover* = 0.75, *mutation* = 0.2 *and elitism* = 0.05. Selection of individuals from the population was performed using a standard tournament based selection method, where the tournament was of size 2. Note that further experiments were conducted using larger tournament sizes to ensure that GP was not being systematically disadvantaged, the results showed no statistically significant differences. The remaining settings for the two groups of GPSR methods using the different representations are presented as follows:

– **GP and GP-PP using the tree-based representation:** Similar to previous research into GP for symbolic regression [22], the function set contains the following operators: $\{+, -, *, \%\}$ and the terminal set contains all features in the respective dataset, *i.e.* $\{x_1, x_2 \cdots, x_p\}$, as well as ephemeral constants which have random values between the range of $(-1, 1)$. As for initialization, *Ramped Half and Half* was chosen to generate the initial population. In regard to the genetic operators the popular *One Point Crossover* and *Uniform Mutation* is used.

- **GP-AWS and GP-AWS-PP using the AWS representation:** Following previous work [23], the following AWS parameters were selected: the number of smoothing spline knots $m = 6$, the smoothing penalty $\lambda = 0$ which means no smoothing, and a degree k of 3 is used. In regard to the genetic operators the $P \cdot K$ *Crossover* and $P \cdot K$ *Mutation* presented in [23] is used.

To investigate the performance of the newly proposed method, 100 independent executions of GP, GP-PP, GP-AWS and GP-AWS-PP are performed on each of the eight real world datasets.

5 Results and Analysis

The effectiveness of GP-AWS-PP on enhancing the generalisation and the interpretability of the learnt GPSR models is shown in this section. It involves a comparison of the hypervolume values between the two multi-objective GP methods, which is intended to highlight the benefits of incorporating EMO and the AWS representation against into GP compared to the traditional tree-based representation. A detailed analysis on the front obtained by the four GP methods is also included. Note that for single-objective GP methods, a "front" is obtained by considering the performance and the number of nodes in the best models for an easy comparison. A demonstration and analysis on the interpretability of the GPSR models in GP-AWS-PP is also presented.

5.1 Comparisons of Hypervolume Indicator

Comparing the performance of GP-AWS-PP to its tree-based counterpart GP-PP, the hypervolume indicator is employed. The mean and standard deviation hypervolume values shown in Table 2 are computed using the popular JMetalPy python library [3,12], which calculates the hypervolume values of the 100 training and testing fronts based on the MSE and the number of parameters. Additionally, the statistical significance based on the non-parametric Mann-Whitney U-test [2] with a significance level of 0.01 is shown in the column titled *SS*. Where a "+" indicates that the respective method has achieved a significantly better result compared to the opposing method, a "−" indicates that the respective method has achieved a significantly worse results than the opposing method, and finally a "=" indicates that both methods are similar in their performance. Examining the training hypervolume results it is observed that GP-AWS-PP performs statistically significantly better as quantified by the hypervolume indicator on 5 of the 8 datasets tested when compared to GP-PP. On the remaining datasets GP-AWS-PP performs equivalently to GP-PP on the Red Wine dataset, and on the Tecator and Communities and Crime datasets GP-PP performs better then GP-AWS-PP. In regard to the testing hypervolume results, the results remain largely consistent with the training hypervolume results seen previously. The only difference observed is on the Red Wine dataset, where GP-PP now shows marginally better hypervolume results compared to GP-AWS-PP on average.

Table 2. Training and Testing Hypervolume Values based on the MSE and the Number of Parameters.

Dataset	Method	Training Avg ± Std	SS	Testing Avg ± Std	SS
Concrete	GP-PP	0.8116 ± 0.0181	−	0.8102 ± 0.0214	−
	GP-AWS-PP	0.9402 ± 0.0034	+	0.9353 ± 0.0042	+
Diabetes	GP-PP	0.2760 ± 0.2598	−	0.2989 ± 0.2703	−
	GP-AWS-PP	0.8850 ± 0.0024	+	0.8441 ± 0.0029	+
Red Wine	GP-PP	0.9790 ± 0.0015	=	0.9787 ± 0.0021	+
	GP-AWS-PP	0.9794 ± 0.0001	=	0.9778 ± 0.0003	−
Boston	GP-PP	0.9532 ± 0.0081	−	0.8576 ± 0.0228	−
	GP-AWS-PP	0.9819 ± 0.0004	+	0.9317 ± 0.0061	+
Pollution	GP-PP	0.9852 ± 0.0024	−	0.9831 ± 0.0037	−
	GP-AWS-PP	0.9917 ± 0.0000	+	0.9884 ± 0.0004	+
Automobile	GP-PP	0.8823 ± 0.0249	−	0.7766 ± 0.0996	−
	GP-AWS-PP	0.9374 ± 0.0077	+	0.8909 ± 0.0148	+
Crime	GP-PP	0.4557 ± 0.0542	+	0.3864 ± 0.0669	+
	GP-AWS-PP	0.3806 ± 0.0224	−	0.3303 ± 0.0248	−
Tecator	GP-PP	0.9711 ± 0.0089	+	0.9722 ± 0.0086	+
	GP-AWS-PP	0.9122 ± 0.0090	−	0.9111 ± 0.0091	-

Analysis of the hypervolume results reveals that in the majority of cases GP-AWS-PP is able to achieve better hypervolume values compared to GP-PP. The experimental results also show that GP-AWS-PP typically has much higher mean and far smaller standard deviation hypervolume values compared to GP-PP, suggesting that GP-AWS-PP learns superior fronts compared to GP-PP on average.

Note that in two cases GP-PP achieved better hypervolume values. This was primarily due to the ability of tree-based GP-PP to more effectively minimise the number of nodes/parameters when compared to GP-AWS-PP (as shown in Figs. 2 and 3 analysed in the following section). Most importantly, GP-AWS-PP consistently generates better performing solutions with respect to the primary objective of the MSE, which is the more salient of the two considered objectives.

5.2   Analyses of Fronts

The final training and testing fronts extracted from 100 independent runs in GP-PP and GP-AWS-PP are shown in Fig. 2 and 3 respectively. The fronts are computed by taking the union of 100 independent executions and taking the best MSE values (f_1) at each discrete increment with respect to the number of nodes/parameters (f_2) and removing all dominated solutions, thus giving the *best non-dominated front*. Additionally, to compare the performance of the multi-objective GP methods with the single-objective GP methods, the non-dominated best-of-run models for GP and GP-AWS from 100 independent runs are shown.

Analyses of Training Fronts – Comparing the training plots of the two GP methods with the AWS representations shown in Fig. 2, it is observed that the solutions generated by GP-AWS-PP typically have a slightly higher training MSE than GP-AWS method on all datasets. These results are to be expected since the GP-AWS method exclusively aims to optimise for the training error, while GP-AWS-PP also optimises for the complexity of the models (*i.e.* the number of active features) which is a conflicting objective with minimizing the training error.

Comparing the training results of GP-AWS-PP with the two tree-based GP methods, it is observed that GP-AWS-PP is far more effective at minimizing the training MSE on all the datasets tested excluding for Communities and Crime, which is consistent with the findings in [23]. This further supports the claim that the AWS representation for GPSR is highly competitive and often superior to the traditional tree-based representation, in both single and multi-objective scenarios.

Analyses of Test Fronts – As shown in Fig. 3, the testing fronts show that GP-AWS-PP generally obtains very promising generalisation performance, which is notably better than the two GP methods using the tree-based representation in seven of the eight tested datasets except for Red Wine. The superior generalisation performance of GP-AWS-PP over GP and GP-PP confirms the benefits of the semi-structured representation at regulating model functional complexity.

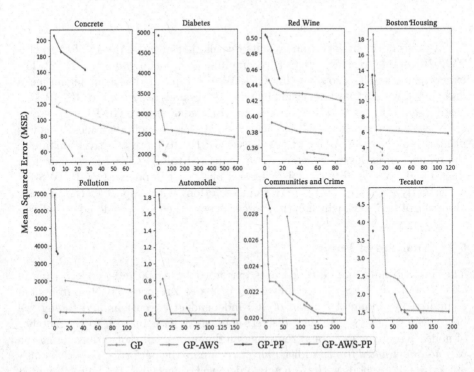

Fig. 2. Best Non-dominated fronts of the **Training MSE** and the **Number of Parameters.**

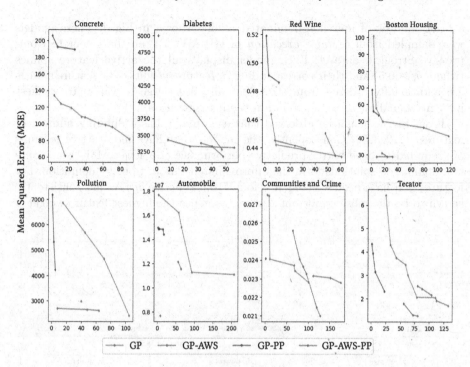

Fig. 3. Best Non-dominated Fronts of the **Testing MSE** and the **Number of Parameters.**

Compared with the single-objective GP-AWS, the pattern is very different from that in the training set. GP-AWS typically constructs highly complex solutions (denoted by the number of parameters/features used) which outperforms GP-AWS-PP on the training sets but poorly generalises onto the unseen testing set. More specifically, it is observed that on Concrete Compressive Strength, Diabetes, Boston Housing, Pollution, Automobile, Communities and Crime and Tecator GP-AWS-PP obtains superior generalisation performance with respect to the testing MSE by also considering the model complexity as a separate objective.

Furthermore, this superior generalisation performance of GP-AWS-PP is often achieved using only a small fraction of the full feature set. This is especially noticeable on Pollution, Automobile and Tecator, where superior generalisation performance is achieved with less then half the number of features used compared to single-objective GP-AWS method. This clearly demonstrates the performance gain of the proposed multi-objective method GP-AWS-PP over its single objective counterpart GP-AWS to learn both highly parsimonious and interpretable regression models, that also generalise well onto unseen data.

5.3   Visualizations and Analyses of GPSR Models in GP-AWS-PP

To further understand the effects of using evolutionary multi-objective optimization in collaboration with the AWS representation, this section provides a brief analysis of four non-dominated models shown in Fig. 4. These models were sampled from a *single execution* of GP-AWS-PP on the Concrete Compressive Strength dataset. Each model displays all the active feature splines (where $\theta_i \geq 0.5$) and their corresponding β_i feature weights. The feature splines are additionally ordered from strongest influence (large β_i value) to weakest influence (smallest β_i value) to aid in the interpretation.

From Fig. 4, it can be observed that each model has a differing number of features, $\{1, 2, 3, 5\}$. Consequently, the models that have more active features are required to have better predictive performance (*i.e.* lower MSE) since only non-dominated solutions form the approximated Pareto front by definition. For features that have been selected, it is found that *concrete age* X_8 has consistently shown to be the most important feature, as it has the highest feature weight β

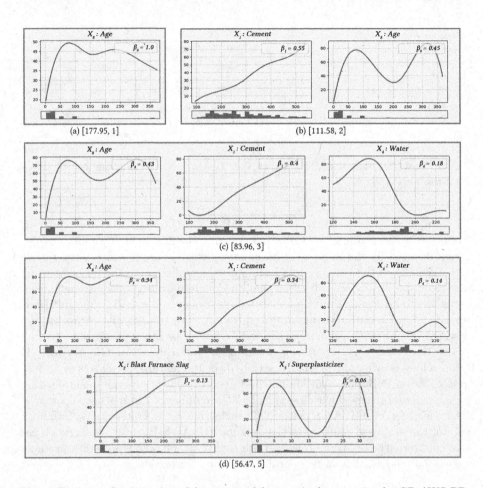

Fig. 4. Four non-dominated models generated from a single execution by GP-AWS-PP on the Concrete Compressive Strength dataset. *Testing* MSE and number of active is displayed below each of the respective sub-figure.

in models (a), (c) and (d) and the second height weight in (b), with a weighting of 45% to the final prediction. A similar pattern occurs for the second most important feature *cement quantity* X_1 (in kgs), which shows the second highest feature weight β in models (a), (c) and (d) and highest in (b), with a weight of 55% to the final prediction.

One benefit of AWS over traditional tree-based GP is that features can easily be inspected by themselves comparably in some respects to what can be done in a linear model. This is useful as it allows one to interpret the effects of a single feature in isolation with respect to the final predicted value. For example, examining X_8 which represents the age of the concrete in days it is observed that in models (a), (b), (c) and (d) the output y value which represents concrete compressive strength is initially very low. This make sense as the concrete is still drying, and requires more time to fully harden and achieve full strength. As age increases it is observed that the compressive strength of the concrete peaks at around 75 before gradually dropping off (there is some variation between models past 150 days due to low data density showing below the plot).

6   Conclusions and Future Work

This paper has conducted the very first investigation into applying evolutionary multi-objective optimization techniques to a semi-structured representation (*i.e.* the AWS representation) for GPSR. The comparisons against traditional tree-based GP methods using both single-objective and multi-objective learning frameworks highlights the highly performant generalisation capabilities of both the single-objective GP-AWS and the newly proposed GP-AWS-PP. Moreover, the experimental investigations also confirms that the models learnt by the new multi-objective GP method have much better interpretablity, compared to the originally single-objective GP-AWS method. A number of interesting findings have also been found regarding interpreting features used in the learnt models highlights some potential future work into utilizing the AWS representation for enhancing the interpretability of many learning algorithms.

References

1. Agapitos, A., Loughran, R., Nicolau, M., Lucas, S., O'Neill, M., Brabazon, A.: A survey of statistical machine learning elements in genetic programming. IEEE Trans. Evol. Comput. **23**(6), 1029–1048 (2019)
2. Arcuri, A., Briand, L.: A practical guide for using statistical tests to assess randomized algorithms in software engineering. In: 2011 33rd International Conference on Software Engineering (ICSE), pp. 1–10. IEEE (2011)
3. Benítez-Hidalgo, A., Nebro, A.J., García-Nieto, J., Oregi, I., Ser, J.D.: jMetalPy: a python framework for multi-objective optimization with metaheuristics. Swarm Evol. Comput. 100598 (2019). http://www.sciencedirect.com/science/article/pii/S2210650219301397
4. Blumer, A., Ehrenfeucht, A., Haussler, D., Warmuth, M.K.: Occam's razor. Inf. Process. Lett. **24**(6), 377–380 (1987)

5. Chen, Q., Zhang, M., Xue, B.: Feature selection to improve generalization of genetic programming for high-dimensional symbolic regression. IEEE Trans. Evol. Comput. **21**(5), 792–806 (2017)
6. Chen, Q., Zhang, M., Xue, B.: Structural risk minimization-driven genetic programming for enhancing generalization in symbolic regression. IEEE Trans. Evol. Comput. **23**(4), 703–717 (2019)
7. Chen, Q., Xue, B., Shang, L., Zhang, M.: Improving generalisation of genetic programming for symbolic regression with structural risk minimisation. In: Proceedings of the Genetic and Evolutionary Computation Conference 2016, pp. 709–716. ACM (2016)
8. Chen, Q., Xue, B., Zhang, M.: Improving symbolic regression based on correlation between residuals and variables. In: Proceedings of the 2020 Genetic and Evolutionary Computation Conference, pp. 922–930 (2020)
9. Chen, Q., Xue, B., Zhang, M.: Rademacher complexity for enhancing the generalization of genetic programming for symbolic regression. IEEE Trans. Cybern. (2020). https://doi.org/10.1109/TCYB.2020.3004361
10. Deb, K., Pratap, A., Agarwal, S., Meyarivan, T.: A fast and elitist multiobjective genetic algorithm: NSGA-II. IEEE Trans. Evol. Comput. **6**(2), 182–197 (2002)
11. Dua, D., Graff, C.: UCI machine learning repository (2017). http://archive.ics.uci.edu/ml
12. Fonseca, C.M., Paquete, L., López-Ibánez, M.: An improved dimension-sweep algorithm for the hypervolume indicator. In: 2006 IEEE International Conference on Evolutionary Computation, pp. 1157–1163. IEEE (2006)
13. Kinzett, D., Johnston, M., Zhang, M.: Numerical simplification for bloat control and analysis of building blocks in genetic programming. Evol. Intel. **2**(4), 151–168 (2009)
14. Koza, J.R., Koza, J.R.: Genetic Programming: On the Programming of Computers by Means of Natural Selection, vol. 1. MIT Press, Cambridge (1992)
15. Koza, J.R., et al.: Genetic Programming II, vol. 17. MIT Press, Cambridge (1994)
16. Le, N., Xuan, H.N., Brabazon, A., Thi, T.P.: Complexity measures in genetic programming learning: a brief review. In: 2016 IEEE Congress on Evolutionary Computation (CEC), pp. 2409–2416. IEEE (2016)
17. Luke, S., Panait, L.: Fighting bloat with nonparametric parsimony pressure. In: Guervós, J.J.M., Adamidis, P., Beyer, H.-G., Schwefel, H.-P., Fernández-Villacañas, J.-L. (eds.) PPSN 2002. LNCS, vol. 2439, pp. 411–421. Springer, Heidelberg (2002). https://doi.org/10.1007/3-540-45712-7_40
18. Luke, S., Panait, L.: Lexicographic parsimony pressure. In: Proceedings of the 4th Annual Conference on Genetic and Evolutionary Computation, pp. 829–836. Morgan Kaufmann Publishers Inc. (2002)
19. Luke, S., Panait, L.: A comparison of bloat control methods for genetic programming. Evol. Comput. **14**(3), 309–344 (2006)
20. McDermott, J., et al.: Genetic programming needs better benchmarks. In: Proceedings of the 14th Annual Conference on Genetic and Evolutionary Computation, pp. 791–798 (2012)
21. Raymond, C., Chen, Q., Xue, B., Zhang, M.: Multi-objective genetic programming for symbolic regression with the adaptive weighted splines representation. In: Proceedings of the 2021 Genetic and Evolutionary Computation Conference Companion, pp. 165–166 (2021)
22. Raymond, C., Chen, Q., Xue, B., Zhang, M.: Genetic programming with rademacher complexity for symbolic regression. In: 2019 IEEE Congress on Evolutionary Computation (CEC), pp. 2657–2664. IEEE (2019)

23. Raymond, C., Chen, Q., Xue, B., Zhang, M.: Adaptive weighted splines: a new representation to genetic programming for symbolic regression. In: Proceedings of the 2020 Genetic and Evolutionary Computation Conference, pp. 1003–1011 (2020)
24. Vanneschi, L., Castelli, M., Silva, S.: Measuring bloat, overfitting and functional complexity in genetic programming. In: Proceedings of 2010 Genetic and Evolutionary Computation Conference, pp. 877–884. ACM (2010)
25. Vlachos, P.: Statlib datasets archive. Department of statistics (1998)
26. Vladislavleva, E.J., Smits, G.F., Den Hertog, D.: Order of nonlinearity as a complexity measure for models generated by symbolic regression via pareto genetic programming. IEEE Trans. Evol. Comput. **13**(2), 333–349 (2008)
27. Wong, P., Zhang, M.: Algebraic simplification of GP programs during evolution. In: Proceedings of the 8th Annual Conference on Genetic and Evolutionary Computation, pp. 927–934 (2006)
28. Zhang, M., Wong, P.: Genetic programming for medical classification: a program simplification approach. Genet. Program Evolvable Mach. **9**(3), 229–255 (2008)

SLUG: Feature Selection Using Genetic Algorithms and Genetic Programming

Nuno M. Rodrigues[1]([✉]) [iD], João E. Batista[1] [iD], William La Cava[3] [iD],
Leonardo Vanneschi[2] [iD], and Sara Silva[1] [iD]

[1] LASIGE Faculty of Sciences, University of Lisbon, Lisbon, Portugal
{nmrodrigues,jebatista,sara}@fc.ul.pt
[2] NOVA Information Management School (NOVA IMS), Universidade Nova de Lisboa,
Campus de Campolide, 1070-312 Lisbon, Portugal
lvanneschi@novaims.unl.pt
[3] Boston Children's Hospital, Harvard Medical School, Boston, MA, USA
william.lacava@childrens.harvard.edu

Abstract. We present SLUG, a method that uses genetic algorithms as a wrapper for genetic programming (GP), to perform feature selection while inducing models. This method is first tested on four regular binary classification datasets, and then on 10 synthetic datasets produced by GAMETES, a tool for embedding epistatic gene-gene interactions into noisy datasets. We compare the results of SLUG with the ones obtained by other GP-based methods that had already been used on the GAMETES problems, concluding that the proposed approach is very successful, particularly on the epistatic datasets. We discuss the merits and weaknesses of SLUG and its various parts, i.e. the wrapper and the learner, and we perform additional experiments, aimed at comparing SLUG with other state-of-the-art learners, like decision trees, random forests and extreme gradient boosting. Despite the fact that SLUG is not the most efficient method in terms of training time, it is confirmed as the most effective method in terms of accuracy.

Keywords: Feature Selection · Epistasis · Genetic Programming · Genetic Algorithms · Machine Learning

1 Introduction

Epistasis can generally be defined as the interaction between genes, and it is a topic of interest in molecular and quantitative genetics [7]. In machine learning (ML), several types of epistatic interactions have been studied. In evolutionary computation, epistasis has traditionally been interpreted as the interaction between characters, sets of characters or, generally speaking, parts of the chromosome representing solutions. This type of epistatic interaction has attracted the interest of researchers mainly because of its effect on fitness landscapes and, consequently, problem hardness. The topic has been studied since the early 90s (see for instance [8,30]), and one of the most popular outcomes of those studies was the NK-landscapes benchmark [2], in which the amount of epistasis is tunable by means of two parameters, N and K. This benchmark has been used in several circumstances for testing the performance of genetic algorithm (GA) variants (see for instance [1,5,22,23,28,37], just to mention a few), and more recently it has also been extended to genetic programming (GP) [41]. An in-depth, although not very recent, survey of studies of epistasis in GA can be found in [31], while in [13] the effect of epistasis on the performance of GA is critically revised, highlighting the difficulty of GA in optimizing epistatic problems. In [19], epistasis was used to select the appropriate basis for basis change space transformations in GA, and in the same year [3] proposed a method to decipher the exact combinations of genes that trigger the epistatic effects, focusing on multi-effect and multi-way epistasis detection. Recently, a new benchmark was proposed [24] where epistasis-tunable test functions are constructed via linear combinations of simple basis functions. A different way of interpreting epistasis in ML is by studying the interactions between features in data. The problem of attribute interdependency is well known in ML. It has been studied in several approaches, using for instance several types of correlation [11] or mutual information [26].

In this paper, we tackle a rather different type of problem: we want to be able to deal with datasets where, among many variables, only a very limited number of them are useful and able to explain the target, and they must be used together for the model to be accurate. In other words, all the few "important" variables must be selected, while the many "confounding" ones must be left out. Furthermore, these few important variables are not necessarily correlated between each other, or have any other relationship of interdependency. This type of behavior can be observed, for instance, in some of Korn's benchmark problems proposed in [15], or in some medical problems, where finding epistasis can be crucial to identify the association between disease and genetic variants, and consequently be able to develop medical treatments and prevention [29]. It is of common intuition that, for problems characterized by such a typology of data, feature selection plays a crucial role, and the objective of this work is to propose a feature selection strategy that, integrated in a very natural way with the modelling algorithm, could be appropriate for working with epistatic datasets. The epistatic datasets studied in this paper have been generated using the GAMETES algorithm, introduced in [38], and have already been used in [16] as a benchmark to validate the M4GP classification method. Similar types of datasets have also been studied in [36], where a GP-based pipeline optimization tool (TPOT-MDR) was proposed to automatically design ML pipelines for bioinformatics problems. For tackling problems characterized by this type of data, Urbanowicz and colleagues recently presented RelieF-based feature selection [40], a unique family of filter-style feature selection algorithms that are sensitive to feature interactions and that can be applied to various types of problems, including classification and regression. In [16] this method has been coupled with M4GP, achieving state-of-the-art results on the GAMETES datasets.

Our proposal consists of using GA for feature selection. The idea, presented for instance in [4,17,21], is framed in a well established research track, and surveys can be found in [12,43]. With the proliferation of data and the consequent development of ML, the use of GA for feature selection increased in the last decade. Numerous recent contributions can be found, for instance, aimed at improving the method in presence of vast amounts of data [6,18], or applying the method in several different real-world scenarios, including medicine [42], economy [34], image processing [33] and sociology [10], just to mention a few. However, we match GA with another evolutionary algorithm, Genetic Programming (GP), obtaining an integrated, and purely evolutionary, method that is able to perform feature selection and at the same time induce good models using the selected features. The GA part acts as a wrapper to the GP part, that is the learner. We call our approach SLUG, and compare it to both standard GP and other GP-based algorithms already used on the GAMETES datasets, such as M3GP [25] and M4GP [16]; we also compare it with other GA-wrapped ML classifiers that also perform feature selection, such as decision trees, random forests and XGBoost. In [35], the authors propose an opposite methodology to SLUG, were they GP for feature selection and GA for feature construction, in an iterative away as opposed to our wrapped approach.

2   SLUG

Our method, feature SeLection Using Genetic algorithms and genetic programming (SLUG), uses a cooperative approach between these two evolutionary algorithms, where the quality of each GA individual is assessed by running GP with the features selected by GA. A schematic showing the behavior of the full SLUG pipeline can be seen in Fig. 1, with the evaluation of the individuals being detailed in Fig. 2.

After splitting the data into training and test sets, a standard GA is applied to the training set (Fig. 1). The individuals of this GA are binary strings of length equal to the number of features in the data. Each bit of the chromosome represents one feature, where 1 or 0 mean that the respective feature is selected or not, respectively. After initializing such a population, it is evaluated. The evaluation of each GA individual requires a complete run of standard GP, using the same training set as the GA but seeing only the features selected by the GA individual. The best fitness achieved in the GP run is the fitness of the GA individual (Fig. 2). Once every GA individual has been evaluated, a new GA population is formed by applying selection and the genetic operators, and after a number of generations the GA finishes and returns both the chromosome with the best selected features and the GP model that achieved the best results when given those features (Fig. 1). Finally, the best GP model is then evaluated using the GA selected features of the test dataset.

Naturally, the GP model does not have to use all the GA selected features, since it also performs its own feature selection. In fact, this is one of the strengths of SLUG for epistatic datasets. On the one hand, the number of useful features on the GAMETES datasets is so low that not even a method like GP, that is so well equipped with feature selection abilities, can isolate them from the numerous other ones. On the other hand, the GA only has to reduce the number of features that GP can potentially use, so its task is facilitated. In other words, the strength of SLUG is that the feature selection step does not need to be accurate: as long as the right features are among a reasonable number of selected ones, GP can do the rest of the job.

3   Data

We test our method on two distinct sets of problems. For the first set, we use four standard binary classification problems: HRT (Heart) [9]; ION (Ionosphere) [9], PRK

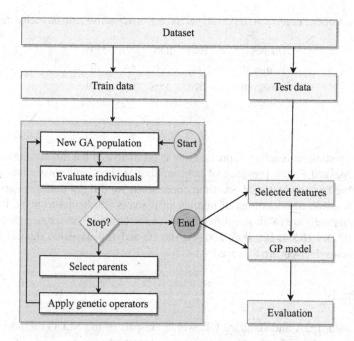

Fig. 1. A graphical representation of the SLUG pipeline.

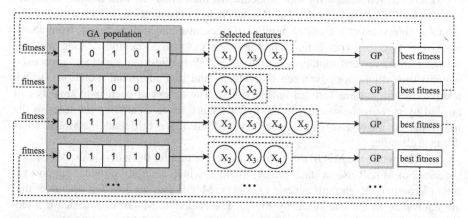

Fig. 2. Illustration of the way the GA individuals are evaluated by running GP with only the selected features. The best fitness of the GP run is the fitness of the respective GA individual.

(Parkinsons) [9] and SON (Sonar) [44]. Details regarding the composition of these datasets can be found in Table 1.

For the second set, we use GAMETES datasets, which are produced by a tool for embedding epistatic gene-gene interactions into noisy genetic datasets [39]. We use 10 different problems that vary according to two measures of difficulty: number of features (10, 100, 1000) and signal-to-noise ratio (0.05, 0.1, 0.2, 0.4). For each problem,

Table 1. Number of features, observations and negative/positive ratio on each dataset.

Datasets	HRT	ION	PRK	SON
Features	13	33	23	61
Observations	270	351	195	208
Neg/Pos Ratio	45/55	65/35	75/25	46/54

a two-way epistatic interaction is present that is predictive of the disease classification, but this is masked by the presence of confounding features and noisy disease classifications. Due to computational and time constraints, we did not perform experiments on all the possible combinations of number of features and signal-to-noise ratio. The 10 selected datasets are (with simplified names in the format $features\_ratio$): 10_005, 10_01, 10_02 and 10_04; 100_005, 100_01, 100_02 and 100_04; 1000_02 and 1000_04. All the gametes datasets are balanced.

4   Methods

Besides standard GA and standard GP, which are part of the SLUG method, we also compare our results with the following GP-based methods:

M3GP: M3GP stands for multidimensional multiclass GP with multidimensional populations [25]. Originally designed for multiclass classification, in M3GP each individual is composed of a mutable number of trees, also called dimensions, from which we extract a set of hyper-features that are then given to a classifier. Along with the standard crossover and mutation operators, M3GP includes an additional crossover, which swaps dimensions between individuals, and two additional mutations, which add/remove dimensions to/from an individual. The fitness of each individual is calculated by running a classifier on the hyper-feature space created by the trees of the individual. On the original implementation of M3GP, this is by default the Mahalanobis distance classifier.

M4GP: While the M3GP uses a tree-based structure for the individuals, M4GP, the successor of M3GP, uses a stack-based structure, which naturally provides support for multiple outputs. Regarding genetic operators, M4GP uses stack-based operators that are equivalent to the ones used by M3GP. For selection, M4GP uses lexicase selection, which out-preformed standard tournament selection, and age-fitness Pareto survival selection in experiments [16].

M4GP+EKF: Expert knowledge filter (EFK) is a preprocessing feature selection algorithm from the RelieF family [14]. In M4GP+EKF it is used to reduce the dataset to the top 10 features before giving it to the M4GP algorithm [16]. From now on we will call this variant M4GP-E.

As part of the discussion, we also present some results obtained by replacing the GP part of SLUG with other ML methods, namely, decision trees (DT), random forests (RF) and extreme gradient boosting, better known as XGBoost (XGB).

5   Experimental Setup

We run SLUG for 50 generations of the GA, using a population of 100 individuals. The GP populations also have 100 individuals, but they evolve for only 30 generations, which our initial experiments revealed to be sufficient to evaluate the quality of the selected features. GP uses the traditional binary arithmetic operators $[+, -, /, *]$ and no random constants. Fitness is the overall accuracy in the training set, measured after transforming the real-valued outputs of GP into class labels. The best fitness of each GP run is passed to the GA as the fitness of each individual, as explained in Sect. 2, and therefore the GA (and therefore SLUG) also uses the overall accuracy as fitness (as do all the other GP and non-GP methods used here). Both GA and GP select the parents of the next generation using tournaments of size 5. Regarding the genetic operators, GP uses the standard subtree crossover and mutation with 50% probability each. GA also uses standard crossover that swaps same-sized blocks between 2 chromosomes with probability of 70%, and standard mutation that performs bit-flip on the chromosome with probability of $1/n$ (where n is the population size) and each bit has probability of $1/m$ of being flipped (where m is the length of the chromosome, i.e., the number of features of the problem). Both GA and GP use some elitism: GP guarantees that the best individual of one generation survives into the next; GA does not guarantee the survival of the best chromosome from one generation to the next, to avoid diversity loss, but it keeps track and returns the best chromosome (and respective GP model) that was ever achieved during the entire run.

Standard GP, M3GP and both M4GP variants all use populations of 500 individuals evolving for 100 generations and, like SLUG, they all use tournaments of size 5. For more specific details on the M3GP and M4GP implementations and settings, the reader should consult Sect. 4 and the papers cited therein. The implementation of the GP methods will be available for download once the paper is accepted.

The STGP and M3GP implementations we use in this work can be found here[1].

Regarding the methods DT, RF and XGB mentioned in the discussion, we use the implementations provided by Scikit-learn [27]. We perform hyperparameter optimization by means of grid search with 5-fold cross-validation on the entire dataset, for each of the three methods. For DT we optimize the split criterion and maximum depth; for RF we optimize the split criterion, number of estimators and maximum depth; for XGB we optimize the learning rate, maximum depth and number of estimators. The GA runs with the exact same parameters as SLUG. In all cases, we randomly split the datasets 30 times, one for each run, into 70% training and 30% test.

6   Results

We measure the overall accuracy of the methods and present the results as boxplots (training and test) of the 30 runs and tables with the (test) medians. To assess the statistical significance of the results, we perform one-way non-parametric ANOVA analysis by means of Kruskal-Wallis with Holm correction, using 0.05 as the significance threshold. The Appendix contains the Holm-corrected p-values obtained in all the datasets.

---

[1] https://github.com/jespb/Python-STGP and https://github.com/jespb/Python-M3GP.

6.1   Regular Classification Tasks

Taking into consideration the results presented in Table 2, Fig. 3 and Appendix Table 4, we can see that our approach performs well, on par with the other GP methods such as M3GP and M4GP. Compared to the baseline of standard GP, SLUG performs better on both HRT and PRK datasets, and presents no significant differences on the remaining two. Regarding the M3GP and M4GP baselines, the results are also positive, with SLUG outperforming both methods on one problem, presenting no significant difference on two others, and being outperformed in the remaining problem. Lastly, regarding M4GP-E, this method outperforms SLUG in one problem, and no significant difference was found between them in the remaining problems. Finally, we could not help but notice one thing that appears to be different between SLUG and the other methods, that is the consistently lower dispersion of the results on training.

Table 2. Median test overall accuracy of the different methods on the non-gametes binary classification tasks. Best results for each problem are identified in green, more than one when there are no statistically significant differences.

	HRT	PRK	ION	SON
GP	0.778	0.831	0.858	0.698
M3GP	0.790	0.881	0.873	0.786
M4GP	0.784	0.864	0.868	0.762
M4GP-E	0.802	0.873	0.854	0.738
SLUG	0.827	0.864	0.877	0.730

6.2   Gametes Classification Tasks

Taking into consideration the results presented in Table 3, Fig. 4 and Appendix Table 5, the first thing to notice is the fact that the standard GP baseline was one of the best methods on the 10-feature gametes problems. It outperformed both M4GP and M4GP-E on the 10_005 dataset, M4GP-E on 10_01, and all except SLUG on 10_02 [2]. We hypothesize that, on these easier problems, the exploration of different dimensional feature spaces that M3GP and M4GP perform is not helpful to the search, preventing the exploitation of better solutions.

Regarding our approach, the results were again highly positive, with SLUG invariably being one of the top performing methods in all problems. The GA of SLUG is able to filter out most, if not all, of the redundant features, which are then further filtered by the standard GP populations, also producing a ready to use model to apply to the problem.

On the 1000_04 dataset, SLUG produced results significantly worse than M4GP-E. We attribute this to the default parameterization of SLUG, which always uses very small

---

[2] We performed 30 runs using the same total number of comparisons as SLUG using the STGP (10000 individuals and 1500 generations). With this, the median test accuracy achieved was 0.4982, while the best was 0.5348.

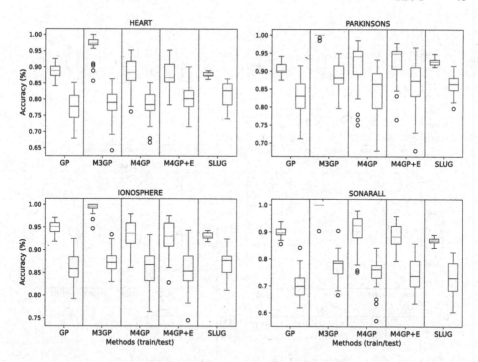

Fig. 3. Performance on the non-gametes binary classification datasets. Each plot contains, for each method, the results on the training (left) and test (right) sets.

populations of 100 individuals. Particularly in the GA, this is too small to appropriately explore the search space on the 1000-feature problems, and therefore the method is not fully capable of filtering out the redundant features. To confirm this hypothesis, we ran SLUG with a larger GA population of 200 individuals. Although this is the double of the previous population size, it is still a very low number of individuals for such a large search space (however, further increasing the size of the population becomes computationally demanding, an issue that is discussed later). We named this variation SLUG Large (SLUG-L). As it can be seen on Fig. 5, particularly on the 1000_04 dataset, SLUG-L is slightly improved, enough to be significantly better than the other solutions, and not significantly worse than M4GP-E.

Once again we notice that SLUG exhibits a much lower dispersion of results than most other methods (Fig. 4), this time not only on training but also on test. This remarkable stability is shared by M4GP-E, although not so strongly.

7   Discussion

From the previous results we can state that SLUG is a powerful method that performs feature selection while inducing high-quality models. On the set of four regular problems, it was one of the best methods in three of them. On the set of 10 gametes problems, it was always one of the best methods, although it required a larger population

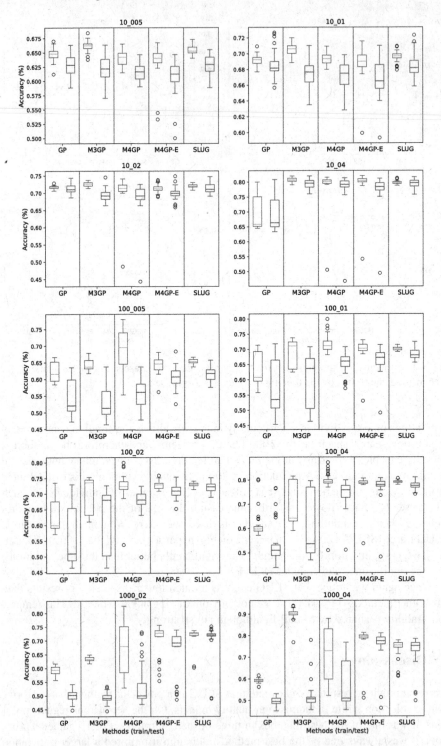

Fig. 4. Performance on the gametes datasets. Each plot contains, for each method, the results on the training (left) and test (right) sets.

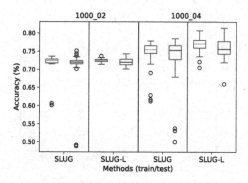

Fig. 5. Performance of different SLUG variants on the two higher dimensional gametes datasets. Each plot contains, for each variant, the results on the training (left) and test (right) sets.

Table 3. Median test overall accuracy of the different methods on the gametes tasks. Best results for each problem are identified in green, more than one when there are no statistically significant differences.

	10_005	10_01	10_02	10_04	100_005	100_01	100_02	100_04	1000_02	1000_04
GP	0.628	0.682	0.710	0.663	0.521	0.535	0.509	0.510	0.502	0.495
M3GP	0.622	0.677	0.692	0.796	0.513	0.637	0.680	0.537	0.490	0.507
M4GP	0.617	0.675	0.692	0.792	0.561	0.661	0.681	0.759	0.500	0.511
M4GP-E	0.613	0.665	0.699	0.784	0.607	0.672	0.709	0.781	0.692	0.775
SLUG	0.629	0.682	0.710	0.797	0.617	0.681	0.722	0.777	0.720	0.753
SLUG-L	-	-	-	-	-	-	-	-	0.720	0.757

size on one of them. On this one exception, one of the hardest problems, the other winner besides SLUG-L was M4GP-E. Published results on M4GP [16] had already shown that wrapping a feature selection method around a powerful classifier can improve the results significantly, and here we confirm that indeed, M4GP-E is often significantly better than M4GP. Reminding that SLUG is also the product of wrapping a feature selection method (GA) around a powerful classifier (GP), our results reconfirm the advantages of such an approach, since SLUG is very often significantly better than standalone GP.

Naturally, we are interested in searching for the best match between wrapper and learner, and we begin by exploring why SLUG performs so well; which of its parts is more important, the GA wrapper of the GP learner. On the one hand, we observe that M4GP is in general a stronger learner than GP; on the other hand, M4GP-E is not stronger than SLUG. Therefore, GA seems to be a better wrapper than the EKF used in M4GP-E, and the main responsible for the success of SLUG. While the combination of GA with M4GP seems like a promising match to explore in the future, for now we try to answer a simple question: is GA such a good wrapper that it can improve also the performance of other ML methods, arguably less powerful than the GP-based ones, like DT, RF and XGB? This question is not only academically interesting, but also important from a practical point of view. Two evolutionary algorithms nested in

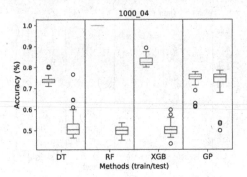

Fig. 6. Performance of different SLUG variants using DT, RF, XGB and GP (the original SLUG) on the gametes 1000_04 problem. Each plot contains, for each variant, the results on the training (left) and test (right) sets.

each other is never an efficient solution in terms of computational effort, so it is not a surprise that SLUG is... sluggish. Any of the three other mentioned ML methods runs much faster than GP, so wrapping GA around any of them could result in a much faster SLUG. Furthermore, like GP, these methods can also perform feature selection on their own, on top of the preselection made by GA. Therefore, we experiment with alternative variants of SLUG where GP is replaced by DT, RF and XGB. The problem chosen to test these variants is the gametes 1000_04, coincidentally the one problem where SLUG-L was required because SLUG was not one of the best methods (see Sect. 6). We chose this particular problem because it has already been used in previous studies [16,32] where the standalone versions of DT, RF and XGB were unable to solve the problem.

The obtained results are shown in Fig. 6 and reveal that, even when wrapped with GA, these methods are not able to solve the problem, and this means that GP is also essential for the success of SLUG. Since the other methods also perform feature selection, the reason why GP is essential is not clear, particularly after observing that in one of the 30 runs the DT method, which is undoubtedly the less powerful one, was able to obtain a high-quality model (highest outlier in test, Fig. 6), and it did so after only 17 generations.

8   Conclusion and Future Work

We have presented SLUG, a method for feature selection using genetic algorithms (GA) and genetic programming (GP). SLUG implements a co-operative approach between these two evolutionary algorithms, where the quality of each GA individual is assessed by doing a GP run with the features selected by GA. The GA acts like a wrapper, selecting features for GP, the learner. At the end of the process, both the set of GA selected features and the best GP induced model are returned, and therefore SLUG comprises the entire pipeline from data preprocessing to predictive modeling. No efforts are put into the optimization of the model, as this is not the main purpose of our research.

We tested SLUG on four regular binary classification datasets, and on 10 synthetic datasets produced by GAMETES, a tool for embedding epistatic gene-gene interactions into noisy datasets. We compared the results of SLUG with the ones obtained by standard GP and other GP-based methods like M3GP and two different M4GP variants, one of them also wrapped by the EKF algorithm for feature selection. SLUG obtained the best results in practically all the problems, with special relevance for the good results obtained on the epistatic datasets, whose difficulty was the driver for this research in the first place.

We discussed the merits and weaknesses of SLUG and the parts that compose it. Its slowness is its obvious limitation, as it requires considerable computational effort to run two evolutionary algorithms nested in each other. We experimented with alternative implementations, replacing the GP backbone of SLUG with faster methods like decision trees, random forests and XGBoost, all wrapped with GA for feature selection. However, even with tuned parameters, none of them was able to catch up with SLUG.

From the above, we conclude that SLUG is a powerful method that performs feature selection while inducing high-quality models, even without putting any efforts on model optimization. In the future, we intend to address the main limitation of SLUG, by reducing its computational demands and therefore making it less sluggish. Many other improvements and extensions are possible, like the ones described below.

The backbone of SLUG is currently standard GP, which is not appropriate for multiclass classification. However, it can be replaced by other methods. The ones we tried did not produce good models, however other options exist, including M3GP and M4GP themselves, which are some of the best GP-based multiclass classification methods available today. Replacing GP with M3GP would give us the added flexibility of being allowed to plug any learning algorithm to the pipeline to work with the hyper-features evolved by M3GP. Instead of GA+GP, we would have a GA+M3GP+$classifier$ pipeline, where GA preselects the features, M3GP uses them to build hyper-features tailored to $classifier$, and $classifier$ finally induces an optimized predictive model, with the added advantage that the classifier can be whatever method best suits the needs of the domain application. Naturally, the same rationale can be used for regression instead of classification.

Regarding the improvement of the wrapper, the main issue with GA is, and has always been, the delicate balance between exploration and exploitation, here with an intense concern regarding computational demands. On the one hand, we want to make GA converge faster to a good subset of selected features, also to save computational effort; on the other hand, it must be able to properly explore the search space, particularly on the most difficult higher dimensional problems, but without requiring large populations which would increase the computational time. We finalize by presenting some ideas on how to deal with this.

In order to accelerate convergence, GP (or any other backbone SLUG is using) could inform GA of what features are actually being used, from the ones preselected. In case the backbone does not perform feature selection itself, it can probably still inform what features are more important. This way, the GA could use more information from the learner than just the fitness achieved with each subset of features, increasing the cooperation between the two methods. It is reasonable to think that, in this case, the

GA binary chromosomes would become real-valued ones, where each bit would now contain a sort of probability of selecting each feature, that the learner could use to build its own models. In order to promote the exploration of the search space without having to increase the population size, and particularly when adding measures for faster convergence, our idea is to use novelty search [20] on the GA in order to increase the bias towards yet unexplored subsets of features.

Acknowledgment. This work was supported by FCT, Portugal, through funding of LASIGE Research Unit (UIDB/00408/2020 and UIDP/00408/2020); MAR2020 program via project MarCODE (MAR-01.03.01-FEAMP-0047); projects BINDER (PTDC/CCI-INF/29168/2017), AICE (DSAIPA/DS/0113/2019), OPTOX (PTDC/CTA-AMB/30056/2017) and GADgET (DSAIPA/DS/0022/2018). Nuno Rodrigues and João Batista were supported by PhD Grants 2021/05322/BD and SFRH/BD/143972/2019, respectively; William La Cava was supported by the National Library Of Medicine of the National Institutes of Health under Award Number R00LM012926.

Appendix

Table 4. Holm corrected p-values using Kruskal-Wallis for the regular classification problems.

HRT	GP	M3GP	M4GP	M4GP-E	SLUG
GP	—	0.9922	1.1556	0.2843	*0.0027*
M3GP	0.9922	—	0.6884	0.8486	*0.0490*
M4GP	1.1556	0.6884	—	0.6599	*0.0124*
M4GP-E	0.2843	0.8486	0.6599	—	0.7852
SLUG	0.0027	0.0490	0.0124	0.7852	—

PRK	GP	M3GP	M4GP	M4GP-E	SLUG
GP	—	*0.0000*	0.7658	0.0627	*0.0441*
M3GP	0.0000	—	0.0597	0.4882	0.1015
M4GP	0.7658	0.0597	—	0.8317	0.7966
M4GP-E	0.0627	0.4882	0.8317	—	0.7220
SLUG	0.0441	0.1015	0.7966	0.7220	—

ION	GP	M3GP	M4GP	M4GP-E	SLUG
GP	—	0.3297	2.2914	1.6595	0.3457
M3GP	0.3297	—	0.9674	0.3734	0.9704
M4GP	2.2914	0.9674	—	1.7345	1.1531
M4GP-E	1.6595	0.3734	1.7345	—	0.3530
SLUG	0.3457	0.9704	1.1531	0.3530	—

SON	GP	M3GP	M4GP	M4GP-E	SLUG
GP	—	*0.0000*	*0.0010*	*0.0154*	0.3311
M3GP	0.0000	—	0.2653	0.3660	0.0232
M4GP	0.0010	0.2653	—	0.6295	0.2414
M4GP-E	0.0154	0.3660	0.6295	—	0.4270
SLUG	0.3311	*0.0232*	0.2414	0.4270	—

Table 5. Holm corrected *p*-values using Kruskal-Wallis for the gametes problems.

10_005	GP	M3GP	M4GP	M4GP-E	SLUG
GP	—	1.1109	0.0673	0.0107	0.9234
M3GP	1.1109	—	0.8996	0.2383	0.5035
M4GP	0.0673	0.8996	—	0.7535	0.0433
M4GP-E	0.0107	0.2383	0.7535	—	0.0117
SLUG	0.9234	0.5035	0.0433	0.0117	—

10_01	GP	M3GP	M4GP	M4GP-E	SLUG
GP	—	0.2129	0.0701	0.0194	0.5589
M3GP	0.2129	—	1.3918	0.5030	0.4243
M4GP	0.0701	1.3918	—	0.9644	0.1472
M4GP-E	0.0194	0.5030	0.9644	—	0.0241
SLUG	0.5589	0.4243	0.1472	0.0241	—

10_02	GP	M3GP	M4GP	M4GP-E	SLUG
GP	—	0.0000	0.0017	0.0021	1.4559
M3GP	0.0000	—	0.7673	0.4077	0.0001
M4GP	0.0017	0.7673	—	0.8110	0.0020
M4GP-E	0.0021	0.4077	0.8110	—	0.0109
SLUG	1.4559	0.0001	0.0020	0.0109	—

10_04	GP	M3GP	M4GP	M4GP-E	SLUG
GP	—	0.0000	0.0000	0.0000	0.0000
M3GP	0.0000	—	0.8301	0.1779	1.3901
M4GP	0.0000	0.8301	—	0.3962	1.3785
M4GP-E	0.0000	0.1779	0.3962	—	0.0975
SLUG	0.0000	1.3901	1.3785	0.0975	—

100_005	GP	M3GP	M4GP	M4GP-E	SLUG
GP	—	0.3509	0.3911	0.0012	0.0001
M3GP	0.3509	—	0.0213	0.0000	0.0000
M4GP	0.3911	0.0213	—	0.0000	0.0000
M4GP-E	0.0012	0.0000	0.0000	—	0.3713
SLUG	0.0001	0.0000	0.0000	0.3713	—

100_01	GP	M3GP	M4GP	M4GP-E	SLUG
GP	—	0.9823	0.0148	0.0060	0.0001
M3GP	0.9823	—	0.0599	0.0072	0.0000
M4GP	0.0148	0.0599	—	0.2304	0.0006
M4GP-E	0.0060	0.0072	0.2304	—	0.0796
SLUG	0.0001	0.0000	0.0006	0.0796	—

100_02	GP	M3GP	M4GP	M4GP-E	SLUG
GP	—	0.3664	0.0040	0.0000	0.0000
M3GP	0.3664	—	0.2970	0.0001	0.0000
M4GP	0.0040	0.2970	—	0.0005	0.0000
M4GP-E	0.0000	0.0001	0.0005	—	0.0365
SLUG	0.0000	0.0000	0.0000	0.0365	—

100_04	GP	M3GP	M4GP	M4GP-E	SLUG
GP	—	0.0728	0.0000	0.0000	0.0000
M3GP	0.0728	—	0.0539	0.0000	0.0001
M4GP	0.0000	0.0539	—	0.0015	0.0084
M4GP-E	0.0000	0.0000	0.0015	—	0.1311
SLUG	0.0000	0.0001	0.0084	0.1311	—

1000_02	GP	M3GP	M4GP	M4GP-E	SLUG	SLUG-L
GP	—	0.4726	0.5740	0.0000	0.0000	0.0000
M3GP	0.4726	—	0.0718	0.0000	0.0000	0.0000
M4GP	0.5740	0.0718	—	0.0000	0.0000	0.0000
M4GP-E	0.0000	0.0000	0.0000	—	0.0003	0.0000
SLUG	0.0000	0.0000	0.0000	0.0003	—	0.9174
SLUG-L	0.0000	0.0000	0.0000	0.0000	0.9174	—

1000_04	GP	M3GP	M4GP	M4GP-E	SLUG	SLUG-L
GP	—	0.3560	0.0676	0.0000	0.0000	0.0000
M3GP	0.3560	—	0.2035	0.0000	0.0000	0.0000
M4GP	0.0676	0.2035	—	0.0000	0.0000	0.0000
M4GP-E	0.0000	0.0000	0.0000	—	0.0114	0.1650
SLUG	0.0000	0.0000	0.0000	0.0114	—	0.3762
SLUG-L	0.0000	0.0000	0.0000	0.1650	0.3762	—

References

1. Aguirre, H.E., Tanaka, K.: Genetic algorithms on NK-landscapes: effects of selection, drift, mutation, and recombination. In: Cagnoni, S., et al. (eds.) Applications of Evolutionary Computing, pp. 131–142. Springer, Heidelberg (2003). https://doi.org/10.1007/978-3-540-78761-7

2. Altenberg, L.: B2.7.2. NK fitness landscapes. In: Handbook of Evolutionary Computation. pp. B2.7:5–B2.7:10. IOP Publishing Ltd. and Oxford University Press, London (1997)

3. Ansarifar, J., Wang, L.: New algorithms for detecting multi-effect and multi-way epistatic interactions. Bioinformatics **35**(24), 5078–5085 (2019). https://doi.org/10.1093/bioinformatics/btz463

4. Chaikla, N., Qi, Y.: Genetic algorithms in feature selection. In: IEEE SMC 1999 Conference Proceedings. 1999 IEEE International Conference on Systems, Man, and Cybernetics (Cat. No. 99CH37028). vol. 5, pp. 538–540 (1999). https://doi.org/10.1109/ICSMC.1999.815609

5. Chan, K., Aydin, M., Fogarty, T.: An epistasis measure based on the analysis of variance for the real-coded representation in genetic algorithms. In: The 2003 Congress on Evolutionary Computation, 2003, CEC 2003. vol. 1, pp. 297–304 (2003). https://doi.org/10.1109/CEC.2003.1299588

6. Chiesa, M., Maioli, G., Colombo, G.: GARS: Genetic algorithm for the identification of a robust subset of features in high-dimensional datasets. BMC Bioinform. **21**(54) (2020). https://doi.org/10.1186/s12859-020-3400-6

7. Cordell, H.J.: Epistasis: what it means, what it doesn't mean, and statistical methods to detect it in humans. Hum. Mol. Gene. **11**(20), 2463–2468 (2002). https://doi.org/10.1093/hmg/11.20.2463

8. Davidor, Y.: Epistasis variance: a viewpoint on GA-hardness. Found. Gen. Algorithms **1**, 23–35 (1991). https://doi.org/10.1016/B978-0-08-050684-5.50005-7

9. Dua, D., Graff, C.: UCI Machine Learning Repository (2017). http://archive.ics.uci.edu/ml

10. García-Dominguez, A., et al.: Feature selection using genetic algorithms for the generation of a recognition and classification of children activities model using environmental sound. Mob. Inf. Syst. **2020**, 12 p (2020). 8617430. https://doi.org/10.1155/2020/8617430

11. Hall, M.A.: Correlation-based feature selection for machine learning. Ph.D. thesis, The University of Waikato (1999)

12. Hussein, F., Kharma, N., Ward, R.: Genetic algorithms for feature selection and weighting, a review and study. In: Proceedings of Sixth International Conference on Document Analysis and Recognition, pp. 1240–1244 (2001). https://doi.org/10.1109/ICDAR.2001.953980

13. Jafari, S., Kapitaniak, T., Rajagopal, K., Pham, V.-T., Alsaadi, F.E.: Effect of epistasis on the performance of genetic algorithms. J. Zhejiang Univ.-Sci. A **20**(2), 109–116 (2018). https://doi.org/10.1631/jzus.A1800399

14. Kononenko, I.: Estimating attributes: analysis and extensions of relief. In: ECML (1994)

15. Korns, M.F.: Genetic programming symbolic classification: A study. In: Banzhaf, W., Olson, R.S., Tozier, W., Riolo, R. (eds.) Genetic Programming Theory and Practice XV, pp. 39–54. Springer, Cham (2018). https://doi.org/10.1007/978-3-319-90512-9

16. La Cava, W., Silva, S., Danai, K., Spector, L., Vanneschi, L., Moore, J.H.: Multidimensional genetic programming for multiclass classification. Swarm Evol. Comput. **44**, 260–272 (2019). https://doi.org/10.1016/j.swevo.2018.03.015

17. Lanzi, P.: Fast feature selection with genetic algorithms: a filter approach. In: Proceedings of 1997 IEEE International Conference on Evolutionary Computation (ICEC 1997). pp. 537–540 (1997). https://doi.org/10.1109/ICEC.1997.592369

18. Lavine, B.K., White, C.G.: Boosting the performance of genetic algorithms for variable selection in partial least squares spectral calibrations. Appl. Spectrosc. **71**(9), 2092–2101 (2017)

19. Lee, J., Kim, Y.H.: Epistasis-based basis estimation method for simplifying the problem space of an evolutionary search in binary representation. Complexity **2019**, 2095167, 13 pages (2019)

20. Lehman, J., Stanley, K.O.: Exploiting open-endedness to solve problems through the search for novelty. In: Proceedings of the Eleventh International Conference on Artificial Life, Alife XI. MIT Press, Cambridge (2008)

21. Li, A.D., Xue, B., Zhang, M.: Multi-objective feature selection using hybridization of a genetic algorithm and direct multisearch for key quality characteristic selection. Inf. Sci. **523**, 245–265 (2020). https://doi.org/10.1016/j.ins.2020.03.032

22. Mathias, K.E., Eshelman, L.J., Schaffer, J.D.: Niches in NK-landscapes. In: Martin, W.N., Spears, W.M. (eds.) Foundations of Genetic Algorithms, vol. 6, pp. 27–46. Morgan Kaufmann, San Francisco (2001). https://doi.org/10.1016/B978-155860734-7/50085-8

23. Merz, P., Freisleben, B.: On the effectiveness of evolutionary search in high-dimensional NK-landscapes. In: 1998 IEEE International Conference on Evolutionary Computation Proceedings. IEEE World Congress on Computational Intelligence (Cat. No. 98TH8360), pp. 741–745 (1998). https://doi.org/10.1109/ICEC.1998.700144

24. Mo, H., Li, Z., Zhu, C.: A kind of epistasis-tunable test functions for genetic algorithms. Concurr. Comput. Pract. Exp. **33**(8), e5030 (2021). https://doi.org/10.1002/cpe.5030

25. Muñoz, L., Silva, S., Trujillo, L.: M3GP- multiclass classification with GP. In: EuroGP (2015)

26. Nazareth, D.L., Soofi, E.S., Zhao, H.: Visualizing attribute interdependencies using mutual information, hierarchical clustering, multidimensional scaling, and self-organizing maps. In: 2007 40th Annual Hawaii International Conference on System Sciences (HICSS 2007), pp. 53–53 (2007). https://doi.org/10.1109/HICSS.2007.608

27. Pedregosa, F., et al.: Scikit-learn: machine learning in python. J. Mach. Learn. Res. **12**, 2825–2830 (2011)

28. Pelikan, M., Sastry, K., Goldberg, D.E., Butz, M.V., Hauschild, M.: Performance of evolutionary algorithms on NK landscapes with nearest neighbor interactions and tunable overlap. In: Proceedings of the 11th Annual Conference on Genetic and Evolutionary Computation, GECCO 2009, pp. 851–858. Association for Computing Machinery, New York (2009). https://doi.org/10.1145/1569901.1570018

29. Petinrin, O.O., Wong, K.C.: Protocol for epistasis detection with machine learning using GenEpi package. Methods Mol. Biol. **2212**, 291–305 (2021)

30. Reeves, C.R., Wright, C.C.: Epistasis in genetic algorithms: an experimental design perspective. In: Proceedings of the 6th International Conference on Genetic Algorithms. pp. 217–224. Morgan Kaufmann Publishers Inc., San Francisco (1995)

31. Rochet, S.: Epistasis in genetic algorithms revisited. Infor. Sci. **102**(1), 133–155 (1997). https://doi.org/10.1016/S0020-0255(97)00017-0

32. Rodrigues, N.M., Batista, J.E., Silva, S.: Ensemble genetic programming. In: Hu, T., Lourenço, N., Medvet, E., Divina, F. (eds.) Genetic Programming, pp. 151–166. Springer, Cham (2020). https://doi.org/10.1007/978-3-319-30668-1

33. Seo, K.-K.: Content-Based Image Retrieval by Combining Genetic Algorithm and Support Vector Machine. In: de Sá, J.M., Alexandre, L.A., Duch, W., Mandic, D. (eds.) ICANN 2007. LNCS, vol. 4669, pp. 537–545. Springer, Heidelberg (2007). https://doi.org/10.1007/978-3-540-74695-9_55

34. Shik Shin, K., Lee, Y.J.: A genetic algorithm application in bankruptcy prediction modeling. Expert Syst. Appl. **23**, 321–328 (2002)

35. Smith, M.G., Bull, L.: Feature construction and selection using genetic programming and a genetic algorithm. In: Ryan, C., Soule, T., Keijzer, M., Tsang, E., Poli, R., Costa, E. (eds.) Genetic Programming, pp. 229–237. Springer, Heidelberg (2003). https://doi.org/10.1007/978-3-319-30668-1

36. Sohn, A., Olson, R.S., Moore, J.H.: Toward the automated analysis of complex diseases in genome-wide association studies using genetic programming. In: Proceedings of the Genetic and Evolutionary Computation Conference, GECCO 2017, pp. 489–496. Association for Computing Machinery, New York (2017). https://doi.org/10.1145/3071178.3071212

37. Tinós, R., Whitley, D., Chicano, F.: Partition crossover for pseudo-Boolean optimization. In: Proceedings of the 2015 ACM Conference on Foundations of Genetic Algorithms XIII, FOGA 2015, pp. 137–149. Association for Computing Machinery, New York (2015). https://doi.org/10.1145/2725494.2725497

38. Urbanowicz, R., Kiralis, J., Sinnott-Armstrong, N., et al.: GAMETES: a fast, direct algorithm for generating pure, strict, epistatic models with random architectures. BioData Mining **5**(16) (2012). https://doi.org/10.1186/1756-0381-5-16

39. Urbanowicz, R.J., Kiralis, J., Sinnott-Armstrong, N.A., Heberling, T., Fisher, J.M., Moore, J.H.: Gametes: a fast, direct algorithm for generating pure, strict, epistatic models with random architectures. BioData Mining **5**, 16–16 (2012)
40. Urbanowicz, R.J., Meeker, M., La Cava, W., Olson, R.S., Moore, J.H.: Relief-based feature selection: Introduction and review. J. Biomed. Inf. **85**, 189–203 (2018). https://doi.org/10.1016/j.jbi.2018.07.014
41. Vanneschi, L., Castelli, M., Manzoni, L.: The K landscapes: a tunably difficult benchmark for genetic programming. In: Proceedings of the 13th Annual Conference on Genetic and Evolutionary Computation, GECCO 2011, Association for Computing Machinery, New York (2011). https://doi.org/10.1145/2001576.2001773
42. Wutzl, B., Leibnitz, K., Rattay, F., Kronbichler, M., Murata, M., Golaszewski, S.M.: Genetic algorithms for feature selection when classifying severe chronic disorders of consciousness. PLoS ONE **14**(7), 1–16 (2019). https://doi.org/10.1371/journal.pone.0219683
43. Xue, B., Zhang, M., Browne, W.N., Yao, X.: A survey on evolutionary computation approaches to feature selection. IEEE Trans. Evol. Comput. **20**(4), 606–626 (2016). https://doi.org/10.1109/TEVC.2015.2504420
44. Zhang, S.: sonar.all-data (2018). https://www.kaggle.com/ypzhangsam/sonaralldata

Evolutionary Design of Reduced Precision Levodopa-Induced Dyskinesia Classifiers

Martin Hurta[1]([⊠])(iD), Michaela Drahosova[1](iD), Lukas Sekanina[1](iD),
Stephen L. Smith[2](iD), and Jane E. Alty[3,4](iD)

[1] Faculty of Information Technology, Brno University of Technology,
Brno, Czech Republic
{ihurta,drahosova,sekanina}@fit.vut.cz

[2] Department of Electronic Engineering, University of York, York, UK
stephen.smith@york.ac.uk

[3] Wicking Dementia Centre, University of Tasmania, Hobart, Australia
jane.alty@utas.edu.au

[4] Neurology Department, Leeds Teaching Hospitals NHS Trust, Leeds, UK

Abstract. Parkinson's disease is one of the most common neurological conditions whose symptoms are usually treated with a drug containing levodopa. To minimise levodopa side effects, i.e. levodopa-induced dyskinesia (LID), it is necessary to correctly manage levodopa dosage. This article covers an application of cartesian genetic programming (CGP) to assess LID based on time series collected using accelerators attached to the patient's body. Evolutionary design of reduced precision classifiers of LID is investigated in order to find a hardware-efficient classifier together with classification accuracy as close as possible to a baseline software implementation. CGP equipped with the coevolution of adaptive size fitness predictors (coASFP) is used to design LID-classifiers working with fixed-point arithmetics with reduced precision, which is suitable for implementation in application-specific integrated circuits. In this particular task, we achieved a significant evolutionary design computational cost reduction in comparison with the original CGP. Moreover, coASFP effectively prevented overfitting in this task. Experiments with reduced precision LID-classifier design show that evolved classifiers working with 8-bit unsigned integer data representation, together with the input data scaling using the logical right shift, not only significantly outperformed hardware characteristics of all other investigated solutions but also achieved a better classifier accuracy in comparison with classifiers working with the floating-point numbers.

Keywords: Cartesian genetic programming · Coevolution · Adaptive size fitness predictors · Energy-efficient · Hardware-oriented · Fixed-point arithmetic · Levodopa-induced dyskinesia · Parkinson's disease

E. Medvet et al. (Eds.): EuroGP 2022, LNCS 13223, pp. 85–101, 2022.
https://doi.org/10.1007/978-3-031-02056-8_6

1   Introduction

Parkinson's disease (PD) is one of the most common neurological conditions affecting approximately 1% of the population over 65 years of age [1,6]. PD is of unknown cause, and there is no known cure. Patient care consists primarily of suppressing symptoms and thus maintaining the quality of life for as long as possible. The key clinical features of PD comprise bradykinesia, rigidity, tremor and postural instability, which result from dopamine deficiency in part of the brain called substantia nigra. These symptoms are often treated with the dopamine-replacement drug levodopa. The right dosage is very important in order to suppress PD symptoms and sign and, at the same time to avoid the drug's troublesome side effects, including involuntary and often violent muscle spasms, i.e. *levodopa-induced dyskinesia (LID)*. Easy and accurate detection of motor abnormalities that people with PD experience, such as bradykinesia and dyskinesia, is thus crucial for sufficient dosage adjustment. A small low-power solution that could be implemented directly into a home wearable device would enable long-term continuous monitoring of people with PD in their own homes and allow clinicians accurate assessment of their patient's condition and the advised adjustment of levodopa dosage.

Many studies are concerned with a determination of motor difficulties that people with PD experience, including bradykinesia, tremor or LID, while focused mainly on the accuracy of classifiers [1]. Thus, approaches using extracted high-level features, spectral analysis and artificial neural networks are common.

Efforts at designing energy-efficient solutions are then usually focused on the low power design of sensor units sending data to other devices for additional evaluation [2,5,8]. Zhu et al. [14] proposed an energy-efficient solution for tremor detection that considers the power estimation of individual features and uses fixed-point arithmetic together with a decision tree. However, this solution involves an invasive source of data, in the form of a local field potential recordings from deep brain stimulation lead implanted to patients.

Lones et al. [6] introduced an approach consisting in the use of genetic programming (GP) and symbolic classifier models based upon low-level features of the movement data (e.g. raw acceleration values) contrary to the use of neural networks and higher-level features (e.g. signal energy and spectral powers over frequency ranges). They developed a non-invasive wearable monitoring system for assessing dyskinesia in people with PD. Sensing modules comprised a tri-axial accelerometer and tri-axial gyroscope, and stored data in local memory. In clinical studies, the data was downloaded to a computer for further processing.

We have adopted their work with the goal to evolve LID-classifiers with respect to hardware implementation. The subject aspects include area on a chip, delay and power consumption. Our target is a highly optimized energy-efficient implementation of a trained classifier that could easily be instantiated in an application-specific integrated circuit (ASIC) along with the classification accuracy as close as possible to a baseline software implementation.

In order to consume less energy, we replace standard floating-point operations with arithmetic operations with reduced precision in the fixed-point representation because they are less energy demanding. Sze et al. [13] illustrate an impact of using 8-bit fixed point on energy and area: An 8-bit fixed-point add consumes 3.3 times less energy and 3.8 times less area than a 32-bit fixed-point add, considering that the energy and area of a fixed-point add scale approximately linearly (of a fixed-point multiply approximately quadratically) with the number of bits of operands. Moreover, reducing the precision also reduces the energy and area cost for storage. The energy and area of memory scale approximately linearly with the number of bits.

To develop candidate LID-classifiers, we use cartesian genetic programming equipped with coevolution of adaptive fitness predictors (CGPcoASFP) [3] in order to accelerate classifier evolution. Formerly CGPcoASFP was applied in a symbolic regression task where coevolved predictors were used to estimate a fitness function in terms of *score* and in the image filter design task where an estimated fitness was *peak signal-to-noise ratio* (PSNR) [3]. Thus the evolution of classifier employing the AUC-based (i.e. Area Under the receiver operating characteristics Curve) fitness function can be seen as a new application for CGPcoASFP.

2   LID-Classifier Design

2.1   Clinical Study Data

In this work, we adopt two clinical studies that are used by Lones et al. [6] and that were conducted at Leeds Teaching Hospitals NHS Trust, UK. Ethics approval was granted and all participants gave written informed consent. Participants were recruited from the Neurology clinics if they had a confirmed diagnosis of PD and also objective evidence of LID. In both studies, sensing modules containing accelerometers and gyroscopes, each able to record movement data in the three spatial and three rotational planes at a sample rate of 100 Hz, were fitted to the patient's legs, arms, torso, head and trunk. At the same time, a camera was used to record patients' movements. Then trained clinicians analysed the video to mark up periods of LID while using the standard UDysRS (Unified Dyskinesia Rating Scale) scoring system. This scoring system grades LID from 0 (no dyskinesia) to 4 (severe dyskinesia). A summary of data collected from the studies is shown in Table 1. Moreover, marked periods contain information about patients movement activities, e.g. (patient is) sitting at rest, walking, drinking from cup, talking, etc.

Table 1. Number of examples of each dyskinesia grade (according to UDysRS) collected from the two studies [6].

LID grade	Study 1	Study 2
0 (normal, no dyskinesia)	2939	1747
1 (slight dyskinesia)	1227	971
2 (mild dyskinesia)	1688	652
3 (moderate dyskinesia)	681	183
4 (severe dyskinesia)	64	361

2.2 Data Preprocessing

The clinical studies provide the data sampled using a triaxial accelerometer and a triaxial gyroscope. There are six values (i.e. three spatial and three rotational values) at each time index. Each data item also contains a LID grade determined by clinicians as described above.

For further processing, the acceleration values at each time index are modified, as well as in [6], by calculating the magnitude, using the formula:

$$|a| = \sqrt{(|a_1|^2 + |a_2|^2 + |a_3|^2)}. \tag{1}$$

As the proposed solution should be suitable for an ASIC, it is suggested to use a fixed-point representation (FX) contrary to a floating-point representation (FP). Hence, we propose to employ the following data representations: signed 8-bit integer (FX-8s), unsigned 8-bit integer (FX-8u), signed 16-bit integer (FX-16s) and unsigned 16-bit integer (FX-16u). The range of values, calculated using Eq. 1, is between 23.33 and 7064.46 for spatial records, which fits only FX-16s and FX-16u data representations when these values are rounded down. However, it is necessary to scale the values to the ranges required for FX-8s and FX-8u. In our initial experiments, we used a formula for scaling to the 8-bit ranges:

$$d_i = \frac{x_i - x_{min}}{x_{max} - x_{min}} \cdot (d_{max} - d_{min}) + d_{min}, \tag{2}$$

where $x_i \in M$ denotes the original (FP) value in the set of all magnitude values M calculated using Eq. 1, and values x_{max} and x_{min} represent the maximum, and the minimum respectively, values in M. Values d_{max} and d_{min} are the maximum, and the minimum of, respectively, possible target values. In our experiments, we use scaling to $[-128, 127]$ and $[0, 127]$ to evolve LID-classifiers with FX-8s and scaling to $[0, 255]$ for FX-8u.

Although the use of Eq. 2 has shown promising results (see Fig. 4a), an alternative method based on a bit shift operation, which is easier to implement in hardware than Eq. 2, is examined in further experiments. As the logical right shift by five bits is very close to the result of Eq. 2 (i.e. division by around 28), the examined data scaling consists in binary input value shifting right by 3 up to 8 bits, i.e. three up to eight least-significant bits of the classifier input values are lost.

2.3 Classifier Model

In order to automatically design LID-classifiers, we have adopted the classifier model introduced by Lones et al. [6], except the training algorithm. As each record of patient's movements is cut into periods, of different lengths, according to the UDysRS LID grade it characterizes, each period (i.e. a time series) is used as a single *fitness case* for LID-classifier training.

A fitness case consists of L calculated magnitudes of acceleration. The fitness case is processed during classification in the following way: $L - 31$ overlapping

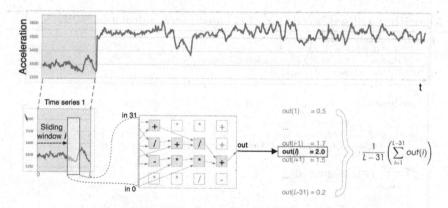

Fig. 1. LID-classifier model. The resulting response determines the LID grade by applying a threshold to the response range of the classifier.

windows of length 32 $(0.32\,\mathrm{s})$ generate $L-31$ vectors for the classifier inputs. The classifier generates an output for each of the $L-31$ vectors, and the resulting response from the classifier is then expressed as the mean of output values. The resulting response determines the LID grade (i.e. one of five classes) by applying a threshold to the response range of the classifier. The procedure of fitness case classification is illustrated in Fig. 1.

2.4 Classifier Training

For the automated design of LID-classifier, we propose to use GP, which is suitable for searching for executable structures, such as classifiers. We employ a variant of GP, the cartesian genetic programming (CGP) [10], which has been repeatedly used in solving problems of prediction and classification while achieving very good results [9]. In addition, CGP was successful in various related topics, such as the design of efficient digital circuits [7] and medical applications [12]. Many variants and improvements of CGP are summarized in [11]. In previous research, Lones et al. [6] employed implicit-context CGP to train LID-classifiers. We experience standard CGP representation [10] and the CGP equipped with the coevolution of adaptive size fitness predictors (CGPcoASFP) [3] in order to accelerate classifier evolution.

As the considered classifiers operate over a sliding window consisting of 32 samples, each candidate classifier can utilise up to 32 inputs, i.e. $n_i = 32$, of the following data representations: FP, 8-bit FX, and 16-bit FX. These data representations are also used in a classifier response in a form of single value, i.e. $n_0 = 1$, and in the set of functions Γ, working over two operands i_1 and i_2. Classifier evolution is operated using a simple $(1 + \lambda)$ evolutionary algorithm.

As a fitness function determining the quality of classifiers we use AUC (Area Under the receiver operating characteristics Curve), which allows accurate assessment of the ability to distinguish classes without defining a threshold value. Algorithm 1 provides a pseudo-code of AUC-based fitness calculation procedure.

Algorithm 1: Pseudo-code for AUC-based fitness calculation

```
Function calculate_auc(responses):
    TPR = 0; FPR = 0; AUC = 0;    // True & False Positive Rate, Area Under the Curve
    TPR_step = 1/count_N_target_responses(responses);
    FPR_step = 1/count_P_target_responses(responses);
    coords = [(0,0)];        // The ROC curve has the TPR on y axis and the FPR on x axis

    sort(responses);                        // Sort responses in descending order

    // Calculate TPR and FPR for all thresholds
    for (i = 0, i < count(responses), i++) do
        if responses[i].target == P then       // TP classifier response, TPR increase
            | TPR += TPR_step;
        else                                    // FP classifier response, FPR increase
            | FPR += FPR_step;
        end
        /* Append current FPR and TPR to coordinates for ROC construction; for more
           items with the same response, coordinates appended only once        */
        if responses[i].output != responses[i+1].output then
            | coords.append((FPR,TPR));
        end
    end

    // Calculate the area under the curve using the trapezoidal rule
    for (i = 0, i < count(coords)-1, i++) do
        | AUC += (coords[i+1].x - coords[i].x) * 0.5 * (coords[i].y + coords[i+1].y);
    end
    return AUC
```

Besides standard CGP, we employ CGPcoASFP in this task to accelerate the time demanding fitness evaluations. Drahosova et al. [3] developed a combination of fitness prediction with coevolution in CGP to reduce the number of expensive full fitness evaluations. The method replaces some of the objective fitness evaluations with an estimated fitness calculated using only a small part of training set and thus accelerates the training process.

In the CGPcoASFP algorithm, candidate programs are evolved using the usual $(1 + \lambda)$ evolutionary strategy together with a population of fitness predictors evolved with a simple genetic algorithm. Two archives of the best solutions supplement these two populations. An archive of the best fitness predictor is used for the fitness evaluation of candidate programs. An archive called fitness trainers with the best candidate programs, partially filled with random programs, is used for predictors evaluation. In addition, these fitness predictors adapt their size, i.e. the number of fitness cases they use for fitness estimation, using a heuristic method proposed in [3]. The variable size of fitness predictor helps to evaluate classifiers on the proper amount of input data, i.e. to find a good trade-off between the time and quality of evaluation.

3   Experimental Setup

Training Data Set: In order to train classifiers, we use solely the first data set, i.e. clinical study 1 described in Sect. 2.1, where, due to the size of sliding window, only data items with a minimal length of 32 samples are employed.

Table 2. Groups of data items from clinical study 2 structured to evaluate classifiers by LID grades and patient's activities separately. Due to the sliding window size (i.e. 32 samples), data items (from the two clinical studies, Table 1) of a length lower than 32 samples are excluded for training and evaluation.

Group	LID grade class N	number of data items N	LID grade class P	number of data items P
LID 1	0	1588	1	895
LID 2	0	1588	2	628
LID 3	0	1588	3	179
LID 4	0	1588	4	361
Walking	0	90	3, 4	21
Sitting-at-rest	0	733	3, 4	170

As described in [6], only data of LID grade 0, understood to be LID negative (N), and merged grades 3 and 4, understood to be LID positive (P), are used for training. The reason is that it is easier to generate robust classifiers when grades 1 and 2 are not involved during training, as described in [6]. It means that the training set consists of 2939 fitness cases with target class N and 745 fitness cases with target class P. Therefore, the resulting classifier is binary. The severity of LID (see Table 1), i.e. one of five classes, is then decided by applying a threshold to the response range of the classifier according to LID grades that occurred in clinical study 1.

Test Data Set: Classifiers are evaluated using the second data set, i.e. clinical study 2 described in Sect. 2.1, in order to obtain an evaluation on unseen data. The second data set is divided into four groups, each containing the data items of grade 0 and data items of one of the remaining grades, see Table 2. This allows measuring the quality of LID-classifier (in terms of AUC) for each LID grade separately. As each data item in the clinical studies contains information about patient movement activity, two additional groups of data items of *walking* and *sitting-at-rest* patient activities are utilised. These groups contain only data of LID grades 0, as class N, and merged grades 3 and 4, as class P.

3.1 Experiments

In order to evolve LID-classifiers that can be easily implemented in an ASIC, we applied CGP to design classifiers working with FX-16u, FX-16s, FX-8u, and FX-8s. To evaluate the proposed approach, the following experiments are investigated:

Experiment E1: All examined LID-classifiers are designed using standard CGP and CGP equipped with the coevolution of adaptive size fitness predictors (CGPcoASFP). These approaches are compared in terms of the quality of evolved classifiers (AUC) and the time of evolutionary design. This experiment aims to examine CGPcoASFP in a new task, i.e. the classifier design employing the AUC-based fitness function.

Experiment E2: In order to investigate the possibility of evolved LID-classifiers with reduced precision along with classification accuracy as close as possible to a baseline software implementation, we compare the AUC of LID-classifiers working with 8-bit and 16-bit FX with the AUC of evolved classifier working with 32-bit FP. In our experiments, we consider the following five data representations: 1) FP, 2) FX-8u, 3) FX-8s, 4) FX-16u, and 5) FX-16s.

In addition to these experiments, we examine two ways of input values scaling for 8-bit processing: (1) using Eq. 2, as described in Sect. 2.2, and (2) using the bit-shift operation, i.e. scaling of binary input value using shifting right by 3 up to 8 bits (SR-3, SR-4, SR-5, SR-6, SR-7, SR-8). These experiments aim to assess the impact of the data scaling on the ability to classify LID correctly.

Experiment E3: Three evolved LID-classifiers working with FX are selected according to their AUC on the training set, test set respectively, and synthesised using a standard design flow. Then, their hardware characteristics, i.e. area on the chip, delay, power consumption, and power delay product (PDP), are compared.

3.2 CGP Setup

The initial parameters of CGP were based on the results of work [6], i.e. the grid size of 6×6 with the set of functions $\Gamma = \{+, -, \times, \div, mean, min, max, abs\}$. However, our search for suitable parameters shows that the grid size of 1×36 together with the L-back of 36 leads to faster convergence. Next, the $(1 + 4)$ evolutionary strategy and the Goldman mutation operator [4] is used to produce a new generation.

3.3 CGPcoASFP Setup

The coevolution setup is based on [3] and customized for this task according to our initial experiments. The setup of CGP while coevolving with predictors is the same as the setup of standard CGP in Sect. 3.2.

Our preliminary experiments with different settings of predictor evolution reveal that six fitness trainers in the archive and eight fitness predictors in the predictor population are enough to produce a satisfactory predictor. The evolution of fitness predictors is conducted using a simple GA, where one-point crossover and mutation with probability 0.01 per gene operators are used. A new generation of predictors consists of three top-ranked predictors from the previous generation, one randomly generated predictor and four offspring whose parents are selected using a 2-tournament selection. Previous experiments [3] have revealed that a frequent interaction (generation to generation) between populations does not lead to programs with desired quality in a reasonable time because of very fast changes in involved populations. Hence, one generation in the predictor evolution executed each 30 generations of program evolution is enough to produce satisfactory predictors in this task.

The size of fitness predictor is initialized with 300 fitness cases, which is around 8% of the original training set. The length of fitness predictors is then based on the detected phase of evolution and adjusted when a new fitness predictor is being evolved after finding a new candidate program with the best subjective fitness or after a predefined number of generations. Decision conditions and their priority for updating the size of predictor are used the same as in [3], except the *prediction error threshold* (I_{thr}) parameter. This parameter depends on the fitness function. We have found that the error threshold of $I_{thr} = 1.04$ is suitable for our task, particularly it leads to the rapid convergence of CGP utilising the AUC-based fitness function.

3.4 Time of Stabilization of LID-Classifier Evolution

For evaluation of proposed approaches, we propose the *time of stabilization* of LID-classifier evolution. Time of stabilization denotes a time of evolution in which most of the runs (of proposed approach) are able to adapt the evolved LID-classifier on the training set. We define the time of stabilization, t_s, as the moment in which median fitness increase stagnation (out of 100 runs) is detected together with 95% confidence interval narrowing, i.e. $\Delta_{fitness}(t_i) < 0.0001$ (for next 10 s) and $w_{confidence}(t_i) < 0.005$, where $\Delta_{fitness}(t_i)$ is the difference between median fitness values in t_i and $t_i + 10$ s and $w_{confidence}(t_i)$ is the width of confidence interval in t_i.

4 Results

All presented results are based on one hundred independent runs for each of algorithm settings. All experiments are performed on the Barbora supercomputer, part of IT4Innovations National Supercomputing Center, where the nodes used for the calculations are equipped with a pair of Intel Cascade Lake 6240 processors. CGP and CGPcoASFP employed the same amount of resources.

4.1 Experiment 1: Comparisons of CGP and CGPcoASFP

We compare the design of classifiers using standard CGP and its extended variant CGPcoASFP. Table 3 summarizes mean AUC of LID-classifiers evolved using proposed approaches on the training set and the test set after 60 s of evolution and at the time of stabilization t_s. It can be seen that CGPcoASFP achieves the stabilisation of evolution approximately nine times faster, together with comparable or better mean AUC, than CGP on both training and test data. Mean AUC improvement occurs even if we compare it after 60 s of evolution. Next, CGP evolving FX-16u, FX-16s and FX-8s LID-classifiers need significantly more time than other proposed combinations to achieve satisfactory fitness. Boxplots showing AUC on the test groups at the time of stabilization of evolution, t_s, are shown in Fig. 3.

The mean training set size, i.e. the fitness predictor size, in the moment of stabilization of evolution, t_s, is shown in Table 3. In comparison to the initial 8%, CGPcoASFP uses approximately 1.33% of the original training set in t_s.

Table 3. For each data representation, the mean AUC of LID-classifiers evolved using CGP and CGPcoASFP (shortly ASFP in this table) on the training set and on the test set (for significant dyskinesia - LID 3, 4) after 60 s of evolution and at the time of stabilization t_s. In this table, FX-8u LID-classifiers work with data scaled using SR-5, FX-8s using Eq. 2. For comparison of CGP and CGPcoASFP, the higher AUC is marked in bold font for each data representation. The mean training set size (fitness predictor size) in t_s is shown in the last row.

Data representation		FP		FX-16u		FX-8u		FX-16s		FX-8s	
Algorithm		CGP	ASFP	CGP	ASFP	CGP	ASFP	CGP	ASFP	CGP	ASFP
Time of stabilization t_s [s]		48	25	1189	65	63	50	549	65	421	27
Training set	Mean AUC in t_s	0.899	**0.902**	0.899	0.899	0.898	**0.908**	0.903	**0.904**	**0.896**	0.894
	Mean AUC in $t = 60$ s	0.899	**0.903**	0.851	**0.899**	0.898	**0.908**	0.846	**0.904**	0.817	**0.898**
Test set	Mean AUC in t_s	0.889	0.889	0.872	**0.895**	0.915	**0.926**	**0.894**	0.893	0.871	**0.878**
	Mean AUC in $t = 60$ s	0.888	0.888	0.834	**0.893**	0.916	**0.926**	0.826	**0.893**	0.750	**0.889**
Mean training set size [%] in t_s		100	1.52	100	1.35	100	1.21	100	1.26	100	1.32

Figure 2 shows the median AUC on the training set (red line) and on the test groups of FX-8u LID-classifiers evolved using CGP (Fig. 2a) and CGPcoASFP (Fig. 2b) during evolution. In order to determine AUC on the test groups, the top-ranked LID-classifier from each generation is (after evolution) re-evaluated using the test groups to show the ability to generalize on unseen data. It can be

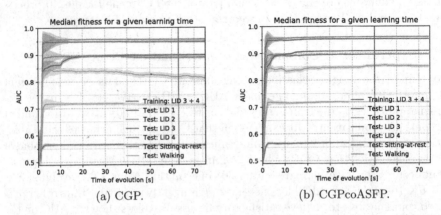

(a) CGP.   (b) CGPcoASFP.

Fig. 2. Median AUC on the training set (red line) and on the test groups of FX-8u (SR-5) LID-classifiers evolved using CGP and CGPcoASFP during evolution. The graph is obtained out of 100 runs with highlighted 95% confidence interval. Red vertical lines show the determined t_s. (Color figure online)

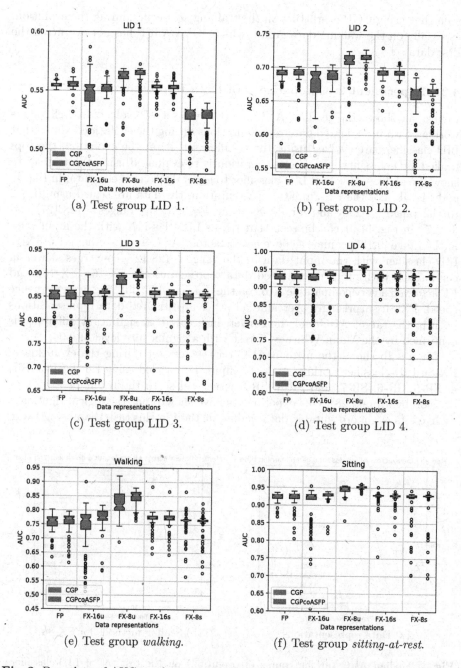

(a) Test group LID 1.

(b) Test group LID 2.

(c) Test group LID 3.

(d) Test group LID 4.

(e) Test group *walking*.

(f) Test group *sitting-at-rest*.

Fig. 3. Box plots of AUC on the test groups at the time of stabilization of evolution, t_s. These figures show the AUC of LID-classifiers working with all investigated data representations evolved using CGP and CGPcoASFP. Investigated data representations include FP, FX-16u, FX-8u (SR-5), FX-16s and FX-8s (Eq. 2 [−128, 127]).

seen that using CGP overfitting on the training set occurs during the evolution, especially on the walking data group, while CGPcoASFP has not overfitted the first data set.

4.2   Experiment 2: Comparisons of Data Representations

Figure 4a shows the median AUC on the test set of evolved LID-classifiers working with investigated data representations during the evolution. Notice that LID-classifiers are evolved using the training set. After the evolution, the top-ranked LID-classifier from each generation is re-evaluated using the test set to show the ability of evolved LID-classifier to generalize on unseen data, in Fig. 4a and Fig. 4b. For the FX-8u data representation, the data are scaled using Eq. 2 to the range [0, 255] and for FX-8s using Eq. 2 to the ranges [−128,127] and [0,127], in Fig. 4a. It can be seen that FX-8s LID-classifier with the input data in the range [0,127] cannot achieve a satisfactory AUC and together with FX-8s LID-classifier with the input data in the range [−128,127] converges slower in comparison with other investigated data representations. FX-16s, FX-16u and FP achieved a very comparable AUC on the test set while differing in convergence speed. FX-8u surprisingly overcame all other investigated data representations both in the target AUC and the convergence speed. A significant difference is confirmed by the Mann-Whitney U test with a significance level of 0.05.

Figure 4b shows the median AUC on the test set during the evolution of FX-8u LID-classifier working with the input data scaled using Eq. 2, SR-3, SR-4, SR-5, SR-6, SR-7, and SR-8. SR-5 is very close to the result of Eq. 2 (i.e. division by around 28). Our experiments have shown that the logical right shift by five bits is a more suitable data scaling method in this task than using Eq. 2.

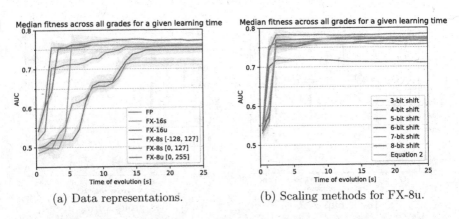

(a) Data representations.   (b) Scaling methods for FX-8u.

Fig. 4. Median AUC (in the course of evolution) on the test set of LID-classifiers evolved using CGPcoASFP obtained out of 100 runs with highlighted 95% confidence interval: (a) shows AUC during the evolution of classifiers working with investigated data representations; (b) shows AUC during the evolution of FX-8u classifiers with the use of investigated scaling methods.

Table 4. Mean AUC presented in [6] and mean AUC out of 100 runs for standard CGP with FP, CGPcoASFP with FP, standard CGP with FX-8u (SR-5) and CGPcoASFP with FX-8u (SR-5). For each test group, the best result is marked in bold font.

		LID 1 [AUC]	LID 2 [AUC]	LID 3 [AUC]	LID 4 [AUC]	*Sitting-at-rest* [AUC]	*Walking* [AUC]
CGP	FP	0.55	0.69	0.85	0.93	0.92	0.75
CGPcoASFP	FP	**0.56**	0.69	0.85	0.93	0.92	0.76
CGP	FX-8u (SR-5)	**0.56**	**0.71**	**0.89**	0.95	**0.95**	0.84
CGPcoASFP	FX-8u (SR-5)	**0.56**	**0.71**	**0.89**	**0.96**	**0.95**	**0.85**
Lones et al. [6]		**0.56**	0.69	0.85	0.93	0.92	0.73

Proposed solutions utilising both CGP and CGPcoASFP for designing FP LID-classifiers achieve mean AUC comparable with the approach presented in [6], see Table 4. Comparisons of the FX-8u (SR-5) LID-classifier (evolved using CGPcoASFP) and the existing solution presented in [6] in Table 4 shows that the proposed method achieves slightly better mean AUC across the test groups and the significantly better mean AUC = 0.85 for the test group *walking* compared to Lones et al. [6] mean AUC = 0.73, despite the fact that the proposed classifiers are working with the reduced precision.

Results of Experiment E2 suggest that it is easier to find significant discriminatory patterns using FX-8u processing together with SR-5 data preprocessing than using other investigated approaches, see Fig. 3. The most evident AUC increase is for the test group walking. It is possible that limiting the precision shaves off some noise and hence the overfitting tendencies. This denotes the suitability of this model for long-term home monitoring, as patients go through their daily activities, which should be a subject of further study.

4.3   Experiment 3: Hardware Characteristics of Evolved Classifiers

Three LID-classifiers, evolved using CGPcoASFP and working with the FX representation, are selected for a hardware implementation. The first classifier C1 works with FX-8u and data scaled using SR-5, see Fig. 5a. The second classifier C2 (Fig. 5b) and third classifier C3 (Fig. 5c) are evolved to operate FX-16u and the original data.

Classifiers C1 and C2 are chosen based on their fitness on training data. Classifier C3 is an expensive solution because it contains area-demanding components contributing to the higher AUC on the test set. Table 5 shows the AUC of selected classifiers on the test data groups.

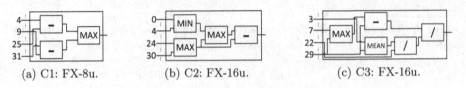

(a) C1: FX-8u.   (b) C2: FX-16u.   (c) C3: FX-16u.

Fig. 5. LID-classifiers used for hardware characteristics evaluation.

Table 5. AUC of the selected LID-classifiers on the test groups.

	LID 1	LID 2	LID 3	LID 4	Walking	Sitting
C1 (8-bit)	0.57	0.72	0.89	0.96	0.82	0.95
C2 (16-bit)	0.55	0.68	0.84	0.92	0.75	0.91
C3 (16-bit)	0.55	0.69	0.85	0.94	0.76	0.93

Table 6. Hardware characteristics of synthesized LID-classifiersfor for a 45 nm technology.

LID-Classifier	Area on chip [μm^2]	Delay [ns]	Power [mW]	PDP [pJ]
C1: FX-8u	258.58	0.94	0.17	0.16
C2: FX-16u	901.53	3.36	0.36	1.20
C2: FX-32u	1936.80	6.63	0.80	5.28
C3: FX-16u	6417.68	40.54	2.78	112.77
C3: FX-32u	27156.98	179.69	10.32	1854.11

Classifiers C2 and C3 are also successfully verified to give comparable AUC results even with an unsigned 32-bit FX (FX-32u). In order to determine the hardware cost, Synopsys Design Compiler targeting 45 nm ASIC technology is employed as a synthesis tool.

Table 6 shows the hardware characteristics of presented classifiers working with various data representations. We can immediately see that the classifier C2 (utilising simpler functions such as maximum, minimum, and subtraction) has significantly better characteristics than the classifier C3 utilising expensive multiplication and division operations.

In Table 6, it can be seen 7.54 times lower energy consumption of classifier C1 in comparison with the classifier C2 working with 16-bit and 709× lower in comparison with classifier C3 working with 32-bit.

Figure 6a shows receiving operating curve (ROC) of the classifier C1, which is the best evolved (in terms of AUC on the training set) for test groups LID 1, LID 2, LID 3 and LID 4. The classifier C1 outperforms all of the other investigated classifiers in terms of AUC on the test groups as well as in terms of hardware characteristics. Figure 6b compares ROCs of classifier C1 and the best evolved software implementation (operating with float) for test groups

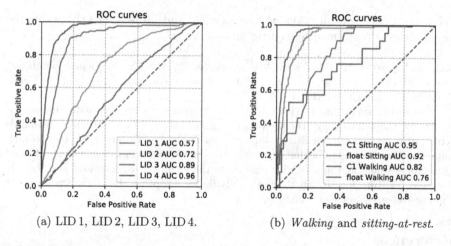

(a) LID 1, LID 2, LID 3, LID 4.   (b) *Walking* and *sitting-at-rest*.

Fig. 6. The ROC curves: (a) of the classifier C1 on LID grades; (b) of the top-ranked FP classifier and classifier C1 on *walking* and *sitting-at-rest* test groups to allow comparisons of FP and FX-8u (SR-5) classifiers.

sitting-at-rest and walking, where the improvement of classifier quality is evident. Notice that the best-evolved and energy-efficient LID-classifier is a very simple solution as it contains only three function instances (see Fig. 5a).

5   Conclusions

In this paper, we have shown that cartesian genetic programming equipped with the coevolution of adaptive size fitness predictors is able to design classifiers that can be used to determine presence and the severity of levodopa-induced dyskinesia. The method was applied to designing classifiers working with five various data representations. This approach outperformed the original CGP in terms of computational cost in all of the investigated experiments and effectively prevented overfitting when evolving FX-8u LID-classifiers.

We have investigated the design of an LID-classifier working with a reduced precision in order to find a hardware efficient classifier with a classification accuracy as close as possible to a baseline software implementation (using float data representations). We have observed that classifiers working with FX-8u, together with input data preprocessing using the logical right shift by five bits, achieved better classifier accuracy (AUC) than classifiers working with FP or FX-16u and FX-16s. Moreover, the FX-8u LID-classifier significantly outperformed the hardware characteristics of all other investigated solutions.

We will analyse why such a simple solution works and exploit this analysis in developing even better classifiers. We plan to extend this approach, to evolve classifiers of other movement abnormalities, such as bradykinesia. Hence, we think of developing a method in which hardware properties, i.e. area on chip, delay and power consumption, will be included and utilised directly during the design process performed by genetic programming.

Acknowledgements. This work was supported by the Czech science foundation project 21-13001S and by the Ministry of Education, Youth and Sports of the Czech Republic through the e-INFRA CZ (ID:90140).

The author would like to thank Dr. Vojtech Mrazek for his help with circuit synthesis. We also acknowledge the patients and clinical staff of Leeds Teaching Hospitals NHS Trust, particularly Dr Stuart Jamison and Dr Jeremy Cosgrove, for their contribution to the clinical study that generated the data used in this research, Dr Michael Lones for his help and advice with regards to the technical aspects, and also the UK National Institute for Health Research (NIHR) for adopting the study within in its Clinical Research Network Portfolio.

References

1. Ahlrichs, C., Lawo, M.: Parkinson's disease motor symptoms in machine learning: a review. Health Inform. Int. J. **2**(4), 1–18 (2013). https://doi.org/10.5121/hiij.2013.2401

2. Dinesh, K., Xiong, M., Adams, J., Dorsey, R., Sharma, G.: Signal analysis for detecting motor symptoms in Parkinson's and Huntington's disease using multiple body-affixed sensors: a pilot study. In: 2016 IEEE Western New York Image and Signal Processing Workshop (WNYISPW), pp. 1–5 (2016). https://doi.org/10.1109/WNYIPW.2016.7904834

3. Drahosova, M., Sekanina, L., Wiglasz, M.: Adaptive fitness predictors in coevolutionary Cartesian genetic programming. Evol. Comput. **27**(3), 497–523 (2019). https://doi.org/10.1162/evco_a_00229

4. Goldman, B.W., Punch, W.F.: Reducing wasted evaluations in cartesian genetic programming. In: Krawiec, K., Moraglio, A., Hu, T., Etaner-Uyar, A.Ş, Hu, B. (eds.) EuroGP 2013. LNCS, vol. 7831, pp. 61–72. Springer, Heidelberg (2013). https://doi.org/10.1007/978-3-642-37207-0_6

5. Locatelli, P., Alimonti, D., Traversi, G., Re, V.: Classification of essential tremor and Parkinson's tremor based on a low-power wearable device. Electronics (Basel) **9**(10), 1–18 (2020). https://doi.org/10.3390/electronics9101695

6. Lones, M.A., et al.: A new evolutionary algorithm-based home monitoring device for Parkinson's Dyskinesia. J. Med. Syst. **41**(11), 176:1–176:8 (2017). https://doi.org/10.1007/s10916-017-0811-7

7. Manazir, A., Raza, K.: Recent developments in Cartesian genetic programming and its variants. ACM Comput. Surv. **51**(6), 1–29 (2019). https://doi.org/10.1145/3275518

8. Milano, F., et al.: Parkinson's disease patient monitoring: a real-time tracking and tremor detection system based on magnetic measurements. Sensors (Basel, Switzerland) **21**(12) (2021). https://doi.org/10.3390/s21124196

9. Miller, J.F.: Cartesian genetic programming. In: Cartesian Genetic Programming, pp. 17–34. Springer, Berlin (2011). https://doi.org/10.1007/978-3-642-17310-3

10. Miller, J.F., Thomson, P.: Cartesian genetic programming. In: Proceedings of the 3rd European Conference on Genetic Programming EuroGP'2000. LNCS, vol. 1802, pp. 121–132. Springer, Cham (2000). https://doi.org/10.1007/978-3-540-46239-2_9

11. Miller, J.F.: Cartesian genetic programming: its status and future. Gene. Program. Evol. Mach. **21**(1), 129–168 (2019). https://doi.org/10.1007/s10710-019-09360-6
12. Smith, S.L., Lones, M.A.: Medical applications of Cartesian genetic programming. In: Stepney, S., Adamatzky, A. (eds.) Inspired by Nature. ECC, vol. 28, pp. 247–266. Springer, Cham (2018). https://doi.org/10.1007/978-3-319-67997-6_12
13. Sze, V., Chen, Y., Yang, T., Emer, J.S.: Efficient processing of deep neural networks: a tutorial and survey. Proc. IEEE **105**(12), 2295–2329 (2017). https://doi.org/10.1109/JPROC.2017.2761740
14. Zhu, B., Taghavi, M., Shoaran, M.: Cost-efficient classification for neurological disease detection. In: 2019 IEEE Biomedical Circuits and Systems Conference (BioCAS), pp. 1–4 (2019). https://doi.org/10.1109/BIOCAS.2019.8918702

Using Denoising Autoencoder Genetic Programming to Control Exploration and Exploitation in Search

David Wittenberg[✉][iD]

Johannes Gutenberg University, Mainz, Germany
wittenberg@uni-mainz.de

Abstract. Denoising Autoencoder Genetic Programming (DAE-GP) is a novel neural network-based estimation of distribution genetic programming (EDA-GP) algorithm that uses denoising autoencoder long short-term memory networks as a probabilistic model to replace the standard mutation and recombination operators of genetic programming (GP). At each generation, the idea is to flexibly identify promising properties of the parent population and to transfer these properties to the offspring where the DAE-GP uses denoising to make the model robust to noise that is present in the parent population. Denoising partially corrupts candidate solutions that are used as input to the model. The stronger the corruption, the stronger the generalization of the model. In this work, we study how corruption strength affects the exploration and exploitation behavior of the DAE-GP. For a generalization of the royal tree problem (high-locality problem), we find that the stronger the corruption, the stronger the exploration of the solution space. For the given problem, weak corruption resulting in a stronger exploitation of the solution space performs best. However, in more rugged fitness landscapes (low-locality problems), we expect that a stronger corruption resulting in a stronger exploration will be helpful. Choosing the right denoising strategy can therefore help to control the exploration and exploitation behavior in search, leading to an improved search quality.

Keywords: Genetic Programming · Estimation of Distribution Algorithms · Probabilistic Model-Building · Denoising Autoencoders

1 Introduction

Estimation of distribution genetic programming (EDA-GP) algorithms are meta-heuristics for variable-length combinatorial optimization problems that sample from a learned probabilistic model, replacing the standard mutation and recombination operators of genetic programming (GP). At each generation, the idea is to first learn the properties of promising candidate solutions of the parent population (*model building*) and to then sample from the model to transfer the learned properties to the offspring (*model sampling*) [9].

An example of an EDA-GP is denoising autoencoder genetic programming (DAE-GP) that uses denoising autoencoder long short-term memory networks (DAE-LSTMs) as a probabilistic model [25]. In comparison to previous EDA-GP approaches, it has the advantage that the model does not impose any assumptions about the relationships between problem variables which allows the DAE-GP to flexibly identify and model relevant properties of the parent population. The DAE-GP captures dependencies between problem variables by first encoding candidate solutions (in prefix notation) to the latent space and then reconstructing the candidate solutions from the latent space. For model building, the DAE-GP is trained to minimize the reconstruction error between the encoded and decoded candidate solutions. For model sampling, candidate solutions are propagated through the trained model to transfer the learned properties to the offspring [25].

The DAE-GP uses denoising to prevent the model from learning the simple identity function [25]. The idea is to partially corrupt input candidate solutions to make the model robust to noise that is present in the parent population. The stronger the corruption, the stronger the generalization of the model [24]. Previous work on estimation of distribution algorithms (EDA), where candidate solutions have a fixed length of size n, found that exploration and exploitation in search can be controlled by the strength of corruption [16]. Exploration increases the diversity of a population by introducing new candidate solutions into search; exploitation reduces diversity by focusing a population of candidate solutions on promising areas of the solution space [19]. Adjusting the corruption strength can therefore help to balance exploration and exploitation leading to a more successful search: we either increase diversity to overcome local optima avoiding premature convergence, or we decrease diversity to exploit promising solution spaces [16].

In this work, we study how corruption strength affects the exploration and exploitation behavior of the DAE-GP. Wittenberg et al. [25] used subtree mutation to corrupt input candidate solutions. Subtree mutation randomly selects a node in a tree and replaces the subtree at that node with a new random subtree generated by ramped half-and-half. The use of subtree mutation has the advantage that it leads to a variation in tree size (the number of nodes in parse tree) [25]. However, applying subtree mutation complicates the control of corruption strength: as subtree mutation randomly selects a subtree to be replaced by a new random subtree, corruption is stronger if the root of the selected subtree is nearer to the root of the parse tree. Furthermore, increasing or decreasing corruption strength is difficult.

Therefore, this paper introduces Levenshtein edit as a new and improved denoising strategy. Levenshtein edit is based on the Levenshtein distance [12] and operates on the string representation of a candidate solution (prefix expression). It uses insertion (add one node), deletion (remove one node), and substitution (replace one node by another node) as edit operators to corrupt a candidate solution. The advantage of using Levenshtein edit over subtree mutation is that we can accurately adjust corruption strength. The more nodes we edit, the stronger the corruption, and the more we force the DAE-GP to focus on general properties of the parent population.

We compare the performance of the DAE-GP with Levenshtein edit and different levels of corruption strength (2%, 5%, 10%, 20%) to a DAE-GP with subtree mutation and standard GP, and analyze the impact of corruption strength on search. We find that corruption strength strongly influences both the performance and the exploration and exploitation behavior of the DAE-GP: the stronger we corrupt input candidate solutions, the stronger the exploration. However, exploration is useful, only if we want to escape from local optima. For the generalization of the royal tree problem (which is an easy problem with high locality), we find that the DAE-GP with weak corruption (Levenshtein edit with 5% corruption strength) performs best. However, when facing more rugged fitness landscapes, a stronger degree of exploration can be helpful. We therefore believe that the denoising strategy is the key to the success of the DAE-GP: it allows us to control the level of exploration and exploitation in search helping us to improve search quality.

In Sect. 2, we present related work on EDA-GP. We describe DAE-LSTMs in Sect. 3, where we focus on the architecture, the denoising strategy, and on model building and sampling. In Sect. 4, we introduce the experiments and discuss the results. We draw conclusions in Sect. 5.

2   Related Work

We can categorize research on EDA-GP into two research streams [9,21]: The first one uses probabilistic prototype trees (PPT) as a model. Given the maximum arity a of the functions in the function set (the interior nodes of a GP parse tree), a PPT is a full tree of arity a where we set the depth of the PPT equal to the maximum tree depth d_{max}. At each node of the PPT, the idea is to first build a multinomial probability distribution over the set of allowed functions (internal nodes) and terminals (leaf nodes) and to then update the distributions according the candidate solutions that are presented to the model. In 1997, Salustowicz and Schmidhuber [20] introduced PPTs as the first probabilistic model in EDA-GP called probabilistic incremental program evolution (PIPE) [20]. Based on PIPE that evolves univariate probability distributions, EDA-GP models have been developed that capture dependencies between nodes in a PPT tree. Examples are the bivariate estimation of distribution programming (EDP) [28] or the multivariate program optimization with linkage estimation (POLE) [4,6]. Hasegawa and Iba [6] report that POLE needs less fitness evaluations than standard GP to solve the MAX, the deceptive MAX, and the royal tree problem [6].

The second stream of research uses grammars as EDA-GP model [9,21]. Here, Ratle and Sebag [18] presented stochastic grammar-based genetic programming (SG-GP) as the first grammar-based approach in 2001. SG-GP uses stochastic context-free grammar (SCFG) as a probabilistic model. The idea is to first identify a set of production rules for a problem with weights attached to the production rules and to then update these weights according to usage counts of the production rules in a parent population [18]. Since SG-GP assumes the production rules to be independent, more sophisticated EDA-GP models capturing more complex grammars have been developed. Consequently, program with annotated grammar estimation (PAGE) is an extension that uses expectation maximization (EM) or variational Bayes (VB) to learn production rules with latent annotations. A latent annotation can be, e.g., the position or the depth of a node in a tree [5]. Another extension is grammar-based genetic programming with a Bayesian network (BGBGP) that was introduced by Wong et al. [26] in 2014. BGBGP uses Bayesian networks with stochastic context-sensitive grammars (SCSG) as a model. Compared to SCFG, SCSG additionally incorporate contextual information allowing the Bayesian network to learn dependencies between production rules [26]. To further refine the BGBGP, Wong et al. [27] added (fitness) class labels to the model. The authors argue that this allows the model to differentiate between good and poor candidate solutions helping the model to find better solutions. For the deceptive MAX and the asymmetric royal tree problem, the model outperforms POLE, PAGE-EM, PAGE-VB, and grammar-based GP in the number of fitness evaluations [27].

One example of an EDA-GP model that does not rely on PPTs or grammars is the n-gram GP proposed by Poli and McPhee [14], where n-grams are used to model relationships between a group of n consecutive sequences of instructions that can learn dependencies in linear GP. Similarly, Hemberg et al. [7] suggested operator free genetic programming (OFGP), which learns n-grams of ancestor node chains. An n-gram of ancestors is the sequence of a node and its n-1 ancestor nodes in a GP parse tree. However, for the Pagie-2D problem, OFGP could not outperform standard GP [7].

Wittenberg et al. [25] recently suggested DAE-GP that uses denoising autoencoder long short-term memory networks (DAE-LSTMs) as a probabilistic model. For a generalization of the royal tree problem, the DAE-GP outperforms standard GP. The DAE-GP can better identify promising areas of the solution space compared to standard GP resulting in a more efficient search in the number of fitness evaluations, especially in large search spaces [25]. The authors argue that, compared to previous EDA-GP approaches, the flexible model representation is the key reason for the high performance, allowing the model to identify in parallel, both position as well as context of relevant substructures [25].

The idea of using DAE as probabilistic models in EDA has earlier been presented by Probst [15] who introduced DAE-EDA. DAE-EDA was designed for problems where candidate solutions follow a fixed-length representation [15]. For the NK landscapes, deceptive traps and HIFF problem, Probst and Rothlauf [16] show that the DAE-EDA yields competitive results compared to the Bayesian optimization algorithm (BOA). However, DAE-EDA is better parallelizable, making it the preferred choice especially in large search spaces. Furthermore, the authors show that corruption strength has a strong impact on exploration and exploitation in search. Adjusting the level of corruption can therefore help to either increase exploration which helps to overcome local optima, or to exploit relevant solution spaces making search more efficient [16].

3   Denoising Autoencoder LSTMs

DAE-LSTMs are artificial neural networks that consist of an encoding and a decoding LSTM: the encoding LSTM encodes a candidate solution (a linear sequence in prefix expression) to the latent space; the decoding LSTM decodes the latent space back to a candidate solution. Since we train the DAE-LSTM to reconstruct the input, the architecture is also referred to as autoencoder long short-term memory network (AE-LSTM) [22], where we use denoising on input candidate solutions to prevent the model from learning the simple identity function. Denoising transforms the AE-LSTM into a DAE-LSTM. When using DAE-LSTMs as a probabilistic model in EDA-GP (DAE-GP), we repeat the following two steps at each generation: first, we train the model to learn relevant properties of our parent population (model building). Then, we propagate candidate solutions through the trained DAE-LSTM to transfer the learned properties to the offspring (model sampling).

In the following sections, we first explain the architecture of AE-LSTMs and the concept of denoising, where we introduce Levenshtein edit as a new denoising strategy. Then, we describe the training as well as the sampling procedure where syntax control is used to restrict the sample space to syntactically valid candidate solutions.

3.1   Autoencoder LSTMs

Figure 1 shows the architecture of an AE-LSTM with one input layer, one hidden layer (consisting of LSTM memory cells), and one output layer. It is based on the architecture presented in [25]. x and o represent the input and output candidate solution of length m and k, respectively. h is the hidden state at time step t, where the total number of time steps corresponds to $T = m + k$ $(m, k \in \mathbb{N})$. The encoding LSTM (left) first sequentially encodes a candidate solution x, with x_t, $t \in \{1, 2, .., m\}$ through the encoding function $g(x)$, where each x_t represents a function or terminal of a candidate solution in our parent population. At each time step t (except $t = 0$), the LSTM memory cell then receives three inputs: the current input x_t, the previous hidden state h_{t-1} and the previous cell state c_{t-1} (not shown here). The idea of transferring information from one time step to the next is to capture long-term dependencies in training data [8]. After complete processing of the input candidate solution x, we copy h_m and c_m, and transfer it to the decoding LSTM, thus $h_{m+1} = h_m$ and $c_{m+1} = c_m$. The decoding LSTM (right) then uses the decoding function $d(h)$ and decodes h_t back to an output candidate solution o, with the aim to reconstruct the input candidate solution x. Using o_t as input in o_{t+1} helps to further reduce the reconstruction error [22]. Similar to [22] and [25], we reverse the input candidate solution x to allow the model to learn low range correlations in training data.

3.2   Suggesting a New Denoising Strategy: Levenshtein Edit

The aim of the AE-LSTM is to reconstruct the input. Given that the hidden layer is sufficiently large, a trivial way to solve this task is to learn the simple

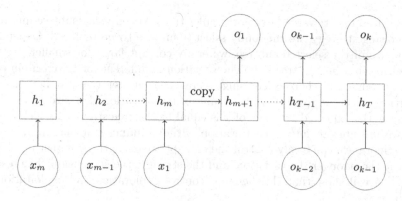

Fig. 1. Autoencoder LSTM assuming one hidden layer

identity function, which means that the AE-LSTM simply replicates the candidate solutions given as input. Since we want to learn a more useful representation of the properties of our parent population, we apply denoising on input candidate solutions, transforming the AE-LSTM into a DAE-LSTM. Based on the first DAE presented by Vincent et al. [24] in 2008, the idea is to partially corrupt input candidate solutions making the model robust to noise that is present in our parent population.

At each generation g, we use the corruption function $c(x)$ to denoise the candidate solutions that were previously selected as promising candidate solutions from population P_g. We can formally describe the process by

$$\tilde{x}^i = c(x^i) \ \forall i \in \{1, .., N\}, \tag{1}$$

where $\tilde{x}^i$ is the corrupted version of the ith candidate solution x in the training set X (of size N) [25].

As a new corruption function $c(x)$, we introduce Levenshtein edit. Levenshtein edit operates on the string representation of x (prefix expression) and uses insertion (add one node), deletion (remove one node), and substitution (replace one node by another node) to transform x into $\tilde{x}$. We control the corruption strength by a priori defining a corruption percentage p ($0 < p < 1$). Given a function set F, a terminal set T, and a candidate solution x, with x_j, $j \in \{1, 2, .., m\}$, we corrupt x by iteratively processing each node x_j, where each x_j has a chance of p to be corrupted: with uniform probability, we either insert a random symbol $s \in F \cup T$ at index j (insertion), we delete x_j (deletion), or we delete x_j *and* insert a random symbol $s \in F \cup T$ at index j (substitution). Note that these edit operations may produce corrupted candidate solutions $\tilde{x}$ that do not follow GP syntax. However, sampling with syntax control (see Sect. 3.4) ensures that output candidate solutions o are syntactically valid. Using Levenshtein edit as denoising strategy has several advantages: similar to subtree mutation presented in [25], we introduce variance in tree size. This is desirable since it introduces additional variation into $\tilde{x}$. However, this variation should not lead to a bias towards larger or smaller trees. When using subtree mutation as denoising strategy, we randomly select a subtree to be replaced. Depending on the size of the selected subtree, we easily corrupt larger or smaller parts of x resulting in a bias in tree size. The situation is different for Levenshtein edit: here, we randomly choose denoising operators that iteratively either increase (insertion), decrease (deletion), or maintain (substitution) the size of x. Thus, for any p, the expected tree size of $\tilde{x}$ is equal to the tree size of x, which means that we are able to introduce variation without inducing a bias in tree size. Furthermore, we can easily control the corruption strength by adjusting p. The larger p, the stronger the variation, and the stronger the corruption. The results in Sect. 4 will show that this helps to control exploration and exploitation in search.

3.3   Training Procedure

At each generation g, we train a DAE-LSTM (from scratch) according to the training procedure shown in Algorithm 1. It is similar to the training procedure presented in [25]. We first initialize the trainable parameters θ of our network, where W', b', and W'', b'' (Algorithm 1, line 1) denote the trainable weights and biases of the encoding and decoding LSTM, respectively. Then, we iteratively adjust the values of the trainable parameters θ using gradient descent. Given the corruption percentage p, we first transform the candidate solution x^i into $\tilde{x}^i$ (Algorithm 1, line 4). Then, we propagate $\tilde{x}^i$ through the DAE-LSTM, using the encoding function $g(x)$ (Algorithm 1, line 5) and the decoding function $d(x)$ (Algorithm 1, line 6). We compute the reconstruction error using the multiclass cross entropy loss function by

$$\theta := \min_{\theta} \sum_{i=1}^{N} Err(x^i, o^i), \tag{2}$$

where o^i is the output candidate solution and x^i the original (not the corrupted) input candidate solution. We update the parameters θ into the direction of the negative gradient and control the strength of the update using the learning rate α $(0 < \alpha < 1)$ (Algorithm 1, line 7).

Algorithm 1. Pseudocode for training a DAE-LSTM

1: **Initialize** $\theta = \{W', b', W'', b''\}$
2: **while** not converged **do**
3:     **for each** candidate solution x^i in training set X **do**
4:         $\tilde{x}^i = c(x^i; p)$
5:         $h = g(\tilde{x}^i; \theta)$
6:         $o^i = d(h; \theta)$
7:         $\theta := \theta - \alpha * \frac{\partial Err(x^i, o^i)}{\partial \theta}$
8:     **end for**
9: **end while**

We use early stopping to prevent the DAE-LSTM from overfitting. Given a hold-out validation set U, we stop training as soon as the validation error $Err(x^j, o^j)$, with $x^j, o^j \in U$, converges. We measure error convergence by observing the number of epochs that the validation error does not improve. As soon as we reach 200 epochs of no improvement, we stop training and use those parameters θ for sampling that minimize the validation error.

3.4 Sampling with Syntax Control

We use the DAE-LSTM with the trained parameters θ to sample new candidate solutions o forming the offspring population P_{g+1}. The procedure is shown in Algorithm 2 and based on [1, 16, 25]. Given θ (Algorithm 2, line 1), we first randomly pick a candidate solution x of our training set X (Algorithm 2, line 2). Then, we corrupt x into $\tilde{x}$ (Algorithm 2, line 3) using the same denoising strategy as during training and propagate $\tilde{x}$ through the DAE-LSTM (Algorithm 2, lines 4–5), where we add the resulting output candidate solution o to P_{g+1} (Algorithm 2, line 6).

Algorithm 2. Pseudocode for sampling from a DAE-LSTM

1: **Given** the trained DAE-LSTM with $\theta = \{W', b', W'', b''\}$
2: **Pick** $x \in X$ randomly
3: $\tilde{x} = c(x, p)$
4: $h = g(\tilde{x}; \theta)$
5: $o = d(h; \theta)$
6: **Add** o to new population P_{g+1}

Furthermore, we introduce a syntax control mechanism that only allows syntactically valid candidate solutions to be sampled. The mechanism proceeds as follows: at each time step t, with $t \in \{m+1, m+2, .., T\}$, when decoding h back to o (Algorithm 2, line 5), the DAE-LSTM generates a probability distribution q over the set of functions and terminals (defined by F and T). Similar to grow initialization [11], we first identify the set of functions and terminals that generate a syntactically valid candidate solution. Then, we set the classes of invalid functions and terminals in q to zero and normalize the remaining probabilities in q back to one, where we use the updated probability distribution to sample o_t.

Without denoising, syntax control is usually not needed since the complexity of the DAE-LSTM is sufficient to also learn correct syntax. However, the stronger the corruption, the more difficult it becomes for the DAE-LSTM to sample syntactically valid candidate solutions, since corrupted candidate solutions used as input to the model no longer belong to the same parent population as X. In these cases, syntax control is very useful: we prevent the DAE-LSTM from inefficient resampling and allow the model to explore new solution spaces, which can help to overcome local optima and to avoid premature convergence.

4   Experiments

We present the experimental setup for studying the influence of denoising on search. We find that the DAE-GP with Levenshtein edit and $p = 0.05$ outperforms a DAE-GP with subtree mutation and standard GP. Furthermore, we show that corruption strength p strongly affects search: the stronger the corruption, the stronger the exploration. Adjusting the corruption strength can therefore help to either exploit or explore relevant areas of the solution space.

4.1   Experimental Setup

For our study, we use the generalization of the royal tree problem presented in [25] as test problem. It is based on the royal tree problem introduced by Punch et al. [17] but uses the initialization method ramped half-and-half [11] to generate target candidate solutions x_{opt}. The idea is to define a fitness based on the structure of a candidate solution x by

$$fitness_x = \frac{lev(x, x_{opt})}{max(l_x, l_{x_{opt}})}, \tag{3}$$

where lev is the minimum Levenshtein distance, defined by the minimum number of insertion, deletion, and substitution operations necessary to transform x into x_{opt} [12]. Similar to [25], we divide lev by the maximum size l of x and x_{opt}, resulting in $fitness_x \in [0, 1]$: the closer x to x_{opt}, the better the fitness, where $fitness_x = 0$ means that x is identical to x_{opt} [25]. We tune the complexity of the problem by adjusting the minimum and maximum tree depths d_{min} and d_{max}, respectively. The larger the solution space, the more difficult the problem.

We implemented the experiments in Python using the evolutionary framework DEAP [3] and the neural network framework Keras [2]. Table 1 shows the GP and DAE-GP parameters. We use the Pagie-1 [13] function and terminal set and define two different problem settings, where we fix the minimum tree depth to $d_{min} = 3$ and set the maximum tree depth to $d_{max} \in \{4, 5\}$. We choose a population size of 500, use binary tournament selection, and run the experiments for a total of 100 generations. We use ramped half-and-half to generate both the initial population and the target candidate solutions x_{opt} and define 30 different x_{opt} per problem setting. Performing 5 runs per x_{opt} results in a total number of 150 runs that we aggregate per problem setting and algorithm. Since we consider six different algorithm configurations, we conduct 1,800 runs in total.

For GP, we follow the recommendations of Koza [11] and use subtree crossover as variation operator where we set an internal node bias to assure that 90% of the crossover points are functions. For the DAE-GP, we have to a priori define a set of hyperparameters. Note that we did not conduct a hyperparameter optimization. We set the number of hidden layers to one and the number of hidden neurons equal the maximum size l of the candidate solutions used as input to the model. We found that the complexity of the model is sufficient to learn complex relationships in training data while allowing efficient model building

Table 1. GP and DAE-GP Parameters

Parameter	Setting
function set	$F = \{+, -, *, /, sin, cos, exp, log\}$
terminal set	$T = \{x, y, 1\}$
target cand. solutions	30 per problem setting
runs	5 per target candidate solution
population size	500
generations	100
initialization	ramped half-and-half
selection	tournament selection of size 2
tree depths	$d_{min} = 3$ and $d_{max} \in \{4, 5\}$
variation operator	GP: subtree crossover with internal node bias (90% functions, 10% terminals), DAE-LSTM: model building and sampling with Levenshtein edit using $p \in \{0.02, 0.05, 0.1, 0.2\}$ and subtree mutation using $d_{min}, d_{max} = 2$ [25]

and sampling. We split the parent population into 50% training set X and 50% validation set U, and set the batch size to 25 (10% of X). We use a learning rate of $\alpha = 0.001$ and perform adaptive moment estimation (Adam) [10] for gradient descent optimization. To study the impact of denoising on search, we vary the denoising strategy throughout the experiments: we test Levenshtein edit, with $p \in \{0.02, 0.05, 0.1, 0.2\}$, and a DAE-GP using subtree mutation, where previous work recommends to set the depth of the new subtree to $d_{min}, d_{max} = 2$ [25].

4.2   Performance Results

We first study the algorithm success rates for the two problem complexities ($d_{max} \in \{4, 5\}$) and the six different algorithm configurations. A run is successful as soon as the algorithm finds a candidate solution x during search that is identical to the target candidate solution x_{opt} ($fitness_x = 0$). Table 2 shows the average success rates after 100 generations. Each success rate represents the average over 150 runs (5 runs for each of the 30 target candidate solutions x_{opt}). As expected, the average success rates are higher for $d_{max} = 4$ compared to $d_{max} = 5$: the solution space becomes larger when choosing larger tree depths making it harder to find x_{opt}. However, the success rates differ strongly depending on the algorithm considered. For both $d_{max} = 4$ and $d_{max} = 5$, the DAE-GP with Levenshtein edit and $p = 0.05$ performs best, with an average success rate of 72.67% and 58.67%, respectively. Interestingly, increasing or decreasing p results in a loss in search success. While the DAE-GP with $p = 0.02$ and $p = 0.1$ yields similar average success rates compared to standard GP (51.33% vs. 59.33% vs. 50.00% for $d_{max} = 4$ and 38.00% vs. 35.33% vs. 36.67% for $d_{max} = 5$), we achieve low success rates using strong corruption: for $d_{max} = 4$ and $d_{max} = 5$, the DAE-GP with $p = 0.2$ only finds 26.00% and 16.67% of the target solutions, respectively. The DAE-GP with subtree mutation performs worst, with average success rates of 16.00% and 1.33%, respectively. The high performance of the DAE-GP with Levenshtein edit and $p = 0.05$ indicates that the model successfully identifies and models relevant properties of the parent population and is able to transfer these properties to the offspring. However, performance strongly depends on the denoising strategy applied.

Table 2. Average success rates after 100 generations

Algorithm	$d_{max} = 4$	$d_{max} = 5$
Standard GP	50.00%	36.67%
DAE-GP Levenshtein edit $p = 2\%$	51.33%	38.00%
DAE-GP Levenshtein edit $p = 5\%$	72.67%	58.67%
DAE-GP Levenshtein edit $p = 10\%$	59.33%	35.33%
DAE-GP Levenshtein edit $p = 20\%$	26.00%	16.67%
DAE-GP subtree mutation	16.00%	1.33%

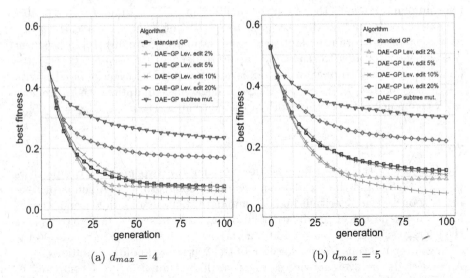

(a) $d_{max} = 4$ (b) $d_{max} = 5$

Fig. 2. Average best fitness over number of generations for problems of varying complexity.

Figure 2 plots the average best fitness over the number of generations. Since we face a minimization problem, we observe a general decrease in the average best fitness over the number of generations. The solution space is larger for $d_{max} = 5$, resulting in a best fitness level that is slightly higher compared to $d_{max} = 4$. Again, for both problem settings, the DAE-GP with Levenshtein edit and $p = 0.05$ performs best, confirming the results from Table 2. Interestingly, in early generations, the DAE-GP with $p = 0.02$ finds similar best fitness candidate solutions compared to $p = 0.05$ but then hardly improves from generation $g = 30$ ($d_{max} = 4$) and $g = 40$ ($d_{max} = 5$), indicating that the algorithm has already converged. In contrast, when setting the corruption strength to $p = 0.1$, we observe a similar best fitness slope of the DAE-GP and standard GP, demonstrating a similar search behavior. When using $p = 0.2$ or subtree mutation as denoising strategy, the performance is much worse.

Given the distribution of the best fitness at the end of each run (generation 100), we conduct several (pairwise) Mann-Whitney U-Tests to test the hypothesis that the best fitness distributions are from the same population. Assuming a significance level of 0.05, we find that the DAE-GP with Levenshtein edit and $p = 0.05$ yields p-values <0.01 for all pairwise comparisons. The results indicate that this DAE-GP is significantly better than all other tested algorithms. When using $p = 0.1$ and comparing the DAE-GP to standard GP, we find p-values of 0.09 ($d_{max} = 4$) and 0.58 ($d_{max} = 5$). Similarly, when setting the corruption strength to $p = 0.02$ and comparing the DAE-GP to standard GP, we find p-values of 0.98 ($d_{max} = 4$) and 0.2 ($d_{max} = 5$). In both cases, the results indicate that the best fitness distributions do not significantly differ from each other, confirming the observation that these algorithms generate similar best fitness candidate solutions.

4.3   The Influence of Denoising on Search

The results above demonstrate that denoising has a strong impact on the performance of the DAE-GP. To better understand the influence of denoising on search, we study the exploration and exploitation behavior of the algorithms. Similar to [25], we approximate exploration and exploitation by examining the number of new candidate solutions over generations that have never been sampled before. Exploitation is stronger, if search introduces a lower number of new candidate solutions during search. In contrast, the more new candidate solutions we introduce into search, the stronger the exploration. According to Rothlauf [19], we need to find an appropriate and problem-specific balance between exploration and exploitation in search. For problems, where small variations on the genotype lead to small variations in fitness (*high-locality problems*), we usually need much less exploration compared to problems, where the fitness landscape is rugged (*low-locality problems*). Thus, depending on the problem at hand, we either need to increase exploitation, making search more efficient, or we need to increase exploration, helping search to keep diversity high and allowing to overcome local optima and to avoid premature convergence [19].

For the generalization of the royal tree problem, we plot results in Fig. 3. As expected, for both variants, we observe a general decrease in the number of candidate solutions over generations. Furthermore, the level of exploration is in general higher for $d_{max} = 5$, again because we face a larger solution space compared to $d_{max} = 4$.

When comparing different denoising strategies with each other, we notice that the level of exploration and exploitation strongly differs throughout the

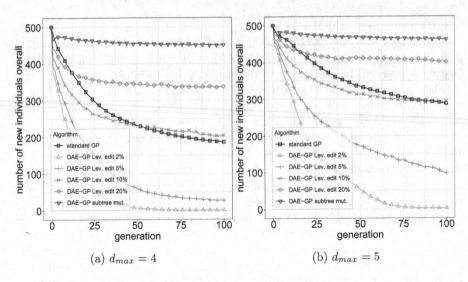

(a) $d_{max} = 4$ (b) $d_{max} = 5$

Fig. 3. Mean number of new candidate solutions over number of generations for problems of varying complexity.

search. For Levenshtein edit, we observe that the larger the corruption strength p, the stronger the exploration. While the DAE-GP with $p = 0.02$ strongly decreases and converges towards zero at generation $g = 50$ ($d_{max} = 4$) and $g = 75$ ($d_{max} = 5$), setting corruption strength to $p = 0.2$ results in a strong exploration of the solution space. Interestingly, as noticed in Sect. 4.2, both settings lead to an inferior performance compared to $p = 0.05$. The DAE-GP with $p = 0.02$ easily gets stuck in local optima (premature convergence) as we tend to replicate the candidate solutions given as input. In contrast, the DAE-GP with corruption strength of $p = 0.2$ introduces too many new candidate solutions, resulting in an inefficient search. Thus, by setting corruption strength to $p = 0.05$, we find a good balance between exploration and exploitation in search.

Another interesting observation is that the level of exploration of standard GP is similar to the one of the DAE-GP, using Levenshtein edit with $p = 0.1$. Thus, we can adjust the corruption strength in a way that allows us to imitate the exploration and exploitation behavior of standard GP, also yielding similar performance results.

For subtree mutation as denoising strategy, we notice that the level of exploration is highest throughout the search, yielding the worst results. We think that the introduction of syntax control (see Sect. 3.4) is the main reason for the bad performance of subtree mutation compared to the results published in [25]. Syntax control allows the DAE-GP to introduce more new candidate solutions into search, which can be helpful to overcome local optima. However, for the generalization of the royal tree problem (high-locality problem), the strong exploration leads to inferior performance. Instead, search with strong exploitation, as shown for Levenshtein edit $p = 0.05$, is more successful.

The results indicate that the denoising strategy is key to the success of the DAE-GP. It strongly influences exploration and exploitation in search and therefore affects performance. Thus, we believe that the denoising strategy should be adjusted depending on the problem at hand: while weaker corruption helps to improve search quality for high-locality problems, we expect stronger corruption to be more successful when we face rugged fitness landscapes (low-locality problems). Here, a stronger exploration of the solution space can help to overcome local optima and to avoid premature convergence.

5   Conclusions

The DAE-GP is an EDA-GP model based on artificial neural networks that flexibly identifies and models hidden relationships in training data. It uses denoising on input candidate solutions to make the model robust to noise that is present in the parent population. This paper introduced Levenshtein edit as a new and improved denoising strategy, allowing us to precisely control corruption strength. Furthermore, we implemented a new syntax control mechanism for sampling from the DAE-GP, allowing a higher level of exploration throughout the search.

We find that denoising strongly influences exploration and exploitation in search and therefore affects performance. The stronger we denoise input candidate solutions, the stronger the exploration. Exploration is especially useful for low-locality problems where we want to escape from local optima. In contrast, for high-locality problems, such as the generalization of the royal tree problem considered in this work, stronger exploitation is needed. Therefore the DAE-GP with low corruption strength (5%) performs best. The results show that the denoising strategy is key to the success of the DAE-GP: it permits us to control the exploration and exploitation behavior in search leading to an improved search quality.

In future work, we investigate the influence of denoising on other problem domains. We will study if we can dynamically control corruption strength throughout search. In addition, we think that Levenshtein edit as denoising strategy can still be improved. The denoising strategy presented in this paper operates on the string of a candidate solution, which easily destroys GP syntax. Thus, Levenshtein edit operating on a parse tree could be a promising approach. Furthermore, a hyperparameter optimization could further improve model quality, as well as other architectures, such as the transformer architecture [23]. Besides this, future work should investigate if a pre-training of the model before evolution helps to improve search quality.

Acknowledgements. I thank my team in Mainz, especially Franz Rothlauf, for insightful discussions on this topic, as well as Dirk Schweim and Malte Probst for previous work on this topic.

References

1. Bengio, Y., Yao, L., Alain, G., Vincent, P.: Generalized denoising auto-encoders as generative models. In: Advances on Neural Information Processing Systems (NIPS 2013), vol. 26, pp. 899–907 (2013)
2. Chollet, F.: keras. https://github.com/fchollet/keras (2015)
3. Fortin, F.A., De Rainville, F.M., Gardner, M.A., Parizeau, M., Gagńe, C.: DEAP: evolutionary algorithms made easy. J. Mach. Learn. Res. **13**(1), 2171–2175 (2012)
4. Hasegawa, Y., Iba, H.: Estimation of Bayesian network for program generation. In: Proceedings of the Third Asian-Pacific Workshop on Genetic Programming, pp. 35–46. Hanoi, Vietnam (2006)
5. Hasegawa, Y., Iba, H.: Estimation of distribution algorithm based on probabilistic grammar with latent annotations. In: Proceedings of the IEEE Congress on Evolutionary Computation, CEC 2007, pp. 1043–1050. IEEE (2007), https://doi.org/10.1109/CEC.2007.4424585
6. Hasegawa, Y., Iba, H.: A Bayesian network approach to program generation. IEEE Trans. Evol. Comput. **12**(6), 750–764 (2008). https://doi.org/10.1109/tevc.2008.915999
7. Hemberg, E., Veeramachaneni, K., McDermott, J., Berzan, C., O'Reilly, U.M.: An investigation of local patterns for estimation of distribution genetic programming. In: Proceedings of the Genetic and Evolutionary Computation Conference (GECCO 2012), pp. 767–774. ACM, Philadelphia (2012). https://doi.org/10.1145/2330163.2330270
8. Hochreiter, S., Schmidhuber, J.: Long short-term memory. Neural Comput. **9**(8), 1735–1780 (1997). https://doi.org/10.1162/neco.1997.9.8.1735
9. Kim, K., Shan, Y., Nguyen, X.H., McKay, R.I.: Probabilistic model building in genetic programming: a critical review. Gene. Program. Evol. Mach. **15**(2), 115–167 (2013). https://doi.org/10.1007/s10710-013-9205-x
10. Kingma, D.P., Ba, J.: Adam: a method for stochastic optimization. In: International Conference on Learning Representations. San Diego (2015)
11. Koza, J.R.: Genetic Programming: On the Programming of Computers by Means of Natural Selection. MIT Press, London (1992)
12. Kruskal, J.B.: An overview of sequence comparison: time warps, string edits, and macromolecules. Soc. Ind. Appl. Math. (SIAM) Rev. **25**(2), 201–237 (1983). https://doi.org/10.1137/1025045
13. Pagie, L., Hogeweg, P.: Evolutionary consequences of coevolving targets. Evol. Comput. **5**(4), 401–418 (1997)
14. Poli, R., McPhee, N.F.: A linear estimation-of-distribution GP system. In: Proceedings of the 11th European Conference on Genetic Programming (EuroGP 2008), pp. 206–217. Springer, Neapel (2008). https://doi.org/10.1007/978-3-540-78671-9
15. Probst, M.: Denoising autoencoders for fast combinatorial black box optimization. In: Proceedings of the Companion Publication of the Annual Conference on Genetic and Evolutionary Computation, pp. 1459–1460. ACM, Madrid (2015)
16. Probst, M., Rothlauf, F.: Harmless overfitting: Using denoising autoencoders in estimation of distribution algorithms. J. Mach. Learn. Res. **21**(78), 1–31 (2020). http://jmlr.org/papers/v21/16-543.html
17. Punch, B., Zongker, D., Goodman, E.: The royal tree problem, a benchmark for single and multi-population genetic programming. In: Angeline, P.J., Kinnear, K.E., Jr. (eds.) Advances in Genetic Programming II, pp. 299–316. MIT Press, Cambridge (1996)

18. Ratle, A., Sebag, M.: Avoiding the bloat with stochastic grammar-based genetic programming. In: Collet, P., Fonlupt, C., Hao, J.-K., Lutton, E., Schoenauer, M. (eds.) EA 2001. LNCS, vol. 2310, pp. 255–266. Springer, Heidelberg (2002). https://doi.org/10.1007/3-540-46033-0_21

19. Rothlauf, F.: Design of Modern Heuristics: Principles and Application, 1st edn. Springer, Berlin (2011). https://doi.org/10.1007/978-3-540-72962-4

20. Salustowicz, R., Schmidhuber, J.: Probabilistic incremental program evolution. Evol. Comput. **5**(2), 123–141 (1997). https://doi.org/10.1162/evco.1997.5.2.123

21. Shan, Y., McKay, R., Essam, D., Abbass, H.: A survey of probabilistic model building genetic programming. In: Pelikan, M., Sastry, K., CantúPaz, E. (eds.) Scalable Optimization via Probabilistic Modeling, pp. 121–160. Springer, Berlin (2006). https://doi.org/10.1007/978-3-540-34954-9

22. Srivastava, N., Mansimov, E., Salakhutdinov, R.: Unsupervised learning of video representations using LSTMs. In: Proceedings of the 32nd International Conference on Machine Learning (ICML 2015), pp. 843–852. ACM, Lille (2015). https://doi.org/10.5555/3045118.3045209

23. Vaswani, A., Shazeer, N., Parmar, N., Uszkoreit, J., Jones, L., Gomez, A.N., Kaiser, L, Polosukhin, I.: Attention is all you need. Adv. Neural Inf. Process. Syst. **30**, 5998–6008 (2017)

24. Vincent, P., Larochelle, H., Bengio, Y., Manzagol, P.A.: Extracting and composing robust features with denoising autoencoders. In: Proceedings of the 25th International Conference on Machine Learning (ICML 2008), pp. 1096–1103. ACM, Helsinki (2008). https://doi.org/10.1145/1390156.1390294

25. Wittenberg, D., Rothlauf, F., Schweim, D.: DAE-GP: denoising autoencoder LSTM networks as probabilistic models in estimation of distribution genetic programming. In: Proceedings of the 2020 Genetic and Evolutionary Computation Conference, pp. 1037–1045. GECCO 2020, ACM, New York (2020). https://doi.org/10.1145/3377930.3390180

26. Wong, P.K., Lo, L.Y., Wong, M.L., Leung, K.S.: Grammar-based genetic programming with Bayesian network. In: IEEE Congress on Evolutionary Computation (CEC'14), pp. 739–746. IEEE, Beijing (2014)

27. Wong, P.K., Lo, L.Y., Wong, M.L., Leung, K.S.: Grammar-based genetic programming with dependence learning and Bayesian network classifier. In: Proceedings of the Genetic and Evolutionary Computation Conference (GECCO 2014), pp. 959–966. ACM, Vancouver (2014). https://doi.org/10.1145/2576768.2598256

28. Yanai, K., Iba, H.: Estimation of distribution programming based on Bayesian network. In: IEEE Congress on Evolutionary Computation (CEC 2003), pp. 1618–1625. IEEE, Canberra (2003). https://doi.org/10.1109/CEC.2003.1299866

Program Synthesis with Genetic Programming: The Influence of Batch Sizes

Dominik Sobania[✉][ID] and Franz Rothlauf[ID]

Johannes Gutenberg University, Mainz, Germany
{dsobania,rothlauf}@uni-mainz.de

Abstract. Genetic programming is a method to generate computer programs automatically for a given set of input/output examples that define the user's intent. In real-world software development this method could also be used, as a programmer could first define the input/output examples for a certain problem and then let genetic programming generate the functional source code. However, a prerequisite for using genetic programming as support system in real-world software development is a high performance and generalizability of the generated programs. For some program synthesis benchmark problems, however, the generalizability to previously unseen test cases is low especially when lexicase is used as parent selection method. Therefore, we combine in this paper lexicase selection with small batches of training cases and study the influence of different batch sizes on the program synthesis performance and the generalizability of programs generated with genetic programming. For evaluation, we use three common program synthesis benchmark problems. We find that the selection pressure can be reduced even when small batch sizes are used. Moreover, we find that, compared to standard lexicase selection, the obtained success rates on the test set are similar or even better when combining lexicase with small batches. Furthermore, also the generalizability of the found solutions can often be improved.

Keywords: Program synthesis · Genetic programming · Generalization

1 Introduction

Genetic programming (GP) [3, 22] is a technique to automatically generate computer programs. For a given set of input/output examples (training cases) defining the requirements, GP searches in an evolutionary process for a program that completely fulfills these requirements. This procedure has similarities to the standard procedure in real-world software development, for example, as in test-driven development [2], where the test cases (e.g., unit tests) are defined first and after that the functional source code is written. GP, which in recent years has made some progress in automatic program synthesis [11], has the potential

© The Author(s), under exclusive license to Springer Nature Switzerland AG 2022
E. Medvet et al. (Eds.): EuroGP 2022, LNCS 13223, pp. 118–129, 2022.
https://doi.org/10.1007/978-3-031-02056-8_8

to replace the second part of this process: writing the functional source code. However, this assumes that GP can find solutions for many everyday programming problems and that these solutions are generalizable which means that they also work on previously unseen test cases (as in production).

In recent work, the success rates (percentage of runs that find a correct solution) for standard program synthesis benchmark problems could be increased significantly [9,14]. This increase is strongly related to the use of lexicase selection [27], in which the training cases are evaluated individually instead of aggregating a program's performance on all training cases and selecting by this overall fitness value (as in tournament selection). However, considering the individual training cases during selection may lead to a strong overfitting on some benchmark problems [18,24]. Usually, such solutions generalize poorly to unseen test cases.

For classification problems, Aenugu and Spector [1] have shown that a variant of lexicase selection using batches combining a set of individual training cases usually leads to a better generalization. However, there are commonly many more training cases available in classification than in program synthesis, since in practice a programmer has to generate all the training cases manually (as there is no oracle function). So, due to the limited number of training cases, the choice of the batch size is also limited in program synthesis. Furthermore, it is still unclear how small batch sizes affect the program synthesis performance and generalization ability of GP.

Therefore, this work studies the influence of small batch sizes used during selection on the success rates and the generalizability of the programs generated by GP. For this analysis, we use three common problems from the general program synthesis benchmark suite [17].

For evaluation, we use a grammar-guided GP approach and use during selection batch sizes ranging from $\beta = 1$, which corresponds to standard lexicase selection, to $\beta = 100$. To analyze the influence of the batch sizes on the success rates as well as on the generalizability of the found solutions, we select three problems from the program synthesis benchmark suite [17] which are known in the literature for their generalization issues. We find in our experiments that using small batch sizes can lead to similar or even better success rates on the test set compared to standard lexicase selection ($\beta = 1$). Furthermore, best generalization rates are achieved with $\beta \geq 2$.

In Sect. 2 we give a brief introduction to lexicase selection and present the relevant work on GP-based program synthesis. Section 3 describes the used benchmark problems and the selection method. In Sect. 4 we present our experiments and discuss the results before concluding the paper in Sect. 5.

2 Lexicase Selection in GP-Based Program Synthesis

In the literature on GP-based program synthesis, variants of lexicase selection are often compared with other selection methods on a wide range of program synthesis benchmark problems and the lexicase variants usually outperform other selection methods like tournament selection, fitness-proportionate selection, or implicit fitness sharing [8,10,12,13,15–17,20,23–25].

Algorithm 1: Lexicase Selection

---

1 cases := shuffle(training_cases);
2 candidates := population;
3 **while** |cases| > 0 & |candidates| > 1 **do**
4 | case := cases.pop(0);
5 | candidates := best_individuals(candidates, case);
6 **end**
7 **if** |candidates| > 1 **then**
8 | **return** choice(candidates);
9 **end**
10 **return** candidates[0];

Algorithm 1 shows the process of selecting an individual for the next generation with standard lexicase selection [16,27] as pseudo-code. First, the training cases are shuffled randomly (line 1) and all solutions from the population are considered as possible candidates for selection (line 2). In the next step, all candidates which do not have the exact lowest error on the first training case are discarded and the first training case is removed from the list (lines 4–5). This step is repeated until either all cases have been considered or only one candidate solution is left (while loop defined in line 3). Finally, either a random solution chosen from the remaining candidates will be returned (lines 7–9) or, if there is only a single solution left, the last remaining candidate solution will be returned (line 10).

Since lexicase selection is computationally intensive in comparison to other selection methods such as tournament or fitness-proportionate selection, de Melo et al. [4] suggested batch tournament selection, which combines the benefits of tournament and lexicase selection. Tested on a set of common regression problems, batch tournament selection achieves a solution quality similar to lexicase selection but is significantly faster. Another approach that is also based on batches of training cases is batch lexicase selection suggested by Aenugu and Spector [1]. For classification problems, they show that batch lexicase selection can improve generalization. In addition to batches, the authors introduce also a threshold parameter which allows individuals to survive the selection process even if they have a larger error than the best individual on the considered batch (depending on the defined threshold). So this parameter allows a further adjustment of the selection pressure (in addition to the selection of the batch size). A selection method based on similar principles that has been applied to program synthesis problems, but without analyzing the generalizability of the found solutions, is summed batch lexicase selection [5].

To prevent pre-mature convergence, Kelly et al. [21] suggested knobelty selection. Based on a defined novelty probability, an individual is selected either based on its novelty or its performance. For the performance-based selection, the authors use lexicase selection.

Recently, Hernandez et al. [19] suggested down-sampled lexicase selection, which operates on a different random subset of the training cases in each generation. Although down-sampled lexicase selection consistently achieves better results than standard lexicase selection, it has not yet been shown that the solutions found generalize better to unseen test cases [18].

However, to our knowledge, there is no work so far studying the influence of small batch sizes on the success rates and the generalizability of programs generated with GP on program synthesis benchmark problems that are known for their low generalization rates.

3 Methodology

To analyze the influence of batch sizes on the performance and generalizability of GP-based program synthesis, we apply a grammar-guided GP approach to common program synthesis benchmark problems. In this section, we present the selected benchmark problems and describe the used grammars as well as the selection method.

3.1 Benchmark Problems

As we want to study if the use of small batches increases generalizability in the program synthesis domain, we selected three problems from the program synthesis benchmark suite [17] that are known for their generalization issues in the literature [24]. The selected problems are:

- **Compare String Lengths**: For three given strings, return true if the strings are sorted in ascending order according to their length. Otherwise, return false.
- **Grade**: For five given integer values, where the first four values define the minimum score required to achieve the grades "A", "B", "C", and "D", and the fifth value defines the score achieved by a student, return the grade for this student. Return an "F" if the achieved score is lower than the score defined by the fourth integer value.
- **Small Or Large**: For a given integer n, return "small" if $n < 1,000$, "large" if $n \geq 2,000$, and an empty string if $1,000 \leq n < 2,000$.

As defined by the benchmark suite, we use 100 training and 1,000 test cases for Compare String Lengths and Small Or Large, and 200 training and 2,000 test cases for the Grade problem.

3.2 Grammars

In our grammar-guided GP approach, we use context-free grammars supporting an expressive subset of the Python programming language including variable assignments, different data types, as well as conditionals. The used grammars are based on the grammars provided by the PonyGE2 framework [7] which follow the principle proposed by Forstenlechner et al. [8] which suggests that program

Table 1. Data types supported by the used grammars for each of the studied program synthesis benchmark problems.

Benchmark Problem	Integer	Boolean	String	Char
Compare String Lengths	✓	✓	✓	
Grade	✓	✓		✓
Small Or Large	✓	✓	✓	

synthesis grammars should, in addition to some basic data types, only support the required data types (e.g., the data types specified by a function's input and output). With this approach, the used grammars and consequently the resulting search space can be kept small.

Table 1 shows for each of the studied program synthesis benchmark problems the data types supported by the used grammars.[1] For all benchmark problems, the basic types Boolean and integer are supported. For Compare String Lengths and Small Or Large, we support in addition also strings. For the Grade problem, we support chars together with the required functions to process char values instead of strings as for this problem no complex string handling is necessary.

3.3 Selection Method

To study the influence of batch sizes in GP-based program synthesis, we extend the lexicase algorithm to include batches. Algorithm 2 shows this extended lexicase variant as pseudo-code.

Algorithm 2: Lexicase Selection with Batches

```
1  cases := shuffle(training_cases);
2  candidates := population;
3  batches := generate_batches(cases, β);
4  while |batches| > 0 & |candidates| > 1 do
5  │   batch := batches.pop(0);
6  │   candidates := best_individuals(candidates, batch);
7  end
8  if |candidates| > 1 then
9  │   return choice(candidates);
10 end
11 return candidates[0];
```

Basically, this method is similar to standard lexicase selection. The only difference is that, instead of individual training cases, batches of training cases of a pre-defined size β are generated (line 3). If β is a divisor of the number

---

[1] Grammars: https://gitlab.rlp.net/dsobania/progsys-grammars-2022-1.

of training cases, then all batches are of equal size. Otherwise, the last batch is smaller. After the batches are created, all candidates that do not have the exact lowest aggregated error/best fitness on the first batch are discarded and the first batch is removed (lines 5–6). As in standard lexicase selection, this step is repeated until either all batches have been considered or only one candidate solution is left (lines 4–7). Finally, a randomly chosen candidate of the list of remaining candidates (lines 8–10) or the last remaining one (line 11) is returned.

For $\beta = 1$, the described method works like standard lexicase selection. In general, the method is a version of batch lexicase selection [1] without the fitness threshold [as we discard all candidates that do not have the exact lowest error/fitness on a considered batch (line 6)] and consequently also similar to summed batch lexicase selection [5] as we aggregate in our experiments the fitness of a batch by calculating the sum of the errors on the contained training cases.

4   Experiments and Results

To study the influence of small batch sizes on the success rates and the generalizability of programs generated by GP we use in our experiments a grammar-guided GP implementation based on the PonyGE2 framework [7]. We set the population size to 1,000 and use position independent grow [6] as initialization method. We set the maximum initial tree depth (for initialization) to 10 and the maximum overall tree depth to 17. For variation, we use sub-tree crossover with a probability of 0.9 and sub-tree mutation with a probability of 0.05. A GP run is stopped after 300 generations.

As batch sizes, we study all divisors of 100, since for the majority of the considered benchmark problems 100 training cases are provided (this allows all batches to be equal in size). Finally, since the results in the program synthesis domain are often subject to high variance [26], we have doubled the number of runs used commonly in the literature (e.g., in [17] and [8]) and use 200 runs per configuration.

4.1   Influence on Selection Pressure

First, we study the influence of the batch sizes on the selection pressure. Therefore, we analyze the development of the average best fitness during a GP run for different batch sizes, where the fitness of an individual is the sum of its errors on the training cases. Furthermore, we analyze for all studied batch sizes the average generation in which a solution that correctly solves all training cases is found for the first time.

Figures 1, 2, 3, 4, 5 and 6 show the results for the benchmark problems considered in this study. The plots on the left (Figs. 1, 3, and 5) show the best fitness over generations for all studied batch sizes and benchmark problems. The results are averaged over 200 runs. The plots on the right (Figs. 2, 4, and 6) show the average generation of a first success on the training cases for all studied

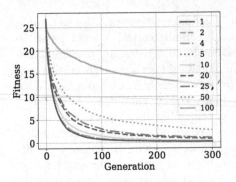

Fig. 1. Average best fitness over generations for the Compare String Lengths problem for all studied batch sizes.

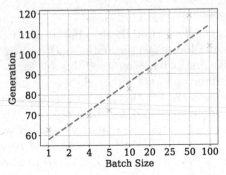

Fig. 2. Average generation of first success on training cases over batch sizes for the Compare String Lengths problem.

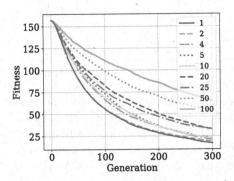

Fig. 3. Average best fitness over generations for the Grade problem for all studied batch sizes.

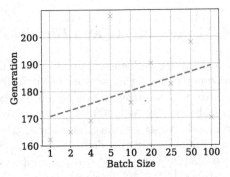

Fig. 4. Average generation of first success on training cases over batch sizes for the Grade problem.

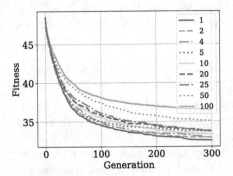

Fig. 5. Average best fitness over generations for the Small Or Large problem for all studied batch sizes.

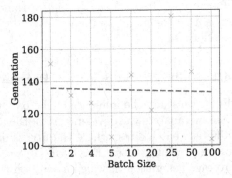

Fig. 6. Average generation of first success on training cases over batch sizes for the Small Or Large problem.

Table 2. Success rates on the training (s_{train}) and the test set (s_{test}) as well as the generalization rate g achieved by the grammar-guided GP approach for different batch sizes β for all studied program synthesis benchmark problems. Best values are printed in **bold** font.

Benchmark Problem	β	s_{train}	s_{test}	g
Compare String Lengths	1	**93.0**	10.0	0.11
	2	91.5	**15.5**	**0.17**
	4	91.5	8.5	0.09
	5	90.5	7.0	0.08
	10	80.0	4.5	0.06
	20	60.0	4.0	0.07
	25	57.5	5.5	0.1
	50	29.5	1.5	0.05
	100	5.5	0.5	0.09
Grade	1	34.0	8.5	0.25
	2	33.5	8.0	0.24
	4	31.0	10.5	0.34
	5	**36.0**	7.5	0.21
	10	25.0	**11.5**	**0.46**
	20	20.5	8.5	0.41
	25	16.5	6.5	0.39
	50	10.5	4.5	0.43
	100	5.5	2.5	0.45
Small Or Large	1	**9.0**	**3.5**	0.39
	2	4.5	3.0	0.67
	4	5.5	2.0	0.36
	5	2.5	1.5	0.6
	10	4.0	1.5	0.38
	20	5.0	**3.5**	0.7
	25	3.0	1.0	0.33
	50	1.0	0.5	0.5
	100	1.5	1.5	**1.0**

benchmark problems and training cases. The dashed regression line illustrates the development/trend for increasing batch sizes.

We see for all studied program synthesis benchmark problems that the fitness decreases more slowly over the generations for increasing batch sizes. The fastest fitness reduction (minimization problem) is always achieved with batch size $\beta = 1$ (standard lexicase selection). Similarly, we observe the slowest fitness reduction for $\beta = 100$. E.g., for the Compare String Lengths problem (Fig. 1), for $\beta = 100$ the average best fitness is around 12 while for $\beta \leq 25$ the average best fitness is close to zero. Overall, the convergence speed is also reduced for small batch sizes ($4 \leq \beta < 20$).

For the generation of first success on the training cases we observe on average increasing values for increasing batch sizes. For the Compare String Lengths problem (Fig. 2) the success generation increases from around 60 for $\beta = 1$ to around 110 for $\beta > 50$ and for the Grade problem (Fig. 4) the generation increases from around 170 to 190. For the Small Or Large problem (Fig. 6), the regression line remains about constant (slight decrease) over the considered batch sizes. However, the results for this problem are based on only a smaller amount of data, compared to the other two benchmark problems, because the success rates on the training set are low for this problem (see Table 2).

In summary, with an increasing batch size β the selection pressure decreases. Additionally, the selection pressure can be reduced even with the use of small batch sizes.

4.2   Analysis of Success Rates and Generalization

To analyze the performance and the generalizability of the solutions found by GP with different batch sizes, Table 2 shows the success rates on the training (s_{train}) and the test set (s_{test}) as well as the generalization rate g achieved by the grammar-guided GP for different batch sizes β for the considered benchmark problems that are known in the literature for their poor generalization with lexicase selection [24]. As the results are based on 200 runs, we report s_{train} and s_{test} in percent. Best values are printed in **bold** font.

As expected, the success rate on the training set s_{train} decreases for an increasing batch size β. Also the success rates on the test set s_{test} are low on all considered benchmark problems for larger batch sizes ($\beta \geq 25$). Nevertheless, using small batch sizes ($2 \leq \beta \leq 10$) often leads to similar or even better success rates on the test set compared to standard lexicase selection ($\beta = 1$). E.g., for the Compare String Lengths problem we achieved a success rate of 15.5 with $\beta = 2$ compared to only 10 with standard lexicase selection.

Furthermore, for all considered benchmark problems, best generalization rates g are achieved with $\beta \geq 2$. Compared to standard lexicase selection, we see for the Grade problem and the Small Or Large problem on average notably larger generalization rates g for $\beta \geq 10$. From a practitioners perspective, a high generalization rate is even more important than a high success rate as it is essential that the found programs work also correctly on previously unseen test cases. An additional check with many test cases is usually not possible in practice as it is expensive to manually create a large test set. However, if a program synthesis method is known for producing generalizable solutions, a programmer can trust this method. If such a method has a low success rate but a high generalization rate, then the search can be easily repeated if no successful solution is found in the first run.

Overall, we find that similar or even better success rates on the test set can be achieved when combining lexicase selection with small batches instead of using standard lexicase selection. In addition, best generalization rates are achieved with $\beta \geq 2$.

5   Conclusions

As GP is able to generate computer programs for a given set of input/output examples automatically, it has the potential to be used in real-world software development. Similar as in test-driven development [2], a programmer could define the input/output examples first and GP could then generate the functional source code. A prerequisite for GP as support system in software development is a good program synthesis performance and a high generalizability of the found programs. However, for some benchmark problems, GP generates programs that generalize poorly to unseen test cases especially when standard lexicase selection is used [24]. For classification problems, however, it has been shown that combining lexicase selection with batches of training cases can improve generalization [1]. Anyway, using batches in a program synthesis context is challenging as usually the number of input/output examples that can be used for training is low.

Therefore, we studied in this work the influence of small batch sizes during selection on the success rates and the generalizability of the programs generated by GP on common program synthesis benchmark problems.

We found that with an increasing batch size the selection pressure is reduced, which can be observed even for small batch sizes ($4 \leq \beta < 20$). Furthermore, we found that, compared to standard lexicase selection, the achieved success rates on the test set are either similar or even better when small batches are used. Overall, best generalization rates are obtained with a batch size $\beta \geq 2$.

So we suggest to use small batches with lexicase selection in GP-based program synthesis as the results are competitive or even better than with standard lexicase selection and also the generalizability of the found solutions can often be improved.

References

1. Aenugu, S., Spector, L.: Lexicase selection in learning classifier systems. In: Proceedings of the Genetic and Evolutionary Computation Conference, pp. 356–364 (2019)
2. Beck, K.: Test-driven Development: by Example. Addison-Wesley Professional (2003)
3. Cramer, N.L.: A representation for the adaptive generation of simple sequential programs. In: Proceedings of an International Conference on Genetic Algorithms and the Applications, pp. 183–187 (1985)

4. De Melo, V.V., Vargas, D.V., Banzhaf, W.: Batch tournament selection for genetic programming: the quality of lexicase, the speed of tournament. In: Proceedings of the Genetic and Evolutionary Computation Conference, pp. 994–1002 (2019)
5. Deglman, J.: Summed batch lexicase selection on software synthesis problems. Scholarly Horizons: Univ. Minnesota, Morris Undergraduate J. **7**(1), 3 (2020)
6. Fagan, D., Fenton, M., O'Neill, M.: Exploring position independent initialisation in grammatical evolution. In: 2016 IEEE Congress on Evolutionary Computation (CEC), pp. 5060–5067. IEEE (2016)
7. Fenton, M., McDermott, J., Fagan, D., Forstenlechner, S., Hemberg, E., O'Neill, M.: PonyGE2: Grammatical evolution in Python. In: Proceedings of the Genetic and Evolutionary Computation Conference Companion, pp. 1194–1201 (2017)
8. Forstenlechner, S., Fagan, D., Nicolau, M., O'Neill, M.: A grammar design pattern for arbitrary program synthesis problems in genetic programming. In: McDermott, J., Castelli, M., Sekanina, L., Haasdijk, E., García-Sánchez, P. (eds.) EuroGP 2017. LNCS, vol. 10196, pp. 262–277. Springer, Cham (2017). https://doi.org/10.1007/978-3-319-55696-3_17
9. Forstenlechner, S., Fagan, D., Nicolau, M., O'Neill, M.: Extending program synthesis grammars for grammar-guided genetic programming. In: Auger, A., Fonseca, C.M., Lourenço, N., Machado, P., Paquete, L., Whitley, D. (eds.) PPSN 2018. LNCS, vol. 11101, pp. 197–208. Springer, Cham (2018). https://doi.org/10.1007/978-3-319-99253-2_16
10. Helmuth, T., Abdelhady, A.: Benchmarking parent selection for program synthesis by genetic programming. In: Proceedings of the 2020 Genetic and Evolutionary Computation Conference Companion, pp. 237–238 (2020)
11. Helmuth, T., Kelly, P.: PSB2: the second program synthesis benchmark suite. In: Proceedings of the Genetic and Evolutionary Computation Conference, pp. 785–794 (2021)
12. Helmuth, T., McPhee, N.F., Spector, L.: The impact of hyperselection on lexicase selection. In: Proceedings of the Genetic and Evolutionary Computation Conference 2016, pp. 717–724 (2016)
13. Helmuth, T., McPhee, N.F., Spector, L.: Lexicase selection for program synthesis: a diversity analysis. In: Riolo, R., Worzel, B., Kotanchek, M., Kordon, A. (eds.) Genetic Programming Theory and Practice XIII. GEC, pp. 151–167. Springer, Cham (2016). https://doi.org/10.1007/978-3-319-34223-8_9
14. Helmuth, T., McPhee, N.F., Spector, L.: Program synthesis using uniform mutation by addition and deletion. In: Proceedings of the Genetic and Evolutionary Computation Conference, pp. 1127–1134 (2018)
15. Helmuth, T., Pantridge, E., Spector, L.: Lexicase selection of specialists. In: Proceedings of the Genetic and Evolutionary Computation Conference, pp. 1030–1038 (2019)
16. Helmuth, T., Pantridge, E., Spector, L.: On the importance of specialists for lexicase selection. Genetic Program. Evol. Mach. **21**(3), 349–373 (2020). https://doi.org/10.1007/s10710-020-09377-2
17. Helmuth, T., Spector, L.: General program synthesis benchmark suite. In: Proceedings of the 2015 Annual Conference on Genetic and Evolutionary Computation, pp. 1039–1046 (2015)
18. Helmuth, T., Spector, L.: Explaining and exploiting the advantages of down-sampled lexicase selection. In: Artificial Life Conference Proceedings, pp. 341–349. MIT Press One Rogers Street, Cambridge, MA 02142–1209 USA (2020)

19. Hernandez, J.G., Lalejini, A., Dolson, E., Ofria, C.: Random subsampling improves performance in lexicase selection. In: Proceedings of the Genetic and Evolutionary Computation Conference Companion, pp. 2028–2031 (2019)

20. Jundt, L., Helmuth, T.: Comparing and combining lexicase selection and novelty search. In: Proceedings of the Genetic and Evolutionary Computation Conference, pp. 1047–1055 (2019)

21. Kelly, J., Hemberg, E., O'Reilly, U.-M.: Improving genetic programming with novel exploration - exploitation control. In: Sekanina, L., Hu, T., Lourenço, N., Richter, H., García-Sánchez, P. (eds.) EuroGP 2019. LNCS, vol. 11451, pp. 64–80. Springer, Cham (2019). https://doi.org/10.1007/978-3-030-16670-0_5

22. Koza, J.R.: Genetic programming: on the programming of computers by means of natural selection, vol. 1. MIT press (1992)

23. Saini, A.K., Spector, L.: Effect of parent selection methods on modularity. In: Hu, T., Lourenço, N., Medvet, E., Divina, F. (eds.) Genetic Programming, pp. 184–194. Springer International Publishing, Cham (2020)

24. Sobania, D.: On the generalizability of programs synthesized by grammar-guided genetic programming. In: Hu, T., Lourenço, N., Medvet, E. (eds.) EuroGP 2021. LNCS, vol. 12691, pp. 130–145. Springer, Cham (2021). https://doi.org/10.1007/978-3-030-72812-0_9

25. Sobania, D., Rothlauf, F.: A generalizability measure for program synthesis with genetic programming. In: Proceedings of the Genetic and Evolutionary Computation Conference, pp. 822–829 (2021)

26. Sobania, D., Schweim, D., Rothlauf, F.: Recent developments in program synthesis with evolutionary algorithms. arXiv preprint arXiv:2108.12227 (2021)

27. Spector, L.: Assessment of problem modality by differential performance of lexicase selection in genetic programming: a preliminary report. In: Proceedings of the 14th Annual Conference Companion on Genetic and Evolutionary Computation, pp. 401–408 (2012)

Genetic Programming-Based Inverse Kinematics for Robotic Manipulators

Julia Reuter[✉][iD], Christoph Steup[iD], and Sanaz Mostaghim[iD]

Institute for Intelligent Cooperating Systems, Faculty of Computer Science,
Otto von Guericke University Magdeburg, Magdeburg, Germany
{julia.reuter,christoph.steup,sanaz.mostaghim}@ovgu.de

Abstract. In this paper, we introduce an inverse kinematics model for a robotic manipulator using Genetic Programming (GP). The underlying problem requires learning of multiple joint parameters of the manipulator to reach a desired position in the Cartesian space. We present a new approach to identify a closed-form solution for the Inverse Kinematics (IK) problem, namely IK-CCGP. The novelty of IK-CCGP is the cooperative coevolutionary learning strategy. Unlike other GP approaches, IK-CCGP is not limited to a certain angle combination to reach a given pose and is designed to achieve more flexibility in the learning process. Moreover, it can operate both as single- and multi-objective variants. In this paper, we investigate whether the inclusion of further objectives, i.e. correlation and the consistency of a solution with physical laws, contributes to the search process. Our experiments show that the combination of the two objectives, error and correlation, performs very well for the given problem and IK-CCGP performs the best on a kinematic unit of two joints. While our approach cannot attain the same accuracy as Artificial Neural Networks, it overcomes the explainability gap of IK models developed using ANNs.

Keywords: Genetic Programming · Cooperative Coevolution · Multi-Objective Optimization · Inverse Kinematics

1 Introduction

Robotic manipulators are at the center of process automation. Most applications today like automatic welding or pick and place tasks require these to operate with high flexibility in movement [24]. At the same time, in special use cases with many manipulators in a small arena like in swarm robotics, we need them to operate in very confined spaces. As a result, a plethora of robotic manipulators were constructed by many companies, which do not follow the standard 6 degrees of freedom (DOF) configuration. One example, is the 5 DOF *KUKA youBot* manipulator that serves as a use case for this paper. By removing one joint [16], the robot takes up less space and is still quite flexible. While these robots fulfill the flexibility and compactness criteria, the kinematic analysis is complicated

E. Medvet et al. (Eds.): EuroGP 2022, LNCS 13223, pp. 130–145, 2022.
https://doi.org/10.1007/978-3-031-02056-8_9

by untypical joint configurations. This is because the standard methods cannot be applied anymore. Consequently, understanding the kinematics, i.e., relation between the DOF and the resulting movement of the rigid body of an arbitrary robotic manipulator, is crucial.

The general structure of a robotic manipulator is an open kinematic chain. It consists of multiple, typically rotational joints, which are connected by links. Non-rotational joints such as prismatic joints are left out of consideration in this paper. The joint rotation parameters θ_i, $i = 1, \ldots, |DOF|$ are variable. In general, a robotic manipulator operates in a 6-D environment $X = [p, o]^T = [x, y, z, \theta_x, \theta_y, \theta_z]^T$. In this pose representation, the vector $p = [x, y, z]^T$ indicates the position of the end-effector, while $o = [\theta_x, \theta_y, \theta_z]^T$ represents the end-effector orientation using three Euler angles [13,21].

The goal of the forward kinematics (FK) denoted by g is to find the pose of the end-effector given the robot joint angles, i.e., $X = g(\theta_1 \ldots \theta_{|DOF|})$. This calculation is straightforward as there is exactly one pose for every joint-angle combination, feasible or not. A common standard to describe the kinematic model of a robot is the Denavit-Hartenberg (D-H) convention, which requires only four parameters per joint. These are the link length a_i, the link twist α_i, the link offset d_i, and the joint angle θ_i [25]. For any given rotational link, three of these quantities are constant, while only θ_i is variable and defines the actual movement [13].

The inverse kinematics (IK) problem aims at the opposite, with the goal to find the robot joint angles given a target pose, i.e., $\theta = g^{-1}(X)$. In contrast to the FK, there are multiple solutions to the IK problem. This makes the problem considerably more complex than the forward kinematics. In general, finding a closed form solution is of great interest, i.e., finding an explicit relationship between a joint variable θ_i and the elements of the 6-D pose vector X. Since multiple valid joint configurations can be found for a given pose, closed-form solutions allow for real-time movements and can furthermore provide decision rules to prefer a particular configuration over another [21]. Moreover, an explicit relationship enables the mathematical analysis of safety-relevant edge cases. A variety of closed-form solution approaches have emerged for different applications within the last decades [2,5]. Classical analytical approaches provide IK solutions in real-time. However, they are often not applicable to robots with non-standard axis configurations, since such robots do not always have unique solutions to the IK problem. Modern computational approaches like Artificial Neural Networks (ANN) can overcome this issue, but lack transparency and explainability. Between these conflicting priorities, finding a fast, explainable solution for a non-standard configured robot is a complex task.

In this paper, we develop a novel approach to learn an IK model of a robotic manipulator. We use Genetic Programming (GP) as the learning mechanism. GP produces equations that are human-readable and can be executed in real-time, while still providing explainability and allow the adaptation of non-standard robotic configurations. We propose the novel Cooperative Coevolutionary Genetic Programming for Inverse Kinematics (IK-CCGP) approach, which tackles the need of an IK model for multiple outputs, i.e., one value per joint of the kinematic chain.

We examined the proposed IK-CCGP on a *KUKA youBot* with 5 DOF and performed several experiments on various settings of the problem. Furthermore, we compare our results with the reported results based on ANN in [1,22]. Our experiments show that we can achieve very good results in certain areas of the workspace. However, an ANN still provides more accurate solutions with smaller failure rates. Nevertheless, the solutions produced by GP can considerably contribute to the explainability of the solutions, which is one of the major goals of this paper.

2   Related Work

Addressing the IK problem with GP is mainly driven by Chapelle et al., who published two papers in 2001 and 2004 [3,4]. In both papers, the problem was modeled as a single-objective problem with a length-penalizing RMSE of the joint angle as a fitness function. All joint equations were learned sequentially starting from joint one, feeding the result to the next joint and so forth. The proposed setting reached an accuracy of 10^{-2} radians for the first joint θ_1 and 10^{-1} radians for the last joint θ_6. The maximum error on the tested instances was 0.3 radians. Next to the mentioned works, the principles of evolution are mostly applied to find off-line, i.e. not real-time capable, IK solutions for given robotic manipulators. Parker et al. [19] developed an Evolutionary Algorithm (EA) model that approximates the joint values for a given end-pose. This approach incorporates the FK equations and uses the positioning error between the desired and the learned poses as the objective to be minimized. Kalra et al. [14] used EAs to find multiple solutions for the IK problem.

Another application of GP in the robotic field is the calibration of manipulators. Dolinsky et al. [8] used GP to approximate an error function between the desired and the actual position of the end-effector caused by mechanical inaccuracies of the real-world robot compared to its simulation. The authors proposed a coevolutionary algorithm, as multiple joint corrections need to be calculated at the same time which all mutually affect each other.

The Artificial Neural Networks (ANN) have been applied to the IK problem for simple manipulators [9,12] and additionally for 6 DOF standard manipulators [6]. These approaches solely give the target pose as an input to predict the corresponding joint angle values. They mainly focus on improving the parameters of the model, such as the number of hidden neurons or the learning rate. Almusawi et al. [1] proposed to include the current joint configurations of a 6 DOF robot in the input parameters, which improved accuracy, especially for continuous trajectories such as drawing a circle with a pen. A different error measure was suggested by Srisuk et al. [22]: Instead of comparing the learned and desired joint angles of the 4 DOF manipulator, the authors implemented the FK equations to compute the end-effector pose from the learned angles. The error function is thus a distance measure between the learned pose and the desired pose. By incorporating the FK equations, this approach allows learning the underlying kinematic behavior without limiting good results to pre-defined joint angles. This helps to overcome the singularity problem of a robot, where multiple joint configurations lead to the same end pose.

In a comparative study, El-Sherbiny et al. [10] opposed different modern IK approaches, namely ANNs, Adaptive Neuro Fuzzy Inference Systems and Genetic Algorithms, to solve the IK problem for a 5 DOF manipulator. ANNs outperformed the other methods. For broader overview about modern IK approaches, refer to [2, Chapter 6].

3   Genetic Programming-Based Inverse Kinematics

In the following, we first present our approach on modelling the IK problem using several objective functions. Afterwards, we introduce the proposed universal, problem-independent algorithm IK-CCGP.

3.1   Fitness Functions to Model the IK Problem

As already mentioned in the introduction, we aim to learn a model to solve the IK problem. In order to reach a certain pose in Cartesian space, two different error functions can be utilized during the training of the GP, which both lead to the same final pose: The joint angle error $f_1(\theta)$ and the pose error $\boldsymbol{f}_1(X)$, where θ represents the angle and X the pose. In addition, we consider other objective functions such as correlation coefficient and dimension penalty, as first introduced by [26].

Fitness Function (f_1): $f_1(\theta)$ describes the difference between the given and the produced joint value in [rad] and is to be minimized for each of the joints in the kinematic chain. This objective function designed to enforce the GP to learn the exact angle values given in the training data to reach a certain pose. Hence, a genetic program is to be identified that transforms the input pose into the desired joint angle value by optimizing for $f_1(\theta)$:

$$f_1(\theta) = \sqrt{\frac{1}{\kappa}\sum_{i=1}^{\kappa}(\hat{\theta}_i - \theta_i)^2} \qquad (1)$$

where κ refers to the number of data points involved. An alternative to $f_1(\theta)$ is $\boldsymbol{f}_1(X)$. Due to the kinematic setup of a robotic manipulator, multiple joint configurations can lead to the same end pose, i.e. more than one valid solutions exist for the given problem. While the $f_1(\theta)$ error function limits the GP to precisely learn the target joint values to reach the desired position, the $\boldsymbol{f}_1(X)$ error function allows for more flexibility in the learning process. Instead of comparing each learned joint value to its given target value, their resulting pose is computed using the FK equations and compared to the desired pose. We consider the position and orientation of a pose as separate objectives, since they also come in different units. Hence, the optimization problem can be formulated using two objectives:

$$\boldsymbol{f}_1(X) = [f_1(p), \ f_1(o)]^T = \left[\sqrt{\frac{1}{\kappa}\sum_{i=1}^{\kappa}||\hat{p}_i - p_i||^2}, \ \sqrt{\frac{1}{\kappa}\sum_{i=1}^{\kappa}||\hat{o}_i - o_i||^2}\right]^T \quad (2)$$

where p is a vector of the position parameters x, y, z and o a vector of the orientation parameters θ_x, θ_y, θ_z. $\boldsymbol{f}_1(X)$ refers to the combined pose error function, considering the position and orientation error as separate objectives. The position error $f_1(p)$ and orientation error $f_1(o)$ use the Euclidean distance between the desired and the learned output.

Correlation Coefficient (f_2): As an additional objective to enhance the learning process, a transformed version of the Spearman correlation coefficient is used as introduced in [26]. It describes the correlation between the produced and the desired output of a genetic program. The main idea behind employing correlation next to the error is to evolve programs that are not yet numerically meaningful but already produce results that correlate with the desired output. Ideally, only small changes in these programs are necessary to produce numerically accurate outputs. Also, a high negative correlation can contribute positively to the learning process, as only one mathematical operation is necessary to invert the results. Therefore, we use the absolute value of the correlation coefficient: $f_2 := 1 - |\rho|$. When using the angle error $f_1(\theta)$ as the first objective, ρ represents the correlation between the produced and the desired angle values. For the pose error $\boldsymbol{f}_1(A)$, three parameters for positioning and three for orientation, need to be considered. To this end, one correlation coefficient is calculated for each position and orientation. The final ρ is equal to the mean of the two absolute values of the position and orientation correlation coefficients.

Dimension Penalty (f_3): Dealing with different physical units such as [rad] and [m] in the same genetic program is a challenging task, especially since trigonometric functions convert these units. The third objective f_3 is formulated to guide the algorithm to evolve programs which do not violate physical laws and match the target unit (i.e., [rad] for each joint angle of the manipulator). Different implementations of a dimension penalty in GP can be found in literature [15,17,18,23]. In this paper, we compute the objectives f_1 and f_2 solely based on their numerical values without any unit feasibility check. For f_3, we traverse the GP tree using post-order traversal and check each operation within an individual for unit matching. Penalties are aggregated throughout the individual, whereby each infeasible operation increases the penalty value by 1. Given that an operation is performed on incompatible units, the unit of the first input argument is handed over to the next operation, i.e. when an angle in [rad] and a length in [m] are added, this operation is penalized with a value of 1 and the unit [rad] is handed over to the next operation. Similarly, when an individual produces a unit that does not match the target unit, a value of 1 is added to the penalty variable. The objective function for the dimension penalty can be formulated as $f_3 := \text{dimPen}_{op} + \text{dimPen}_{out}$, where $dimPen_{op}$ represents the aggregated

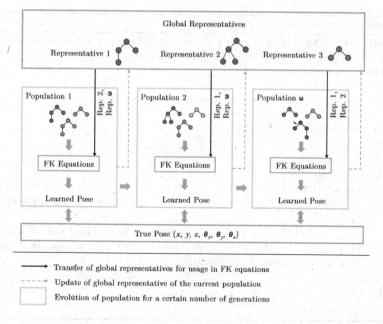

Fig. 1. One iteration of the IK-CCGP approach

dimension penalties produced by non-physical operations within the individual and $dimPen_{out}$ is either 0 or 1, depending on whether the output unit is equal to the target unit.

3.2 Cooperative Coevolutionary GP for Inverse Kinematics

Cooperative coevolution is a concept in evolutionary algorithms that simultaneously evolves multiple so-called subpopulations to solve a given problem. There are several variants of cooperation between the subpopulations. In some studies, the evolved solutions in each subpopulation are merged into a single solution to be evaluated [20]. In this paper, we keep the solutions separate, but evaluate them in a combined fitness measure denoted as collective evaluation. Here, one subpopulation per joint is evolved, while the other subpopulations are represented each by one representative individual. For the collective evaluation, we employ the FK equations to minimize the error between the desired pose and the learned pose in Cartesian space, which also attained good result in [8,22]. This is the main idea in the proposed Cooperative Coevolutionary GP for Inverse Kinematics (IK-CCGP).

Figure 1 depicts one iteration of the IK-CCGP approach, as described in lines 6-15 in the complete Algorithm 1. The coevolutionary learning process is defined by multiple phases: While one subpopulation is evolved, the remaining subpopulations stand idle and are not changed. Global representatives for each

---

Algorithm 1: IK-CCGP Algorithm

> **Input** : Training data X, number of subpopulations ω, subpopulation size N,
> number of generations k, number of iterations l
> **Output**: Set of archives A_j, $j = 1, \ldots, \omega$

1 **for** $j \leftarrow 1$ **to** ω **do**
2 | $P_j \leftarrow$ randomly initialize subpopulation with size N
3 | $r_j \leftarrow$ select global representative from P_j
4 | $A_j \leftarrow$ initialize empty archive
5 **end**
6 **for** $iter \leftarrow 1$ **to** l **do**
7 | **for** $j \leftarrow 1$ **to** ω **do**
8 | | **for** $i \leftarrow 1$ **to** N **do**
9 | | | evaluate $(P_{j,i}, X, r, j)$ `// evaluation in Algorithm 2`
10 | | **end**
11 | | $P_j, A_j \leftarrow GP(k, X, P_j, A_j)$ `// evaluation in Algo. 2`
12 | | $P_j, A_j \leftarrow MutOnlyGP(k, X, P_j, A_j)$ `// evaluation in Algo. 2`
13 | | $r_j \leftarrow$ update global representative using A_j
14 | **end**
15 **end**
16 **return** $\bigcup_{j=1}^{\omega} A_j$

---

subpopulation that is currently not under training guarantee the common evaluation using the FK equations. Next to the coevolutionary setting, we employ two important concepts in our algorithms that contribute to the learning process.

In the first concept, we introduce a two phase training strategy. In the first training phase, Function GP (Algorithm 1, line 11) calls a standard GP algorithm for k generations with crossover and mutation probabilities $p_c = p_m$ [26]. In case of crossover, either one-point crossover or leaf-based one-point crossover is chosen at random. Mutation selects randomly between uniform mutation, node replacement, insertion mutation and shrink mutation. In the second phase, we only use mutation for k generations to refine the current individuals in terms of slight changes in the primitives and prevent uncontrolled growth. Thus, Function $MutOnlyGP$ (Algorithm 1, line 12) only selects from mutation operations, i.e. node replacement with a probability of 2/3 and shrink mutation with 1/3. In both Functions GP and $MutOnlyGP$, the archive A_j is updated according to the Pareto-dominance criterion. It means that only non-dominated solutions can be kept in the archive.

For the second concept, we provide information about the angles of the previous joints to the currently trained joint to steer the learning process towards a closed form solution. This idea arises from the fact that there are multiple joint configurations for the same pose. Thus, even when all other joint values are learned using the objective function $f_1(\theta)$, deviations in only one joint value can lead to an extremely inaccurate final pose. Inverse input transformation reverts the influence of all joints that are located before the currently learned joint in

---

Algorithm 2: IK-CCGP Evaluation Procedure for One Individual

Input : Individual ind_j, Training Data X, Set of Representatives r, Joint
         Index j
Output: Objective values

1 $inds \leftarrow (r_0, \ldots, r_{j-1}, ind_j, r_{j+1}, \ldots, r_\omega)$
2 ${}^1X_\omega \leftarrow X$
3 **for** $i \leftarrow 1$ **to** ω **do**
4 | $\theta_i \leftarrow$ parse ${}^iX_\omega$ through $inds_i$
5 | ${}^{i+1}X_\omega \leftarrow tf(\theta_i, i)\,{}^iX_\omega$
6 **end**
7 $\hat{X} \leftarrow g(\theta_i, \ldots, \theta_\omega)$
8 $f \leftarrow [f_1(X), f_2, f_3]^T$
9 **return** f

---

the kinematic chain. To revert the influence of joint i, denoted by θ_i, from the
target pose ${}^iX_\omega$, we compute

$$
{}^{i+1}X_\omega = (\text{Rot}_{\alpha_i})^{-1}(\text{Trans}_{a_i})^{-1}(\text{Trans}_{d_i})^{-1}(\text{Rot}_{\theta_i})^{-1}\,{}^iX_\omega = tf(\theta, i)\,{}^iX_\omega \quad (3)
$$

where α_i denotes the orientation offset, a_i the link length and d_i the position
offset of the joint i. ${}^{i+1}X_\omega$ is the transformed target pose in the coordinate frame
of joint $i + 1$, which is used in the training of joint $i + 1$. The offset parameters
are constant for a given joint.

Algorithm 2, lines 2-6, describes this consecutive transformation for all joints
of the kinematic chain: the training data is parsed through the representative
of the first joint and translates the training data by the resulting angle values
using Eq. 3. The transformed pose is used as input data for the individual of the
second joint and so on.

These two concepts are included in Algorithm 1. The algorithm requires a
set of training data X, the number of joints ω and the subpopulation size N.
Additional input parameters are the number of generations per training phase k
and the number of training iterations l. Initially, one representative is randomly
selected from each of the initial subpopulations (lines 1-4). In the main loop
(lines 6-15), the subpopulations are evolved using the above two-phase training
strategy. The evaluation procedure for an individual in *GP* and *MutOnlyGP*
calls Algorithm 2. First (line 1), a list of representatives and the individual to be
evaluated is created in the order of the joints in the kinematic chain. For example, when joint $j = 2$ is currently trained and the kinematic chain consists of
$\omega = 4$ joints, the list contains the elements $[r_1, ind_2, r_3, r_4]$, denoted by $inds$. This
list is used to perform the inverse transformation of the training data in lines
3-6, as introduced previously. The resulting joint angles $\theta_1 \ldots \theta_\omega$ are fed into the
FK equations to compute the resulting pose $\hat{X}$ (Algorithm 2, line 7). This pose
can then be compared to the true pose X using the objective function $f_1(X)$.
Depending on the application, additional objectives can be computed. After k
generations of the two-phase training, one representative from the subpopulation

is selected, which is used to determine the joint value for this subpopulation during the evolution of the remaining subpopulations. After l iterations of the main loop, the algorithm terminates and returns a Pareto-dominance-based archive of cooperative solutions. Each solution is a non-dominated individual of a subpopulation, together with the representatives of the other subpopulations that were used during the evaluation and calculation of the objective values. In general, the proposed approach can be applied to either the entire kinematic chain of a robot or a kinematic unit within the kinematic chain that consists of multiple consecutive joints.

4   Experimental Evaluation

To evaluate the proposed approach, we take an inverse kinematics model $\theta = g^{-1}(X)$ for the *KUKA youBot* as application scenario. The function g has the domain $dom(g) = [-0.4 \ m; 0.4 \ m]^3 \times [-\pi \ rad; \pi \ rad]^3$, which is essentially the reachable area of the *KUKA youBot*. The co-domain is given by the possible range of the joints angles $\theta_1 \ldots \theta_5$. This manipulator comes with a special setup: The first joint plays an important role as it determines the plane, in which the target position is located. This plane can be defined by two configurations of the base joint $\pm\pi$ apart from each other. When the robot bends over itself, the first joint is directed towards the opposite side of the target position. Hence, an angle error of $f_1(\theta) = \pm\pi$ rad can be produced when a GP learns an angle that also defines the plane but is shifted by π. We consider two different variants of input angles of joint 1 for the training of joints > 1: First, the true joint 1 angle including bend-overs (this requires a bend-over handling strategy). Second, the projected angle resulting from the projection of the target pose onto the x-y-plane, which excludes bend-overs. The projected angle can be calculated with the simple equation $\theta_1 = \frac{169}{180}\pi - \arctan2(y, (x - 0.024))$, where $\frac{169}{180}\pi$ and 0.024 are known offset parameters of the first joint. The major goals of the experiments are to find out, which combination of objective functions performs best, and how the proposed IK-CCGP performs on a kinematic unit of two joints compared to a kinematic chain of three consecutive joints. Furthermore, we intend to measure to what extent the outcome is affected by transforming the input data for joints 2 and 3 by the *projected* angle of joint 1 compared to transforming by the *ground truth* angle of joint 1.

4.1   Data Processing

To generate the training data for the IK problem, we used a FK implementation for the *youBot*: For each of the 5 joints, 20 discrete positions are selected evenly distributed within the movement range of the joint. For all 20^5 combinations of joint values, the end effector pose in Cartesian space is computed using the FK equations. A robot simulation environment performs a feasibility check on each data instance, i.e. whether the configuration leads to a feasible pose or causes intersections of the arm. All infeasible samples are removed from the training

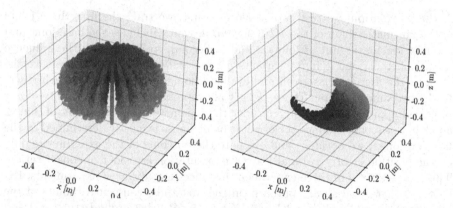

Fig. 2. Data samples in the workspace of the manipulator. Colors represent angle values for joint 2. Left: Input data for joint 1. No transformation. Right: Input data for joint 2. Influence of the first joint is removed by inverse transformation.

data set, leaving 949,593 feasible data samples within the robot workspace that can be employed for training the IK-CCGP algorithm. We extract a representative training dataset with 10,000 samples evenly distributed over the entire workspace. For the sake of computational cost, the algorithms are trained on batches of data with a batch size of 200. The samples per batch are defined beforehand to facilitate a fair comparison between the algorithmic variants. For the final evaluation of the found solutions, we employ 20,000 data samples randomly drawn from the workspace.

Each training sample incorporates the pose parameters x, y, z, θ_x, θ_y, θ_z and corresponding joint angles θ_1, θ_2, θ_3, θ_4, θ_5. As described in the previous section, we transform the input data for joints > 1 according to Eq. 3 to remove the influence of previous joints. Figure 2 shows an exemplary distribution of the training data, where (left) displays input data for training the first joint, and (right) input data for the second joint. It has a planar shape since the influence of the first joint is removed. In this way, the target position depends on only two instead of three variables.

4.2 Experiment Setup

We run experiments in two stages: In preliminary experiments, we identify the best combination of fitness functions for the given problem by performing the training of joint 2 on the angle error $f_1(\theta)$ and the additional objectives f_2 and f_3. We select joint 2 as a use case since a simple equation is not known beforehand, other than for the first joint, where we either require a bend-over handling technique for the ground truth angles or use the simple formula for projected angles. The best combination of objective functions is employed in the advanced experiments, where we challenge our proposed IK-CCGP approach. To compare the performance of our approach on different numbers of joints involved in the coevolution, we test two scenarios: First, we train the first three joints of the kinematic chain of the *KUKA youBot*, which includes the base joint and the first kinematic unit of joints 2 and 3. Second, to understand the influence of the different joint 1 input variants *ground truth* and *projected*, we take the angle of the first joint as given and evaluate how the proposed approach reacts to the two different input types. To get an impression about the quality of our proposed approaches, we only consider the kinematic unit consisting of joint 2 and 3 in this scenario. Since the orientation of a pose is mostly determined by the last two joints, we optimize and evaluate the outcome of the experiments only on the position error $f_1(p)$ and leave the orientation error out of consideration. This makes a total of three experiment instances for advanced experiments: IK-CCGP-3 that applies our approach on the first three consecutive joints of the kinematic chain, IK-CCGP-2G and IK-CCGP-2P using ground truth (G) and projected (P) joint 1 input data respectively applied to the kinematic unit of joints 2 and 3.

All experiments use the same function set $\mathcal{F} = \{+, -, \cdot, /, \cos(\circ), \sin(\circ), \tan(\circ), \arccos(\circ), \arcsin(\circ), \arctan2, -\circ, \circ^2, \sqrt{\circ}, \circ \bmod 2\pi\}$, where $\circ$ represents the input of unary operators. The terminal set $\mathcal{T}$ varies for each experiment and consists of the six parameters that define the (ground truth or projected) target pose and additionally a set of constants $\mathcal{C}$ containing the offset parameters of the joints that are currently trained: $\mathcal{T} = \{x, y, z, \theta_x, \theta_y, \theta_y\} + \mathcal{C}$. For each algorithmic variant, 31 independent runs are performed. The parameters are set as follows: In the single-objective optimization, we use tournament selection with a tournament size of 3. We use NSGA-II algorithm for multi-objective optimization [7]. The population size is $\mu = \lambda = 1500$ for all experiments. We use crossover and mutation probabilities of 0.5, except for the mutation-only phase, with a mutation probability of 1.0. The leaf-biased crossover selects a leaf with a probability of 0.8. The maximum depth of a solution tree is set to 20 with a maximum of 30 nodes. The preliminary experiments execute ten algorithmic iterations, one of which consists of ten generations of crossover and mutation followed by ten generations of mutation-only, summing up to 200 generations in total. As the advanced experiments intend to solve a more complex problem and coevolution requires more time for mutual adjustment between the subpopulations, $l = 20$ iterations of the IK-CCGP algorithm are performed, where each subpopulation is trained for $k = 10$ generations in each phase of the two-phase training. This makes a total of 800 generations for IK-CCGP-2G and IK-CCGP-2P and 1200 for the three joint experiment IK-CCGP-3. All algorithms are implemented using the **deap**-framework version 1.3.1 [11] and the **pint** package[1] version 0.16.1.

4.3   Preliminary Experiments

In the preliminary experiments, we test the performance of the combinations of objectives $\boldsymbol{f} = [f_1(\theta)]$, $\boldsymbol{f} = [f_1(\theta), f_2]^T$, $\boldsymbol{f} = [f_1(\theta), f_3]^T$ and $\boldsymbol{f} = [f_1(\theta), f_2, f_3]^T$.

---

[1] https://github.com/hgrecco/pint.

We always include the error function $f_1(\theta)$, since it is the main objective we want to minimize. The individual with the lowest angle RMSE according to $f_1(\theta)$ on the evaluation dataset is selected as the best solution for each of the 31 runs. Thus, for each experiment variant, 31 RMSE values are employed to determine the quality of the learned solutions. We conduct the pairwise Wilcoxon-Mann-Whitney rank sum test with a level of significance $\alpha = 0.05$ to compare the general performance of the different objective function variants.

The results of the statistical test indicate that the multi-objective variant $f = [f_1(\theta), f_2]^T$ is superior to the single-objective variant $f = [f_1(\theta)]$. This implies that the correlation as an additional objective enhances the quality of the results. The combination $f = [f_1(\theta), f_3]^T$ yields the worst results. The three-objective variant, that also incorporates correlation, can partially compensate the drawbacks of the dimension penalty objective. Nonetheless, it is outperformed by the two-objective variant using $f = [f_1(\theta), f_2]^T$.

4.4 Advanced Experiments

Based on the preliminary experiments, all advanced experiments are conducted using the combination of objectives $f = [f_1(p), f_2]^T$.

Figure 3 (left) shows the convergence behavior of the position error for the advanced experiments. This data is deduced from the training process, which starts 400 generations later for IK-CCGP-2G and IK-CCGP-2P, as they do not include the training for joint 1. From this plot, one may infer that experiment variant IK-CCGP-3 performed the worst. Especially the zigzag pattern of the gray curve indicates that the learning process did not follow a continuous improvement, but rather oscillated around a slowly declining curve. This behavior can be explained by the fact that joint 1 is an additional variable in IK-CCGP-3. Since the first joint defines the plane in which the final position lies within the workspace, errors in this joint can lead to large deviations in the final position. It can be observed that it is of great advantage when the angle value of the first joint is already known, as for IK-CCGP-2G and IK-CCGP-2P. In this way, the algorithm only operates towards finding the correct position on the predefined plane, which shrinks the search space tremendously. IK-CCGP-2G and IK-CCGP-2P follow more the expected fitness development with poor results in the beginning, which rapidly improve in the first quarter of the evolution process and converge towards the end. In general, both experiments produce position errors in the magnitude of a few centimeters.

For further analyses, we select the solution with the smallest position RMSE among the 31 experiment runs for each of the experiment variants. Figure 3 (right) displays the distribution of position errors on the evaluation dataset for these best solutions. It becomes apparent that the best solution of IK-CCGP-3 performs the worst over all other solutions, with a median error of $0.0671\ m$. The other variants range between 2 and 3 centimeters of median error. No severe difference between using the ground truth or projected joint 1 angles as input data can be observed. The overall best solution with an RMSE of $0.0343\ m$, a maximum absolute error (MAE) of $0.1712\ m$ and a median error of $0.0213\ m$ was obtained by experiment variant IK-CCGP-2P.

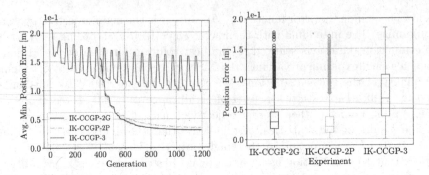

Fig. 3. Results of the advanced experiments. Left: Convergence behavior of the three experiment variants. Right: Error distribution on the evaluation dataset with 20,000 samples using the best solution of each experiment variant.

Furthermore, we analyze the percentage of large error values of more than $0.1\,m$. Again, IK-CCGP-3 with 28.3% has the largest percentage of error. The approach with the smallest percentage of large errors is IK-CCGP-2P with 0.8%, compared to IK-CCGP-2G with 2.1%. Figure 4 gives additional clues about the distribution of large errors within the workspace. For all data samples which caused large position errors, the original positions are plotted to identify problematic regions. The IK-CCGT-2P algorithm had mainly problems finding joint values for positions at the top of the reachable area and very few outliers in the remaining workspace. Additionally, IK-CCGT-2G produced large errors at the bottom of the workspace and the edge of the reachable area.

The algorithm found more consistent solutions throughout the workspace when the projected joint 1 angles were given as inputs, i.e. IK-CCGT-2P, compared to the ground truth angles in IK-CCGT-2G. An explanation for this observation is that IK-CCGT-2G is trained on the ground truth data of joint 1. Thus, it was possible that the algorithm received input values of joint 1 that were $\pm\pi$ apart but arrived at positions that are very close to each other, once with a bend over and once without. To the contrary, IK-CCGT-2P received very consistent input angles of joint 1, i.e. positions that are very close to each other also originated from the same joint 1 angle. This continuous input helped the algorithm to learn a consistent formula for most positions within the workspace. Two possible explanations for the cluster of large errors above the center of the x-y-plane with z-values between $0.33\,m$ and $0.47\,m$ arise from this assumption: First, these positions can only be reached by a bend over due to the kinematic configuration of the robot. Or second, the algorithm has issues learning joint angles that completely extend the arm to the top.

4.5   Discussion

Our main goal to prefer genetic programming over ANNs in this paper is the explainability of the produced solutions. However, the accuracy is the typical

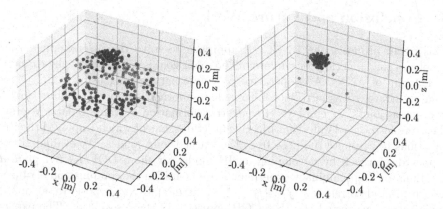

Fig. 4. Distribution of large position errors >0.1 m evaluated on 20,000 data samples. Left: IK-CCGP-2G. Right: IK-CCGP-2P, z values of cluster in the center range from 0.33 m to 0.47 m

criterion that an IK model is assessed on. Most IK models developed with ANNs are evaluated using continuous trajectory tracking: once the start position of the trajectory is found, the subsequent positions are close to the current position. Our evaluation method uses 20,000 independent positions instead of a continuous trajectory, which makes it difficult to compare our accuracy to ANNs. Nevertheless, multiple papers show that the position error of ANNs is in the magnitude of millimeters, while the best solution developed by our approach has a median error of 2.13 cm [1,22]. Since the existing GP approaches for the IK problem use an angle error in [rad], a fair comparison between our approach using position errors in [m] and the existing GP approaches is not possible [3,4]. Even though the position accuracy of our approach leaves space for future research, we obtain human-readable equations that can be analyzed mathematically. This is especially necessary for manipulator operations in safety-relevant areas. An equation obtained by experiment IK-CCGP-2P for joint 3 is $\theta_3 = \left(x + \frac{155}{180}\pi + \frac{56}{180}\pi - \frac{(\sin(0.033)+0.155)\cdot(\sin(\theta_z+0.033))}{\theta_x}\right)^2 \bmod 2\pi$. The numbers are known offset parameters of the joints. Due to the transformation of input poses, θ_x only takes on the values 1.570 or −1.570 for joint 3. Since $\sin(v) = v$, $v < 0.1$ can be assumed, the equation evaluates to $\theta_3 = \left(x + \frac{211}{180}\pi \pm 0.12 \cdot \sin\left(\theta_z + 0.033\right)\right)^2 \bmod 2\pi$. Thus, our algorithm developed an equation in which θ_3 only depends on x and the orientation parameter θ_z as well as the sign given by θ_x. This equation is more comprehensible than the usually multidimensional matrices produced by ANNs. Nevertheless, it makes use of non-physical operations, such as $\theta_z + 0.033$, where an angle and a length are added. This is an expected behavior, as the dimension penalty objective was not optimized in our approach.

5   Conclusion and Future Work

This paper proposes the IK-CCGP approach to solve the inverse kinematics problem using genetic programming. The main goal is to overcome the explainability gap of ANNs. A cooperative coevolutionary setting using a two-phase training strategy was introduced. To include information about the joint angles of previous joints, we employed inverse transformation of training data. We furthermore introduced different objective functions, one of which employed the FK equations to compute the pose from the learned joint angles. We evaluated the proposed approach by developing an IK model for the 5 DOF *KUKA youBot* manipulator. In preliminary experiments, we identified the combination of objectives error and correlation, $f = [f_1, f_2]^T$, as fitting for our purpose. In advanced experiments, we tested the IK-CCGP approach in three scenarios. The experiments for learning three consecutive joints of the kinematic chain performed worst. On the other hand, experiments that learned a kinematic unit of two joints generated promising results in the magnitude of a few centimeters of position error. The proposed approach overcomes the explainability gap of ANNs and is generally applicable to a variety of robotic configurations. For future research, further analysis of the resulting equations, such as a boundary value analysis, can be conducted. Moreover, the remaining two joints of the kinematic chain can be analyzed using a geometric IK approach. This can decrease the overall position error compared to the current position error.

References

1. Almusawi, A.R., Dülger, L.C., Kapucu, S.: A new artificial neural network approach in solving inverse kinematics of robotic arm (Denso vp6242). Comput. Intell. Neurosci. **2016** (2016)
2. Aristidou, A., Lasenby, J., Chrysanthou, Y., Shamir, A.: Inverse kinematics techniques in computer graphics: a survey. Comput. Graph. Forum **37**(6), 35–58 (2018)
3. Chapelle, F., Bidaud, P.: A closed form for inverse kinematics approximation of general 6R manipulators using genetic programming. In: IEEE International Conference on Robotics and Automation, vol. 4, pp. 3364–3369 (2001)
4. Chapelle, F., Bidaud, P.: Closed form solutions for inverse kinematics approximation of general 6r manipulators. Mech. Mach. Theory **39**(3), 323–338 (2004)
5. Craig, J.J.: Introduction to Robotics: Mechanics and Control. Pearson Education Inc., 3rd edn. (1989)
6. Daunicht, W.J.: Approximation of the inverse kinematics of an industrial robot by defanet. In: IEEE International Joint Conference on Neural Networks, pp. 1995–2000 (1991)
7. Deb, K., Pratap, A., Agarwal, S., Meyarivan, T.: A fast and elitist multiobjective genetic algorithm: NSGA-II. IEEE Trans. Evol. Comput. **6**(2), 182–197 (2002)
8. Dolinsky, J.U., Jenkinson, I., Colquhoun, G.J.: Application of genetic programming to the calibration of industrial robots. Comput. Ind. **58**(3), 255–264 (2007)
9. Eckmiller, R., Beckmann, J., Werntges, H., Lades, M.: Neural kinematics net for a redundant robot arm. In: IEEE International Joint Conference on Neural Networks, vol. 2, pp. 333–339 (1989)

10. El-Sherbiny, A., Elhosseini, M.A., Haikal, A.Y.: A comparative study of soft computing methods to solve inverse kinematics problem. Ain Shams Eng. J. **9**(4), 2535–2548 (2018)
11. Fortin, F.A., De Rainville, F.M., Gardner, M.A., Parizeau, M., Gagné, C.: DEAP: evolutionary algorithms made easy. J. Mach. Learn. Res. **13**, 2171–2175 (2012)
12. Hakala, J., Fahner, G., Eckmiller, R.: Rapid learning of inverse robot kinematics based on connection assignment and topographical encoding (cate). In: IEEE International Joint Conference on Neural Networks, vol. 2, pp. 1536–1541 (1991)
13. Jazar, R.N.: Theory of Applied Robotics: Kinematics, Dynamics, and Control. Springer Science Business Media, Heidelberg (2010)
14. Kalra, P., Mahapatra, P., Aggarwal, D.: An evolutionary approach for solving the multimodal inverse kinematics problem of industrial robots. Mech. Mach. Theory **41**(10), 1213–1229 (2006)
15. Keijzer, M., Babovic, V.: Dimensionally aware genetic programming. In: Proceedings of the 1st Annual Conference on Genetic and Evolutionary Computation, vol. 2, pp. 1069–1076 (1999)
16. Kucuk, S., Bingul, Z.: Inverse kinematics solutions for industrial robot manipulators with offset wrists. Appl. Math. Model. **38**(7–8), 1983–1999 (2014)
17. Li, D., Zhong, J.: Dimensionally aware multi-objective genetic programming for automatic crowd behavior modeling. ACM Trans. Model. Comput. Simulat. **30**(3), 1–24 (2020)
18. Mckay, R.I., Hoai, N.X., Whigham, P.A., Shan, Y., O'neill, M.: Grammar-based genetic programming: a survey. Genetic Program. Evol. Mach. **11**(3–4), 365–396 (2010)
19. Parker, J.K., Khoogar, A.R., Goldberg, D.E.: Inverse kinematics of redundant robots using genetic algorithms. In: IEEE International Conference on Robotics and Automation, vol. 1, pp. 271–276 (1989)
20. Rodriguez-Coayahuitl, L., Morales-Reyes, A., Escalante, H.J., Coello, C.A.C.: Cooperative co-evolutionary genetic programming for high dimensional problems. In: Parallel Problem Solving from Nature, pp. 48–62 (2020)
21. Spong, M.W., Hutchinson, S., Vidyasagar, M.: Robot Modeling and Control. John Wiley & Sons, Inc., New York (2005)
22. Srisuk, P., Sento, A., Kitjaidure, Y.: Forward kinematic-like neural network for solving the 3d reaching inverse kinematics problems. In: 14th International Conference on Electrical Engineering/Electronics, Computer, Telecommunications and Information Technology, pp. 214–217 (2017)
23. Wappler, S., Wegener, J.: Evolutionary unit testing of object-oriented software using strongly-typed genetic programming. In: Proceedings of the 8th Annual Conference on Genetic and Evolutionary Computation, pp. 1925–1932 (2006)
24. Wei, Y., Jian, S., He, S., Wang, Z.: General approach for inverse kinematics of NR robots. Mech. Mach. Theory **75**, 97–106 (2014)
25. Zhang, Y., Li, Y., Xiao, X.: A novel kinematics analysis for a 5-dof manipulator based on kuka youbot. In: IEEE International Conference on Robotics and Biomimetics, pp. 1477–1482 (2015)
26. Zille, H., Evrard, F., Reuter, J., Mostaghim, S., van Wachem, B.: Assessment of multi-objective and coevolutionary genetic programming for predicting the stokes flow around a sphere. In: Conference Proceedings EUROGEN 2021 (2021)

On the Schedule for Morphological Development of Evolved Modular Soft Robots

Giorgia Nadizar[1] [iD], Eric Medvet[2(✉)] [iD], and Karine Miras[3] [iD]

[1] Department of Mathematics and Geosciences, University of Trieste, Trieste, Italy
[2] Department of Engineering and Architecture, University of Trieste, Trieste, Italy
emedvet@units.it
[3] Artificial Intelligence Department, Rijksuniversiteit Groningen, Groningen,
The Netherlands

Abstract. Development is fundamental for living beings. As robots are often designed to mimic biological organisms, development is believed to be crucial for achieving successful results in robotic agents, as well. What is not clear, though, is the most appropriate scheduling for development. While in real life systems development happens mostly during the initial growth phase of organisms, it has not yet been investigated whether such assumption holds also for artificial creatures. In this paper, we employ a evolutionary approach to optimize the development—according to different representations—of Voxel-based Soft Robots (VSRs), a kind of modular robots. In our study, development consists in the addition of new voxels to the VSR, at fixed time instants, depending on the development schedule. We experiment with different schedules and show that, similarly to living organisms, artificial agents benefit from development occurring at early stages of life more than from development lasting for their entire life.

Keywords: Adaptation · Evolutionary Robotics · Embodied cognition · Development · Body-brain evolution

1 Introduction and Related Works

Phenotypic development is pervasive in nature and it can happen in different dimensions, e.g., lifetime body adaptations to cope with environmental seasonal changes [1], brain plasticity through learning [2], body training [3], behavioral environmental regulation [4], etc. Additionally to these forms of development, there is a very fundamental one: growth. Notably, growth starts during morphogenesis and may continue for a long period during the lifetime of a creature, according to its species. In humans, the fluctuations of phenotypic growth depend on genetic and environmental factors during prepubertal and pubertal development [5]. Because of the complexity of these factors, the difficulty of establishing growth standards has been discussed [6]. Moreover, different body traits develop

E. Medvet et al. (Eds.): EuroGP 2022, LNCS 13223, pp. 146–161, 2022.
https://doi.org/10.1007/978-3-031-02056-8_10

at distinct ages. For instance, while the significant height growth happens until adolescence [7], male muscle mass peaks around their 20 to 30 years old [8].

Curiously, while body growth in animals is rapid in early life, it then progressively slows, and the reasons for this are not yet quite understood [7], though its association to possible advantages of delaying fertility maturation has been discussed [9]. Furthermore, animal brain development is lifelong, happening prenatally, during infancy and adolescence, and even in adulthood [10]. In fact, because of its complexity, the human frontal cortex is not fully developed until the mid twenties [4]. Note that this developmental maturation does not necessarily mean growth in the brain, but a better organization of the neural structures, requiring some form of pruning [4]. Interestingly, synaptic pruning—i.e., removing some of the connections in the neural network constituting the brain—has been shown to be potentially beneficial also for evolved artificial agents [11,12].

While the dynamics of growth, including the interplay between body and brain development, is unclear, we could hardly doubt that this complex dynamics is fundamental for the behavioral complexity observed in diverse species. Therefore, the field of Evolutionary Robotics has great motivation to study growth development. Nevertheless, not only is the field focused mostly on evolving the controller without evolving the body [13], but also has development received relatively little attention.

Some developmental representations have become popular [14,15], but they have been mostly used for morphogenesis only. One instance of a development study has demonstrated the benefits of environmental regulation for lifetime phenotypic plasticity so that bodies and brains of robots could adapt in response to environmental changes [16,17]. Another approach experimented with reconfigurable robots that relied on manually designed bodies [18]. Furthermore, a field of research called morphogenetic engineering has been introduced to promote models of complex self-architecture systems [19]. Some other examples of development studies are the use of pre-programmed lifetime changes that could be compared to growth: investigating the impact of development on evolvability [20,21], and exploring the effects of using stages of morphological development as a way of scaffolding behavior [22].

Although the aforementioned works represent an important step for the investigations of development within artificial life, there is still a lot to be explored. There is a pressure for an increase in this type of investigation, with the purpose of expanding our perspective about how development can be carried out, and in which conditions determined effects shall be observed.

Aiming at furnishing the literature with new insights, in this paper we address a specific question related to growth development: does the development schedule impact on the effectiveness of evolved agents? Namely, is a continuous, lifelong development better or worse than a development that occurs mostly at the beginning of the life of the agent? To this extent, we design various development representations for 2-D simulated modular Voxel-based Soft Robots (VSRs) [23] which can be optimized via suitable evolutionary algorithms (EAs): we hence combine development with evolution, allowing robots to undergo alterations on different timescales. Due to their expressive power, VSRs are ideal for experimenting with morphological development and they have already been used in [21,24]: differently from the present paper, the two cited works do not study the development schedule, but the overall impact of development on evolution, in [21], and the possibility of exploiting environmental feedback for determining the development, in [24].

Even though our work focuses on morphological development, involving only the body of the agent, the robot controller is tightly coupled with its morphology: therefore, we also design evolvable brains which can effectively control different bodies. To assess the effects of development, we evaluate the performance of robots in a locomotion task. For providing more context, our study encompasses also agents which do not undergo development, considered as a baseline. Our results show that, for all representations, the most appropriate scheduling of development for artificial agents resembles that of living organisms. Namely, we find that early development yields to better performing robots than those which experience continuous growth. Moreover, the comparison with non-developing robots confirms the potentially beneficial effects of development for artificial agents.

2   Background: Voxel-Based Soft Robots

We experiment with Voxel-based Soft Robots (VSRs), a kind of modular soft robots. Each VSR module consists of a deformable cube (*voxel*), which can vary in volume in order to achieve movement. The final volume of each voxel is determined by two factors: (a) external forces acting on the voxel, which is deformable by construction, and (b) a control signal, regulating active expansion/contraction of the voxel. In this study, we consider a 2-D variant of said robots that are simulated in discrete time [25]. Working in 2-D reduces the computational cost of the simulation, while yielding results that are conceptually portable to the 3-D case.

A VSR is defined by its *morphology* and its *controller*, describing respectively the arrangement of voxels in a 2-D grid and the law which determines each voxel control signal.

2.1   VSR Morphology

The morphology of a VSR describes the voxel arrangement in a 2-D grid. Each voxel is a soft deformable square, modeled with (a) four masses at the corners, to prevent excessive deformations and rigidly connect neighbors, (b) spring-damper systems, to ensure softness and elasticity, and (c) ropes, to avoid uncontrolled expansion. We refer the reader to [26] for further details on the voxel mechanical model utilized.

VSRs accomplish movement similarly to biological muscles, thanks to the contraction and expansion of individual voxels. The behavior of each voxel is determined by a control signal and by the interaction with other bodies, exerting their forces on it, e.g., the ground or other voxels. At each simulation time step k, the controller feeds every i-th voxel with a control signal $a_i^{(k)} \in [-1,1]$, -1 corresponding to maximum requested expansion, and 1 corresponding to maximum requested contraction. In the simulator employed [25], contraction and expansions are modeled as linear variations of the rest-length of the spring-damper system, proportional to the control signal received.

Voxels are equipped with sensors. We use three types of sensors, whose readings can be exploited by the VSR controller: (a) *area* sensors, perceiving the ratio between the current area of the voxel and its rest area, (b) *touch* sensors, sensing if the voxel is in contact with the ground or not, and (c) *velocity* sensors, which perceive the velocity of the center of mass of the voxel along the x- and y-axes (thus corresponding to the union of a v_x and a v_y sensor). We normalize sensor readings in such a way that, at each simulation time step, the readings $s_i^{(k)}$ of the i-th voxel are defined in $[-1, 1]^4$.

2.2   VSR Controller

At each simulation time step k, the VSR controller is fed with the sensor readings $s^{(k)} = [s_1^{(k)} \; s_1^{(k)} \dots]$ and outputs the control signals $a^{(k)} = (a_1^{(k)}, a_2^{(k)}, \dots)$ for all voxels.

In this study, we consider two different kinds of controllers: the phase controller [21,23,27] and the neural controller [28,29]. For both controllers, in this work, even though we compute the control signal at each simulation time step, we actually apply it to the voxel every $t_{step} = 0.5\,s$ and keep it constant in between variations. In other words, we employ a step like control signal derived by the original control signal. We do this because we aim at preventing vibrating behaviors, which have been found to be a strong attractor in evolution of VSRs [30].

Phase Controller. In the phase controller, each control signal is computed from the current time, according to a sinusoidal function. Namely, the control signal of the i-th voxel at simulation time step k is computed as $a_i^{(k)} = \sin\left(2f\pi k \Delta t + \phi_i\right)$, where f is the sine wave frequency, Δt is the simulation time interval, and ϕ_i is the voxel phase. In most works where they have been used, these controllers have been optimized only in the phases ϕ_i, whereas f is set a priori to the same value for each voxel: for this reason, these are called phase controllers.

Note that this is an open-loop type of controller, which does not exploit sensor readings $s^{(k)}$.

Neural Controller. VSR neural controllers are based on Artificial Neural Networks (ANNs), which are employed to process sensor readings and produce voxel control signals. Neural controllers have been demonstrated beneficial for the achievement of good performance in VSRs [28,31], due to their sensing abilities.

We use the *distributed* neural controller presented in [29], consisting of a number of fully-connected feed-forward ANNs, i.e., multi-layer perceptrons (MLPs), one per voxel. At every simulation time step k, each MLP processes the local sensor readings $s_i^{(k)}$ together with the information coming from the neighboring voxels, in order to produce the local control signal $a_i^{(k)}$ and the information to be passed to neighboring voxels. The information passed between neighboring voxels consists of a vector of n_signal values, or a zero-vector of the same size for voxels at the boundaries. Such vector is processed with one time step of delay, i.e., every MLP processes the vectors produced by neighboring MLPs at the previous simulation time step. The control signal of the i-th voxel is hence determined as $\left[a_i^{(k)} \; m_{i,N}^{(k)} \; m_{i,E}^{(k)} \; m_{i,S}^{(k)} \; m_{i,W}^{(k)}\right] =$ MLP$_\theta\left(\left[s_i^{(k)} \; m_{i_N,S}^{(k-1)} \; m_{i_E,W}^{(k-1)} \; m_{i_S,N}^{(k-1)} \; m_{i_W,E}^{(k-1)}\right]\right)$, where $m_{i,N}^{(k)} \in [-1,1]^{n_\text{signal}}$ is the information output by the i-th voxel for its neighbor at north (the same for the other three neighbors), $m_{i_N,S}^{(k-1)} \in [-1,1]^{n_\text{signal}}$ is the information output by the neighbor at north for the i-th voxel (that is its neighbor at south) at previous time step $k-1$, and $\theta \in \mathbb{R}^p$ is the vector of the parameters (or weights) of the MLP.

In this study, we utilize an identical MLP in each voxel, both in terms of architecture and weights θ. This design choice arises from the fact that this controller can be employed for a variable amount of voxels without any changes, so it is particularly suitable for a developing body. Moreover, [30] showed experimentally that using the same MLP in each voxel is not worse than using MLPs with different weights.

3   Development of VSRs

We consider morphological development, i.e., a mechanism according to which, at given time instants during the life of the VSR, new voxels are added to the VSR body.

For the purpose of this study, we say that the development of a VSR is completely described by a schedule and a development function. We define the *schedule* as a sequence $S = (t_j)_j$ of time instants when the addition of a new voxel occurs. We define the *development function* as a function d that, given a number of voxels n, outputs a VSR $d(n)$ consisting of at most n voxels. We impose the requirements for the function d that, for all n, (a) the morphology of the VSR $d(n)$ differs from the morphology of the VSR $d(n+1)$ for at most one voxel and (b) $d(n)$ has no more voxels than $d(n+1)$.

Given a starting size n_0, a schedule S, and a development function d, we can perform a simulation of a VSR $d(n_0)$ that starts with a morphology of (at most) n_0 voxels at $t = 0$ and, at each $t_j \in S$, develops to a VSR $d(n_0 + j)$ that is not smaller than the previous one.

The main goal of this study is to gain insights into the impact of the schedule on the effectiveness of evolved developing VSRs. To achieve this goal, we set the schedule to a few predefined sequences, let the evolution optimize the developing function, and compare the outcomes.

3.1   Representations for the Development Function

For broadening the generality of our experimental findings, we consider four different ways of representing the developing function in a way that allows its optimization by the means of evolution.

For the ease of presentation, we describe the development function d in terms of a function d_{morph}, that determines the morphology of the VSR, and a function $d_{\mathrm{controller}}$, that determines the controller of the VSR. Moreover, we directly describe how the outputs of $d_{\mathrm{morph}}(n, g)$ and $d_{\mathrm{controller}}(n, g)$ are computed, given a genotype g and a number n.

Vector-Based Morphology Representation. Given a real vector $v \in \mathbb{R}^{n_{\mathrm{side}}^2}$, we obtain a morphology of n voxels as follows.

We denote by $M = d_{\mathrm{morphology}}(n, v)$ the Boolean matrix describing the obtained morphology, where the voxel at position i, j is present if and only if the corresponding element $m_{i,j}$ is set. First, we reshape the vector v to a matrix V of n_{side}^2 real values. Second, we determine the greatest element of V and set the corresponding element of M. Then, we repeat the following two steps until $\min(n, n_{\mathrm{side}}^2)$ elements of M have been set: (1) we consider the subset of M unset elements that are adjacent to set elements and (2) we set the element of the subset with the largest corresponding value in V.

Note that, with this representation, it is guaranteed that the morphology will have exactly n voxels, provided that n_{side}, a parameter of the representation, is large enough.

Figure 1 provides a schematic representation of an example of application of this function with $n_{\mathrm{side}} = 5$ and $n = 4$.

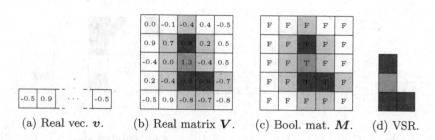

| (a) Real vec. v. | (b) Real matrix V. | (c) Bool. mat. M. | (d) VSR. |

Fig. 1. Schematic view of the grid-based morphology representation $d_{\mathrm{morph}}(n, v)$, with $n_{\mathrm{side}} = 5$, $n = 4$, and an example $v \in \mathbb{R}^{25}$. Dark orange is used to highlight the first element chosen (the one with highest value), whereas lighter orange is used to indicate the other chosen elements. The gray area indicates the candidate voxels for a possible future development (i.e., $n = 5$ with this same v). (Color figure online)

Tree-Based Morphology Representation. Given an ordered tree T in which each node is a number in $\mathbb{R}$ and has either 0 or 4 child nodes, we obtain a morphology of up to n voxels as follows.

Each node of the tree corresponds to an element of the matrix M describing the morphology and the four children of a node correspond to the four neighboring elements at north, south, east, and west. Given a node corresponding to the $m_{i,j}$ element, the first child corresponds to $m_{i,j-1}$, the second to $m_{i,j+1}$, etc.

First, we transform T into a tree T' by mapping each node of T to a node in T' being a pair (v, u), where $v \in \mathbb{R}$ is the node real value and $u \in \{\text{SET}, \text{UNSET}, \text{USED}\}$—initially, $u = \text{UNSET}$ for every node in T'. Second, we set the root u to SET. Then, we repeat the following three steps until n nodes in T' have $u = \text{SET}$ or there are no more T' nodes with $u = \text{UNSET}$: (1) we consider the subset of nodes with $u = \text{UNSET}$ and whose parent node has $u = \text{SET}$, (2) we choose the node in the subset with the largest v, and (3) set $u = \text{SET}$ for the chosen node and $u = \text{USED}$ for all the other nodes representing the same position and with $u = \text{UNSET}$. Finally, we obtain the morphology M by setting the element $m_{0,0}$—for convenience, we assume that the indexes of the elements of M can assume values in $\mathbb{Z}$—and setting every other element i, j for which there is a SET node in T' whose relative position to the root is i, j.

Note that, with this representation, a morphology with less than n voxels could be obtained for a given tree T. In the extreme case, if T consists of the root node only, then the morphology will have just one voxel. On the other hand, the representation is parameter-free and does not impose an upper bound on the number of voxels in the VSR. Note also that, for each position of the matrix M there are up to four nodes in the tree T, but at most one is used depending on ancestors of the node: i.e., this representation is redundant [32] and exhibits epistasis [33].

Figure 2 provides a schematic representation of an example of application of this function with $n = 4$.

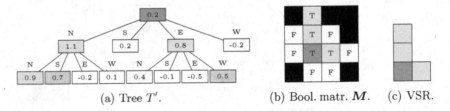

(a) Tree T'.   (b) Bool. matr. M.   (c) VSR.

Fig. 2. Schematic view of the tree-based morphology representation $d_{\text{morph}}(n, T)$, with $n = 4$. Colors in T' nodes represent the value of u, while numbers are the ones of T (not shown here for brevity). Dark orange is used to highlight the root of the tree, whereas lighter orange is for $u = \text{SET}$, white for $u = \text{UNSET}$, and gray for $u = \text{USED}$. The same colors are used in the Boolean matrix M and in the obtained VSR morphology. Black cells in M correspond to nodes that are not present in the tree, hence such cells could never be used with this T, regardless of n. (Color figure online)

Vector-Based Phase Controller Representation. Given a real vector $v \in \mathbb{R}^{n_{\text{side}}^2}$, we obtain a phase controller for a VSR whose morphology M can be contained in a $n_{\text{side}} \times n_{\text{side}}$ grid of voxels as follows.

First, we reshape the vector v to a matrix V of $n_{\text{side}} \times n_{\text{side}}$ real values. Second we build a phase controller in which the phase ϕ of the voxel at position i, j, if any, is given by the corresponding element in V. If there is no voxel at i, j, the corresponding element in V does not contribute to the controller.

Vector-Based Neural Controller Representation. Given a real vector $v \in \mathbb{R}^p$ and a description of the topology of an MLP consisting on the numbers $l_1, \ldots, l_m$ of neurons for each layer (with $p = \sum_{i=1}^{i<m} l_{i+1}(l_i + 1)$), we obtain a neural controller by simply setting the parameters vector $\boldsymbol{\theta}$ of the MLP to $\boldsymbol{v}$.

Note that, since the MLP is the same for all voxels, this controller is applicable to any VSR, regardless of its morphology, provided that (a) l_1 is compatible with the dimension $n_{\text{sensor}} = |\boldsymbol{s}_i^{(k)}|$ of sensor readings in the voxels and with the value of n_{signal} and (b) l_m is compatible with the value of n_{signal}. More precisely, given n_{sensor} and n_{signal}, $l_1 = n_{\text{sensor}} + 4n_{\text{signal}}$ and $l_m = 1 + 4n_{\text{signal}}$ must hold. Since n_{sensor} is determined by the morphology ($n_{\text{sensor}} = 4$ in this work, see Sect. 2.1), it follows that the free parameters for this representations are n_{signal}, m, and the values of l_j for $2 \leq j < m$.

Tree-Based Phase Controller Representation. This controller representation is tightly coupled with the tree-based morphology representation: in fact, we only use it in combination with that representation. Given an ordered tree T in which each node is a pair of numbers $v, \phi \in \mathbb{R}^2$ and has either 0 or 4 child nodes, we obtain a phase controller for the VSR mapped from the v-part of T according to the tree-based morphology representation, as follows. Let M be the morphology obtained as described above, we associate with each voxel in the morphology the ϕ value of the corresponding element in T.

The rationale for this representation, is to tightly couple v values, determining the morphology, and ϕ values, determining the controller, by embedding them in the same tree. Together with appropriate genetic operators, this link should prevent destructive effects resulting from the misalignment between the part of the genotype describing the morphology and the one describing the brain [34].

Full Development Function Representations. Summarizing, we consider the four representations resulting from the following combinations of a d_{morph} and a $d_{\text{controller}}$ representation:

- *Grid-phase*, in which the genotype is a vector $\boldsymbol{v} \in \mathbb{R}^{2n_{\text{side}}^2}$: we obtain the robot by mapping the leading half of $\boldsymbol{v}$ with the vector-based morphology representation and the trailing half with the vector-based phase controller representation.
- *Grid-neural*, in which the genotype is a vector $\boldsymbol{v} \in \mathbb{R}^{n_{\text{side}}^2+p}$: we obtain the robot by mapping the leading n_{side}^2 elements of $\boldsymbol{v}$ with the vector-based morphology representation and the trailing p elements with the vector-based neural controller representation.
- *Tree-phase*, in which the genotype is a tree T with nodes in $\mathbb{R}^2$ with either 0 or 4 children: we obtain the robot by mapping the tree of the first elements of T nodes with the tree-based morphology representation and T with the tree-based phase controller representation.

– *Tree-neural*, in which the genotype is a pair T, v composed of a tree T with nodes in $\mathbb{R}$ with either 0 or 4 children and a vector $v \in \mathbb{R}^p$: we obtain the robot by mapping T with the tree-based morphology representation and v with the vector-based neural controller representation.

3.2 Evolution of the Development Function

To evolve a development function, we employ a single, standard EA that we adapt, in the initialization and genetic operators, to the four different representations presented above.

In our EA, we iteratively evolve a population of n_{pop} solutions for n_{gen} generations. At each generation, we build the offspring by repeating n_{pop} times the following steps: (1) we randomly select the crossover (with probability p_{cross}) or the mutation (with probability $1 - p_{cross}$) genetic operator; (2) we select one or two parents (depending on the chosen operator) with a tournament selection of size n_{tour}; (3) we apply the operator to the parents obtaining a new individual. Then, we merge the parents and the offspring, we keep only the n_{pop} best individuals, and proceed to the next generation.

For initializing the population, we sample $U(-1, 1)$ for each element of the vector-based representations, and we use the ramped half-and-half initialization (with depth in $[d_{min}, d_{max}]$) for the tree-based representation. For the latter, we sample $U(-1, 1)$ for the values of the nodes.

Concerning the genetic operators, we do as follows. In the vector-based representations (grid-phase and grid-neural), we use the extended geometric crossover, where the child $v \in \mathbb{R}^n$ is determined from the parents $v_1, v_2 \in \mathbb{R}^n$ as $v = v_1 + \alpha(v_2 - v_1) + \beta$, where $\alpha \in \mathbb{R}^n$ is sampled as $\alpha_i \sim U(-0.5, 1.5)$, and $\beta \in \mathbb{R}^n$ is sampled as $\beta_i \sim N(0, \sigma_{cross})$. As mutation, we use the Gaussian mutation, where $v = v_1 + \beta$, with betas sampled from $N(0, \sigma_{mut})$.

In the tree-based representations, we use the standard subtree crossover, which consists in replacing a random subtree of one parent with a randomly chosen subtree of the other parent: both subtrees are picked to ensure the child tree has a maximum depth of d_{max}. As mutation, we use the standard subtree mutation, in which one random subtree is replaced with a newly generated tree, ensuring a maximum depth of d_{max} for the child. Only with the tree-phase representation, with 50 % probability, we apply a noise sampled from $N(0, \sigma_{mut})$ to each ϕ element of the tree instead of applying the standard subtree mutation.

In the combined representation (tree-neural), we do crossover by applying standard subtree crossover and extended geometric crossover to the two parts of the genotype. Similarly, we do mutation by applying Gaussian mutation and standard subtree mutation.

4   Experimental Evaluation

We performed several experiments to answer to the following research questions: What is the most appropriate development schedule for artificial agents? Does it depend on the representation of the development function?

For answering to said questions, we evolved development functions to develop VSRs suited for the task of *locomotion*, in which the goal for the robot is to travel as far as possible on a terrain in a given amount of time. We employed two different development schedules, together with no development, to be considered as a baseline. A detailed description of the experimental procedure and results follows.

Concerning the representation, we used the following parameters: $n_{side} = 10$, $f = 1\,Hz$, $n_{signal} = 2$, $m = 4$, and $l_2 = l_3 = l_1 = 4 + 4 \cdot 2 = 12$ (i.e., we used MLPs with two inner layers with the same size of the input layer). Regarding the EA, we used the following parameters: $n_{pop} = 96$ and $n_{gen} = 209$ (corresponding to 20 000 total fitness evaluations), $p_{cross} = 0.75$, $n_{tour} = 10$, $\sigma_{cross} = 0.1$, $\sigma_{mut} = 0.35$, $d_{min} = 3$, and $d_{min} = 6$. We verified that, for the chosen value of n_{pop} and n_{gen}, evolution was in general capable of converging to a solution, i.e., longer evolutions would have resulted in negligible fitness improvements.

To evaluate the effectiveness of an individual, i.e., a development function, given a schedule S, we proceeded as follows. At the beginning of the simulation, we (1) used the development function to obtain an initial VSR $d(n_0)$ from n_0 and (2) we placed it right above the terrain at the starting position. Then, at each $t_i \in S$ during the simulation, we (1) removed the VSR $d(n_{i-1})$ from the simulation, taking note of the x-coordinate x_{left} of its leftmost voxel, (2) used the development function to develop the VSR to $d(n_i)$ and (3) placed the developed VSR in the simulation right above the terrain in a position such that its leftmost part was at x_{left}. We stopped the simulation after 210 s (simulated time), took note of the run distance Δx, as the difference between the initial and final x-coordinate of the center of mass of the VSR, and used Δx as fitness.

We removed and added (i.e., *re-spawn*) the VSR just before and right after each development because the new voxel might have been added in positions that conflict with the current posture of the robot (e.g., under a foot, "inside" the terrain). As a consequence, each development step led to a re-spawning of the VSR, where its gait was interrupted.

We characterized the performance of the representations in conjunction with two development schedules, both encompassing 14 stages: *early* development $S_{early} = (10, 20, 30, \ldots, 120, 130)$, resembling biological development, and *uniform* development $S_{uniform} = (15, 30, 45 \ldots, 180, 195)$, accounting for continuous growth (numbers are in s). In addition, to have a baseline for comparisons, we also employed a non-developmental schedule $S_{no-devo} = \emptyset$: in this case VSRs were initialized according to the initial development, and no voxels were ever added to them. To ensure fairness in terms of re-spawning (as such events could slow down the VSR), we interrupted the gait to lift the VSR in the air according to $S_{uniform}$, even though no development was occurring.

Concerning the initial size n_0 of the VSRs, we aimed at being as fair as possible, since larger robots could, in principle, benefit from having more power. Hence, we chose $n_{0,early} = 6$, $n_{0,uniform} = 8$, and $n_{0,no-devo} = 14$ in order to have approximately the same weighted average VSR size during the simulation ($\bar{n}_{early} \approx 14.7$, $\bar{n}_{uniform} = 14.5$, and $\bar{n}_{no-devo} = 14$). In other words, the chosen values of n_0 resulted in all VSRs having approximately the same integral of size over the simulations.

For each of the $4 \cdot 3$ combinations of representation and schedule, we performed 10 independent, i.e., based on different random seeds, evolutionary optimizations, obtaining a total of 120 runs. When comparing results of pairs of combinations, we performed the Mann-Whitney U test, after having verified the proper requirements, with the null hypothesis of equality of the means—we report the p-values. Note that, since we performed multiple pairwise comparisons simultaneously, we applied the required Bonferroni corrections for evaluating the significance of results.

We used 2D-VSR-Sim [25] for the simulation setting all parameters to default values; in particular, we set the simulation time interval $\Delta t = \frac{1}{60}$ s. We made the code for the experiments publicly available at https://github.com/giorgianadizar/VSREvoDevo.

4.1   Results and Discussion

The experimental results are reported in Figs. 3, 4 and 5. The most high level finding of our experiments is displayed in Fig. 3, which depicts the distributions of the fitness Δx of the best individuals at the end of evolution for each representation and schedule. From such plots, we are able to compare the outcomes deriving from S_{early} and S_{uniform}: given the distributions and the p-values, we can conclude that, in general, early development is not worse than uniform development, and that for phase controllers it is significantly better. We can hence infer that development in artificial life is somehow similar to development in real life, and, even though creatures that continuously grow end up being larger, such trait does not really benefit their overall performance. We hypothesize that early development is more effective as the optimization of the controller of the agent is favored by the fact that the brain is able to interact with a fixed body for a longer amount of time (the last development stage, which is longer than the other ones). Therefore, we speculate that evolution finds a way to optimize the controller for the last body, since being optimal during this longer stage could result in more distance gain, hence in higher fitness. On the other hand, continuous growth seems to hinder brain development, as evolution cannot find an optimal controller to almost equally fit all the bodies the controller interacts with.

Comparison Against No Development. Reasoning further on Fig. 3, it is interesting to also compare the results achieved by non-developing VSRs. From the previous assumptions, we would expect such outcomes to be significantly better than both early and uniformly developed VSRs, as in this case the brain is optimized for just one body. However, the results shown in the plots are less clear, as there is no evident winner among the non-developed, early-developed, and uniformly-developed VSRs. We explain these mixed findings by reasoning on two factors: the re-spawning and the lack of development. Concerning the re-spawning, it likely slowed VSRs down, even though they were not really developing, preventing them from exhibiting a fluid and effective gait. In addition, we speculate that the lack of actual development could have been detrimental for the overall performance achieved, consistently with [21].

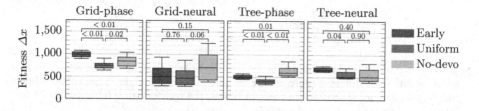

Fig. 3. Box plots of the fitness Δx of the best development functions at the end of evolution for different representations (plot columns) and development schedules (color). p-values are shown above pairs of boxes. We consider $\alpha = 0.05/3 \approx 0.017$ for statistical significance, due to the Bonferroni correction.

Analysis of VSR Velocity. To gain further insight on the obtained results, we also measured the velocity of VSRs along development: we define $v_{x,i}$ as the average velocity achieved by a VSR in its i-th stage of development. Figure 4 depicts the distribution of the velocity of VSRs during the last development stage for each representation and schedule. These outcomes are aligned with the previous findings: early development yields to not slower VSRs compared to uniform development, whereas non developed VSRs tend to exhibit fuzzier relationships with the others. However, more interesting conclusions can be drawn if we interpret Fig. 4 taking into consideration that VSRs in the last (i.e., 14-th) stage have different sizes according to the chosen schedule, namely $n_{14,\text{early}} = 19$, $n_{14,\text{uniform}} = 21$, and $n_{14,\text{no-devo}} = 14$. In fact, we can observe that, surprisingly, larger VSRs do not correspond to higher velocity. To explain this, we resort to the same motivation provided before. Namely, early development generates VSRs that are mostly optimized for the last stage of their lives, not only because the last robots are bigger in size, but also because the body-brain interaction is longer.

To conclude the velocity analysis, we provide in Fig. 5 a display of the $v_{x,i}$ throughout the simulation. From these plots, the previously laid hypothesis as to why early development is more successful seems to be confirmed. In addition, we can note that both early and uniform development follow a general growing trend for the velocity, suggesting that also size plays a significant role in the achievement of good performance at locomotion.

Comparison Among Representations. Last, it is interesting to reason on the different outcomes produced by the representations we experimented with, both in terms of fitness Δx (Fig. 3) and velocity $v_{x,14}$ in the last development stage (Fig. 4). We summarize the outcomes of the statistical significance tests between pair of representations in Table 1, where we use colored dots (the color

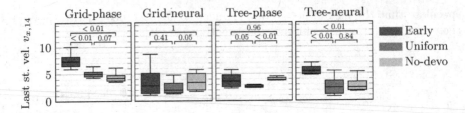

Fig. 4. Box plots of the last stage velocity $v_{x,14}$ of the best development functions at the end of evolution for different representations (plot columns) and development schedules (color). p-values are shown above pairs of boxes. We consider $\alpha = 0.05/3 \approx 0.017$ for statistical significance, due to the Bonferroni correction.

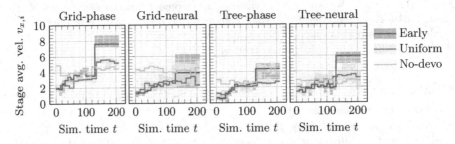

Fig. 5. Average velocity $v_{x,i}$ (median with lower and upper quartiles across the 10 repetitions) of the developing VSRs at different stages during the simulation, for different representations (plot columns) and development schedules (color).

encoding the development schedule) to annotate distributions which are significantly different (p-value $< \alpha = 0.05/6 \approx 0.008$). From the table we can immediately notice that the results obtained without development almost never significantly depend on the employed representation, whereas the outcomes coming from early or uniform development show more interesting variety among representations. Taking into account Figs. 3 and 4 and Tables 1a and 1b, we can conclude that the grid-phase representation is in general not worse than the others, and is significantly better for a subset of schedules and representations. We speculate that this could depend on two factors: the direct representation and the superiority of a phase controller to a neural controller for developing VSRs. Namely, we hypothesize that it is easier for evolution to find suitable phases values for a growing body, than optimizing a single MLP to fit all voxels of a wide gamut of bodies.

To conclude the discussion on the experiments we show in Fig. 6 an example of a developing VSR obtained at the end of one evolution with the grid-phase representation and the uniform schedule: in the figure, each frame shows the VSR during a developing stage. The corresponding video is available at https://youtu.be/DD4D20EH1sA.

Table 1. Statistical significance results for different metrics and representations. Each cell is annotated with a dot if the p-value on the two representations with the same schedule is $< \alpha = 0.05/6 \approx 0.008$ (due to the Bonferroni correction).

	GP	GN	TP	TN			GP	GN	TP	TN		
GP	–	•	•••	••		GP	–	•	••	••		• Early
GN	•	–				GN	•	–				• Uniform
TP	•••		–	••		TP	••		–	•		• No-devo
TN	••		••	–		TN	••		•	–		
	(a) Fitness Δx.						(b) Last stage vel. $v_{x,14}$.					

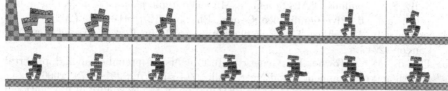

Fig. 6. View of a developing VSR (uniform schedule with the grid-phase representation). Each image is taken $\approx 0.5\,\mathrm{s}$ after a voxel has been added to the VSR body, to leave time to the robot to fall and exhibit its posture on the ground. Voxels color encodes the ratio between its current area and its rest area (red for contraction, yellow for rest, green for expansion). (Color figure online)

5   Concluding Remarks

In this work, we investigated the effects of different schedules for morphological development of Voxel-Based Soft Robots (VSRs), a kind of modular soft robots. To this extent, we evolved development functions, i.e., functions which can build and extend VSRs bodies and controllers, to generate and develop VSRs capable of successfully performing the task of locomotion. Aiming at achieving general results, our study encompassed four representations for development functions, based on different combinations of body-brain encodings, and we also included non-developing VSRs, as a baseline. Our experimental findings show that, similarly to living organisms, VSRs benefit from early development, whereas continuous growth tends to hinder the overall performance of the agent. In particular, we have noticed that, despite having more power, bigger VSRs deriving from continuous growth are not more effective than the early developed smaller ones, concluding that an appropriate development schedule plays a key role in determining the effectiveness of a VSR.

As an extension of this work, it might be of interest to experiment with additional representations, e.g., based on neural cellular automata, and to take into account environmental feedback [24] in development. Moreover, the concept of early mortality [16] could be introduced in our framework.

Acknowledgements. The experimental evaluation of this work has been partially supported by a Google Faculty Research Award granted to E.M.. K.M. was supported by the Hybrid Intelligence Center, a 10-year program funded by the Dutch Ministry of Education, Culture and Science through the Netherlands Organization for Scientific Research (https://www.hybrid-intelligence-centre.nl), grant number 024.004.022.

References

1. Liknes, E.T., Swanson, D.L.: Phenotypic flexibility of body composition associated with seasonal acclimatization in passerine birds. J. Thermal Biol. **36**(6), 363–370 (2011)
2. Fusco, G., Minelli, A.: Phenotypic plasticity in development and evolution: facts and concepts (2010)
3. Kelly, S.A., Panhuis, T.M., Stoehr, A.M.: Phenotypic plasticity: molecular mechanisms and adaptive significance. Compr. Physiol. **2**(2), 1417–1439 (2011)
4. Sapolsky, R.M.: Behave: The Biology of Humans At Our Best and Worst. Penguin, London (2017)
5. Thomis, M.A., Towne, B.: Genetic determinants of prepubertal and pubertal growth and development. Food Nutr. Bull. **27**(4_suppl5), S257–S278 (2006)
6. Butte, N.F., Garza, C., de Onis, M.: Evaluation of the feasibility of international growth standards for school-aged children and adolescents. J. Nutr. **137**(1), 153–157 (2007)
7. Lui, J.C., Baron, J.: Mechanisms limiting body growth in mammals. Endocr. Rev. **32**(3), 422–440 (2011)
8. Batsis, J.A., Buscemi, S.: Sarcopenia, sarcopenic obesity and insulin resistance. In: Medical Complications of Type 2 Diabetes. IntechOpen (2011)
9. Jones, J.H.: Primates and the evolution of long, slow life histories. Current Biol. **21**(18), R708–R717 (2011)
10. Thompson, R.A., Nelson, C.A.: Developmental science and the media: early brain development. Am. Psychol. **56**(1), 5 (2001)
11. Nadizar, G., Medvet, E., Pellegrino, F.A., Zullich, M., Nichele, S.: On the effects of pruning on evolved neural controllers for soft robots. In: Proceedings of the Genetic and Evolutionary Computation Conference Companion, pp. 1744–1752 (2021)
12. Nadizar, G., Medvet, E., Huse Ramstad, H., Nichele, S., Pellegrino, F.A., Zullich, M.: Merging pruning and neuroevolution: towards robust and efficient controllers for modular soft robots. Knowl. Eng. Rev. **37**, 1–13 (2022)
13. Prabhu, S.G.R., Seals, R.C., Kyberd, P.J., Wetherall, J.C.: A survey on evolutionary-aided design in robotics. Robotica **36**(12), 1804–1821 (2018)
14. Lindenmayer, A.: Mathematical models for cellular interactions in development I. Filaments with one-sided inputs. J. Theoret. Biol. **18**(3), 280–299 (1968)
15. Stanley, K.O.: Compositional pattern producing networks: a novel abstraction of development. Genetic Program. Evol. Mach. **8**(2), 131–162 (2007)
16. Miras, K., Cuijpers, J., Gülhan, B., Eiben, A.: The impact of early-death on phenotypically plastic robots that evolve in changing environments. In: ALIFE 2021, The 2021 Conference on Artificial Life, MIT Press (2021)
17. Miras, K., Ferrante, E., Eiben, A.: Environmental regulation using Plasticoding for the evolution of robots. Front. Robot. AI **7**, 107 (2020)
18. Daudelin, J., Jing, G., Tosun, T., Yim, M., Kress-Gazit, H., Campbell, M.: An integrated system for perception-driven autonomy with modular robots. Sci. Robot. **3**(23), eaat4983 (2018)

19. Doursat, R., Sayama, H., Michel, O.: Morphogenetic Engineering: Toward Programmable Complex Systems. Springer, Cham (2012). https://doi.org/10.1007/978-3-642-33902-8

20. Kriegman, S., Cheney, N., Corucci, F., Bongard, J.C.: Interoceptive robustness through environment-mediated morphological development. arXiv preprint arXiv:1804.02257 (2018)

21. Kriegman, S., Cheney, N., Bongard, J.: How morphological development can guide evolution. Sci. Rep. 8(1), 1–10 (2018)

22. Bongard, J.: Morphological change in machines accelerates the evolution of robust behavior. Proc. Natl. Acad. Sci. 108(4), 1234–1239 (2011)

23. Hiller, J., Lipson, H.: Automatic design and manufacture of soft robots. IEEE Trans. Robot. 28(2), 457–466 (2012)

24. Walker, K., Hauser, H., Risi, S.: Growing simulated robots with environmental feedback: an eco-evo-devo approach. In: GECCO 2021, New York, NY, USA, pp. 113–114. Association for Computing Machinery (2021)

25. Medvet, E., Bartoli, A., De Lorenzo, A., Seriani, S.: 2D-VSR-Sim: a simulation tool for the optimization of 2-D voxel-based soft robots. SoftwareX 12, 100573 (2020)

26. Medvet, E., Bartoli, A., De Lorenzo, A., Seriani, S.: Design, Validation, and Case Studies of 2D-VSR-Sim, an Optimization-friendly Simulator of 2-D Voxel-based Soft Robots. arXiv-2001 (2020)

27. Corucci, F., Cheney, N., Giorgio-Serchi, F., Bongard, J., Laschi, C.: Evolving soft locomotion in aquatic and terrestrial environments: effects of material properties and environmental transitions. Soft Robot. 5(4), 475–495 (2018)

28. Talamini, J., Medvet, E., Bartoli, A., De Lorenzo, A.: Evolutionary synthesis of sensing controllers for voxel-based soft robots. In: Artificial Life Conference Proceedings, pp. 574–581. MIT Press (2019)

29. Medvet, E., Bartoli, A., De Lorenzo, A., Fidel, G.: Evolution of distributed neural controllers for voxel-based soft robots. In: Proceedings of the 2020 Genetic and Evolutionary Computation Conference, pp. 112–120 (2020)

30. Medvet, E., Bartoli, A., Pigozzi, F., Rochelli, M.: Biodiversity in evolved voxel-based soft robots. In: Proceedings of the Genetic and Evolutionary Computation Conference, pp. 129–137 (2021)

31. Ferigo, A., Iacca, G., Medvet, E.: Beyond body shape and brain: evolving the sensory apparatus of voxel-based soft robots. In: Castillo, P.A., Jiménez Laredo, J.L. (eds.) EvoApplications 2021. LNCS, vol. 12694, pp. 210–226. Springer, Cham (2021). https://doi.org/10.1007/978-3-030-72699-7_14

32. Rothlauf, F., Goldberg, D.E.: Redundant representations in evolutionary computation. Evol. Comput. 11(4), 381–415 (2003)

33. Vanneschi, L., Castelli, M., Manzoni, L.: The k landscapes: a tunably difficult benchmark for genetic programming. In: Proceedings of the 13th Annual Conference on Genetic and Evolutionary Computation, pp. 1467–1474 (2011)

34. Pagliuca, P., Nolfi, S.: The dynamic of body and brain co-evolution. Adapt. Behav. 1059712321994685 (2020)

An Investigation of Multitask Linear Genetic Programming for Dynamic Job Shop Scheduling

Zhixing Huang⬚, Fangfang Zhang^(✉)⬚, Yi Mei⬚, and Mengjie Zhang⬚

School of Engineering and Computer Science, Victoria University of Wellington,
PO Box 600, Wellington 6140, New Zealand
{zhixing.huang,fangfang.zhang,yi.mei,mengjie.zhang}@ecs.vuw.ac.nz

Abstract. Dynamic job shop scheduling has a wide range of applications in reality such as order picking in warehouse. Using genetic programming to design scheduling heuristics for dynamic job shop scheduling problems becomes increasingly common. In recent years, multitask genetic programming-based hyper-heuristic methods have been developed to solve similar dynamic scheduling problem scenarios simultaneously. However, all of the existing studies focus on the tree-based genetic programming. In this paper, we investigate the use of linear genetic programming, which has some advantages over tree-based genetic programming in designing multitask methods, such as building block reusing. Specifically, this paper makes a preliminary investigation on several issues of multitask linear genetic programming. The experiments show that the linear genetic programming within multitask frameworks have a significantly better performance than solving tasks separately, by sharing useful building blocks.

Keywords: Multitask · Linear genetic programming ·
Hyper-heuristic · Dynamic job shop scheduling

1 Introduction

Job shop scheduling (JSS) is a typical combinatorial optimization problem and has a large commercial value in manufacturing systems. There are a set of machines and a set of jobs in the job shop. The job shop processes the set of jobs by the given machines so that some objectives, such as tardiness and makespan, are optimized. For dynamic job shop scheduling (DJSS), there are some dynamic events such as new job arrivals, which need to be considered when making schedules. In DJSS with new job arrivals, the information of the new jobs is not known in advance. Such characteristic requires optimization techniques to be able to make an instant reaction (e.g., re-scheduling or repairing existing schedules) to the newly arrived jobs. It also limits the application of some existing exact optimization algorithms such as branch-and-bound and dynamic programming whose computation burden may be too large for the instant reaction.

© The Author(s), under exclusive license to Springer Nature Switzerland AG 2022
E. Medvet et al. (Eds.): EuroGP 2022, LNCS 13223, pp. 162–178, 2022.
https://doi.org/10.1007/978-3-031-02056-8_11

Hyper-heuristic methods (HH) have been successfully applied to many applications [18]. They try to search a suitable scheduling heuristic for a certain problem by selecting or recombining some existing scheduling heuristics [6]. Different from heuristic methods whose search space consists of solutions (i.e., complete schedules), HH methods search in a heuristic space given by users. Specifically, the heuristics in JSS are also known as dispatching rules. It has been shown that HH methods can obtain more sophisticated and effective priority dispatching rules than human designed ones in DJSS [1,5,28]. Genetic programming-based hyper heuristic (GPHH) is one of the most popular branches of HH methods [5,14]. Specifically, for GPHH, scheduling heuristics are encoded into genetic programming (GP) individuals. These heuristics will be modified by genetic operators and evaluated on problem instances. The performance of heuristics on the problem instances will be regarded as the fitness of those heuristics. The quality of scheduling heuristics are improved generation by generation.

Although there have been many advanced techniques to assist GPHH to find more effective heuristics in solving a certain DJSS problem [15,24–26], it is a tedious and expensive task for GPHH methods to search effective heuristics for each single scenario. In recent years, some researchers found that sharing knowledge among different scenarios is a potential research direction to enhance GPHH in solving different DJSS scenarios [16,22]. Given that many DJSS scenarios share similarities in objective functions or job shop environments, they may require the same building blocks (e.g., subtrees in tree-based GP) to form an effective scheduling heuristic.

Evolutionary multitask optimization is an emerging topic of evolutionary computation area, which aims to fully utilize the search information among different tasks [20]. The evolutionary multitask methods will accept more than one optimization tasks and solve them simultaneously by an evolutionary computation method within a unified search space. The evolutionary multitask optimization has a wide spectrum of applications nowadays, such as vehicle routing [2,29], time series prediction [7,11], and robot path planning [21]. The evolutionary multitask techniques in these applications are validated to be more effective than solving the problems separately.

To adapt multitask techniques to GPHH methods for dynamic scheduling, several GPHH-specific multitask techniques are proposed. For example, Park et al. [16] proposed a niched GP to improve the generalization ability with different machine breakdown levels (i.e., different optimization tasks). Specifically, the term "niched" means the GP method has a light-weight grouping mechanism. Every group in niched GP is assigned to a specific task. The breeding and selection of GP population were also designed based on these groups. Besides, Zhang et al. respectively made an investigation on multitask GPHH methods [23] and proposed a multitask multi-population GPHH method to design dispatching rules for dynamic flexible JSS [22]. To improve the training efficiency and precisely share the search information, Zhang et al. [27] further proposed a surrogate-assisted multitask GPHH method. Their designed surrogate model successfully enhances the GPHH in terms of test performance and convergence speed.

However, most of existing studies of multitask GPHH are designed based on tree-based GP [13]. Since the tree-like structures usually only have one output, GP individuals have to be assigned to a specific task in the off-the-shelf evolutionary multitask optimization frameworks. On the other hand, linear genetic programming (LGP) [4], which can reuse useful building blocks easily, may be more suitable for multitask optimization. Though LGP has some advantages over tree-based GP in designing multitask frameworks, none of the existing studies apply LGP to multitask optimization frameworks.

To consolidate the foundation of applying LGP to multitask framework, this paper serves as a preliminary work to investigate the performance and behaviour of linear genetic programming with multitask optimization frameworks. Basically, this paper makes an investigation about several key issues of developing multitask linear genetic programming-based hyper heuristic (LGPHH). These issues are summarised into the following three research questions:

- Which existing multitask framework (e.g., multifactorial evolutionary framework and multitask multi-population framework) is most suitable with LGPHH?
- How effective is LGPHH compared with the existing tree-based GPHH for multitask DJSS?
- How does multitask LGPHH share information among the individuals for different tasks?

The rest of the paper is organised as follows. Section 2 gives the introduction to DJSS, LGP, and two existing multitask frameworks. Section 3 develops two LGPHH-based multitask methods for solving DJSS problems. The experiment settings and the result analysis are respectively introduced in Sect. 4 and 5. Finally, Sect. 6 draws out some conclusions.

2   Background

2.1   Dynamic Job Shop Scheduling

DJSS with new job arrival start with an empty job shop whose set of machines M are given beforehand. The jobs will come into the job shop to form the job set J over time. Their information cannot be known until their arrival. Every job j has a sequence of operations $(o_{j1}, ..., o_{ji}, ..., o_{jl_j})(1 \leq i \leq l_j)$, an arrival time α_j, a due date d_j, and a weight ω_j. The operation o_{ji} will be processed by a certain machine $\pi(o_{ji}) \in M$ with a processing time $\delta(o_{ji})$. A machine can only process one operation at any time and its process is assumed to be uninterruptable. The operation sequence of job j specifies the process order of those operations. $o_{ji+1}(i+1 \leq l_j)$ can only be processed after o_{ji} is completed.

This paper mainly considers the flowtime and the tardiness as the performance metrics of the job shop. To formulate these metrics, we denote the actual

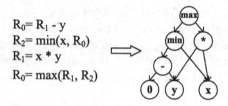

$R_0 = R_1 - y$
$R_2 = \min(x, R_0)$
$R_1 = x * y$
$R_0 = \max(R_1, R_2)$

Fig. 1. An example program of LGP

starting time of an operation o_{ji} as $x(o_{ji})$ and denote the finishing time of job j as c_j, where $c_j = x(o_{jl_j}) + \delta(o_{jl_j})$. The flowtime and the tardiness are further specified as maximum flowtime (F_{max}), mean flowtime (F_{mean}), mean weighted flowtime (WF_{mean}), maximum tardiness (T_{max}), mean tardiness (T_{mean}), and mean weighted tardiness (WT_{mean}). They are formulated as below.

- $F_{max} = \max_{j \in J}(c_j - x(o_{j1}))$
- $F_{mean} = \frac{\sum_{j \in J}(c_j - x(o_{j1}))}{|J|}$
- $WF_{mean} = \frac{\sum_{j \in J}(c_j - x(o_{j1})) \cdot \omega_j}{|J|}$
- $T_{max} = \max_{j \in J}(\max(c_j - d_j, 0))$
- $T_{mean} = \frac{\sum_{j \in J}(\max(c_j - d_j, 0))}{|J|}$
- $WT_{mean} = \frac{\sum_{j \in J}(\max(c_j - d_j, 0) \cdot \omega_j)}{|J|}$

2.2 Linear Genetic Programming

LGP [4] is a GP variant which has been successfully applied to classification [3, 9,12,17] and symbolic regression problems [8,19]. LGP individuals are sequences of register-based instructions. The instructions in a same sequence are executed sequentially to form a completed computer program. The linear arrangement of instructions and the sequential execution are two core meaning of the term "linear". For every single instruction in LGP, it contains three parts: source register, operation, and destination register. The values in the source registers serve as the inputs of the operation. The output from the operation is assigned to the destination register and passed to the subsequent instructions. To output the final result, at least one output register is needed for LGP. By default, the first register is regarded as the output register. Figure 1 is a simple example of LGP individual to represent a mathematical formula "$\max(xy, \min(x, -y))$". R_0, R_1 and R_2 are three registers. They serve as both source and destination registers. These registers are initialized by a certain value, such as zero in this example. The LGP individual can also be transformed into a directed acyclic graph (DAG) to be more compact.

The evolutionary framework of LGP is quite similar with the one of standard GP. But because of the different representation, LGP has two kinds of different genetic operators from standard GP [13]. The first type of genetic operators is macro variation. The term "macro" means that this kind of genetic operators produce offspring mainly by affecting the total number of instructions. The other type of genetic operators is micro variation. Contrarily, micro variation does not change the total number of instructions, but only changes the primitives inside instructions to produce offspring.

2.3   Related Work

In the literatures, there are two popular evolutionary multitask frameworks for existing GPHH methods. One is multifactorial evolutionary algorithm (MFEA) and the other is multitask multi-population GPHH (M^2GP).

Multifactorial Evolutionary Algorithm. MFEA was firstly proposed by Gupta et al. [10]. The main idea of MFEA is to use an evolutionary algorithm with a single population of individuals to solve different optimization tasks simultaneously. All of these individuals are encoded into a unified search space and can be transformed into a problem-specific representation to solve different tasks. To evolve the individuals for different tasks simultaneously, MFEA introduces four key properties, i.e., factorial cost, factorial rank, scalar fitness, and skill factor. Based on these properties, the effectiveness of an individual in solving a certain task can be represented by the factorial cost and rank. The individuals good at solving different tasks can be identified by different skill factors. The individuals with different skill factors can also make a fair comparison together based on the scalar fitness. To enable individuals to share the information among different tasks, Gupta et al. developed an assortative mating algorithm which allows individuals with different skill factors to perform crossover with a pre-defined probability. A vertical cultural transmission is also developed together with the assortative mating to propagate the skill factor from parent individuals to offspring.

Multitask Multi-population GPHH. M^2GP is proposed by Zhang et al. [22], which is a GP-specific multitask optimization framework. Specifically, M^2GP splits a GP population into several sub-populations, each for a single task. Every sub-population evolves GP individuals with the conventional evolutionary framework of GP. GP individuals in M^2GP are trained on different problem instances in different generations. GP individuals in M^2GP share their knowledge by swapping sub-trees across different sub-populations. Different from MFEA in which individuals may change their skill factor (i.e., corresponding task) by imitating different parents, GP individuals in M^2GP only evolve for a certain task and will not migrate to the other sub-populations. To improve the efficiency of multitask learning, M^2GP further proposes an origin-based offspring reservation strategy, which only keeps the offspring generated based on the parent from the corresponding sub-population and discards the other offspring in crossover. The empirical results show that M^2GP has a better performance than MFEA in solving dynamic flexible JSS problems.

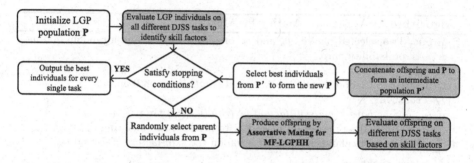

Fig. 2. Flowchart of MF-LGPHH

3 Multitask LGPHH

In this paper, we aim to make a preliminary investigation on the performance and the behaviour of LGP with off-the-shelf GPHH-specific multitask optimization techniques. Specifically, two multitask LGPHH methods are developed based on MFEA and M²GP respectively.

3.1 Multi-factorial LGPHH

Multi-factorial LGPHH (MF-LGP) is developed based on MFEA. The evolutionary framework of MF-LGP is shown in Fig. 2 where the dark boxes are the key differences from basic LGPHH methods. Initially, LGP individuals are randomly generated and evaluated on all different DJSS tasks to identify their skill factors. The minimum ranking among different tasks is regarded as the fitness of LGP individuals (i.e., scalar fitness). In every generation, parent individuals are randomly selected from the population. The offspring are generated by a newly developed LGP-specific assortative mating algorithm. This algorithm generates offspring by mutating instructions or exchanging instruction segments of parent individuals based on the skill factors of parents and a predefined random mating probability (rmp). The skill factors of offspring are also updated by inheriting from one of the parents. To improve the training efficiency, every LGP individual will be evaluated on only one corresponding DJSS scenario, which is specified by the skill factor. The performance of LGP heuristic is regarded as the fitness of individuals. Then, both of parent and offspring individuals are concatenated into an intermediate population. The best individuals of the intermediate population will be selected greedily and form the new population in next generation. To ensure the fitness of LGP individuals are comparable, all LGP individuals are evaluated on a same DJSS problem instance.

To be more specific, the newly developed LGP-specific assortative mating (shown in Algorithm 1) is designed based on [10] and the three basic genetic operators of LGP (i.e., crossover, macro mutation, and micro mutation). The algorithm accepts two randomly selected parents from the population. If the two parent individuals have the same skill factor or a randomly generated number is

---

Algorithm 1: Assortative Mating for MF-LGP

Input: Two selected parents p_a and p_b, crossover rate r_c, and a random mating
probability rmp.

Output: Two offspring c_a and c_b.

1 Generate two random numbers $rand1$ and $rand2$ between 0 and 1;

    `// crossover`

2 **if** *(p_a and p_b have same skill factor) or ($rand1 < r_c$)* **then**

3   Perform LGP crossover on p_a and p_b to produce two offspring c_a and c_b;

4   Perform vertical cultural transmission on the skill factors of c_a and c_b;

    `// macro mutation`

5 **else if** $rand2 < 0.5$ **then**

6   Apply LGP macro mutation on p_a and p_b respectively to produce offspring
    c_a and c_b;

    `// micro mutation`

7 **else**

8   Apply LGP micro mutation on p_a and p_b respectively to produce offspring
    c_a and c_b;

9 **Return** c_a and c_b.

---

smaller than the random mating probability, the crossover is performed on the parent individuals to produce offspring. The skill factors of offspring are updated based on the vertical cultural transmission proposed in [10]. If the two parents have different skill factors and the random mating probability is not satisfied, macro and micro mutation will be performed. In this algorithm, macro and micro mutation have the same probability in producing offspring. Since macro and micro mutation only accept one parent individual each time, the skill factor of the generated offspring is the same as that of the parent in mutation.

However, MF-LGP only uses one DJSS problem instance during evolution, and the performance of MF-LGP may be limited by the insufficient training instances. To have a comprehensive investigation, a MFEA-based LGPHH with GP selection paradigm is also developed. It replaces the selection paradigm of conventional MFEA into the one of standard GP, which applies tournament selection to select parents and replaces the old population by offspring. Since there is no concatenation of parents and offspring, the problem instances can be rotated every generation. This variant of MFEA-based LGPHH is denoted as MF-LGP$_{rotate}$.

3.2 Multitask Multi-population LGPHH

In this paper, we extend M^{2}GP to LGP to develop a new algorithm called M^{2}LGP. The flowchart of M^{2}LGP is shown in Fig. 3. The dark boxes in Fig. 3 also highlight key differences from basic LGP. Basically, it firstly initializes multiple populations of LGP individuals randomly. The individuals in a sub-population are only evaluated on a certain DJSS scenario. When the stopping conditions are not satisfied, M^{2}LGP reproduces offspring by origin-based offspring reservation

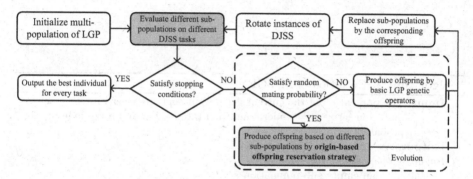

Fig. 3. Flowchart of M²LGP

strategy or basic LGP genetic operators based on a probability specified by a random mating probability. The sub-populations are then replaced by the offspring. The DJSS problem instance is rotated every generation. Finally, the best LGP individuals in the different sub-populations are outputted to test data.

Specifically, the evolution of M²LGP produces offspring by three basic kinds of LGP genetic operators. The pseudo code of the evolution is shown in Algorithm 2. To share the search information, the origin-based offspring reservation strategy proposed by Zhang et al. is also extended to LGP crossover. When the random number is smaller than rmp, LGP selects two parent individuals from different sub-populations. Then, LGP exchanges the instruction segments of the parent individuals and only retains the offspring from the parent individual of the corresponding sub-population. The old sub-population will be replaced by the newly generated offspring population.

4   Experiment Design

4.1   Multitask DJSS Scenarios

Based on the categorization in [22], there are two types of multitask settings in DJSS, i.e., heterogeneous and homogeneous multitask optimization. Specifically, heterogeneous multitask problems contain a set of DJSS problems whose optimization objectives are different but having a same utilization level. On the contrary, the DJSS problems in homogeneous multitask problems have a same optimization objective but different utilization levels. We develop three scenarios for each type of multitask settings. These six scenarios are listed in Table 1. The notation "$<x, y>$" denotes a task whose optimization objective is x and utilization level is y.

There are 10 machines for every problem instance. The new arrival jobs have a sequence of operations whose length ranges from 2 to 10. The processing time of operations is a continuous value from 1 to 99. Every job has a weight. Specifically, 20%, 20%, and 60% of the new jobs have a weight of 1, 4, and 2

Algorithm 2: Evolution of M²LGP

Input: The population of the current generation *pop*, crossover rate r_c, macro mutation rate r_{macro}, micro mutation rate r_{micro}, and a random mating probability *rmp*.

Output: An updated LGP population.

1 **for** *all sub-population s in pop* **do**
2 | Initialize an empty sub-population s_n;
3 | Load elite individuals from s to s_n by an elitism selection;
4 | **while** *size of s_n < size of s* **do**
5 | Generate a random number *rand1* between 0 and 1;
6 | Use tournament selection to select a parent individual p_a from s;
        // crossover
7 | **if** *rand1 < r_c* **then**
8 | Generate a random number *rand2* between 0 and 1;
9 | **if** *rand2 < rmp* **then**
10 | Select p_b from another sub-population $s'(s' \neq s)$ by tournament selection;
              // origin-based offspring reservation
11 | Swap an instruction segment from p_b to p_a to produce offspring c_a;
12 | $s_n = s_n \bigcup \{c_a\}$;
13 | **else**
14 | Select p_b from s by tournament selection;
15 | Perform LGP crossover on p_a and p_b to produce two offspring c_a and c_b;
16 | $s_n = s_n \bigcup \{c_a, c_b\}$;
        // macro mutation
17 | **else if** *rand1 < $r_c + r_{macro}$* **then**
18 | Apply LGP macro mutation on p_a to produce offspring c_a;
19 | $s_n = s_n \bigcup \{c_a\}$;
        // micro mutation
20 | **else if** *rand1 < $r_c + r_{macro} + r_{micro}$* **then**
21 | Apply LGP micro mutation on p_a to produce offspring c_a;
22 | $s_n = s_n \bigcup \{c_a\}$;
23 | **else**
24 | reproduce p_a to s_n.
25 | $s = s_n$;
26 **Return** *pop*.

Table 1. Problem settings of the multitask scenarios

Scenarios	task1	task2	task3
	homogeneous multitask		
homoFmean	$<F_{mean}, 0.95>$	$<F_{mean}, 0.85>$	$<F_{mean}, 0.75>$
homoTmean	$<T_{mean}, 0.95>$	$<T_{mean}, 0.85>$	$<T_{mean}, 0.75>$
homoWTmean	$<WT_{mean}, 0.95>$	$<WT_{mean}, 0.85>$	$<WT_{mean}, 0.75>$
	heterogeneous multitask		
heteFTMax	$<F_{max}, 0.95>$	$<T_{max}, 0.95>$	
heteFTMean	$<F_{mean}, 0.95>$	$<T_{mean}, 0.95>$	
heteWFTMean	$<WF_{mean}, 0.95>$	$<WT_{mean}, 0.95>$	

Table 2. The terminal set

Notation	Description
NIQ	the number of operations in the queue of a machine
WIQ	the total processing time of operations in the queue of a machine
MWT	the waiting time of the machine
PT	the processing time of the operation
NPT	the processing time of the next operation
OWT	the waiting time of the operation
NWT	the waiting time of the next to-be-ready machine
WKR	the total remaining processing time of the job
NOR	the number of remaining operations of the job
WINQ	total processing time of operations in the queue of the machine which specializes in the next operation of the job
NINQ	number of operations in the queue of the machine which specializes in the next operation of the job
rFDD	the difference between the expected due date of the operation and the system time
rDD	the difference between the expected due date of the job and the system time
W	the weight of the job
TIS	the difference between system time and the arrival time of the job
SL	the difference between the expected due date and the sum of the system time and WKR

respectively. During the simulation, the first 1000 jobs will be regarded as warm-up jobs to ensure that heuristics are evaluated in a steady state of job shops. The performance of a heuristic is evaluated by the subsequent 5000 jobs. For every scenario, 30 independent runs with different random seeds are carried out, and each output heuristic is tested on 50 unseen DJSS instances.

4.2 Comparison Methods

To investigate the three research questions, two comparison methods are developed. Firstly, a baseline method of LGPHH is adopted. It simply runs the LGPHH for each single task separately. In other words, there is no knowledge transfer among the tasks. LGPHH serves as a baseline for other multitask optimization techniques. Secondly, the state-of-the-art GPHH-specific multitask method, M²GP, is adopted. M²GP is based on tree-based GP.

Table 3. The mean (and standard deviation) of test performance in all multitask scenarios

Scenario	Task	LGPHH	M²GP	M²LGP	MF-LGP	MF-LGP$_{rotate}$
homo Fmean	$<F_{mean}, 0.95>$	1584.4(21.0)	**1569.3(10.5)**	1577.0(12.8)	1609.8(26.7)	1580.6(13.2)
	$<F_{mean}, 0.85>$	870.7(6.8)	**861.5(2.7)**	863.8(3.5)	874.4(6.1)	867.2(5.6)
	$<F_{mean}, 0.75>$	658.7(1.7)	**654.8(1.3)**	**655.0(1.6)**	656.9(2.2)	655.8(1.7)
homo Tmean	$<T_{mean}, 0.95>$	1129.3(8.7)	**1125.1(15.1)**	1125.3(11.9)	1165.3(26.9)	1134.3(13.8)
	$<T_{mean}, 0.85>$	427.1(5.9)	**415.9(2.1)**	417.1(2.9)	429.4(7.0)	419.2(4.2)
	$<T_{mean}, 0.75>$	218.9(1.7)	**215.0(1.1)**	**215.2(1.0)**	217.9(2.1)	**215.7(1.3)**
homo WTmean	$<WT_{mean}, 0.95>$	1817.0(29.4)	**1771.6(27.7)**	1804.9(27.3)	1839.2(24.9)	1787.5(26.3)
	$<WT_{mean}, 0.85>$	731.1(9.1)	**724.5(4.8)**	731.2(4.6)	745.5(12.0)	728.5(6.4)
	$<WT_{mean}, 0.75>$	394.3(2.5)	**391.5(1.6)**	393.8(2.0)	400.2(4.1)	**392.6(2.2)**
heteFT Max	$<F_{max}, 0.95>$	**4470.5(108.0)**	4551.7(173.5)	**4450.1(114.2)**	4794.1(203.6)	**4461.0(96.0)**
	$<T_{max}, 0.95>$	3945.2(117.3)	3991.2(117.1)	3878.4(90.5)	4272.7(170.8)	**3849.6(82.3)**
heteFT Mean	$<F_{mean}, 0.95>$	1579.8(10.6)	**1570.2(8.4)**	1570.1(11.7)	1620.1(31.0)	**1572.2(15.0)**
	$<T_{mean}, 0.95>$	1132.9(23.0)	**1119.1(9.7)**	**1121.8(13.5)**	1167.0(28.1)	**1122.1(14.0)**
heteW FTMean	$<WF_{mean}, 0.95>$	2793.7(31.7)	**2763.7(23.0)**	2783.0(34.6)	2813.9(26.0)	2781.5(35.6)
	$<WT_{mean}, 0.95>$	1803.4(30.2)	**1771.4(25.6)**	1799.4(35.4)	1823.1(26.5)	1792.9(33.8)
	Average rank	3.40	2.09	2.51	4.42	2.57

bold font: a method is significantly better than most of other methods on a certain task.
M²LGP: Multitask Multi-population LGPHH; MF-LGP: Multi-factorial LGPHH;
MF-LGP$_{rotate}$: Multi-factorial LGPHH with training instance rotation.

The parameters of these methods are designed based on [22]. Basically, the population size and the number of sub-populations vary with the number of tasks. When there are k tasks, there will be k sub-populations for the methods based on M²GP, and there will be totally $k \times 200$ individuals for all LGP methods ($k \times 400$ individuals for tree-based GP methods). The total number of generations is 102 for LGP methods and 51 for tree-based GP methods. Every LGP individual has a maximum of 50 instructions. Each manipulates four available registers. The first register is regarded as the output register. To facilitate the knowledge transfer among tasks, LGP adopts a kind of effective macro mutation and a linear crossover to produce offspring. Specifically, the effective macro mutation inserts (or removes) an effective instruction into (from) heuristics, and will remove all ineffective instructions after mutation. The maximum crossover length and the maximum length difference of the linear crossover are both 30. Specifically, the crossover, macro and micro mutation rate of M²LGP are 60%, 10%, and 25% respectively. The hyper parameters of tree-based GP are set the same as the ones of [22]. A terminal set including sixteen terminals is designed for the GP methods, which is shown in Table 2.

5   Results and Discussion

5.1   Test Performance

To analyze the effectiveness of multitask LGPHH, the test performance of the five methods are compared, as shown in Table 3. A Friedman test with a significance level of 0.05 is also applied to the test performance analysis. The average rank below the table shows the overall ranking of all algorithms based on the Friedman test. The p-value of the Friedman test on the test performance is 1.3e−08, which means there is a significant difference among all of these algorithms. Therefore, a pairwise Wilcoxon test with false discovery rate correction (by the Benjamini and Hochberg method) and a significance level of 0.05 is further applied to every pair of these methods. The bold results in the table highlight the methods which are significantly better than most of other methods.

To answer the first research questions, i.e., which existing multitask framework is suitable to LGPHH, the baseline LGPHH, M^2LGP and the two MFEA-based LGPHH are compared. Generally speaking, M^2LGP and MF-LGP$_{rotate}$ have a quite competitive performance with each other. They show a similar average ranking about 2.5. They also have a significantly better performance than the baseline method in most of the scenarios based on the Wilcoxon test. However, the simple combination of LGPHH and MFEA does not work very well in all these scenarios. Its average rank is 4.42 among the five algorithms. Given that the optimization problems in the paper are minimization problems, MF-LGP has the worst performance in most cases. The results of the three multitask LGPHH methods imply that simply replacing LGPHH into the existing multitask frameworks is not always a good way. It is likely for multitask LGPHH to work poorly, especially when there are some unsuitable designs for LGPHH in multitask frameworks. Based on the results, it is advisable for LGPHH to be adopted in M^2LGP and MF-LGP$_{rotate}$ which enable LGPHH to have sufficient training instances by GP selection methods.

To investigate the effectiveness of multitask LGPHH compared with tree-based GPHH, M^2GP, M^2LGP, and MF-LGP$_{rotate}$ are further compared. Basically, M^2LGP and MF-LGP$_{rotate}$ are less effective than the state-of-the-art method, i.e., M^2GP. The results of the average rank show that M^2LGP and MF-LGP$_{rotate}$ have a bigger value than M^2GP. It implies that M^2GP has a better overall performance than the two LGPHH-based multitask algorithms. Although the performance of M^2LGP and MF-LGP$_{rotate}$ are quite competitive with M^2GP in the three heterogeneous scenarios, they are inferior to M^2GP in the three homogeneous multitask scenarios based on the Wilcoxon test. The test effectiveness of multitask LGPHH methods should be further improved.

5.2   Example Program Analysis

To analyze how LGPHH shares useful knowledge among different tasks, we sample some example heuristics from all independent runs. Here, three heuristics from an independent run of M²LGP in solving homoWTmean and two heuristics from an independent run of MF-LGP in solving heteFTMax are selected. These LGP-based heuristics are transformed into DAGs and are shown in Fig. 4. The nodes of the DAGs represent different operations or terminals (oval for operations and rectangle for terminals). Each node has at most two output edges. These output edges accept the result from the node that it points to. The "0" and "1" beside edges respectively denote the first and second argument of operations. The final heuristic value is outputted from the top node.

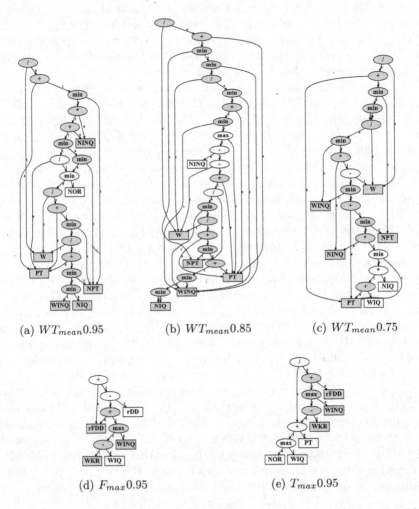

(a) $WT_{mean}0.95$ (b) $WT_{mean}0.85$ (c) $WT_{mean}0.75$

(d) $F_{max}0.95$ (e) $T_{max}0.95$

Fig. 4. Three example programs from homoWTmean and two example programs from heteFTMax

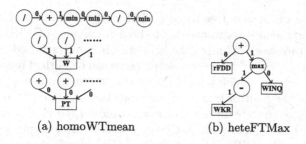

(a) homoWTmean   (b) heteFTMax

Fig. 5. Examples of common patterns in heuristics

If we have a closer look on these DAGs, some common patterns with at least three nodes can be found among the scheduling heuristics from a same scenario. The common patterns of these scheduling heuristics are highlighted in grey. Figure 5 shows some example common patterns in these heuristics. For the tasks of WT_{mean}, the three heuristics share common building blocks of dividing job weight and adding the processing time of next operation multiple times. These building blocks are also reused multiple times in these heuristics. It implies that it is advisable to select the operations with large weight and short processing time in minimizing the weighted mean tardiness. Besides, LGP-based heuristics can also share some "high-level" structures of operation combinations. The "$/, +, \min$" structure is adopted by two of the heuristics at the top of the DAGs. For the tasks of F_{max} and T_{max}, the two heuristics share a building block of "$rFDD + \max(WINQ, -WKR)$". It implies that, to minimize the maximum flowtime and tardiness, prioritizing the operations which are close to the due date (i.e., small $rFDD$) and have a lot of remaining work (i.e., large WKR) is a useful strategy. Besides, the operations which do not suffer from bottle neck machines (i.e., small $WINQ$) should also be processed as soon as possible. Averagely, more than half of the nodes are covered by at least one repeated patterns in these five heuristics. The results validate that LGP-based heuristics can share useful building blocks and operation combinations in the two existing multitask frameworks.

6 Conclusion

This paper makes an investigation of LGPHH methods with different evolutionary multitask frameworks. To extend LGPHH to two existing multitask frameworks, we have developed two LGPHH-based multitask methods, which are MF-LGP and M²LGP, based on the characteristics of LGPHH. These methods are examined on six different multitask scenarios, including three homogeneous and three heterogeneous scenarios. Some conclusions are drawn out based on the comparison. Firstly, the results show that M²GP and MFEA with training instance rotation help LGPHH to have an effective test performance in multitask learning. It implies that LGPHH is suitable to those frameworks with more GPHH characteristics. Secondly, the multitask LGPHH methods based on off-the-shelf frameworks are worse than tree-based GPHH methods in terms of test effectiveness. Designing a multitask framework to further enhance LGPHH performance will be our future work. Thirdly, the heuristics in multitask LGPHH can share some common patterns. These common patterns can be both of reusable building blocks and operation combinations. By sharing these common patterns among different tasks, the multitask LGPHH methods can be more effective than solving these tasks separately. In our future work, more LGP characteristics will be considered in the design of multitask frameworks, to further enhance the performance of multitask LGPHH. For example, LGP individuals can have multiple output registers to solve different tasks, and some selective crossovers can be developed based on different output registers.

References

1. Al-Sahaf, H., et al.: A survey on evolutionary machine learning. J. R. Soc. N. Z. **49**(2), 205–228 (2019)
2. Ardeh, M.A., Mei, Y., Zhang, M.: A novel multi-task genetic programming approach to uncertain capacitated Arc routing problem. In: Proceedings of the Genetic and Evolutionary Computation Conference, pp. 759–767 (2021)
3. Brameier, M., Banzhaf, W.: A comparison of linear genetic programming and neural networks in medical data mining. IEEE Trans. Evol. Comput. **5**(1), 17–26 (2001)
4. Brameier, M., Banzhaf, W.: Linear Genetic Programming, vol. 53. Springer, Boston (2007). https://doi.org/10.1007/978-0-387-31030-5
5. Branke, J., Nguyen, S., Pickardt, C.W., Zhang, M.: Automated design of production scheduling heuristics: a review. IEEE Trans. Evol. Comput. **20**(1), 110–124 (2016)
6. Burke, E.K., Hyde, M.R., Kendall, G., Ochoa, G., Özcan, E., Woodward, J.R.: A classification of hyper-heuristic approaches: revisited. In: Gendreau, M., Potvin, J.-Y. (eds.) Handbook of Metaheuristics. ISORMS, vol. 272, pp. 453–477. Springer, Cham (2019). https://doi.org/10.1007/978-3-319-91086-4_14
7. Chandra, R., Ong, Y.S., Goh, C.K.: Co-evolutionary multi-task learning for dynamic time series prediction. Appl. Soft Comput. J. **70**, 576–589 (2018)
8. Dal Piccol Sotto, L.F., De Melo, V.V.: A probabilistic linear genetic programming with stochastic context-free grammar for solving symbolic regression problems. In: Proceedings of the Genetic and Evolutionary Computation Conference, pp. 1017–1024 (2017)
9. Downey, C., Zhang, M., Liu, J.: Parallel linear genetic programming for multi-class classification. Genet. Program Evolvable Mach. **13**(3), 275–304 (2012). https://doi.org/10.1007/s10710-012-9162-9
10. Gupta, A., Ong, Y.S., Feng, L.: Multifactorial evolution: toward evolutionary multitasking. IEEE Trans. Evol. Comput. **20**(3), 343–357 (2016)
11. Huang, S., Zhong, J., Yu, W.J.: Surrogate-assisted evolutionary framework with adaptive knowledge transfer for multi-task optimization. IEEE Trans. Emerg. Top. Comput. **9**(4), 1930–1944 (2019)
12. Kantschik, W., Banzhaf, W.: Linear-tree GP and its comparison with other GP structures. In: Miller, J., Tomassini, M., Lanzi, P.L., Ryan, C., Tettamanzi, A.G.B., Langdon, W.B. (eds.) EuroGP 2001. LNCS, vol. 2038, pp. 302–312. Springer, Heidelberg (2001). https://doi.org/10.1007/3-540-45355-5_24

13. Koza, J.R.: Genetic programming as a means for programming computers by natural selection. Stat. Comput. **4**(2), 87–112 (1994). https://doi.org/10.1007/BF00175355

14. Nguyen, S., Mei, Y., Zhang, M.: Genetic programming for production scheduling: a survey with a unified framework. Complex Intell. Syst. **3**(1), 41–66 (2017). https://doi.org/10.1007/s40747-017-0036-x

15. Nguyen, S., Zhang, M., Tan, K.C.: Surrogate-assisted genetic programming with simplified models for automated design of dispatching rules. IEEE Trans. Cybern. **47**(9), 2951–2965 (2017)

16. Park, J., Mei, Y., Nguyen, S., Chen, G., Zhang, M.: Evolutionary multitask optimisation for dynamic job shop scheduling using niched genetic programming. In: Mitrovic, T., Xue, B., Li, X. (eds.) AI 2018. LNCS (LNAI), vol. 11320, pp. 739–751. Springer, Cham (2018). https://doi.org/10.1007/978-3-030-03991-2_66

17. Provorovs, S., Borisov, A.: Use of linear genetic programming and artificial neural network methods to solve classification task. Sci. J. Riga Tech. Univ. Comput. Sci. **45**(1), 133–139 (2012)

18. Sanchez, M., Cruz-Duarte, J.M., Ortiz-Bayliss, J.C., Ceballos, H., Terashima-Marin, H., Amaya, I.: A systematic review of hyper-heuristics on combinatorial optimization problems. IEEE Access **8**, 128068–128095 (2020)

19. Wilson, G., Banzhaf, W.: A comparison of cartesian genetic programming and linear genetic programming. In: O'Neill, M., et al. (eds.) EuroGP 2008. LNCS, vol. 4971, pp. 182–193. Springer, Heidelberg (2008). https://doi.org/10.1007/978-3-540-78671-9_16

20. Xu, Q., Wang, N., Wang, L., Li, W., Sun, Q.: Multi-task optimization and multitask evolutionary computation in the past five years: a brief review. Mathematics **9**(8), 1–44 (2021)

21. Yi, J., Bai, J., He, H., Zhou, W., Yao, L.: A multifactorial evolutionary algorithm for multitasking under interval uncertainties. IEEE Trans. Evol. Comput. **24**(5), 908–922 (2020)

22. Zhang, F., Mei, Y., Nguyen, S., Tan, K.C., Zhang, M.: Multitask genetic programming-based generative hyperheuristics: a case study in dynamic scheduling. IEEE Trans. Cybern. 1–14 (2021). https://doi.org/10.1109/TCYB.2021.3065340

23. Zhang, F., Mei, Y., Nguyen, S., Zhang, M.: A preliminary approach to evolutionary multitasking for dynamic flexible job shop scheduling via genetic programming. In: Proceedings of Genetic and Evolutionary Computation Conference Companion, pp. 107–108 (2020)

24. Zhang, F., Mei, Y., Nguyen, S., Zhang, M.: Collaborative multifidelity-based surrogate models for genetic programming in dynamic flexible job shop scheduling. IEEE Trans. Cybern. 1–15 (2021). https://doi.org/10.1109/TCYB.2021.3050141

25. Zhang, F., Mei, Y., Nguyen, S., Zhang, M.: Correlation coefficient-based recombinative guidance for genetic programming hyperheuristics in dynamic flexible job shop scheduling. IEEE Trans. Evol. Comput. **25**(3), 552–566 (2021)

26. Zhang, F., Mei, Y., Nguyen, S., Zhang, M.: Evolving scheduling heuristics via genetic programming with feature selection in dynamic flexible job-shop scheduling. IEEE Trans. Cybern. **51**(4), 1797–1811 (2021)

27. Zhang, F., Mei, Y., Nguyen, S., Zhang, M., Tan, K.C.: Surrogate-assisted evolutionary multitasking genetic programming for dynamic flexible job shop scheduling. IEEE Trans. Evol. Comput. **25**(4), 651–665 (2021)

28. Zhang, F., Nguyen, S., Mei, Y., Zhang, M.: Genetic Programming for Production Scheduling - An Evolutionary Learning Approach. Springer, Singapore (2021). https://doi.org/10.1007/978-981-16-4859-5
29. Zhou, L., Feng, L., Zhong, J., Ong, Y.S., Zhu, Z., Sha, E.: Evolutionary multitasking in combinatorial search spaces: a case study in capacitated vehicle routing problem. In: IEEE Symposium Series on Computational Intelligence (2016)

Cooperative Co-evolution and Adaptive Team Composition for a Multi-rover Resource Allocation Problem

Nicolas Fontbonne[1]([⊠]), Nicolas Maudet[2], and Nicolas Bredeche[1]

[1] Sorbonne Université, CNRS, ISIR, 75005 Paris, France
nicolas.fontbonne@sorbonne-universite.fr
[2] Sorbonne Université, LIP6, 75005 Paris, France

Abstract. In this paper, we are interested in ad hoc autonomous agent team composition using cooperative co-evolutionary algorithms (CCEA). In order to accurately capture the individual contribution of team agents, we propose to limit the number of agents which are updated in-between team evaluations. However, this raises two important problems with respect to (1) the cost of accurately estimating the marginal contribution of agents with respect to the team learning speed and (2) completing tasks where improving team performance requires multiple agents to update their policies in a synchronized manner. We introduce a CCEA algorithm that is capable of learning how to update just the right amount of agents' policies for the task at hand. We use a variation of the El Farol Bar problem, formulated as a multi-robot resource selection problem, to provide an experimental validation of the algorithms proposed.

Keywords: ad hoc autonomous agent teams · multi-agent systems · marginal contribution · team composition · multi-robots · cooperative co-evolutionary algorithms (CCEA) · evolutionary computation · evolutionary robotics

1 Introduction

When multiple individuals get together to solve a task, it is sometimes difficult to identify who is actually contributing, and who is not. This is especially problematic when the benefits are equally shared among individuals, including with free-riders who invest a minimal amount of effort. Nature abounds from such examples and various strategies evolved to mitigate the detrimental cost of free-riding, such as partner choice or reputation [11,22].

The problem of identifying the marginal contribution of individuals has also been studied extensively in cooperative game theory [18]. However, exact methods such as computing the Shapley value [17] require strong assumptions (e.g. ability to replay coalitions) and unrealistic computation time, which have led to a flourishing research into the design of approximate methods [21,23,24]. The basic idea

E. Medvet et al. (Eds.): EuroGP 2022, LNCS 13223, pp. 179–193, 2022.
https://doi.org/10.1007/978-3-031-02056-8_12

of such methods is to identify the individual's contribution by computing the difference between the group performance with and without this very individual (e.g. by removing it or by replacing it with an individual with a default strategy).

In this research, we are interested in ad hoc autonomous agent teams where agents must act together without pre-coordination [19], which implies that the environment is non-stationary as all agents learn in parallel. This requires using methods that can only alter individuals' strategy, with neither a default strategy being known nor the possibility to remove temporarily one particular individual.

Such problem settings have been explored in evolutionary computation for multiagent systems, and notably with Cooperative Co-Evolutionary Algorithms (CCEA) which were first introduced in [13,14] and largely explored since then (see [10] for a review of variants and applications). In particular, CCEA have been explored in setups involving multiple robotic agents in tasks such as exploration and foraging [7] and environment monitoring [15,16,25].

In this paper, we address the problem of isolating team members so as to identify their contribution within the collective. On the one hand, one could allow only a single agent to learn at a given time, making it possible to measure accurately its contribution as other agents' strategies would remain stationary. On the other hand, several (or all) of the agents' policies could be iterated at the same time, possibly speeding up learning thanks to parallelization.

Balancing between providing accurate estimation of an individual contribution and parallelization of learning actually depends on the context at hand. When rewards are sparse and depend on a single individual's behavioural innovation, it is preferable to bootstrap learning with large-scale exploration. However, whenever team performance increases it is more efficient to turn towards a more conservative search so as to retain previous improvements. Finally, one less obvious situation arises when the synergy between individuals is required to improve performance, for example when two robots are required to open a door, none of which would gain any benefit by acting alone.

The rest of the paper is organized as follows. Section 2 presents the problem of team composition in CCEA. Section 3 presents two CCEA algorithms that enable to tune the number of learning agents within one learning step. The two algorithms differ with respect to how the balance between contribution estimation accuracy and learning parallelization is set: fixed, or self-adaptive. Section 4 presents the problem used for evaluation, which is a modified version of the famous Bar El Farol problem [1] formulated as a multi-robot resource allocation problem where coordination is required (i.e. several resources must be harvested and harvesting is extremely beneficial it the optimal fixed number of robots is met). Results are presented in Sect. 5 for both the ad hoc version of and the self-adaptive versions of the algorithm.

2   Cooperative Coevolutionary and Team Composition

In its most simple setup, cooperative co-evolutionary algorithms (CCEA) rely on a collection of independent evolutionary algorithms, with each dedicated to optimizing the policy of one particular agent of the team [4, 5]. Each independent algorithm works to improve the performance of one agent's control parameters using an assessment of the team performance.

Each algorithm maintains a population of parameter sets, which define candidate policies for the agent this algorithm is in charge of. At each generation, performance assessment is computed for various teams. Then, each instance of the CCEA tries to improve its agent's performance by using classic evolutionary operators of selection, mutation and recombination.

The problem faced by CCEA is thus a black-box optimization problem, with the additional twist that evaluation is for the *whole* team, and optimization is performed at the individual level, thus implying a weak link between team evaluation and the actual individual behaviour. Defining $\boldsymbol{\theta}$ as the vector containing the parameters provided by each algorithm of the CCEA, F as the fitness function used to assess team performance and f the fitness value, we have:

$$F : \text{team parameters } \boldsymbol{\theta} \longrightarrow \text{fitness value } f$$

Figure 1 illustrates the learning loop of a simple multi-agent black-box optimization procedure for cooperative co-evolution. A given algorithm in charge of a particular agent i will provide policy parameters θ^i for this agent to be evaluated in a team. These parameters will be evaluated alongside parameters provided by the other agents. The team is then evaluated and a fitness value is returned.

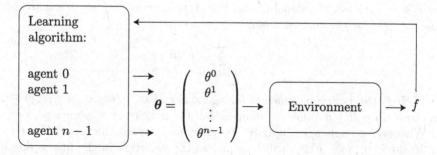

Fig. 1. The learning loop of interaction. All agents submit their own parameters independently for evaluation. They are evaluated at the same time on the environment or task. This return the fitness f of the whole team. Finally this feedback is used by all agent to update their parameters submission for next iteration.

After an evaluation, each agent has to evaluate if the new set of parameters proposed θ^i has contributed to the team fitness in a negative, positive or neutral manner. It is necessary to extract from the fitness $f = F(\boldsymbol{\theta})$, the part which depends only on the parameters of the agent i, $F^i(\theta^i)$.

From an agent's viewpoint, an increase in team performance may be due to others, and may even shadow a decrease in the very contribution the agent performs. In order to mitigate the intrinsically noisy fitness evaluation due to team heterogeneity (team composition changes over time), multiple evaluations of the same set of policy parameters will be performed for a given agent, so that different versions of θ^i can be ranked and further selected to create new candidate policies for the next generation. However, obtaining an exact assessment of one individual's contribution to the team remains elusive unless all other individuals follow static policies. Considering teams formed of n team agents, with each agent's evolutionary algorithm maintaining a population of p candidate policies, complexity would be $\mathcal{O}(p^n)$ at each generation.

In order to provide results in a reasonable time, CCEA generally relies on a partial evaluation of agents' policy contribution, by evaluating a subset of all possible team compositions at each iteration. Though such implementation breaks down complexity, CCEA algorithms have been shown to have a tendency to prematurely converge to stable states because of a deceptive fitness landscape created by the choice of collaborators for evaluation [6,12]. Several methods have been proposed to address these issues, including novelty-based rewards to escape local minima [7] or automatically merging populations when agents' behaviours are similar to address scalability issues [8,9]. However, the contribution of one specific agent remains approximated rather than precisely measured.

3   Cooperative Co-evolutionary Algorithms with Limited Team Composition Update

In the simplest case, the global fitness $F(\boldsymbol{\theta})$ is the sum of each agent's individual fitness $F^i(\theta^i)$ for the current team:

$$F(\boldsymbol{\theta}) = \sum_{i \in \text{agents}} F^i(\theta^i)$$

With θ^i the policy parameters for agent i, and $\boldsymbol{\theta} = (\theta^0, \ldots, \theta^i, \ldots, \theta^{N-1})$, i.e. the team policy parameters composed of the policies of N agents.

Whenever a single agent updates its policy parameters, the variation in overall fitness $F(\boldsymbol{\theta}_{t+1}) - F(\boldsymbol{\theta}_t)$ will be equal to the variation in the fitness due to the change in behaviour of the agent concerned δF^i. This can be written as:

$$\begin{aligned}
F(\boldsymbol{\theta}_{t+1}) - F(\boldsymbol{\theta}_t) &= F^{-i}(\theta_{t+1}^{-i}) + F^i(\theta_{t+1}^i) - F^{-i}(\theta_t^{-i}) - F^i(\theta_t^i) \\
&= F^i(\theta_{t+1}^i) - F^i(\theta_t^i) \qquad\qquad (1) \\
&= \delta F^i
\end{aligned}$$

With $F^{-i}(\theta^{-i})$ the performance of all individuals minus the agent i, assuming θ^{-i} is stationary between t and $t+1$. Though an exact value for the contribution of agent i remains unavailable, δF^i gives a proxy which provides sufficient information to measure both the direction and amplitude of the change due to agent i's new policy.

Assuming agents are independent, the above equation holds true and can be used as long as only one agent's policy is changed at a time. However, this assumption incurs two important limitations:

- The computational cost of iterating over a single agent's strategy at a time is high (see previous Section), and there is a trade-off between the quality of one agent's contribution estimation and the expected gain at the level of the team (e.g. whenever a single robot is needed to significantly improve team performance, trying with all robots is relevant);
- The task may require coupling between the agents' behaviour, and any team fitness improvements may require that *several* agents change their policy parameters simultaneously (e.g. moving a heavy object can only be done with two robots). If not, a CCEA can get stuck on a local minimum if we assume independence between agents and change only one agent at a time.

In order to address these issues and still retain the benefit of accurate estimation of the agents' contribution, we propose a CCEA algorithm where it is possible to modulate the number of agents that are updated in-between team evaluations. We use a collection of $(1+1)$-GA algorithm where each $(1+1)$-GA algorithm i provides the policy parameters θ^i for its corresponding agent i, and the whole team is evaluated using all agents with their policy parameters, i.e. $\theta = (\theta^0, \ldots, \theta^{N-1})$.

Algorithm 1: CC-$(1+1)$-GA$_{k_{\text{fixed}}}$
Introducing k mutants per iteration

---

1   $k \leftarrow$ number of team members to be updated;
2   $N \leftarrow$ total number of agents;
3   $\theta_{\text{parent}} \leftarrow$ parameters initialisation;
4   $f_{\text{parent}} \leftarrow F(\theta_{\text{parent}})$;
5   **for** *gen < nb max generation* **do**
6 | ID $\leftarrow$ randomly sample k agents;
7 | $\theta_{\text{child}}^{ID} \leftarrow$ mutate$(\theta_{\text{parent}}^{ID})$;
8 | $f_{\text{child}} \leftarrow F(\theta_{\text{child}}^{ID}, \theta_{\text{parent}}^{-ID})$;
9 | **if** $f_{child} \geq f_{parent}$ **then**
10 | | $\theta_{\text{parent}}^{ID} \leftarrow \theta_{\text{child}}^{ID}$;
11 | | $f_{\text{parent}} \leftarrow f_{\text{child}}$;
12 | **end**
13 **end**

Algorithm 1 details the complete CCEA, which runs multiple instance of $(1+1)$-GA in parallel, which we will refer to as the CC-$(1+1)$-GA$_{k_{\text{fixed}}}$ algorithm from now on. Each $(1+1)$-GA algorithm maintains a population of two individuals [3], a parent θ_{parent}^i and a child θ_{child}^i. Both are candidate policy parameters for agent i. The parent is replaced when the child fares better, and a new child is created by applying mutation on the new parent. Whenever a child fails to outperform its parent, it is replaced by a new child mutated from the current parent. The mutation operator depends on the problem (e.g. Gaussian mutation, bit-flip, uniform draw).

At each new iteration, k agents are drawn and randomly changed in the team, with $0 < k \leq N$. The k parameter is used to tune the amount of renewal k/N for the team composition in-between iterations of the CCEA algorithm. The k new team members are kept only if they provide an increase in the team fitness. Therefore, the challenge is to find the most efficient size k of the number of team agents to be modified at each CCEA steps. So far, k is fixed beforehand by the user, and may benefits from prior knowledge on the task regarding possible required coupling between agents, in terms of number of agents to change simultaneously to reach the global optimum in terms of team efficiency.

However, such prior knowledge may not be available and a relevant value of k not only depends on the problem (e.g. some problems may require coupling between agents, others may not), but also on the current state of the optimization (e.g. broad initial search steps vs. refined tuning near the optimal solution). In order to address this, we propose the CC-(1+1)-GA$_{k_{\text{adaptive}}}$, where the k parameter is learned during the course of evolution (see Algorithm 2). We propose to choose the number of team members to be updated by using the adversarial bandit learning algorithm EXP3 (Exponential-weight algorithm for Exploration and Exploitation [2]) that tracks the success rate of various possible values for k so far, which means both exploiting the current best value and exploring alternate values. The goal of the adaptation mechanism is to converge to the best possible value for k for the context at hand, i.e. the value that leads to the largest increase of fitness, whether through rare but important increases or through small but frequent increases.

As described in Algorithm 2, we define a set of J possible values for k $(k_0, ..., k_{J-1})$, each associated with a weight $W(k_j)$ monitoring the success rate of a particular k_j. Lines 10–13 of the algorithm detail which k_j is selected for a particular iteration. We compute the probability distribution of each k_j which depends on the weight $W(k_j)$ and the parameter γ of the algorithm. $\gamma \to 1$ favours exploration (i.e. the choice of k_j will be almost uniform). On the contrary, $\gamma \to 0$ favours exploitation, taken into account the importance of the weights $W(k_j)$. The fitness gain is normalized between $[0, 1]$ (Line 20) and then used to update the weight $W(k_j)$ (Line 21).

4   The Multi-rover Resource Selection Problem

We define a problem that is a variation of the well-known El Farol bar problem [1, 24] where each individual must choose a day to go to the bar among M possible choices with the criterion of not being too numerous each days. In our setup, we consider the problem where N independent robots must spread over M resources, and where each resource has an optimal capacity c in terms of number of robots

---

Algorithm 2: CC-(1+1)-GA$_{k_{adaptive}}$
Replacing a varying number of team agents per iteration

---

1   $K \leftarrow$ table of possible number of team members to update simultaneously ;
2   $W \leftarrow$ table of weights for each k;
3   $P \leftarrow$ table of probability for each k;
4   $k \leftarrow$ number of team members to be updated ;
5   $N \leftarrow$ total number of agents;
6   $\theta_{parent} \leftarrow$ parameters initialization;
7   $\gamma \leftarrow$ real $\in [0, 1]$, parameter for the **EXP3** algorithm ;
8   $f_{parent} \leftarrow F(\theta_{parent})$;
9   **for** *gen < nb max generation* **do**
10   **for** $j = 1, \ldots, J$ **do**
11     $P[j] \leftarrow (1 - \gamma)\frac{W[j]}{\sum_{i=1}^{J} W[i]} + \frac{\gamma}{J}$
12   **end**
13    $k_j \leftarrow$ random draw in $K[]$ with probabilities $P[]$;
14   ID $\leftarrow$ randomly sample k agents;
15    $\theta_{child}^{ID} \leftarrow$ mutate(θ_{parent}^{ID});
16    $f_{child} \leftarrow F(\theta_{child}^{ID}, \theta_{parent}^{-ID})$;
17   **if** $f_{child} \geq f_{parent}$ **then**
18     $\theta_{parent}^{ID} \leftarrow \theta_{child}^{ID}$;
19     $f_{parent} \leftarrow f_{child}$;
20     $R \leftarrow \tanh\left(\frac{f_{child}}{f_{parent}}\right)$;
21     $W[j] \leftarrow W[j]\exp\left(\frac{\gamma R}{P[j]J}\right)$;
22   **end**
23 **end**

---

necessary to optimally harvest it. This is illustrated in Fig. 2, which provides an example where each robot chooses a resource.

Team performance f is obtained by adding each resource's satisfaction ϕ_c. For each resource, its satisfaction ϕ_c depends on the number of robots r who chose it. This satisfaction is described by the following equation:

$$\phi_c(r) = \begin{cases} Mr\exp(\frac{-r}{c}) & \text{if } r = c \\ r\exp(\frac{-r}{c}) & \text{else.} \end{cases} \qquad (2)$$

where r represents the amount of robots on the resource, M the total number of resources, and c controls the optimal number of robots required for the resource.

The satisfaction function diverges from the original formulation of the El Farol Bar problem as the best team performance always implies that the number of robots per resource must be optimal (exactly c robots per resource), even if it implies some resources are left aside or only partially filled. The satisfaction boost for the $r = c$ case ensures that filling a maximum number of resources with the c robots is the optimal strategy. An example of such function with $c = 10$ is plotted on Fig. 3.

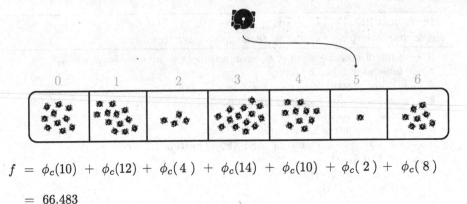

$$f = \phi_c(10) + \phi_c(12) + \phi_c(4) + \phi_c(14) + \phi_c(10) + \phi_c(2) + \phi_c(8)$$

$$= 66.483$$

Fig. 2. The $N = 60$ robots are represented here as little rovers that each must choose between $M = 7$ resources. Here the selected agent chooses resource 5. When all robots have made their choices, the satisfaction for each resources are computed and summed to obtain the fitness f of the team.

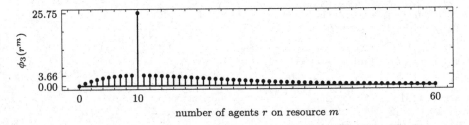

Fig. 3. Satisfaction function with $c = 10$ of a given resource, depending on the number of robots that picked it

The fitness of a team is then the sum of the satisfaction for all resources:

$$f = \sum_{m \in [0, M-1]} \phi_c(r^m)$$

where r^m is the number of robots at resource m. The robots must coordinate to optimally fill a maximum number of resources.

To increase the value of this function, it is then necessary to move individuals from crowded resources to resources with fewer robots, up to the extent that resources with the exact number of robots are favoured.

The number of robots N, the number of resources M, and the optimal number of robots per resource c can be modified to change the structure of the problem. In the next section, different instances of this problem are used to study various properties of the algorithms we proposed in the previous section. In particular, it is possible to set up the problem so that either single or multiple changes in the team composition may always yield too few or too many permutations in the team distribution over resources for team performance to increase.

5   Results

5.1   Experimental Setting

We use the Multi-Rover Resource Selection problem, with different number of resources M, number of agents N, and optimal number of robots per resource c. The three setups used are:

- **Setup 1** with $N = 120$, $M = 300$, and $c = 30$. There are many resources, each requiring a large number of robots. The maximum performance could be reached by a team of exactly $M \times c = 300 \times 30 = 9000$ agents. Given the limited number of agents, they must spread over a few of the resources ($N/c = 120/30 = 4$ resources) so that the team reaches optimal performance;
- **Setup 2** with $N = 900$, $M = 300$, and $c = 3$. The number of robots involved makes it possible to reach the optimal team performance value for this setup ($N = M \times c$) if all agents are uniformly spread over the resources;
- **Setup 3** with $N = 60$, $M = 7$, and $c = 10$. There exists several configurations of pairing agents and resources which are local optima *and* cannot be escaped by updating only one agent in the team. Figure 4 gives an example of a sub-optimal configuration for which using $k = 1$ is detrimental. When the algorithm gets into such a configuration, all possible updates of a unique agent will decrease the team fitness. Escaping such a local optimum requires either exploring new configurations at the cost of a (hopefully temporary) decrease in team performance (see [7] for example using novelty search in CCEA, which is out-of-scope of the current paper) or modifying several agents at the same time (which is possible with $k > 1$).

In the following, we use both the CC-$(1+1)$-GA$_{k_{\text{fixed}}}$ algorithm with either $k = 1$, 10 or 30, and the CC-$(1+1)$-GA$_{k_{\text{adaptive}}}$ algorithm (using EXP3) for learning the value of k in $\{1, 10, 30\}$. All experiments are replicated 32 times. Mean and standard deviation for all algorithm variants are traced. Evaluations is used on the x-axis to provide a fair comparison in terms of computational effort.

5.2   Fixed vs. Adaptive Methods for Team Composition Update

Starting with the three variants of the CC-$(1+1)$-GA$_{k_{\text{fixed}}}$ algorithm, we can observe different learning dynamics depending both on the value of k and the setup at hand.

In the first setup (Fig. 5(a)), we observe a clear benefit for using $k = 10$ and $k = 30$ during the first iterations. But this initial gain in performance does not allow it to converge faster when using $k = 1$. In particular, a value of $k = 30$ is extremely deleterious for the convergence as it fails to reach the optimum value within the allocated evaluation budget. This tendency is even more visible in the

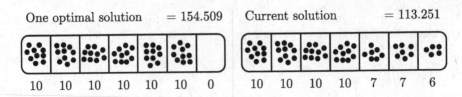

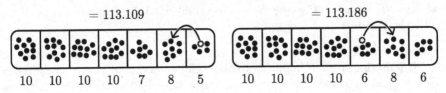

Beneficial mutations from the current solution

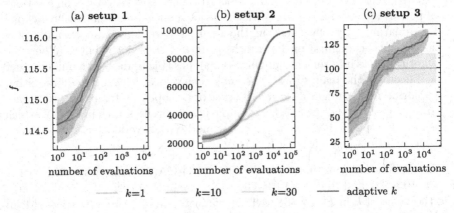

Fig. 4. The resource selection problem has local minimums that can't be escaped by mutating only one agent. In this example, 60 agents must spread on 7 resources by being 10 on 6 of them. In the state where 4 resources are selected by 10 agents, 2 are selected by 7, and 1 by 6, modifying the selection of one agent can only decrease the fitness of the system.

Fig. 5. Performance of the CC-(1+1)-GA$_{k_{\text{fixed}}}$ algorithm with either $k = 1$, $k = 10$ and $k = 30$, as well as CC-(1+1)-GA$_{k_{\text{adaptive}}}$ with $k \in \{1, 10, 30\}$. Performance f is plotted as mean (solid lines) and standard deviation for the three setups considered with respect to the number of fitness evaluations. Curves are plotted on a x-log scale. There are 32 replications for each algorithm and for each experiment.

second setup (Fig. 5(b)). Using larger values for k provides a slight advantage at the beginning but is quickly lost for both $k = 10$ and $k = 30$.

The outcome is rather different in the third setup (Fig. 5(c)) as using $k > 1$ allows to reach better performances and prevent the algorithm to get stuck on a local optimum. Indeed, the algorithm becomes stalled when using $k = 1$, the structure of the problem making it impossible to improve team performance without considering coupled synergies when updating team members.

Figures 5(a) and (b) show that the CC-(1+1)-GA$_{k_{\text{adaptive}}}$ algorithm follows the curves of the best performing algorithms using a fixed value of k. Figure 5(c) also shows that the adaptive algorithm is able to adapt to a situation where the CC-(1+1)-GA$_{k_{\text{fixed}}}$ algorithm would fail because of its fixed k value (here, using $k = 1$ withholds convergence to an optimal team composition). Overall, dynamically modulating the number of policies updated in the team composition always results in performance curves closely matching the best out of the algorithmic variants using a fixed value of k. This remains true even when the best variant with a fixed k value is outperformed by another variant with a different value of k, which confirms the relevance of the adaptive algorithm to act as an anytime learning algorithm. In other words, the CC-(1+1)-GA$_{k_{\text{adaptive}}}$ algorithm presents the best choice when the problem and the evaluation budget are not known.

5.3   Dynamics of Adapting the Number of Team Agents to Update

We analyze how the CC-(1+1)-GA$_{k_{\text{adaptive}}}$ algorithm is changing the value of k throughout evolution for the three setups at hand. Figure 6 represents the median value of k over the 32 repetitions for each of the three experimental setups. We observe that the algorithm switches between the different values for k, and follows different dynamics depending on the setup.

In the first setup, the method slightly favours $k = 1$ and $k = 10$ after a few iterations of exploration. This bias is consistent with the performances observed for k fixed, where the $k = 30$ version is less efficient (see Fig. 5). In the second setup, the value of k decreases during the learning process to stabilize at $k = 1$, allowing for some fine-tuning of team composition. The third setup displays somewhat different dynamics for the value of k, quickly switching from one value to the other. The difference in performance between the different group sizes is not large enough to make a clear-cut choice, and the method chooses k uniformly at each step without impacting the performances.

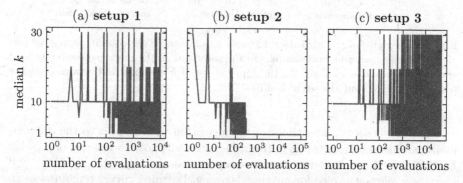

Fig. 6. Median value of k over the 32 repetitions for the first (left), second (middle) and third setups (right). Curves are plotted on a x-log scale.

5.4   Sensitivity of Meta-parameters

As described in Algorithm 2, CC-(1+1)-GA$_{k_{adaptive}}$ uses two meta-parameters, which are:

- $K = (k_0, ..., k_{J-1})$, the set of possible values for k;
- the egalitarianism factor γ that determines at each step whether k should be chosen at random (uniform sampling), or selected with respect to the weights of the k values, obtained from the cumulative fitness gain for each particular value of k. The value of γ balances between exploitation and exploration, and the EXP3 algorithm for multi-armed bandit problems has been extensively studied elsewhere [2, 20];

In the previous section, these meta-parameters were fixed as follow: the set of possible k was limited to $\{1, 10, 30\}$, the egalitarianism factor γ was set to 0.1.

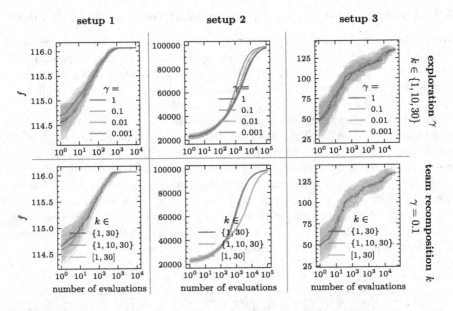

Fig. 7. Sensitivity of the algorithm to meta-parameters. Each column represents one of the different experimental setups. On the rows, one of the meta-parameter is fixed and the other one is varying. On the top, the set of k are fixed but γ varies. At the bottom, γ is fixed but the set of k varies.

Figure 7 shows the sensitivity of the algorithm with respect to the different meta-parameters. From top to bottom, the sensitivity to γ and the set of possible k. The general conclusion from this study is that the algorithm is robust and remains a relevant choice for anytime learning. Learning curves remain close to what has been shown previously, with some exceptions for extreme values. In particular, we can observe that:

- γ does not have a significant impact on the algorithm, provided that it is not too small nor too high to efficiently modulate the exploration and exploitation of k's
- the algorithm is somewhat also sensitive to the cardinal of the set of possible values for k. When there are too many possibilities to explore, the evaluation of each choice takes more time and is, therefore, less accurate if the context changes too fast. The effect of this exploration can especially be observed for the second setup where the algorithm is less accurate when the value for k can be chosen among 30 possible values ($k \in [1, 30]$).

6   Conclusion

In this paper, we present a cooperative co-evolutionary algorithm (CCEA) that implements a collection of (1+1)-GA algorithms, each endowed with the task to optimize the policy parameters of a specific agent while performance is assessed at the level of the team. Our algorithm acts on team composition by continuously updating a limited number of team agents, depending on the task at hand and the level of completion. Therefore, the main contribution of this paper is to describe an algorithm with a self-adapting team composition update mechanism used throughout learning.

We showed that modulating through time the number of new policies added to the current team makes it possible to provide efficient anytime learning, without requiring *a priori* knowledge on the problem to be solved. Moreover, we show that the algorithm can deal with problems where coupling between agents during learning is mandatory to improve team performance.

Experimental validation was conducted using a variant of the El Farol Bar problem, a famous problem in collective decision making, which was modified to capture a multi-agent resource selection problem. Our algorithm is indeed also relevant for multi-robotic setups, which have been recently studied using various CCEA algorithms [7–9,15,16,25], and future works are currently being conducted in this direction.

Acknowledgements. This work is funded by ANR grant ANR-18-CE33-0006.

References

1. Arthur, W.B.: Inductive reasoning and bounded rationality. Am. Econ. Rev. **84**(2), 406–411 (1994)
2. Auer, P., Cesa-Bianchi, N., Freund, Y., Schapire, R.E.: The nonstochastic multi-armed bandit problem. SIAM J. Comput. **32**(1), 48–77 (2002)
3. Beyer, H.-G., Schwefel, H.-P.: Evolution strategies - a comprehensive introduction. Nat. Comput. **1**(1), 3–52 (2002). https://doi.org/10.1023/A:1015059928466
4. De Jong, K.A.: Evolutionary computation: a unified approach. In: Proceedings of the 2016 on Genetic and Evolutionary Computation Conference Companion, pp. 185–199 (2016)

5. Eiben, A.E., Smith, J.E.: Introduction to Evolutionary Computing, vol. 53. Springer, Heidelberg (2003). https://doi.org/10.1007/978-3-662-05094-1
6. Funes, P., Pujals, E.: Intransitivity revisited coevolutionary dynamics of numbers games. In: Proceedings of the 7th Annual Conference on Genetic and Evolutionary Computation, GECCO 2005, pp. 515–521. Association for Computing Machinery, New York (2005)
7. Gomes, J., Mariano, P., Christensen, A.L.: Novelty-driven cooperative coevolution. Evol. Comput. 25(2), 275–307 (2017)
8. Gomes, J., Mariano, P., Christensen, A.L.: Dynamic team heterogeneity in cooperative coevolutionary algorithms. IEEE Trans. Evol. Comput. 22(6), 934–948 (2018)
9. Gomes, J., Mariano, P., Christensen, A.L.: Challenges in cooperative coevolution of physically heterogeneous robot teams. Nat. Comput. 18(1), 29–46 (2016). https://doi.org/10.1007/s11047-016-9582-1
10. Ma, X., et al.: A survey on cooperative co-evolutionary algorithms. IEEE Trans. Evol. Comput. 23(3), 421–441 (2019)
11. Noë, R., Hammerstein, P.: Biological markets: supply and demand determine the effect of partner choice in cooperation, mutualism and mating. Behav. Ecol. Sociobiol. 35(1), 1–11 (1994). https://doi.org/10.1007/BF00167053
12. Panait, L.: Theoretical convergence guarantees for cooperative coevolutionary algorithms. Evol. Comput. 18(4), 581–615 (2010)
13. Potter, M.A., De Jong, K.A.: A cooperative coevolutionary approach to function optimization. In: Davidor, Y., Schwefel, H.-P., Männer, R. (eds.) PPSN 1994. LNCS, vol. 866, pp. 249–257. Springer, Heidelberg (1994). https://doi.org/10.1007/3-540-58484-6_269
14. Potter, M.A., De Jong, K.A.: Cooperative coevolution: an architecture for evolving coadapted subcomponents. Evol. Comput. 8, 1–29 (2000)
15. Rahmattalabi, A., Chung, J.J., Colby, M., Tumer, K.: D++: structural credit assignment in tightly coupled multiagent domains. In: 2016 IEEE/RSJ International Conference on Intelligent Robots and Systems (IROS), pp. 4424–4429. IEEE (2016)
16. Rockefeller, G., Khadka, S., Tumer, K.: Multi-level fitness critics for cooperative coevolution. In: Proceedings of the 19th International Conference on Autonomous Agents and Multiagent Systems (AAMAS 2020), pp. 1143–1151, 9–13 May 2020
17. Shapley, L.S.: A value for n-person games. In: Contributions to the Theory of Games II. Annals of Mathematics Studies, vol. 28, pp. 307–317 (1953)
18. Shoham, Y., Leyton-Brown, K.: Multiagent Systems: Algorithmic, Game-Theoretic, and Logical Foundations. Cambridge University Press, Cambridge (2008)
19. Stone, P., Kaminka, G.A., Kraus, S., Rosenschein, J.S.: Ad hoc autonomous agent teams: collaboration without pre-coordination. In: Proceedings of the Twenty-Fourth AAAI Conference on Artificial Intelligence, AAAI 2010, pp. 1504–1509. AAAI Press (2010)
20. Sutton, R.S., Barto, A.G.: Reinforcement Learning: An Introduction, 2nd edn. MIT Press, Cambridge (2018)
21. Tumer, K., Agogino, A.K., Wolpert, D.H.: Learning sequences of actions in collectives of autonomous agents. In: Proceedings of the First International Joint Conference on Autonomous Agents and Multiagent Systems: Part 1, pp. 378–385 (2002)
22. West, S.A., Griffin, A.S., Gardner, A.: Social semantics: altruism, cooperation, mutualism, strong reciprocity and group selection. J. Evol. Biol. 20(2), 415–32 (2007)

23. Wolpert, D.H., Tumer, K.: Optimal payoff functions for members of collectives. Adv. Complex Syst. **4**(2/3), 265–279 (2001)
24. Wolpert, D.H., Tumer, K.: An introduction to collective intelligence. Technical report, NASA (2008)
25. Zerbel, N., Tumer, K.: The power of suggestion. In: Proceedings of the 19th International Conference on Autonomous Agents and Multiagent Systems (AAMAS 2020), pp. 1602–1610, 9–13 May 2020

Short Presentations

Synthesizing Programs from Program Pieces Using Genetic Programming and Refinement Type Checking

Sabrina Tseng$^{(\boxtimes)}$, Erik Hemberg, and Una-May O'Reilly

Massachusetts Institute of Technology, Cambridge, MA 02139, USA
stseng@alum.mit.edu, {hembergerik,unamay}@csail.mit.edu

Abstract. Program synthesis automates the process of writing code, which can be a very useful tool in allowing people to better leverage computational resources. However, a limiting factor in the scalability of current program synthesis techniques is the large size of the search space, especially for complex programs. We present a new model for synthesizing programs which reduces the search space by composing programs from program pieces, which are component functions provided by the user. Our method uses genetic programming search with a fitness function based on refinement type checking, which is a formal verification method that checks function behavior expressed through types. We evaluate our implementation of this method on a set of 3 benchmark problems, observing that our fitness function is able to find solutions in fewer generations than a fitness function that uses example test cases. These results indicate that using refinement types and other formal methods within genetic programming can improve the performance and practicality of program synthesis.

1 Introduction

Program synthesis, the automatic construction of a computer program from a user specification, is a challenging and central problem in the field of artificial intelligence (AI) [7]. Programming has been classified as "AI-hard" [35] since all problems in AI can reduce to programming, and thus our progress in program synthesis serves as a good benchmark for how close we are to achieving general artificial intelligence [21]. In addition, program synthesis has broad applications in software engineering. For example, software development often entails refactoring old code to improve structure or readability without affecting behavior, which program synthesis can help automate. In addition, program synthesis can allow non-programmers to efficiently perform computational tasks [3].

Two of the main approaches to program synthesis are stochastic search through genetic programming [14], and formal verification methods such as symbolic solving [7]. However, solver-based methods do not scale beyond small programs such as introductory programming problems [9], and many current approaches are constrained in scope [21]. In this paper, we propose a new program synthesis model

E. Medvet et al. (Eds.): EuroGP 2022, LNCS 13223, pp. 197–211, 2022.
https://doi.org/10.1007/978-3-031-02056-8_13

which leverages pre-existing code, in the form of functions that we call "program pieces", and synthesizes the high-level program structure. This model allows for an approach that incorporates refinement type checking [32], a formal verification method, into genetic programming search.

Genetic programming (GP) is a search technique that begins with an initial population of programs from the search space, and evolves and combines the most "fit" programs through non-deterministic processes similar to biological evolution to move towards an optimal solution [25]. In particular, GP proceeds in generations, where in each generation the search selects the most fit programs and varies them to get a new generation of more evolved and more fit programs. In GP systems, the performance of the search depends heavily on the fitness function, since incorrect programs need a good heuristic to optimize [7,22]. A common fitness function is the program's accuracy on a set of example inputs and outputs. However, having a large set of examples is computationally expensive [6], while a small set of examples leads to under-specification and often the wrong generalizations [7]. NetSyn [17] showed that using neural networks to learn a fitness function can improve GP performance. This suggests that there is still room for improvement in the design of the fitness function.

On the other hand, formal verification methods can be used to synthesize programs through symbolic proofs of satisfiability and correctness. One example of a formal verification method is refinement type checking [32], which is a stronger form of type checking that can enforce predicates on types. Specifically, a user can define stricter input and output types for a function using refinement types, so that the refinement type check enforces expected preconditions and postconditions. The liquid type system [28] allows for efficient static checking of refinement type safety, without requiring every expression to be manually annotated. However, as mentioned above, formal methods alone do not scale well beyond small programs.

Our key idea in this paper is to improve scalability by decomposing programs into *program pieces*, which are functions provided by the user or imported from a library. We form candidate programs by composing program pieces. By abstracting away logical units of code into these program pieces, we reduce the search space for the synthesis, thus enabling us to solve larger synthesis problems. Furthermore, this allows users of our system to make use of built-in functions or external libraries, which can provide complex logic for free.

An additional benefit of this decomposition is that we can use refinement types to specify the input and output types of program pieces, which specifies the overall intended behavior of the program we want to synthesize. In our proposed system, we use refinement type checking as a fitness function within our GP algorithm. In particular, we define a novel fitness function based on the number of errors that result from the refinement type check, so that programs with fewer errors have better fitness. Using this fitness function, we observe that the GP search converges towards a program that has no type errors, which we consider to be correct since the refinement types specify the intended behavior. In addition, unlike fitness functions based on input-output examples which are under-specified as mentioned above, refinement types provide a formal specification of the entire input and output spaces.

We present the following contributions in this paper:

- A general-purpose program synthesis model that synthesizes programs by composing preexisting program pieces
- A fitness function on programs composed of pieces that enables GP to find good programs, derived from the number and type of errors that result from refinement type checking
- An evaluation of the new fitness function in this model

We evaluate the performance of our proposed fitness function against a fitness function that uses accuracy on input-output examples. We find that on average, with our refinement type-based fitness function, the GP search finds solutions in about 20% fewer generations than when we use input-output examples.

The remainder of the paper is structured as follows: first, we outline our methods, including how we translate the refinement type check into a fitness function (Sect. 2). Next, we describe our experiments and results (Sect. 3). Finally, we discuss related work (Sect. 4) and conclusions (Sect. 5).

2   Method

We will present our method in 4 sections. First, we describe our program synthesis model, defining program pieces and introducing a running example (Sect. 2.1). Next, we outline our base genetic programming (GP) algorithm and how it synthesizes programs (Sect. 2.2). Next, we briefly introduce refinement types and LiquidHaskell (Sect. 2.3). Then, we present our new fitness function, describing how we integrate information from LiquidHaskell into the base GP algorithm (Sect. 2.4).

2.1   Program Synthesis Model

In our program synthesis model, programs are composed of *program pieces*, which are functions provided by the user or imported from built-in and external libraries. As a running example, we consider a list filtering problem that we call FilterEvens: given a list of integers, return a list containing only the even integers from the input. The example below, and subsequent examples, will use Haskell syntax [11]. A user might provide the following 3 program pieces:

Example 1. Program pieces for FilterEvens

1. condition takes in integer x and returns true if x is even, false otherwise.

```
condition :: Int -> Bool
condition x = x 'mod' 2 == 0
```

2. condition takes in integer x and returns true if x is odd, false otherwise.

```
condition :: Int -> Bool
condition x = x 'mod' 2 /= 0
```

3. `filterEvens` takes in an array of integers `xs` and returns the array containing all members from `xs` for which `condition` is true.

```
filterEvens :: [Int] -> [Int]
filterEvens xs = [a | a <- xs, condition a]
```

A correct program would consist of pieces 1 and 3. Note that piece 2 is not ultimately needed; a user will not have complete knowledge of the implementation, so they may include pieces that the synthesis algorithm chooses not to use.

2.2 Genetic Programming Algorithm

In the context of program synthesis, genetic programming evolves a population of candidate programs over time to find an optimal program [14]. Candidate programs are defined by their *chromosome*, a sequence of integers representing the indexes of the program pieces that compose that program. For example, using our `FilterEvens` problem defined in Example 1, the chromosome $c = [1, 3]$ corresponds to this program consisting of piece numbers 1 and 3:

Example 2. Program defined by chromosome $[1, 3]$, which uses the correct condition to filter a list to only contain even integers

```
condition :: Int -> Bool
condition x = x 'mod' 2 == 0

filterEvens :: [Int] -> [Int]
filterEvens xs = [a | a <- xs, condition a]
```

A sketch of our base genetic programming algorithm is shown in Algorithm 1. We provide a set of parameters Θ which includes the population size, chromosome length, mutation and crossover rate for variation, tournament size, and elite size, and parameter G, the number of generations to run for. We also provide a fitness function f, which computes a heuristic representing how "good" each candidate solution is, along with a set of input/output examples X which we use to test candidate programs to compute fitness (described in more detail below).

The algorithm proceeds in the following steps, labeled with the corresponding line numbers in Algorithm 1:

- **Generate individuals** (1): Let $|c|$ be the chromosome length and $|P|$ the number of program pieces; both are provided in the parameters. We generate a random individual by generating $|c|$ random numbers, each in the range $[0, |P|)$. This list represents the chromosome for that individual. We repeat the process **pop_size** times to generate an initial population.

- **Compute fitness** (2, 6): We use the provided fitness function f to compute fitness for each individual in the population.
- **Selection** (4): To select individuals for variation, we use tournament selection [4]. The tournament size t is provided in the parameters Θ. We will run pop_size tournaments, where each tournament selects t individuals at random from the population and selects the individual with best fitness. Thus, individuals with higher fitness are more likely to be selected for variation.
- **Variation** (5): We use two variation operators to create new individuals.
  - **Mutation** [23]: With probability equal to the mutation rate, we mutate an individual as follows. Given a chromosome c, we choose an index uniformly at random from $[0, |c|)$, and change it to a new value, also chosen uniformly at random from the range of possible values $[0, |P|)$, to get new chromosome c'.
  - **Single-Point Crossover** [24]: With probability equal to the crossover rate we create two new individuals as follows. Given two chromosomes c_1 and c_2, we choose an index uniformly at random to be the crossover point p. We create new individuals c'_1 and c'_2 such that c'_1 contains the left part of c_1, up to index p, and the right part of c_2, from index $p+1$ to the end, and vice versa for c'_2.
- **Replacement** (7): We use an elitism strategy [26] to update the population. Let e be the elite size provided in the parameters Θ. We choose our new population to consist of the e individuals from the current generation before variation with the best fitness, plus the (pop_size $- e$) individuals after variation with the best fitness.

Algorithm 1. Genetic Programming for Program Synthesis
evolve(Θ, G, f, X):

1: $P \leftarrow$ generate_individuals(Θ)	// Generate random initial population
2: $P \leftarrow$ computeFitness($P, f(X, \cdot)$)	// Compute fitness of initial pop
3: **for** G iterations **do**	
4: $P' \leftarrow$ selection(P, Θ)	// Select individuals for variation
5: $P' \leftarrow$ variation(P', Θ)	// Mutation and crossover
6: $P' \leftarrow$ computeFitness($P', f(X, \cdot)$)	// Compute fitness of new pop
7: $P \leftarrow$ replacement(P, P', Θ)	// Update population depending on fitness
8: **end for**	
9: $p^* \leftarrow$ max($\{$p.fitness $: p \in P\}$)	
10: **return** p*	// Return program with max fitness

Fitness Function. In our base algorithm, we use a standard fitness function: the candidate program's accuracy on the example test cases X [14]. In particular, given some chromosome c, fitness is given by

$$f_{IO}(X,c) = \frac{\text{number of correct examples}}{\text{total number of examples}}$$

Under this fitness function, programs which perform better on the example cases will have higher fitness. However, there are potential problems with using input-output examples, as mentioned in Sect. 1. This fitness function only specifies a program's intended behavior for a small set of examples, and a solution that succeeds on these examples may not necessarily generalize to others [13]. This leads us to explore refinement types as an alternate way to compute fitness.

2.3   Refinement Types and LiquidHaskell

Refinement types are types that further restrict the space of possible values by specifying a predicate. For example, we can express the `filterEvens` function from our running example using refinement types as follows, indicating that it takes a list of integers as input and outputs a list of *even* integers:

Example 3. LiquidHaskell Refinement Type Specification for `filterEvens`

```
{-@ type Even = {v:Int | v mod 2 = 0} @-}
{-@ filterEvens :: [Int] -> [Even] @-}
```

LiquidHaskell [34] is a plugin for Haskell which supports refinement types, including static checking of refinement type safety using a symbolic solver such as Z3 [20]. We can express a function like `filterEvens` in Example 3, and LiquidHaskell will verify at compile time that `filterEvens` satisfies the refined type. In this case LiquidHaskell checks that the output of `filterEvens` is always a list of even integers. If the check fails, LiquidHaskell outputs errors showing which refinement type specifications were not satisfied. This static checking is able to not only restrict integer values, but also enforce properties of lists and other complex types, so it is applicable to a broad range of functions.

2.4   Refinement Types Fitness Function

For certain types of problems, such as the `FilterEvens` example we have defined, refinement types are able to express the intended behavior of the program. Because this is a symbolic check, it verifies that behavior over all valid inputs without relying on example test cases.

To make use of this property, we leverage LiquidHaskell's refinement type checking to define a new fitness function for the GP. To do so, we require that the user provide a refinement for each program piece. Since refinements are based only on the intended behavior of a function, and do not depend on the implementation, we assume that users will be able to provide refinements even for library functions that will be used in the synthesized code.

A naive fitness function that simply runs the LiquidHaskell type check would return a binary value (0 if it fails, 1 if it passes), which does not work well as a heuristic. Instead, we can look more closely at LiquidHaskell's output, which includes syntax errors and refinement type errors, to construct a more fine-grained function.

Syntax Errors. We assume that individual program pieces, which are often built-in functions or library functions, are free of syntax errors. Under this assumption, the only syntax errors that can be produced by combining program pieces are multiple definition errors (for pieces that have the same name and function signature), and missing definition errors (for pieces that were declared in other pieces but don't appear in the solution). The maximum number of syntax errors that can result is equal to the length of the chromosome.

Refinement Type Errors. Refinement type checking is only performed after regular syntax checking, so no refinement type errors are reported if a program has incorrect syntax. Otherwise, if the program has no syntax errors, Liquid-Haskell will report one error per refinement (i.e. per function signature) that is not satisfied. Thus, the maximum possible number of refinement type errors is also equal to the length of the chromosome.

Fitness Function. We construct our fitness function using a linear scale based on the number and type of errors reported. In addition, we follow the principle that syntax errors are generally "worse" than refinement type errors; syntax errors indicate structural issues like duplicated or missing program pieces, while refinement type errors mean that the program has the right structure.

Therefore, for a given chromosome c (with length $|c|$) where LiquidHaskell produces s syntax errors and t refinement type errors, we calculate the following fitness function:

$$f_{RT}(c) = \begin{cases} 0.5 - \frac{s}{2|c|} & \text{if } s > 0 \text{ (syntax checking fails)} \\ 1 - \frac{t}{2|c|} & \text{if } s = 0 \text{ (syntax checking succeeds)} \end{cases} \tag{1}$$

From Eq. 1, programs that have syntax errors always have fitness <0.5 while programs that have no syntax errors will have fitness ≥ 0.5. A program that has no syntax or refinement type errors, such as the program given in Example 2, has a fitness value of 1 and is considered to be correct.

As another example, consider the program in our `FilterEvens` specification with the chromosome [2, 3]. We include the LiquidHaskell refinement type specifications as well:

Example 4. Program defined by chromosome [2, 3], which uses the incorrect condition, filtering the list to contain odd integers

```
{-@ condition :: x:Int -> {v:Bool | (v <=> (x mod 2 /= 0))} @-}
condition :: Int -> Bool
condition x = x 'mod' 2 /= 0

{-@ type Even = {v:Int | v mod 2 = 0} @-}
{-@ filterEvens :: [Int] -> [Even] @-}
filterEvens :: [Int] -> [Int]
filterEvens xs = [a | a <- xs, condition a]
```

This program compiles without syntax errors, but the `filterEvens` refinement type specification is not satisfied as the given `condition` yields odd instead of even integers. Thus, this program produces 0 syntax errors and 1 refinement type error, resulting in a fitness value of $1 - \frac{1}{2 \cdot 2} = 0.75$. This program is given a higher fitness than, for example, one that is missing a `condition` function, which would cause syntax errors.

We will use this fitness function with our original GP algorithm as described in Algorithm 1.

3   Experiments and Results

In this section we present an evaluation of our new fitness function based on refinement type checking. Our goal is to assess whether it can provide a performance and scalability improvement over two baselines: a standard fitness function based on input-output examples, and random search. In Sect. 3.1 we specify our benchmark problems and what program pieces we use in the synthesis. In Sect. 3.2 we describe our experimental setup. Next, in Sect. 3.3 we outline the results of our evaluation. Lastly, in Sect. 3.4 we discuss limitations of our technique and possible threats to its validity.

3.1   Program Synthesis Problems

We use a set of 3 program synthesis problems for evaluation. Some are adapted from a general program synthesis benchmark suite [9] and expanded for our program synthesis model as described below. All of them have the property that their behavior can be expressed using refinement types. For program pieces, we chose building blocks that are likely to be part of the standard library for any language, such as checking if an integer is even or filtering a list, as well as domain-specific functions that the user would provide, such as a function that joins two sorted partitions used in sorting algorithms. Below are the problem specifications and a high level description of what program pieces are included.

1. **List Filtering** (adapted from Count Odds in [9]): Given a list of integers, filter the list and return 3 new lists containing just the even integers, just the odd integers, and just the integers greater than 2. We provide several possible filtering conditions as program pieces, including the correct ones as well as others that are not needed for the correct solution.
2. **Insertion Sort:** Given a list of integers, sort them in ascending order using insertion sort. We provide several possible conditions for determining when to insert, as well as a skeleton for the sort. The skeleton provides the control flow, so our search needs to find the correct conditions and operations to fit into the skeleton.
3. **QuickSort:** Given a list of integers, sort them in ascending order using quicksort. We provide a skeleton for the sort function, as in Insertion Sort, as well as different possible ways of partitioning the list for quicksort.

3.2 Experimental Setup

For each selected program synthesis problem, we run 60 trials and report performance as the number of generations taken to find a solution. We compare the following 3 variants of GP search:

1. **RefinementTypes (RT):** GP search using our new fitness function based on counting errors from refinement type checking (Eq. 1).
2. **IOExamples (IO):** GP search using a baseline fitness function using accuracy on a set of input-output example cases, as described in Sect. 2.2. For each problem, we choose a small (<10) but diverse set of examples. Specifically, we ensure that the example sets cover all execution paths in a correct solution.
3. **RandomSearch (RS):** Random generation of individuals. To make this comparable with GP search, we proceed in generations, where `pop_size` individuals are randomly generated and evaluated per generation. As with GP search we can report the number of generations taken to find a solution. Thus, the total number of fitness evaluations is the same (`pop_size` * `generations`), so the running time is approximately equal as well. We include this as a baseline to verify that GP is well suited to our program synthesis model and provides an improvement over naive random search.

We also run each problem on 3 different search space sizes to evaluate scalability; we vary the size of the search space by including or excluding different optional program pieces which are not needed in a correct solution.

The common parameters that we used for all experiments is shown in Table 1. Note that for ease of implementation, we terminate searches after 20 generations and report a run as having taken 20 generations if it does not find a solution.

Table 1. Experiment parameters

Parameter	Value
Mutation rate	0.3
Crossover rate	0.8
Tournament size	3
Elite size	2
Population size	20
Max generations	20
Number of trials	60

We tuned the max generations and population size to find a setting in which most trials find a solution before reaching the max generation limit. We did not tune the other parameters.

Our implementation, including problem specifications and program piece specifications for each problem, is available on GitHub[1].

3.3   Results

Table 2 shows the results of our experiments. For each problem and set of program pieces, the search space size is calculated as $|P|^{|c|}$, where $|P|$ is the number of program pieces and $|c|$ is the length of the chromosome. We present the sample mean $\bar{x}$ and standard deviation s of the number of generations taken to find a solution for each fitness function.

The p-values shown in the table come from comparing the two specified variants using the Mann-Whitney U nonparametric test [18], which tests the null hypothesis that two sets of samples have the same population distribution (in particular, the probability that a random member from population 1 is greater than a random member from population 2 is $1/2$). The p-values have also been adjusted for multiple hypothesis testing using the Bonferroni correction to decrease the likelihood of Type I error [1]; specifically, we multiply p-values by 2, the number of simultaneous hypotheses we are testing.

Table 2. Experiment Results. We run 60 trials per problem, search space size, and variant and record the number of generations taken to find a solution. We report the sample mean $\bar{x}$ and standard deviation s. The p-values come from the Mann-Whitney U nonparametric test and have been adjusted using the Bonferroni correction for multiple hypothesis testing. p-values less than 0.05 are in bold.

| Problem | Search Space Size | Generations to find solution | | | | | | $p_{RT=IO}$ | $p_{RT=RS}$ |
| | | Refinement Types | | IO Examples | | Random Search | | | |
		$\bar{x}$	s	$\bar{x}$	s	$\bar{x}$	s		
List Filtering	5.9e4	8.2	5.4	10.5	6.6	14.2	6.8	0.065	**0.000**
	1.0e5	12.5	6.2	14.8	5.9	15.9	6.0	**0.046**	**0.002**
	1.0e6	12.8	6.6	16.7	5.0	17.8	4.6	**0.000**	**0.000**
Insertion Sort	1e5	5.4	4.8	8.4	7.1	8.4	6.5	**0.042**	**0.010**
	1.6e6	8.0	5.7	8.9	6.9	11.4	6.9	0.700	**0.008**
	1.8e7	9.4	7.0	13.1	6.7	16.4	5.1	**0.008**	**0.000**
QuickSort	2.6e5	9.3	6.1	11.1	7.3	12.7	7.0	0.181	**0.005**
	5.3e5	10.3	6.2	14.6	6.3	15.8	6.5	**0.000**	**0.000**
	1.0e6	9.0	6.2	17.2	4.8	15.5	6.5	**0.000**	**0.000**

We can see from the table that in general, `RefinementTypes` finds a solution in fewer generations than the two baselines. Across all the experiments,

---

[1] https://github.com/sabrinatseng/GAble.

`RefinementTypes` achieves an average improvement of 20% over `IOExamples` and 32% over `RandomSearch`. The p-values show that the improvement is significant ($p < 0.05$) in most cases.

We hypothesize that a key reason for the performance improvement is the difference in fitness values for programs that have syntax errors. For `IOExamples`, all programs that have syntax errors have a fitness value of 0 since the fitness evaluation is not able to run at all (the program cannot be interpreted). We can see in Fig. 1a that for `IOExamples`, many candidate programs (all those with syntax errors) have fitness values of 0, and there are not many distinct fitness values. On the other hand, the `RefinementTypes` fitness function provides a heuristic even if there are syntax errors, as seen in Fig. 1b, where there are four distinct fitness values for programs with syntax errors (fitness <0.5). This is helpful because among programs that have syntax errors, some are still closer to correct (e.g. less errors) and the `RefinementTypes` fitness function can capture that. Therefore, in areas of the search space corresponding to programs that have syntax errors, the new fitness function can still guide the GP search whereas those programs are all evaluated to be equally "unfit" by the `IOExamples` fitness function. In the trial shown in Fig. 1, the search using `IOExamples` is unable to find a solution after 20 generations, whereas the additional heuristic information provided by `RefinementTypes` allows the GP search to find a solution after 10 generations.

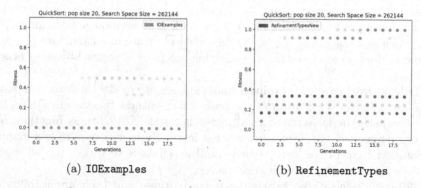

(a) `IOExamples`   (b) `RefinementTypes`

Fig. 1. Scatter plots of population's fitness values over time (generations) for (a) `IOExamples` and (b) `RefinementTypes` fitness functions. Each plots was generated from one trial run on the QuickSort problem with the same search space size and population size. Each point (g, f) represents an individual in generation g with a fitness value of f, and the opacity increases with the number of individuals with fitness value f.

We also see from the table that the p-value generally remains below 0.05 as the search space size increases, which shows that the performance improvements that we observe can potentially scale to larger problems as well.

3.4   Threats to Validity

We note that refinement types are not applicable to every problem; for example, some string manipulations, such as the Double Letters problem from [9], would be difficult to express using refinement types since they involve complex dependencies between indices of the string. In addition, we observed that the GP search overall runs an order of magnitude slower in terms of wall-clock time when using the refinement type check rather than example cases as a fitness function. We did not optimize our implementations; in particular, there are many I/O operations that may be unnecessary in a better implementation, so this difference may change after optimization.

4   Related Work

Since the fitness function is so integral in GP search, many researchers have studied different ways of defining the fitness function. NetSyn [17], mentioned in Sect. 1, uses a neural network to learn a better fitness function based on input-output examples. CROWDBOOST [2] explores evolving the fitness function along with candidate programs during GP. Hemberg et al. [10] show that it is possible to improve search performance by using domain knowledge extracted from the problem description to construct the fitness function. *Implicit fitness sharing* [19], in which multiple individuals that solve the same example case must "share" the reward, can also improve search performance by preserving population diversity. Another related approach is behavioral programming [15, 16], which introduces the use of the full execution trace of a candidate program in the evaluation stage rather than relying solely on a scalar objective fitness function.

Others have investigated using formal methods like model checking and Hoare logic for program verification as the basis for the fitness function in GP [8,12]. Our approach similarly uses formal methods for the GP's fitness function, but we use refinement types, which are often less verbose and require less manual annotation than Hoare logic; with LiquidHaskell, it is very easy to define and verify refinement types for program pieces [33].

Prior works have also explored refinement types and their applicability to program synthesis. SYNQUID [27] uses refinement types for program synthesis without GP by decomposing the type specifications and solving local type constraints. Fonseca et al. [5] suggest an approach for combining GP with refinement types, including a possible fitness function for refinements expressed in their programming language; however, they do not present any experimental data or results.

A similar approach for improving practicality of program synthesis is program *sketching*, where a user provides a partially-complete template of a program, and the synthesis algorithm fills in the missing low-level details [29]. This has been implemented successfully for certain problem domains in systems like SKETCH [31] and PSKETCH [30], which achieve better efficiency because the search space is restricted. Our approach is analogous but inverted: the user provides building blocks and the synthesis algorithm finds a correct composition of those building blocks. This has the same benefit of restricting the search space and can be useful in situations where a user does not have enough knowledge of the program structure to build a sketch.

5   Conclusions

Our results show that it is possible to express complex programs such as sorting using our program piece-based model. Using this model for program synthesis, we can make use of refinement type checking to express correctness properties of the program. We show that in this model, using refinement type checking to evaluate fitness within GP search can provide an improvement over using an example-based fitness evaluation. These results merit further investigation into different approaches to achieving scalability in program synthesis as well as different ways of incorporating symbolic solving within GP search. In future work, we hope to evaluate a wider set of benchmarks, including more complex problems with larger search spaces. We also hope to further explore ways to formalize and potentially automate the construction of program pieces, for example by searching the standard library, or using GP to "fill in" missing pieces.

References

1. Bland, J.M., Altman, D.G.: Multiple significance tests: the Bonferroni method. BMJ **310**(6973), 170 (1995). http://bmj.bmjjournals.com/cgi/content/full/310/6973/170
2. Cochran, R.A., D'Antoni, L., Livshits, B., Molnar, D., Veanes, M.: Program boosting: program synthesis via crowd-sourcing. SIGPLAN Not. **50**(1), 677–688 (2015). https://doi.org/10.1145/2775051.2676973
3. David, C., Kroening, D.: Program synthesis: challenges and opportunities. Philos. Trans. Ser. A Math. Phys. Eng. Sci. **375**(2104), Article ID 20150403 (2017)
4. Fang, Y., Li, J.: A review of tournament selection in genetic programming. In: Cai, Z., Hu, C., Kang, Z., Liu, Y. (eds.) ISICA 2010. LNCS, vol. 6382, pp. 181–192. Springer, Heidelberg (2010). https://doi.org/10.1007/978-3-642-16493-4_19
5. Fonseca, A., Santos, P., Silva, S.: The usability argument for refinement typed genetic programming. In: Bäck, T., et al. (eds.) PPSN 2020. LNCS, vol. 12270, pp. 18–32. Springer, Cham (2020). https://doi.org/10.1007/978-3-030-58115-2_2
6. Giacobini, M., Tomassini, M., Vanneschi, L.: Limiting the number of fitness cases in genetic programming using statistics. In: Guervós, J.J.M., Adamidis, P., Beyer, H.-G., Schwefel, H.-P., Fernández-Villacañas, J.-L. (eds.) PPSN 2002. LNCS, vol. 2439, pp. 371–380. Springer, Heidelberg (2002). https://doi.org/10.1007/3-540-45712-7_36
7. Gulwani, S., Polozov, O., Singh, R.: Program synthesis. Found. Trends® Program. Lang. **4**(1–2), 1–119 (2017). https://doi.org/10.1561/2500000010
8. He, P., Kang, L., Johnson, C.G., Ying, S.: Hoare logic-based genetic programming. Sci. China Inf. Sci. **54**(3), 623–637 (2011). https://doi.org/10.1007/s11432-011-4200-4

9. Helmuth, T., Spector, L.: General program synthesis benchmark suite. In: Proceedings of the 2015 Annual Conference on Genetic and Evolutionary Computation, GECCO 2015, pp. 1039–1046. Association for Computing Machinery, New York (2015). https://doi.org/10.1145/2739480.2754769

10. Hemberg, E., Kelly, J., O'Reilly, U.M.: On domain knowledge and novelty to improve program synthesis performance with grammatical evolution. In: Proceedings of the Genetic and Evolutionary Computation Conference, GECCO 2019, pp. 1039–1046. Association for Computing Machinery, New York (2019). https://doi.org/10.1145/3321707.3321865

11. Hudak, P., et al.: Report on the programming language Haskell: a non-strict, purely functional language version 1.2. SIGPLAN Not. **27**(5), 1–164 (1992). https://doi.org/10.1145/130697.130699

12. Johnson, C.G.: Genetic programming with fitness based on model checking. In: Ebner, M., O'Neill, M., Ekárt, A., Vanneschi, L., Esparcia-Alcázar, A.I. (eds.) EuroGP 2007. LNCS, vol. 4445, pp. 114–124. Springer, Heidelberg (2007). https://doi.org/10.1007/978-3-540-71605-1_11

13. Kitzelmann, E.: Inductive programming: a survey of program synthesis techniques. In: Schmid, U., Kitzelmann, E., Plasmeijer, R. (eds.) AAIP 2009. LNCS, vol. 5812, pp. 50–73. Springer, Heidelberg (2010). https://doi.org/10.1007/978-3-642-11931-6_3

14. Koza, J.R.: Survey of genetic algorithms and genetic programming. In: Proceedings of WESCON 1995, pp. 589– (1995)

15. Krawiec, K.: Behavioral Program Synthesis with Genetic Programming. Springer, Cham (2016). https://doi.org/10.1007/978-3-319-27565-9

16. Krawiec, K., O'Reilly, U.M.: Behavioral programming: a broader and more detailed take on semantic GP. In: Proceedings of the 2014 Annual Conference on Genetic and Evolutionary Computation, GECCO 2014, pp. 935–942. Association for Computing Machinery, New York (2014). https://doi.org/10.1145/2576768.2598288

17. Mandal, S., Anderson, T.A., Turek, J.S., Gottschlich, J., Zhou, S., Muzahid, A.: Learning fitness functions for machine programming (2021)

18. Mann, H.B., Whitney, D.R.: On a test of whether one of two random variables is stochastically larger than the other. Ann. Math. Stat. **18**(1), 50–60 (1947). https://doi.org/10.1214/aoms/1177730491

19. McKay, R.I.B.: Fitness sharing in genetic programming. In: Proceedings of the 2nd Annual Conference on Genetic and Evolutionary Computation, GECCO 2000, San Francisco, CA, USA, pp. 435–442. Morgan Kaufmann Publishers Inc. (2000)

20. de Moura, L., Bjørner, N.: Z3: an efficient SMT solver. In: Ramakrishnan, C.R., Rehof, J. (eds.) TACAS 2008. LNCS, vol. 4963, pp. 337–340. Springer, Heidelberg (2008). https://doi.org/10.1007/978-3-540-78800-3_24

21. O'Neill, M., Spector, L.: Automatic programming: the open issue? Genet. Program Evolvable Mach. **21**, 251–262 (2019). https://doi.org/10.1007/s10710-019-09364-2

22. O'Neill, M., Vanneschi, L., Gustafson, S., Banzhaf, W.: Open issues in genetic programming. Genet. Program Evolvable Mach. **11**(3–4), 339–363 (2010). https://doi.org/10.1007/s10710-010-9113-2

23. Page, J., Poli, R., Langdon, W.B.: Mutation in genetic programming: a preliminary study. In: Poli, R., Nordin, P., Langdon, W.B., Fogarty, T.C. (eds.) EuroGP 1999. LNCS, vol. 1598, pp. 39–48. Springer, Heidelberg (1999). https://doi.org/10.1007/3-540-48885-5_4

24. Poli, R., Langdon, W.B.: Genetic programming with one-point crossover. In: Chawdhry, P.K., Roy, R., Pant, R.K. (eds.) Soft Computing in Engineering Design

and Manufacturing, pp. 180–189. Springer, London (1998). https://doi.org/10.1007/978-1-4471-0427-8_20

25. Poli, R., Langdon, W.B., McPhee, N.F.: A Field Guide to Genetic Programming. Lulu Enterprises, UK Ltd. (2008)

26. Poli, R., McPhee, N.F., Vanneschi, L.: Elitism reduces bloat in genetic programming. In: Proceedings of the 10th Annual Conference on Genetic and Evolutionary Computation, GECCO 2008, pp. 1343–1344. Association for Computing Machinery, New York (2008). https://doi.org/10.1145/1389095.1389355

27. Polikarpova, N., Kuraj, I., Solar-Lezama, A.: Program synthesis from polymorphic refinement types. SIGPLAN Not. **51**(6), 522–538 (2016). https://doi.org/10.1145/2980983.2908093

28. Rondon, P.M., Kawaguci, M., Jhala, R.: Liquid types. In: Proceedings of the 29th ACM SIGPLAN Conference on Programming Language Design and Implementation, PLDI 2008, pp. 159–169. Association for Computing Machinery, New York (2008). https://doi.org/10.1145/1375581.1375602

29. Solar-Lezama, A.: Program synthesis by sketching. Ph.D. thesis, University of California at Berkeley, USA (2008)

30. Solar-Lezama, A., Jones, C.G., Bodik, R.: Sketching concurrent data structures. SIGPLAN Not. **43**(6), 136–148 (2008). https://doi.org/10.1145/1379022.1375599

31. Solar-Lezama, A., Tancau, L., Bodik, R., Seshia, S., Saraswat, V.: Combinatorial sketching for finite programs. SIGARCH Comput. Archit. News **34**(5), 404–415 (2006). https://doi.org/10.1145/1168919.1168907

32. Vazou, N., Rondon, P.M., Jhala, R.: Abstract refinement types. In: Felleisen, M., Gardner, P. (eds.) ESOP 2013. LNCS, vol. 7792, pp. 209–228. Springer, Heidelberg (2013). https://doi.org/10.1007/978-3-642-37036-6_13

33. Vazou, N., Seidel, E.L., Jhala, R.: LiquidHaskell: experience with refinement types in the real world. In: Proceedings of the 2014 ACM SIGPLAN Symposium on Haskell, Haskell 2014, pp. 39–51. Association for Computing Machinery, New York (2014). https://doi.org/10.1145/2633357.2633366

34. Vazou, N., Seidel, E.L., Jhala, R., Vytiniotis, D., Peyton-Jones, S.: Refinement types for Haskell. SIGPLAN Not. **49**(9), 269–282 (2014). https://doi.org/10.1145/2692915.2628161

35. Yampolskiy, R.V.: AI-complete, AI-hard, or AI-easy - classification of problems in AI. In: MAICS (2012)

Creating Diverse Ensembles
for Classification with Genetic
Programming and Neuro-MAP-Elites

Kyle Nickerson[1]([✉]) [iD], Antonina Kolokolova[1], and Ting Hu[2] [iD]

[1] Memorial University of Newfoundland, St. John's, NL, Canada
kln870@mun.ca
[2] School of Computing, Queen's University, Kingston, ON, Canada

Abstract. Model diversity is essential for ensemble classifiers, which make predictions by combining predictions from multiple simpler models. While ensemble classifiers often outperform single-model classifiers, their success crucially depends on the ensemble's construction. Genetic programming (GP) is a powerful evolutionary algorithm that can evolve populations of simple classifiers; however, standard GP algorithms produce populations of models with correlated predictions. Recent work in the broader evolutionary computing community has begun focusing on methods for evolving diverse populations, such as MAP-Elites [24], which can evolve populations that are diverse in a low dimensional *behavior space*. In this work, we demonstrate a novel technique for using MAP-Elites to create diverse GP populations, which can be used as ensemble classifiers. We demonstrate the utility of our framework, which we call Neuro-MAP-Elites, by comparing it with other classification algorithms across a diverse set of classification datasets.

Keywords: Diversity · Linear genetic programming · Ensemble classifiers

1 Introduction

Ensemble classifiers, which make predictions by combining multiple simple models, outperform single model classifiers for many supervised learning tasks. The importance of diversity in ensemble classifiers is well documented, however in general it can be challenging to create diverse ensemble classifiers in a principled way. While there may be various notions of diversity, for ensemble classifiers it is specifically *error diversity* - meaning that individual classifiers make errors on different samples - which matters most [7].

To see the benefit of error diversity, consider a toy problem consisting of only three samples and a set of limited classifiers, each of which can only classify two of the three samples. In this scenario, we can construct an optimal ensemble from three limited classifiers, as long as they are maximally diverse with respect

E. Medvet et al. (Eds.): EuroGP 2022, LNCS 13223, pp. 212–227, 2022.
https://doi.org/10.1007/978-3-031-02056-8_14

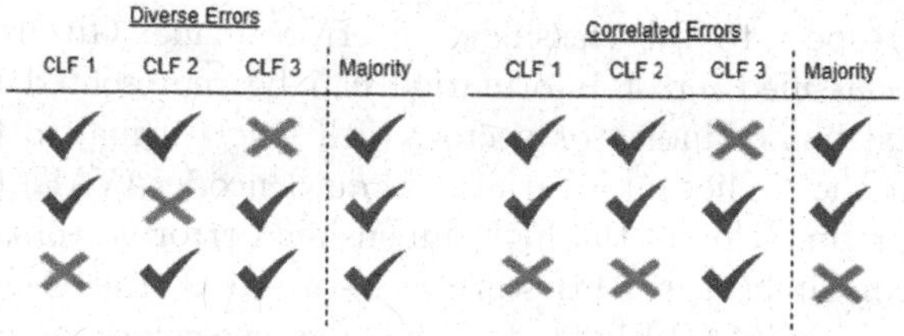

Diverse Errors					Correlated Errors			
CLF 1	CLF 2	CLF 3	Majority		CLF 1	CLF 2	CLF 3	Majority
✓	✓	✗	✓		✓	✓	✗	✓
✓	✗	✓	✓		✓	✓	✓	✓
✗	✓	✓	✓		✗	✗	✓	✗

Fig. 1. Benefit of ensemble diversity. In this toy example, each classifier can only achieve a maximum accuracy of 67%. However, as long as there is diversity in the errors made, a majority vote classifier constructed from these imperfect classifiers will achieve perfect accuracy.

to the errors they make. Conversely, if even two of the three classifiers make the same error, then the ensemble will not be correct in all cases (see Fig. 1).

The fact that evolutionary algorithms (EAs), such as genetic programming, produce populations of solutions makes them seemingly ideal for ensemble creation. However, many standard EAs for evolving classifiers lose diversity as evolution proceeds, causing the predictions of the individuals in the final population to be strongly correlated. This limits our ability to create an effective ensemble classifier directly from a final population. In practice, we can run an EA many times and create a diverse ensemble by selecting the best individual from each run to be in the final ensemble, however there are drawbacks to this method. In addition to being wasteful by not using all models from each run, there are other issues with this approach. For example, it is possible that if the standard algorithm is run too long that independent trails will converge to the same or similar solutions, and if it is not run long enough, the individuals will not be fit enough to be useful in an ensemble.

Within the field of evolutionary computing, there are many examples of the utility of creating diverse sets of solutions as opposed to focusing on a single best solution, such as evolving adaptable robot controllers [10], playing card games [8,12], and generating video game content [14]. Many of these results rely specifically on the MAP-Elites algorithm, a niching EA, which represents the population as a discrete grid of cells and assigns solutions to cells based on their behaviors [24].

In MAP-Elites, candidate solutions only compete with other candidates assigned to the same cell, which allows the population to maintain diversity as evolution proceeds. The mapping from solutions to cells is facilitated by *behavior descriptors*, which maps solutions to a low dimensional behavior space. The behavior space is then partitioned into cells, and solutions are assigned to the cells in which their behavior descriptors lie. This partitioning of the behavior space helps prevent MAP-Elites populations from converging to a set of highly similar solutions by preserving diversity in the behavior space [24].

Defining effective behavior descriptors is an essential aspect of MAP-Elites, as they determine the sorts of diversity which will be produced. As mentioned above, when creating ensemble classifiers, we are particularly concerned about diversity with respect to the classification errors made. Given a fixed set of samples to be classified, error information can be represented naturally as a high dimensional binary indicator vector, with length equal to the number of samples. Our method relies on a variational autoencoder (VAE) to learn a low-dimensional representation of the high dimensional error vectors.

The main contribution of this work is Neuro-MAP-Elites (NME), a novel framework based on MAP-Elites, for evolving ensembles of classifiers with greater error diversity. Using linear genetic programs (LGPs) as our classification model, we show that NME can be used to create diverse populations of classifiers and further that these more diverse populations make more effective ensemble classifiers.

2   Background

In this section, we provide some brief background on the techniques upon which NME is based.

2.1   Linear Genetic Programming

In general, genetic programming (GP) seeks to evolve computational models for making predictions [5]. There are many variants of GP, based on different representations for the computational models being evolved, such as tree GP [19], Cartesian GP [22] and linear GP (LGP) [5]. In this work, we use LGP for our genetic programming model, as it provides good performance on a wide range of classification tasks [5,30]; however, any GP variant can be used with our method. In this section, we give a general overview of LGP, and in Sect. 3, we provide more specific details on the specific LGP implementation used in this work.

Simply put, LGP is a type of GP where computational models (i.e., programs) are represented as sequences of instructions, often resembling imperative programs [5]. Generally, programs have access to a number ($n_{registers}$) of writable *computation registers* used when executing their instruction sequences. Programs also have some registers designated as *input registers*, which, as their name suggests, contain input values to the program. In the context of classification tasks, these input values are the features of the samples that we are classifying. The input registers may be implemented by designating a subset of the writable computation registers as input registers or as a separate set of read-only registers. Instructions typically involve mathematical operations on values stored in registers and result in either information being written to registers, or changes to the program execution (such as skipping instructions). Programs perform classification of samples as follows: first, the samples' features are loaded into the input registers, next the instructions are executed, and finally the final state of the computation registers is then transformed to a prediction. The transformation of the final state of the computation registers may be done in many ways and is dependent on the problem. In the simple case of binary classification tasks, a common approach is to designate a single computation register as the *output register*, and then compare the value of the final register to a predefined threshold to obtain the prediction (i.e., if *output* > *threshold* predict class 1, else predict class 2). In this work, we combine LGP with the MAP-Elites algorithm to help create diverse populations.

2.2   Map-Elites

Map-Elites is an EA designed to evolve diverse populations of solutions in a single run [24]. More specifically, Map-Elites falls under the umbrella of *quality diversity* algorithms, which are EAs designed to evolve populations of high-performing solutions which are also diverse. The way Map-Elites works is fairly straightforward – instead of using an unstructured population, as is typical in EAs, MAP-Elites used a structured grid population to maintain diversity. The structured grid contains a number of cells equal to the maximum population size. Each cell begins empty and may contain no more than one solution during the execution of the algorithm. When a new candidate solution is created, there is a two-step process to determine if the candidate solution is added to the population. First, a *behavior function* maps the candidate solution to a single cell. The candidate solution then competes with the current solution in this cell, or if no solution currently occupies the cell, the candidate solution is automatically added. The simplest way to implement the competition is by simply selecting the solution with the highest fitness and breaking ties randomly.

An essential part of MAP-Elites is determining the mapping from solutions to cells. To this end, when evaluating a possible solution, a *behavior descriptor* is produced, in addition to a fitness score. The *behavior space* is a low-dimensional vector, typically 2D, used to represent a solution in the *behavior space*. The behavior space is partitioned into (usually equal sized) cells so that a program is assigned to the cell in the behavior space in which its descriptor lies. The reason for using low-dimensional descriptors is that higher dimensional descriptors lead to problems stemming from the curse of dimensionality. Specifically, the problem is that if we divide each dimension into k regions (boundaries for the cell), then the total number of cells for a d-dimensional descriptor will be k^d. If we instead try to fix the max population size at N, then there can only be $\lfloor \log_d N \rfloor$ regions per dimension. In practice, we typically want at least ten regions per dimension, so we must stick to low-dimensional descriptors or use other variants of MAP-Elites, such as MAP-Elites-CVT [32].

2.3   Variational Autoencoders (VAEs)

VAEs are a powerful probabilistic modeling framework for representation learning [18]. The VAE framework assumes that high dimensional observed data are generated by a random process acting on unobserved latent factors. VAEs are composed of two feed-forward neural net models, often called the encoder and decoder networks. The encoder network learns to infer a distribution over low-dimensional representations of the high dimensional data, and the decoder learns a generative model from latent factors to the samples from the original high dimensional space.

To train a VAE, the weights of both the encoder and decoder are optimized together, using an unsupervised objective. During training, the high-dimensional original data x are passed through the encoder, which outputs a probability distribution over encodings of x. Specifically, this is done by outputting a mean vector μ_x, and variance vector σ_x, which are interpreted as parameters to a Normal distribution with a diagonal only co-variance matrix. A sample is then drawn from this distribution, and the sample is fed into the decoder, which aims to reconstruct the original sample x by outputting $\hat{x}$. The loss function used to train a standard VAE is known as the evidence lower bound (ELBO), and contains two terms. The first is the reconstruction error $||x - \hat{x}||^2$, which measures the reconstruction quality. In the loss function, this term incentivizes the VAE towards learning low-dimensional encodings, which are informative about the high dimensional representation. The other term is the KL divergence between the distribution output by the encoder, and a standard Normal distribution $D_{KL}(N(\mu_x, \sigma_x)||N(0, \mathrm{I}))$. This term encourages representations that are approximately normally distributed.

While it may seem beneficial to only focus on the first objective—which is essentially what is done in basic autoencoders [17] – the second objective provides regularization and encourages the encoder to learn smoother encodings. This means small changes in the latent features produce small changes in the high dimensional space, and similar high dimensional vectors are encoded to nearby locations in the low dimensional space. Further, it also produces latent spaces in which the samples are approximately normally distributed, which is useful for some downstream tasks.

There have been many modifications made to VAEs since their original proposal. Here we briefly mention a VAE variant called β-VAE [16], which is used in this work. β-VAE follows the original VAE design but employs a modified version of the ELBO loss function. In β-VAE, the loss contains a constant β, which controls the relative weight of the two terms in the standard VAE loss. The benefit of β-VAE is that it allows us to control the trade-off between the two terms in the ELBO. Specifically, the β-VAE loss function is: $loss = ||x - \hat{x}||^2 + \beta D_{KL}(N(\mu_x, \sigma_x)||N(0, I))$.

2.4 Ensemble Classifiers

Traditionally, GP approaches to classification rely on outputting the single best program as the final predictive model. However, it has been argued that since these algorithms produce populations of programs that are all adapted to the target task, it is logical to make use of the entire population in the final model [13, 29]. One major issue which must be addressed when evolving ensembles is the maintenance of diversity amongst the individual solutions, as predictive diversity has been shown to be crucial in ensemble creation [7].

In work from the GP community on evolving ensembles, there are generally two approaches; *offline* approaches, which construct the ensemble directly from a final population, and *online* approaches, which gradually build the ensemble during evolution [13]. With offline approaches, it is necessary to actively design the population structure to encourage diversity and prevent convergence to a population of identical or similar individuals. In online approaches, while not strictly necessary, diversity preserving populations can be beneficial [29].

More recently, others have used EAs with explicit diversity mechanisms to create ensemble classifiers. Boisvert and Sheppard [4] use an approach based on novelty search [21], to evolve diverse ensembles of decision trees. In this work, the population is represented as a variable-sized *archive*, and new candidate solutions are added to the archive if they meet a criterion based on novelty and fitness. Cardoso et al. [9] also used novelty search in the space of neural network architectures to create diverse ensembles. In their work, the novelty metrics were based explicitly on error diversity. To the best of our knowledge, our work is the first to apply MAP-Elites and GP to create ensemble diversity.

3   Our LGP Implementation

In this section we describe the specific details of the LGP implementation used in this work. In our implementation of LGP, all instructions have the format

$$destination = source1 <op> source2$$

where op is one of the functions in the operator set {ADD, SUBT, MULT, PDIV, SNIG, QUIT}, and *destination, source1, source2* refer to registers which store floating point values (see Table 1 for information on the operators).

Table 1. Operators from LGP system. *dest* refers the destination register and *src1, src2* refer to source registers.

Operators	Description
ADD	$dest = src1 + src2$
SUBT	$dest = src1 - src2$
MULT	$dest = src1 * src2$
PDIV	if $scr1 \neq 0$ $dest = src1/src2$
	else $dest = src1$
SNIG	if $src1 > src2$, skip next instruction
	(skip next if greater)
QUIT	do not execute any more instructions

In our system, all registers are writable, including the input registers. Programs have access to a total of $10 + n_{features}$ registers, where $n_{features}$ is the number of features in the dataset. This setting was determined empirically and worked well with the variety of datasets we tested. Others have advocated using a constant multiple of the number of features [5], however we found that for datasets with many features, this method provides too many registers, and evolution takes much longer to find good solutions. For initialization, the first register is set to 0.0, the following nine are set to constant values, and the remaining $n_{features}$ registers are set to the feature values of the sample which is being classified. Any binary features are represented using 1.0 to represent true and 0.0 for false. A program's prediction is based on the final value of the first register; values greater than 0 are interpreted as a prediction that the class label is "1", values less than 0 are interpreted as a prediction that the class label is "0". Programs that end execution with 0 in the first register are interpreted as not having made a prediction; when computing a program's fitness, no prediction is always scored as an incorrect prediction.

Variation. In our LGP algorithm, we produce variation in programs through both micro and macro mutations. Our macro mutation operator replaces a randomly selected instruction with a new randomly generated instruction, and our micro mutation operator randomly changes either the operator, destination register, or one of the source registers of a randomly selected operation.

When generating random instructions, new instructions obey the following rules, which allows for efficient evolution and ensures all mutations result in legal programs. The first rule simply ensures all instructions refer to valid registers and operators by enforcing bounds on their range. This second rule is that when generating a random value for a destination register of a program, the maximum value is one greater than the current maximum value of a destination register in that program. This rule is inspired by the progressive complexification proposed in NEAT [31] and is designed to encourage mutations to have a higher chance of being effective (Table 2).

Table 2. Rules for random instruction creation. Rule 1 ensures that generated instructions are always legal and meaningful. Rule 2 encourages mutations to have a higher change of being effective. In rule 2, *max_dest* refers to the largest integer representing a destination register in the program for which the instruction is being generated, and is taken to be 0 in the case of a program with no instructions.

Rule	Description
Rule 1	$op \in \{0, 1, ..., 5\}$
	$src1, src2, dest \in \{0, 1, ..., 9 + n_{features}\}$
Rule 2	$dest \in \{0, ..., max\_dest + 1\}$

Fitness. A program's fitness is its balanced accuracy score on the training data, which is computed from the number of true positives (TP), true negatives (TN), false positives (FP) and false negatives (FN): $fitness = \frac{0.5TP}{TP+FN} + \frac{0.5TN}{TN+FP}$. The balanced accuracy score provides a good dataset agnostic measure of the accuracy of a classifier, as it is normalized to account for imbalanced classes [26].

Behaviors. To use MAP-Elites with LGP, we must define suitable behavior descriptors for the LGP programs. Previously there has been only limited work using MAP-Elites together with LGP, such as [11]. In our experiments using basic MAP-Elites with LGP, we use three behavior descriptors to categorize program behaviors: the number of features, instructions, and registers used by the program. The number of instructions counts only instructions that affect the final output of the program, and the number of registers counts the number of unique destination registers used in effective instructions, both of which of indicative of a programs complexity (see Table 3 for information on the descriptors used with each variant).

Table 3. Behavior descriptors used with each variant of MAP-Elites.

ME Type	# of features	# of registers	# of instructions	VAE encoder
Basic ME 0	X	X		
Basic ME 1		X	X	
Basic ME 2	X		X	
Neuro ME				X

4   Neuro MAP-Elites

This section details the Neuro MAP-Elites (NME) algorithm, an offline approach to evolving diverse GP populations, which can be used as accurate predictive ensembles. We begin by outlining an ideal high-dimensional behavior descriptor appropriate for any classifier, particularly linear genetic programs. We then propose a low-dimensional approximation that can be used with MAP-Elites to create accurate ensemble classifiers.

The primary motivation behind our behavior descriptors is that classifiers are designed to make predictions on samples coming from some distribution. When we describe the behavior of a classifier, what really matters is how it behaves on samples from this target distribution. This is similar to the idea of program *semantics*, which has previously been studied in the context of GP [1,2,20,23,25]. The main innovation in this work is proposing a methodology for creating a low-dimensional encoding that captures this notion of behavior.

If we consider a simplified case in which the target distribution is uniform over a finite dataset, we can create a high dimensional descriptor of a classifier behavior by recording its predictions on all samples. In this case, the high dimensional descriptor gives a complete description of the classifier behavior. The question of whether it is possible to obtain a complete low dimensional description of the behavior is equivalent to the question of whether it is possible to compress the high dimensional descriptors to a fixed low dimension without loss - which in general is not possible. This means that for any low dimensional behavior descriptor, some programs with different prediction behaviors will be mapped to the same point in the low dimensional space. The goal of our method is to provide a low dimensional approximation to the ideal high dimensional descriptor. To this end, we employ a VAE which learns to compress the high dimensional ideal descriptors into low dimensional approximations.

The proposed NME algorithm can be divided into 3 phases; mining solutions, VAE training, and a final MAP-Elites run using the encoder to generate behavior descriptors (see Fig. 2 for an overview of the algorithm.)

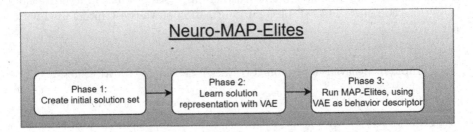

Fig. 2. Overview of Neuro-MAP-Elites. (Phase 1) Create an archive of classifiers and record their predictions on training samples. In our implementation, we create this archive by running MAP-Elites multiple times using various simple descriptors. (Phase 2) A VAE is trained to compress the prediction vectors to a low-dimensional descriptor which can be used to map programs to cells in MAP-Elites. (Phase 3) Run MAP-Elites, using the encoder network to produce behavior descriptors when mapping programs to cells.

4.1   Mine Solutions

The goal of the first phase of NME is to draw a sample from the distribution of errors produced by 'good' programs, which can be used in phase two to train the VAE. In general, and depending on the specific problem, what constitutes a 'good' solution may vary. In this work, we consider any solution which is present in a final population and obtains a balanced accuracy score greater than 0.5 on the training data. To create the sample, we run a basic version of MAP-Elites using various descriptors (Basic ME0, Basic ME1, Basic ME2), and record the predictions made by each individual in the final populations on all training samples.

4.2   VAE Training

The goal of the second phase is to learn a low-dimensional representation of samples from the distribution of errors produced by 'good' programs. To this end, we use the prediction vectors from solutions produced in the first phase as training data and train a β-VAE to encode these vectors into a 2-dimensional representation to be used as a behavior descriptor in MAP-Elites.

Initially, when training the VAE, we used cross-validation to select the optimal β values for each dataset from values in the range $\{0.1, 0.2, ..., 1.5\}$. We found for all datasets that the optimal β was in $\{0.2, 0.3, 0.4\}$, so when running final experiments, we reduced the range of β values tested to only those ≤ 1.0. For each β, we repeat fitting the VAE five times, using different random seeds, as we found that the random initialization impacted the VAEs' ability to learn good representations. The VAE that created the highest entropy distribution in the latent space was selected from these five fitting trials. We experimented with using two and three dimensions for the latent space; however, all experiments in this work are based on two dimensions, as we did not find better performance from increasing the latent space to three dimensions.

The VAE that created the highest entropy distribution in the latent space was selected from these five fitting trials.

4.3   MAP Elites with Encoder

In the final phase, we rerun MAP-Elites, however instead of using the basic descriptors (as in phase 1), we now use the encoder network of the VAE (trained in phase 2) to produce the descriptors. The encoder takes as input a binary prediction vector made by a program on the training data and outputs a 2-dimensional real-valued encoding of the prediction vector. As the encoder was trained as part of a VAE, the distribution of encodings should be approximately a unit normal distribution. We take advantage of this fact when partitioning the latent space into bins to use with MAP-Elites, and set the bin boundaries so that each bin has equal probability mass under a normal distribution.

5   Experiment Setup

To test the efficacy of our method, we compared the predictive accuracy of our method against other standard supervised learning techniques across a diverse set of datasets.

5.1   Dataset Selection

In this work, we use a subset of datasets from the Penn Machine Learning Benchmarks (PMLB) repository [26] which contains a large collection of curated datasets for machine learning evaluation and comparison. PMLB contains a wide assortment of datasets suitable for various machine learning tasks. In this work, we considered datasets that contain a binary classification task. As our algorithm produces an ensemble classifier, we are particularly interested in how it performs relative to other ensemble classifiers. To this end, we selected the datasets based on the performance of a standard ensemble classifier: random forest [6]. Specifically, we selected two datasets where random forest performs much better than other standard classifiers, two datasets where random forest performs much worse, and finally two datasets where all the tested standard algorithms do poorly (see Table 4).

For all classifiers, the datasets were first partitioned into a "full training' and a test set (75%–25% split). The "full training' set is further partitioned into training and validation sets (75%–25% split). The training sets are used to fit the models, the validation sets are used to determine model hyperparameters, and the test sets are used to compute the final metrics.

Table 4. Datasets used for classifier comparison. See [26] for dataset details.

Dataset	Difficult for RF	Difficult for other ML
Breast		X
Monk2		X
HV_without_noise	X	
HV_with_noise	X	
GAMETES_Epistasis	X	X
Parity5+5	X	X

To demonstrate the efficacy of our method, we compare the performance achieved by classifiers generated with NME against the performance of standard machine learning classifiers, as well as genetic programming classifiers evolved using a classic version of MAP-Elites.

5.2   Standard Machine Learning Classifiers

All experiments using standard classifiers used the classifier implementations from *scikit-learn* [27], as well as scikit-learn utilities for tuning their parameters[1]. Specifically, we considered the following five standard machine learning classifiers (scikit-learn names in parentheses); random forest (RandomForestClassifier) [6], k-nearest neighbors (KNeighborsClassifier), logistic regression (LogisticRegressionClassifier) [3], Gaussian naive Bayes (GaussianNB) [15] and support vector machine classifiers (SVC) [28].

5.3   Map-Elites Classifiers

For both basic MAP-Elites and NME, we tested two methods of creating a final classifier from the final population. In the first method, the final classifier is simply the single program with the best fitness from the final population. If multiple programs are tied for the best fitness, the program with the fewest effective instructions is selected (if there is still a tie, the winner is chosen randomly). In the second method, an ensemble is created by combining all programs in the final population with fitness above a threshold t (t is chosen to maximize the

---

[1] See github.com/BigTuna08/nme for the code to tune parameters of all models.

accuracy of the majority vote classifier on the training data). The ensemble classifier outputs the prediction of the majority of the programs, with ties broken randomly. We also considered other methods of combining programs to create the final classifier, such as weighting the programs by their fitness, but this did not improve results.

All runs of MAP-Elites used a 20×20 grid for the population and ran for 1 million evaluations.

6   Results

In this section we present results comparing NME with the variants of basic MAP-Elites described in Table 3. In addition to our results on ensemble accuracy (Sect. 6.3), we show results supporting our methods in Sects. 6.1 and 6.2.

6.1   VAE Efficacy

One possible concern with this methodology is how well the learned encoding captures the information from the original high dimensional descriptors. To investigate this, we examine the decoders' ability to reconstruct the original high dimensional descriptor from the 2-dimensional encoding. Averaged across all datasets, the decoders were able to correctly reconstruct over 88% of the predictions, with the reconstruction ability varying from just below 80% to nearly 100% on the various datasets (see Table 5).

Table 5. Accuracy of VAE at reconstructing predictions. Percent scores indicate the percentage of bits in the error vectors correctly reconstructed by the VAE. Higher scores indicate that the learned descriptors are more informative about the ideal high dimensional descriptors.

Dataset	VAE prediction reconstruction
Breast	98.88%
HV_without_noise	90.25%
HV_with_noise	89.66%
Monk2	89.19%
Parity5+5	84.94%
GAMETES_Epistasis	79.67%
Mean	88.76%

6.2   Diversity Comparison

Here, we compare the predictive diversity of ensembles of LGP programs created by basic variants of MAP-Elites, as well as our proposed NME method. We define the predictive diversity as the average Euclidean distance between prediction vectors within the ensemble. To obtain these results, we conducted 50 independent runs of each MAP-Elites variant (Table 3).

The results from comparing predictive diversity (Table 6) support our claim that NME produces more diverse populations. We found that across all datasets, the average diversity produced by NME in a single run was greater than both (1) the diversity of an ensemble created by combining all final populations created from the three variants of basic MAP-Elites and (2) the diversity of the single best run of basic MAP-Elites. Further, these results show that for four of the six datasets tested, the least diverse single run of NME was still more diverse than the most diverse run of basic MAP-Elites (Table 6).

Table 6. Comparison of LGP prediction diversity with top 2 scores in bold. Here we show the diversity scores obtained from running basic ME 120 times and combining the final populations (Multi), the highest diversity score obtained in a single run (Best Single), the average diversity score from a single run (Mean Single), and the lowest diversity score from a single run (Worst Single). Across all datasets, NME produced populations with the the most diversity. For many datasets, the least diverse single run of NME was more diverse than all variants using basic MAP-Elites.

Dataset	Basic ME			NME	
	Multi	Best Single	Mean Single	Mean Single	Worst Single
GAMETES	4.67	5.74	3.85	**7.64**	**5.78**
HV_noise	7.62	7.54	6.27	**8.69**	**7.93**
HV	4.83	5.18	4.26	**7.11**	**5.66**
Breast	3.28	**3.74**	2.97	**4.29**	3.58
Monk2	3.51	**4.21**	3.29	**4.64**	4.11
Parity5+5	3.98	4.64	3.76	**6.85**	**5.34**

6.3 Ensemble Accuracy

Measured across all datasets, our method compares favorably against both the traditional machine learning classifiers and LGP classifiers evolved using MAP-Elites with basic LGP descriptors.

However, no method is a clear winner across all of the datasets (see Table 7). On the two datasets which were selected for being easy for random forest (Breast and Monk2), random forest was the most accurate. On one of the datasets, which was significantly harder for random forest than other standard classifiers (HV_without_noise), multiple methods achieved perfect accuracy, including NME partial vote; on the other (HV_with_noise), multiple standard methods outperform all evolved classifiers. Finally, on the datasets which were difficult for standard methods (Parity5+5 and GAMETES_Epistasis), evolved classifiers outperformed the standard ones, although in only one of these (GAMETES_Epistasis) was the NME classifier the best.

Another finding evident from Table 7 is that of the methods tested that evolve ensembles, those created with NME significantly outperform ensembles created with the basic variants of MAP-Elites. This is despite the fact that basic MAP-Elites can produce high-quality single solutions, sometimes better than the single solutions produced by NME. This result supports our hypothesis that NME generates populations with more meaningful diversity and that this diversity is beneficial for creating ensembles.

Table 7. Comparison of balanced accuracy scores of common machine learning classifiers and evolved classifiers. Best scores for each dataset are indicated in bold.

Dataset	RF	KNN	LR	GNB	SVC	ME-Best	ME-Vote	NME-Best	NME-Vote
Breast	**.950**	.564	.500	.949	.500	.939	.579	.913	.943
Monk2	**.987**	.709	.447	.456	.697	.729	.502	.642	.785
HV	.646	.637	**1.00**	.523	.949	**1.00**	.426	.986	**1.00**
HV_noise	.575	.520	**.974**	.526	.854	.687	.495	.709	.802
GAMETES	.499	.515	.486	.513	.486	.495	.516	.510	**.569**
Parity5+5	.594	.601	.463	.463	.473	**1.00**	.494	.891	.986
Mean	.709	.591	.645	.572	.660	.808	.502	.775	**.848**

7 Discussion

Using representation learning techniques in combination with quality diversity methods provides a promising avenue for creating diverse classifier ensembles. In this work, we have provided a method for extending MAP-Elites for use with high dimensional descriptors by learning low dimensional approximations to the true descriptors. Here, we focused on diversity with respect to the errors made, but there are other possible high dimensional descriptors that could be used with our method.

One in particular, is information about features used by each classifier. In a similar manner as the high dimensional binary error vectors, information about the features used by a classifier can naturally be represented as a binary indicator vector, which could be compressed by a VAE. There are two main reasons why it may be beneficial to use this methodology with feature information; the first is for working with data with missing or noisy features, and the second is to improve our understanding of what features tend to co-occur in effective classifiers. This second use is perhaps the most interesting and relies on the generative model portion of the VAE (sometimes called the decoder), as opposed to the encoder portion used in NME. If we use a simple generative model, such as a single-layer neural network, we can inspect the model to gain insight into the relationships amongst features.

Another possible direction for this work is to explore other methods for compressing the ideal high-dimensional descriptor outlined in this work. The design of VAE models has recently received much attention from the representation learning community, and it is possible that novel architectures may be more suitable for use in our algorithm. In our experiments, we limited the VAE latent dimension to two, as we found that was sufficient for encoding most of the information in the prediction vectors for most datasets. Clearly, this may be limiting, particularly when the number of samples used for creating the prediction vectors is large. In future work, we plan to examine the relationship between the number of samples included in the high dimensional descriptor, the dimensionality of the encoding, and the performance of NME.

One limitation of our current work is NME requires greater computational resources than traditional GP methods, as it requires us to create an initial set of solutions and train a VAE, before evolving the final population with MAP-Elites. In our current implementation, we create the initial set of solutions by running basic variants of MAP-Elites multiple times, which is a major cause of inefficiency. In future work, we plan to experiment with more efficient ways to create the initial solution set; in particular by using more efficient machine learning classifiers in this step. We also plan to implement a cyclical version of NME, which can continuously alternate between phase two (training VAE) and phase three (MAP-Elites with encoder), until a stopping condition is met. This will hopefully reduce the amount of effort needed in phase 1, as the solution set used to train the VAE will be updated as NME proceeds. By improving the efficiency of NME, we can make it more practically competitive with non-evolutionary classifiers and lead to greater adoption of GP by the larger machine learning community.

References

1. Beadle, L., Johnson, C.: Semantically driven crossover in genetic programming, pp. 111–116, July 2008
2. Beadle, L., Johnson, C.: Semantically driven mutation in genetic programming, pp. 1336–1342, May 2009
3. Berkson, J.: Application of the logistic function to bio-assay. J. Am. Statist. Assoc. 39(227), 357–365 (1944)
4. Boisvert, S., Sheppard, J.W.: Quality diversity genetic programming for learning decision tree ensembles. In: Hu, T., Lourenço, N., Medvet, E. (eds.) EuroGP 2021. LNCS, vol. 12691, pp. 3–18. Springer, Cham (2021). https://doi.org/10.1007/978-3-030-72812-0_1
5. Brameier, M.F., Banzhaf, W.: Linear Genetic Programming, 1st edn. Springer Publishing Company Inc., Cham (2007)
6. Breiman, L.: Random forests. Mach. Learn. 45(1), 5–32 (2001)
7. Brown, G., Wyatt, J., Harris, R., Yao, X.: Diversity creation methods: a survey and categorisation. Inf. Fusion 6(1), 5–20 (2005)
8. Canaan, R., Togelius, J., Nealen, A., Menzel, S.: Diverse agents for ad-hoc cooperation in Hanabi. In: 2019 IEEE Conference on Games (CoG), pp. 1–8 (2019)
9. Cardoso, R.P., Hart, E., Kurka, D.B., Pitt, J.V.: Using novelty search to explicitly create diversity in ensembles of classifiers. In: GECCO 2021, pp. 849–857. ACM, New York, NY, USA (2021)
10. Cully, A., Clune, J., Tarapore, D., Mouret, J.B.: Robots that can adapt like animals. Nature 521, 503–507 (2015)
11. Dolson, E., Lalejini, A., Ofria, C.: Exploring genetic programming systems with map-elites, August 2018

12. Fontaine, M.C., Lee, S., Soros, L.B., De Mesentier Silva, F., Togelius, J., Hoover, A.K.: Mapping hearthstone deck spaces through map-elites with sliding boundaries. In: GECCO 2019, pp. 161–169. ACM, New York, NY, USA (2019)

13. Gagné, C., Sebag, M., Schoenauer, M., Tomassini, M.: Ensemble learning for free with evolutionary algorithms? In: GECCO 2007, pp. 1782–1789. ACM, New York, NY, USA (2007)

14. Gravina, D., Khalifa, A., Liapis, A., Togelius, J., Yannakakis, G.N.: Procedural content generation through quality diversity (2019)

15. Hastie, T., Tibshirani, R., Friedman, J.H.: The Elements of Statistical Learning: Data Mining, Inference, and Prediction, 2nd edn. Springer, Cham (2009). https://doi.org/10.1007/978-0-387-84858-7

16. Higgins, I., t al.: beta-VAE: learning basic visual concepts with a constrained variational framework. In: ICLR (2017)

17. Hinton, G.E., Salakhutdinov, R.R.: Reducing the dimensionality of data with neural networks. Science 313(5786), 504–507 (2006)

18. Kingma, D.P., Welling, M.: Auto-encoding variational bayes (2014)

19. Koza, J.R.: Genetic programming: automatic programming of computers. EvoNews 1(3), 4–7 (1997)

20. Krawiec, K., Lichocki, P.: Approximating geometric crossover in semantic space. In: GECCO 2009, pp. 987–994. ACM, New York, NY, USA (2009)

21. Lehman, J., Stanley, K.O.: Abandoning objectives: evolution through the search for novelty alone. Evol. Comput. 19(2), 189–223 (2011)

22. Miller, J.: Cartesian Genetic Programming, vol. 43, June 2003

23. Moraglio, A., Krawiec, K., Johnson, C.G.: Geometric semantic genetic programming. In: Coello, C.A.C., Cutello, V., Deb, K., Forrest, S., Nicosia, G., Pavone, M. (eds.) PPSN 2012. LNCS, vol. 7491, pp. 21–31. Springer, Heidelberg (2012). https://doi.org/10.1007/978-3-642-32937-1_3

24. Mouret, J., Clune, J.: Illuminating search spaces by mapping elites (2015)

25. Nguyen, Q.U., Hoai, N., O'Neill, M., McKay, R., Galván-López, E.: Semantically-based crossover in genetic programming: application to real-valued symbolic regression. Genetic Program. Evol. Mach. 12, 91–119 (2011)

26. Olson, R.S., La Cava, W., Orzechowski, P., Urbanowicz, R.J., Moore, J.H.: PMLB: a large benchmark suite for machine learning evaluation and comparison. BioData Mining 10(1), 36 (2017)

27. Pedregosa, F., et al.: Scikit-learn: machine learning in Python. J. Mach. Learn. Res. 12, 2825–2830 (2011)

28. Platt, J.C.: Probabilistic outputs for support vector machines and comparisons to regularized likelihood methods. In: Advances in Large Margin Classifiers, pp. 61–74. MIT Press (1999)

29. Rodrigues, N.M., Batista, J.E., Silva, S.: Ensemble genetic programming. In: Hu, T., Lourenço, N., Medvet, E., Divina, F. (eds.) EuroGP 2020. LNCS, vol. 12101, pp. 151–166. Springer, Cham (2020). https://doi.org/10.1007/978-3-030-44094-7_10

30. Sha, C., Cuperlovic-Culf, M., Hu, T.: Smile: systems metabolomics using interpretable learning and evolution. BMC Bioinform. 22(1), 284 (2021)

31. Stanley, K.O., Miikkulainen, R.: Evolving neural networks through augmenting topologies. Evol. Comput. 10(2), 99–127 (2002)

32. Vassiliades, V., Chatzilygeroudis, K., Mouret, J.: Using centroidal voronoi tessellations to scale up the multidimensional archive of phenotypic elites algorithm. IEEE Trans. Evol. Comput. 22(4), 623–630 (2018)

Evolving Monotone Conjunctions
in Regimes Beyond Proved Convergence

Pantia-Marina Alchirch[1]([⊠]) [ID], Dimitrios I. Diochnos[2] [ID],
and Katia Papakonstantinopoulou[1,2] [ID]

[1] Athens University of Economics and Business (TESLAB), Athens, Greece
{marina.alchirch,katia}@aueb.gr
[2] University of Oklahoma, Norman, Oklahoma, USA
{diochnos,katia}@ou.edu

Abstract. Recently it was shown, using the typical mutation mechanism that is used in evolutionary algorithms, that monotone conjunctions are provably evolvable under a specific set of Bernoulli $(p)^n$ distributions. A natural question is whether this mutation mechanism allows convergence under other distributions as well. Our experiments indicate that the answer to this question is affirmative and, at the very least, this mechanism converges under Bernoulli $(p)^n$ distributions outside of the known proved regime.

Keywords: Evolvability · Genetic programming · Monotone conjunctions · Distribution-specific learning · Bernoulli $(p)^n$ distributions

1 Introduction

Automating the creation of computer programs that perform intelligent operations has been driving the research in evolutionary programming and in machine learning – though the approaches used are oftentimes different. Slightly more than a decade ago, these two fields came closer with the introduction of the framework of *evolvability* by Leslie Valiant [16].

Evolvability formulates evolution as a learning process and is a framework for a special type of local search method that ultimately develops *individuals* (that is, computer programs) that have high fitness within their environment. In other words, the goal is to develop a function that has high predictive accuracy on an unknown function c that we want to learn from training examples.

We continue the study of a simple and intuitive class of Boolean functions, that of *monotone conjunctions*, within the framework of evolvability.

1.1 Monotone Conjunctions and Representation

A monotone conjunction is a function that combines a set of variables with a Boolean AND. For example, the function $f = x_1 \wedge x_2 \wedge x_5$ returns TRUE if the first, second and fifth variable are satisfied simultaneously on a truth assignment $a = (a_1, \ldots, a_n) \in \{0, 1\}^n$, otherwise it returns FALSE. When we are working in a space with n Boolean variables, an intuitive representation for monotone conjunctions is that of a bitstring of length n, where a 1 (resp. 0) in a particular bit indicates the presence (resp. absence) of the specific variable in the function. For example, when $n = 8$, we can represent the function $f = x_1 \wedge x_2 \wedge x_5$ as:

| 1 | 1 | 0 | 0 | 1 | 0 | 0 | 0 |

. With $|h|$ we denote the *size* of a monotone conjunction h; the number of variables that are contained in h. Hence, in our example, $|f| = 3$.

On the Importance of Conjunctions Within Machine Learning. Conjunctions, as well as disjunctions, are perhaps the most basic classes of Boolean functions that act as building blocks for more complex functions. Even though these classes of functions are simple, nevertheless they have exponentially many functions on n Boolean variables and therefore provide a basic testbed for various ideas, as well as for understanding general bounds that are proved in the context of machine learning. Furthermore, learning algorithms for such basic classes of functions may provide insights for more sophisticated algorithms or even extend naturally to algorithms for richer classes of functions in certain contexts.

As an example, within the *Probably Approximately Correct (PAC)* model of learning [15], learning functions that are disjunctions of a *constant* number k of conjunctions can be achieved with a learning algorithm that is merely used for learning conjunctions [11]. The idea is that a disjunction of k conjunctions $f_1 \vee f_2 \vee \cdots \vee f_k$ can be converted to a conjunctive formula, where each clause has at most k literals[1] via the distributive law as shown below:

$$f_1 \vee f_2 \vee \cdots \vee f_k = \bigwedge_{u_1 \in f_1, u_2 \in f_2, \ldots, u_k \in f_k} (u_1 \vee u_2 \vee \cdots \vee u_k).$$

Therefore, for every selection (allowing repetitions) of k literals $(u_1, u_2, \ldots, u_k)$ over the original set of n Boolean variables $\{x_1, \ldots, x_n\}$, one can create a new variable $y_{u_1, u_2, \ldots, u_k}$ whose value is defined by $y_{u_1, u_2, \ldots, u_k} = u_1 \vee u_2 \vee \cdots \vee u_k$. Hence, an efficient distribution-independent algorithm for learning conjunctions from the set $\{x_1, \ldots, x_n\}$, may also learn such richer functions efficiently, but this time over the broader set of the y variables, which are $(2n)^k$ in total.

1.2   Related Work and Motivation

Using a simulation argument, a hallmark result in evolvability is one by Vitaly Feldman where it has been shown that evolvability is equivalent to learning using correlational statistical queries under a fixed distribution [5]. However, this simulation result, as has also been pointed out by Feldman, is not necessarily the most intuitive or efficient approach for designing evolutionary algorithms. At the same time intuitive evolutionary mechanisms are desirable and sought for; see, e.g., [9,12]. In this context, it is perhaps not surprising that one of the simplest,

---

[1] A literal is a Boolean variable or its negation.

non-trivial, classes of Boolean functions, that of monotone conjunctions, has received a lot of attention and their evolvability has been studied.

In particular, Leslie Valiant gave a *swapping-type* algorithm for learning monotone conjunctions when the distribution was uniform over $\{0,1\}^n$, when he introduced evolvability [16]. We outline this *swapping algorithm* in Sect. 3.1. The analysis of this algorithm was simplified in [3]. Eventually it was shown that this algorithm converges for Bernoulli $(p)^n$ distributions (defined in Sect. 3), characterized by any $p \in (0,1)$, where the uniform distribution is a special case obtained for $p = 1/2$. Meanwhile, another direction of research towards the learnability of monotone conjunctions has explored the power of *parallel* statistical queries by means of *recombination* [7], and of *horizontal gene transfer* [14].

On the other hand, the problem of learning monotone, or not, conjunctions has been studied within genetic programming (GP) as well. In this direction [9,10] have explored tree-like representations for learning monotone conjunctions under the uniform distribution in the realistic (for machine learning and evolvability) case, where the number of training examples are upper bounded by some polynomial of the input parameters. There has also been done additional work on exploring the learnability of monotone conjunctions, but some of these algorithms may have unrealistic assumptions for the framework of evolvability. For example, the algorithm in [13] uses a genetic approach in which the updates depend on the number of bits in which the candidate solution and the input differ. As another example, in the case of [6] it is assumed that the learner has knowledge of the exact fitness value of various hypotheses.

Along the lines of genetic programming, another mechanism that has been studied is the one inspired by the standard mutation mechanism that is encountered in $(1 + 1)$ evolutionary algorithms (EAs). This mechanism considers all the bits in the bitstring representation of a monotone conjunction (recall the discussion from Sect. 1.1) and tosses a coin that succeeds with probability $1/n$ in each bit. Whenever the coin toss succeeds, the bit at the particular coordinate is flipped. This algorithm has been shown to converge under product distributions where each variable is satisfied with the same probability p (called Bernoulli $(p)^n$ distributions; see Sect. 3), when p takes values in $(0, 1/3] \cup \{1/2\}$ [2]. A natural question that we try to answer in this paper is the following one:

Does the mutation mechanism that is inspired by the (1+1) EA allow the evolvability of monotone conjunctions under a broader set of distributions, compared to what is currently provably known?

Our experimental findings indicate that the answer is *affirmative*.

Structure of the Paper. Section 2 summarizes the computational models that come together in our work. Section 3 provides details on the problem that we study as well as a brief discussion on a related algorithm to our work, from where we draw inspiration on providing specific values to certain parameters that govern the evolutionary mechanism that we study. Section 4 provides details on the implementation of our method and how we define successful executions.

Section 5 presents the values of certain parameters that we use in the experiments as well as discusses the results of our experimental study. Section 6 concludes our work with a summary and ideas for future work.

2   Computational Models Relevant to Our Work

We now describe briefly the computational models that are relevant to our work. Before we do that, however, we make a remark on the terminology.

Remark 1 (Terminology). A candidate solution of an optimization problem, in EAs/GP is typically called an *individual*. On the other hand, in machine learning, a candidate solution to a learning problem, is typically called a *hypothesis* (or a *model*). One may use these terms interchangeably and in particular in our case these correspond to Boolean functions (or, if you prefer, to *computer programs*).

2.1   Evolutionary Algorithms and Evolving Programs

Evolutionary algorithms is a class of algorithms that develop solutions to optimization problems of interest. The development of these solutions proceeds in an iterative manner, such that candidate solution(s) from one iteration to the next are typically obtained after applying modification operators on the representation of the candidate solution(s) of the previous iteration. The function that is being optimized is called a *fitness function.* The idea is that the higher the fitness value of a particular individual (solution) is, the better the individual is for our purposes; i.e., as a solution to the optimization problem that we solve. The simplest mechanism that creates such solutions is shown in Algorithm 1, where we see that given an individual (candidate solution) x encoded as a bitstring of length n, a *mutated* version x' is obtained from x after tossing n times a coin that succeeds with probability $1/n$, and upon success of each coin toss, the respective bit in the binary representation of x is flipped. This modification mechanism is called a *mutation* as it tries to mimic in an elegant and compact way the way mutations occur in nature, and thus allows this algorithmic scheme to explore the binary search space in a randomized way. If x' is at least as fit as its *parent* x, then x' is selected to be the solution used for the next generation; otherwise,

---

Algorithm 1: The (1+1) Evolutionary Algorithm

Input: A function f to be optimized over $\{0,1\}^n$.
Output: A solution x, candidate for optimizing f.
1 $x \leftarrow$ random string from $\{0,1\}^n$;
2 **repeat**
3 $\quad$ Compute x' by flipping each bit of x independently with probability $1/n$;
4 $\quad$ **if** $f(x') \geq f(x)$ **then** $x \leftarrow x'$;
5 **until** some termination condition is met;

---

x is selected for one more generation. This way, the different solutions that we obtain across the different *iterations* (also known as *generations*) monotonically increase the fitness values that correspond to them. The interested reader may find additional discussion and several interesting results in [4].

A closely related field to EAs is that of genetic programming (GP) [8]. Similarly to EAs, the goal of GP is to develop a solution/individual that maximizes a fitness function. However, in the case of GP, the individuals correspond to different *functions* (computer programs), rather than to mere numerical points or truth assignments, from the domain of the fitness function. The most usual representation of these individuals is with the use of tree structures, as then on one hand such a representation is convenient (in a manner similar to decision trees) and on the other hand it is easy to define modification operators inspired by nature, such as mutation and recombination, and give rise to new individuals to be considered as candidate solutions that may survive in the next generation.

Our work in this paper falls under the broader umbrella of supervised machine learning, where the goal of the learner is to develop a function that approximates well some ground truth function. In other words, the goal of the learner is very well aligned with the goal of GP. On the other hand, the functions that we consider in our case have a very natural representation using bitstrings, as it was discussed in Sect. 1.1, and thus we can ultimately use Algorithm 1.

2.2 Supervised Machine Learning and Evolvability

In supervised machine learning the learner is typically presented with a set $S = \{(x_i, c(x_i))\}_{i=1}^m$ of *training examples* that exhibit the behavior of some *ground truth* function c on certain instances of the domain $\mathcal{X}$. Based on this information, the learner forms a *hypothesis* (or a *model*) h that approximates the ground truth c. For example, one typical approach for selecting a hypothesis h from a set of possible hypotheses $\mathcal{H}$, is that of *empirical risk minimization*, where the $h \in \mathcal{H}$ that is selected is the function that has the best predictive accuracy on the training examples S that were given to the learner.

Evolvability on the other hand is a special framework for supervised machine learning. In particular, in evolvability, the learner only gets to know how well their hypotheses approximate the ground truth function c, based on *aggregate* information that is computed from training examples. This information is equivalent to a noisy estimate of the risk (error rate) of the various hypotheses. The idea is that evolvability casts the whole process of evolution as a learning problem and the modifications that occur on the individuals (hypotheses) during the evolution should be favoring the fittest ones for survival to the next generation. In that sense, the encoding of the individuals at the genotype level cannot depend on individual experiences, but rather on some aggregate signal that is received from the environment, which thus describes how fit the particular individual is for this environment. Algorithms for evolvability are called *ecorithms*.

After this brief high-level discussion on supervised learning and evolvability, we will now provide more details for the framework of evolvability. We are looking at Boolean functions where the output values TRUE and FALSE are represented by 1 and -1 respectively. Evolvability works in a local search fashion, where at each step of the evolution a (parent) hypothesis h is considered together with the hypotheses that are obtained after applying a mutation operator on the particular (parent) hypothesis h, forming a neighborhood $N(h)$. Eventually, each hypothesis in the neighborhood $N(h)$ is evaluated using a *fitness* function, called *performance*, and ultimately this function is driving the search. For a *target function* c that we are trying to learn[2] and a distribution D over $\{0,1\}^n$, the performance of a hypothesis h, also called the *correlation* of h and c, is

$$Perf_D(h,c) = \mathbf{E}_{x \sim D}[h(x) \cdot c(x)]. \tag{1}$$

Note that from the above definition we also have that:

$$Perf_D(h,c) = \sum_{x \in \{0,1\}^n} h(x)c(x)\mathbf{Pr}_{x \sim D}(x) = 1 - 2 \cdot \mathbf{Pr}_{x \sim D}(h(x) \neq c(x)). \tag{2}$$

An approximate value $\widehat{Perf}_S(h,c)$ of $Perf_D(h,c)$ is obtained empirically for each hypothesis using a sample S; we denote this value with v_h for brevity. Then, for a real constant t, called *tolerance*, we obtain the sets:

$$\begin{cases} \mathtt{Bene} = \{h' \in N(h) \mid v_{h'} > v_h + t\} \\ \mathtt{Neut} = \{h' \in N(h) \mid v_{h'} \geq v_h - t\} \setminus \mathtt{Bene}. \\ \mathtt{Del} = \{h' \in N(h) \mid v_{h'} < v_h - t\} \end{cases} \tag{3}$$

Hence, for the next iteration, a hypothesis from the set $\mathtt{Bene}$ is selected, should $\mathtt{Bene} \neq \emptyset$. Otherwise, a hypothesis from $\mathtt{Neut}$ is selected; note that $\mathtt{Neut} \neq \emptyset$ since $\mathtt{Neut}$ always contains the parent hypothesis h. Thus, while the set $\mathtt{Del}$ of deleterious mutations is needed for partitioning the neighborhood $N(h)$, it is of little interest as no hypothesis will ever be selected from $\mathtt{Del}$. *The goal of the evolution* is to produce in $poly(1/\varepsilon, 1/\delta, n)$-time a hypothesis h such that

$$\mathbf{Pr}\left(Perf_D(h,c) < Perf_D(c,c) - \varepsilon\right) < \delta. \tag{4}$$

3   The Learning Problem that We Study

We are interested in learning monotone conjunctions in the framework of evolvability. In particular, we focus on Bernoulli $(p)^n$ distributions $\mathcal{B}_{n,p}$ over $\{0,1\}^n$. These distributions are specified by the probability p of setting each variable x_i equal to 1. Thus, a truth assignment $(a_1, \ldots, a_n) \in \{0,1\}^n$ has probability $\prod_{i=1}^n p^{a_i}(1-p)^{1-a_i}$. Given a monotone conjunction c that we want to learn and a hypothesis h, we can partition the variables that appear in either c or h as shown below:

$$c = \bigwedge_{i=1}^m x_i \wedge \bigwedge_{k=1}^u y_k \quad \text{and} \quad h = \bigwedge_{i=1}^m x_i \wedge \bigwedge_{\ell=1}^r w_\ell. \tag{5}$$

---

[2] The function c is also called *ideal function*, as it represents the *ideal behavior* in a certain environment.

Therefore, the x's are *mutual* variables, the y's are called *undiscovered* (or *missing*) variables, and the w's are the *wrong* (or *redundant*) variables. Variables in the target c are called *good*, otherwise they are called *bad*. Given this decomposition, we can calculate the quantity $\mathbf{Pr}_{x \sim \mathcal{B}_{n,p}} (h(x) \neq c(x))$ under a $\mathcal{B}_{n,p}$ distribution, with the following two observations:

- $h(x) = +1$ and $c(x) = -1$: This happens on truth assignments where the x_i's are satisfied, the w_ℓ's are satisfied, and at least one of the y_k's is falsified. Therefore, this will happen with probability $p^m p^r (1 - p^u)$.
- $h(x) = -1$ and $c(x) = +1$: Similar analysis implies that this will happen with probability $p^m p^u (1 - p^r)$.

Adding the above two we get: $\mathbf{Pr}_{x \sim \mathcal{B}_{n,p}} (h(x) \neq c(x)) = p^{m+r} + p^{m+u} - 2p^{m+r+u}$. As a consequence, (2) reduces to,

$$\mathrm{Perf}_{\mathcal{B}_{n,p}} (h, c) = 1 - 2p^{m+r} - 2p^{m+u} + 4p^{m+r+u} . \tag{6}$$

Definition 1 (Short, Medium, Long). *Given integers q and ϑ, a monotone conjunction f is* short *when* $|f| \leq q$, medium *when* $q < |f| \leq q + \vartheta$, *and* long *otherwise.*

Definition 1 partitions the class of functions that we want to learn in three groups and will allow us to define a criterion (Criterion 1) that we will use in order to determine if a particular experimental run is successful or not. We will also need the following definition.

Definition 2 (Best q-Approximation). *A hypothesis h is called a best q-approximation of c if $|h| \leq q$ and $\forall h' \neq h, |h'| \leq q : \mathrm{Perf}_D (h', c) \leq \mathrm{Perf}_D (h, c)$.*

3.1   A Related Algorithm: The Swapping Algorithm

Before we discuss details of our implementation, we briefly describe a related algorithm to our work, the *swapping algorithm* for monotone conjunctions, that was introduced by Valiant in [16].

The swapping algorithm has been shown to converge [1] under Bernoulli $(p)^n$ distributions that are characterized by any $0 < p < 1$ using the general evolutionary scheme that was described in Sect. 2.2, where at every step of the evolution the neighborhood $N(h)$ is partitioned into the sets Bene, Neut, and Del, and selection first favors the set Bene, otherwise the set Neut. The algorithm is important for our work because we intend to use some of its parameters and ideas in the evolutionary mechanism that we want to study.

In the swapping algorithm, the neighborhood $N(h)$ of a monotone conjunction h is the set of monotone conjunctions that arise by *adding* a variable (neighborhood $N^+(h)$), *removing* a variable (neighborhood $N^-(h)$), or *swapping* a variable with another one (neighborhood $N^\pm(h)$), plus the conjunction itself. Thus, $N(h) = N^-(h) \cup N^+(h) \cup N^\pm(h) \cup \{h\}$. As an example, let $h = x_1 \wedge x_2$, and $n = 4$. Then, $N^-(h) = \{x_1, x_2\}$, $N^+(h) = \{x_1 \wedge x_2 \wedge x_3, x_1 \wedge x_2 \wedge x_4\}$, and $N^{\pm}(h) = \{x_3 \wedge x_2, x_4 \wedge x_2, x_1 \wedge x_3, x_1 \wedge x_4\}$. Note that $|N(h)| = \mathcal{O}(n|h|)$ in general. Finally, for the parameters q and ϑ that appear in Definition 1, the swapping algorithm uses the following values:

$$q = \lceil \log_{1/p}(3/\varepsilon) \rceil \quad \text{and} \quad \vartheta = \lfloor \log_{1/p}(2) \rfloor . \tag{7}$$

4   Implementation

Regarding the implementation, our starting point is the algorithm for the evolution of monotone conjunctions that was used in [2], which in turn is based on the $(1 + 1)$ EA (Algorithm 1). Our evolutionary mechanism is shown in detail in Algorithm 2. This algorithm is known to converge [2] to a hypothesis that satisfies (4), which is the goal for evolution, for Bernoulli $(p)^n$ distributions that are characterized by $p \in (0, 1/3] \cup \{1/2\}$. However, we are interested in studying this evolutionary mechanism, at the very least, for other values of p that characterize Bernoulli $(p)^n$ distributions and it is this particular case that we explore in this paper. Below we explain the functions that appear in Algorithm 2.

Algorithm 2: MUTATOR function based on the $(1 + 1)$ EA

---

1 $q \leftarrow \lceil \log_{1/p}(3/\varepsilon) \rceil$;
2 $h' \leftarrow$ MUTATE(h);
3 **if** $p < 1/3$ **then** $t \leftarrow p^{q-1} \min\{4p^q/3, 1 - 3p\}$;
4 **else if** $p = 1/3$ **then** $t \leftarrow 2 \cdot 3^{-1-2q}$;
5 **else if** $p = 1/2$ **then** $t \leftarrow 2^{-2q}$;
6 **else if** $p > 1/3$ *and* $p < 1/2$ **then**
7 | $\vartheta \leftarrow 0$;
8 | $\Lambda \leftarrow 1 - 2p$;
9 | $\mu \leftarrow \min\{2p^{q+\vartheta}, \Lambda\}$;
10 | $t \leftarrow p^{q-1}\mu(1 - p)$;
11 **else**
12 | $k \leftarrow \lfloor \log_{1/p}(2) \rfloor$;
13 | $\vartheta \leftarrow k$;
14 | $\Lambda \leftarrow \min\{|2p^k - 1|, |1 - 2p^{k+1}|\}$;
15 | $\mu \leftarrow \min\{2p^{q+\theta}, \Lambda\}$;
16 | $t \leftarrow p^{q-1}\mu(1 - p)$;
17 **if** $|h'| > q$ **then return** h;
18 $\nu_h \leftarrow$ EVALUATEHYPOTHESIS(h);
19 $\nu_{h'} \leftarrow$ EVALUATEHYPOTHESIS(h');
20 **if** $\nu_{h'} > \nu_h + t$ **then return** h';
21 **else if** $\nu_{h'} >= \nu_h - t$ **then return** USELECT(h, h');
22 **else return** h;

EVALUATEHYPOTHESIS returns the performance $Perf_D(h, c)$ of a hypothesis h. In the experiments we do that using (6), by using the values m, u, and r, of the mutual, undiscovered, and redundant variables.

The function MUTATE takes as input the bit vector that represents the initial hypothesis, flips each bit with probability $1/n$, and returns the new mutated hypothesis. This is the mutation mechanism that was described in Algorithm 1.

The function USELECT is responsible for selecting uniformly at random a hypothesis from the two that are passed as parameters. In particular, the two hypotheses are h and h', where h is the initial hypothesis and h' the mutated one that occurred from function MUTATE.

Finally, we would like to make the following remark. As discussed in Sect. 2.2, the evolutionary mechanism has access to a noisy value $\widehat{Perf_S}(h, c)$, that is obtained from an appropriately large sample S, as a proxy for the true value $Perf_D(h, c)$ for some hypothesis h. However, by using (6) directly in EVALUATEHYPOTHESIS we obtain the true value *exactly*. We argue that this should not be a problem, as the neighborhood is split into the sets Bene, Neut, and Del based on the tolerance t. The idea is that when one may try in the future to prove rigorously our experimental findings from Sect. 5, it should be enough to identify the minimum non-zero difference in the performance between *any two* hypotheses in the hypothesis space. Assuming this value is equal to Δ, then by setting the tolerance equal to $\Delta/2$ and requiring approximation of each $Perf_D(h, c)$ to be done within $\Delta/2$ of their true value, then the sets Bene, Neut, and Del, will be entirely correct in the partitioning of the hypotheses in the neighborhood, to beneficial, neutral, and deleterious.

4.1 Setting the Parameters q and ϑ

Two important parameters that we use in Algorithm 2 are the parameters q and ϑ and the values that we use are given by (7). Regarding q, its value has been the same in [1–3] and therefore it is only natural to maintain this definition in our work as well. Regarding ϑ, we introduce it because it was useful for proving the convergence of the swapping algorithm when $p \geq 1/2$. One of the ideas from [1] is that when the function c that we want to learn is of medium size (i.e., $q < |c| \leq q + \vartheta$) and the distribution $\mathcal{B}_{n,p}$ is governed by some $p \geq 1/2$, then convergence is proved when a hypothesis h is formed that is a best q-approximation of c (per Definition 2). Hence, our hope is that this phenomenon will transcend from the swapping algorithm where it has been proved to work, to the (1+1) EA mechanism that we explore in this work.

4.2 Guessing a Good Value for the Tolerance t

Beyond q and ϑ for which we use the values of (7), another important parameter for evolution is that of the tolerance t. As the algorithm that we use (Algorithm 2) comes from [2], we use the values indicated by [2] in the proved regime; i.e., when $p \in (0, 1/3] \cup \{1/2\}$. In the unproved regime (i.e., when $p \notin (0, 1/3] \cup \{1/2\}$) we attempt to use the tolerance that is indicated in [1] which allows the swapping algorithm to converge for every $p \in (0,1)$ that characterizes the Bernoulli $(p)^n$ distribution that governs the instances. In particular, the tolerance in [1] is

$$t_{\text{swapping}} = p^{q-1}\mu(1-p),\tag{8}$$

where $\mu = \min\{2p^{q+\vartheta}, \Lambda\}$. Regarding the quantity Λ, if $0 < p < 1/2$ we have

$$\Lambda_{p<1/2} = 1 - 2p.\tag{9}$$

When $p \in [1/2, 1)$, the quantity Λ is defined by first looking if p is of the form $2^{-1/k}$, with $k \in \{1,\ldots,n\}$, or if p belongs to a sub-interval of $[1/2, 1)$ of the form $(2^{-1/k}, 2^{-1/(k+1)})$; in other words, we care about the two consecutive points from the family of points $2^{-1/k}$ (with $k \in \{1,\ldots,n\}$) that contain p. It is this latter case which corresponds to the values of $p > 1/2$ that we examine in this work in the unproved regime (i.e., $p \in \{0.6, 0.7, 0.8, 0.9\}$). Note that the interval of interest $(2^{-1/k}, 2^{-1/(k+1)})$ is obtained for $k = \lfloor \log_{1/p}(2) \rfloor$. Eventually, a quantity that is good enough for our purposes is to set

$$\Lambda_{p>1/2} = \min\{|2p^k - 1|, |1 - 2p^{k+1}|\}.\tag{10}$$

In other words, using (9) and (10) we can define

$$\Lambda = \begin{cases} \Lambda_{p<1/2}, & \text{if } 1/3 < p < 1/2, \\ \Lambda_{p>1/2}, & \text{if } 1/2 < p < 1. \end{cases}\tag{11}$$

Now, one can use (11) in (8) and compute the desired tolerance that will be used for the experiments depending on the p that we want to test.

4.3   Successful Executions

The following criterion was used for proving convergence in [1] and we adopt it.

Criterion 1 (Success Criterion).   *We define a single run to be successful if we accomplish the following:*

(a) When c is short, identify c precisely.
(b) When c is medium, generate a best q-approximation of c.
(c) When c is long, generate a hypothesis h such that $\text{Perf}_{\mathcal{B}_{n,p}}(h,c) \geq 1 - \varepsilon$.

Therefore, for a given Bernoulli $(p)^n$ distribution and a given target c, we run Algorithm 2 in an endless loop until we satisfy our Criterion 1. In fact, we consider such an execution successful if we satisfy Criterion 1 *for 10 consecutive iterations*, thus signifying that the solution that we have found has some notion of stability and therefore it is not the case that we satisfy perhaps Criterion 1 during one iteration but then in a subsequent iteration the hypothesis drifts away and evolves to a solution that has performance less than $1 - \varepsilon$.

Remark 2 (On the Strictness of the Success Criterion). Criterion 1 is probably more strict than what is really needed in some cases. To see this, consider the following situation: say, $p = 0.2$, $\varepsilon = 0.01$ ($\Rightarrow q = 4$), and the target function that we want to learn is $c = x_1 \wedge x_2 \wedge x_3 \wedge x_4$. Then, according to Criterion 1, this is case (a), and we would like to evolve h such that $h = c$. However, the hypothesis $h' = x_5 \wedge x_6 \wedge x_7 \wedge x_8$ is very different from c (as none of the variables that appear in h also appears in c) but nevertheless, using (6), we see that it holds $Perf_{\mathcal{B}_{n,p}}(h', c) = 1 - 2 \cdot 0.2^4 - 2 \cdot 0.2^4 + 4 \cdot 0.2^8 \approx 0.99361$. In other words, even if h' does not satisfy the stringent requirement of case (a) of our criterion for successful execution, since $\varepsilon = 0.01$ it nevertheless satisfies (4) which is really the goal of evolution, as it has performance at least $1 - \varepsilon$.

5   Experimental Results and Discussion

Using Algorithm 2 we perform experiments[3] for $\mathcal{B}_{n,p}$ distributions such that $p = j/10$, where $j \in \{1, 2, \ldots, 9\}$. By testing the values $p \in \{0.1, 0.2, 0.3, 0.5\}$ we can understand the rate of convergence when p is in the regime of proved convergence (based on [2]). Moreover, we can also use these numbers as baselines for forming conclusions regarding the rate of convergence when we perform experiments under distributions $\mathcal{B}_{n,p}$ that are characterized by values of p, when p is outside of the known regime of $(0, 1/3] \cup \{1/2\}$ where we have proved convergence.

5.1   Details on the Experimental Setup

Dimension of the Instance Space. In all of our experiments we set the dimension of our instance space to be equal to $n = 100$. This value of $n = 100$ allows a rich hypothesis space while at the same time it allows the repetitive execution of Algorithm 2 in a fairly reasonable amount of time for our experiments.

Target Sizes that we Test. For each p value mentioned above we generate targets that have sizes taken from the sets S_a, S_b, and S_c shown below:

$$\begin{cases} S_a = \{1, 2, q/4, q/2, 3q/4, q-1, q\} \\ S_b = \{q+1, q+\vartheta/2, q+\vartheta\} \\ S_c = \{q+\vartheta+1, q+\vartheta+(n-q-\vartheta)/4, \\ \qquad q+\vartheta+2(n-q-\vartheta)/4, \\ \qquad q+\vartheta+3(n-q-\vartheta)/4, n\}. \end{cases} \tag{12}$$

In particular, the target sizes from the set S_a are used for testing case (a) of Criterion 1, the target sizes from the set S_b are used for testing case (b) of Criterion 1, and the target sizes from the set S_c are used for testing case (c) of Criterion 1. Note that when $p < 1/2$, then $\vartheta = 0$. In such a case we consider the set S_b to be empty. That is, the target size that is indicated as having size $q+1$ is available in the set S_c where now $q+\vartheta+1 = q+0+1 = q+1$.

Epochs (Repetitions). For each pair $(p, |c|)$ that we test, we perform 100 different epochs (repetitions) starting from the empty hypothesis (i.e., h is a bitstring of

---

[3] Source code available at: https://gitlab.com/marina_pantia/evolvability_code.

length n where each entry has the value of 0) until convergence. The epochs smooth the experimental results and allow us to better understand the average case of execution.

Numerical Values of the Parameters $q, \vartheta,$ and t. Table 1 summarizes the values that the parameters $q, \vartheta,$ and t obtain, when $p = j/10$ for $j \in \{1, 2, \dots, 9\}$.

5.2   High-Level Summary of Results

We note that in every single one of our experiments we were able to satisfy Criterion 1. Table 2 presents the average number of iterations that was necessary so that we can satisfy Criterion 1 in every case that we tested.

Table 1. Values of q, ϑ, and tolerance t corresponding to each probability p that we tested in our experiments. Note that the values for the tolerance t should be multiplied by 10^{-6}. In every case the dimension of the instance space is $n = 100$.

p	0.1	0.2	0.3	0.4	0.5	0.6	0.7	0.8	0.9
q	3	4	5	7	9	12	16	26	55
ϑ	0	0	0	0	1	1	1	3	6
$t\ (10^{-6})$	13.3	17	26.2	8.05	3.81	3.79	6.62	2.33	1.09

Table 2. Average number of iterations until convergence (as computed using 100 epochs), depending on the target size and the probability used. Note that when $p < 1/2$, then $\vartheta = 0$ and therefore in these situations it is the case that $q + 1 > q + \vartheta/2$ as well as $q + 1 > q + \vartheta$. Therefore, some values may be repeated or appear out of order. However, for uniformity we keep these rows everywhere in accordance to the presentation of the sets $S_a, S_b,$ and S_c in (12) from Sect. 5.1. In addition, when $p \in \{0.5, 0.6, 0.7\}$, then $\vartheta = 1$ and hence $q + 1 = q + \vartheta/2 = q + \vartheta$ as we use rounding in order to treat decimals (i.e., round($\vartheta/2$) = round(1/2) = 1).

Target size $|c|$	Probability p								
	0.1	0.2	0.3	0.4	0.5	0.6	0.7	0.8	0.9
1	9355.3	8240.16	6109.52	4494.06	1846.62	292.16	263.67	231.91	264.03
2	18373.48	13234.84	8878.63	6757.35	3460.26	1275.46	1189.7	413.5	432.55
$q/4$	9355.3	8240.16	6109.52	6757.35	3460.26	2377.29	2285.82	1251.94	1147.72
$q/2$	18373.48	13234.84	8878.63	13631.78	6485.19	4388.57	4522.01	2340.74	1482.84
$3q/4$	18373.48	22613.09	22200.21	15894.43	11988.98	7071.61	6480.98	3718.52	2071.57
q	39011.15	33743.87	40434.23	37737.39	26736.85	15716.76	15174.42	6951.12	3826.76
$q + 1$	12.56	13.56	14.82	15.67	24303.88	23337.84	28692.53	7449.52	3608.87
$q + \vartheta/2$	39011.15	33743.87	40434.23	37737.39	24303.88	23337.84	28692.53	9728.63	4553.08
$q + \vartheta$	39011.15	33743.87	40434.23	37737.39	24303.88	23337.84	28692.53	14651.58	9382.01
$q + \vartheta + 1$	12.56	13.56	14.82	15.67	17.2	20.4	27.54	39.87	102.61
$q + \vartheta + (n - q - \vartheta)/4$	12.49	13.78	14.4	15.04	17.15	20.53	25.37	38.43	100.97
$q + \vartheta + 2(n - q - \vartheta)/4$	12.67	13.68	14.93	14.79	16.88	20.8	25.24	38.15	92.61
$q + \vartheta + 3(n - q - \vartheta)/4$	13.03	13.9	14.92	14.45	17.31	20.72	25.4	38.95	97.44
n	12.22	13.93	15.04	14.77	17.21	20.87	25.92	37.27	94.81

On the Convergence against Long Targets. As it can be seen from Table 2, case (c) in Criterion 1, corresponding to $|c| > q + \vartheta$, is perhaps the easiest one to accomplish. The intuitive reason from the work of [1] is that q and ϑ have been selected in such a way, so that *any* hypothesis h that has size q, *regardless* of its composition of *good* and *bad* variables among the q variables that it contains, will satisfy the equation $Perf_{\mathcal{B}_{n,p}}(h,c) \geq 1-\varepsilon$. In particular, the intuitive idea is that c and h contain enough many variables and hence they make positive predictions on a small subspace of the n-dimensional hypercube $\{0,1\}^n$. As a consequence c and h agree almost everywhere, since almost everywhere they make a negative prediction. As a further consequence, their correlation is at least $1 - \varepsilon$. Indeed, in our experiments when $|c| > q + \vartheta$, regardless of the underlying value of p that governs the distribution, we see that h satisfies the criterion $Perf_{\mathcal{B}_{n,p}}(h,c) \geq 1-\varepsilon$ very quickly.

On the Convergence against Short and Medium Targets. Moreover, quite remarkably, based on the results shown in Table 2 for short and medium targets, the evolutionary mechanism that we study appears to be converging faster to a solution that satisfies Criterion 1 when p is outside of the known proved regime of $(0,1/3] \cup \{1/2\}$. As characteristic examples one can compare the entries corresponding to $p = 0.4$ versus $p = 0.3$, or $p = 0.8$ versus $p = 0.5$.

The conclusions that we draw for the different values of p that we test are similar. Therefore in Sect. 5.3 below we focus on one particular case where $p = 0.4$, while in Sect. 5.4 we complement Table 2 and the discussion of Sect. 5.3 by showing boxplots with more refined information on the convergence rate of every case that we tested.

5.3 Details on the Convergence When $p = 0.4$

Figure 1a presents the average number of iterations against target sizes up to $q + 2$ when $p \in \{0.3, 0.4, 0.5\}$ and $n = 100$. Table 1 informs us that for $p = 0.3$,

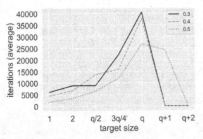
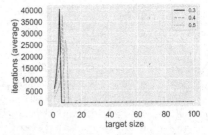

(a) Iterations until convergence when $n = 100$ and $p = 0.4$, compared to $p = 0.3$ and $p = 0.5$ where it is known that the algorithm converges efficiently. On the horizontal axis we see target sizes as a function of q, so that we can study better case (a) of Criterion 1.

(b) Iterations until convergence when $n = 100$ and $p = 0.4$, compared to $p = 0.3$ and $p = 0.5$ where it is known that the algorithm converges efficiently. We can see the convergence rate when $p = 0.4$ across the entire spectrum of possible target sizes.

Fig. 1. Iterations until convergence when $n = 100$ and $p \in \{0.3, 0.4, 0.5\}$. In Fig. 1a we focus in the situation where $|c| \in \{1, 2, q/2, 3q/4, q, q + 1\}$ which covers case (a) of Criterion 1, even though q is different for the different p values; see, e.g., Table 1. When $|c| > q + 1$ the convergence is very fast for all cases. In Fig. 1b we see the complete picture for target sizes between 1 and $n = 100$.

$p = 0.4$, and $p = 0.5$ we have $q = 3$, $q = 4$, and $q = 5$ respectively. Even though these values of q are different, nevertheless, they all correspond to the situation where the target is short – case (a) of Criterion 1 – and for this reason we decided to put labels on the x axis that are related to q. Of course, since the q values are different, one can also consider a plot similar to Fig. 1b and be able to see the complete picture for target sizes between 1 and $n = 100$ in each case. Regardless if one uses Fig. 1a or b, we observe that (i) the algorithm converges for every target size, and (ii) the rate of convergence when $p = 0.4$ is very similar to what we observe for $p = 0.3$ and $p = 0.5$ where it has been proved that the algorithm converges. Similar results are discussed below for other values of p.

5.4 Further Details on the Experiments of Every $(p, |c|)$ Pair Tested

We complement Table 2 and the discussion of Sect. 5.3 by providing further statistics for the executions of Algorithm 2. Figure 2 presents *boxplots* regarding the number of iterations that was needed so that Criterion 1 was satisfied for every $p = i/10$, with $i \in \{1, 3, 4, 5, 6, 7, 8, 9\}$ and for every target size that belonged to one of the sets S_a, S_b, and S_c that were described in (12). (Due to space limitations we omitted the case for $p = 0.2$.) Each boxplot shows the median value for the execution of the algorithm regarding a particular $(p, |c|)$ pair. Furthermore, the thick part of the boxplot indicates the range of values that belong between the 25th and the 75th percentile. The whiskers are drawn so that they are in 1.5 times the inter-quartile range and finally in some cases we may also see some outliers which correspond to executions that took unexpectedly long/short time.

5.5 Discussion

As a summary, for every value $p = j/10$ with $j \in \{1, 2, \ldots, 9\}$ that characterizes a Bernoulli $(p)^n$ distribution, Algorithm 2 satisfied the goal of evolution and converges to a function that satisfies (4). This is true against *any target function that we tested*. Moreover, the average case analysis indicates that the running time needed to converge to such a good solution is in fact comparable to the running time that is needed (on average) by a simpler variant of this algorithm, that is obtained when the algorithm is tested against values of $p \in (0, 1/3] \cup \{1/2\}$, where it is has been proved that the algorithm converges efficiently [2].

Implications. One first implication of these experimental results is that the (1+1)-EA variant that we examined, appears to be equally powerful as the swapping algorithm which provably evolves monotone conjunctions for Bernoulli $(p)^n$ distributions governed by any $p \in (0, 1)$ satisfying (4). A second implication is that the success criterion that we set beforehand (Criterion 1) indeed appears to capture fairly accurately what is happening on successful executions that also generate stable solutions. As a consequence of these two, a third implication is that the experimental convergence that we explored motivates future work for a formal approach on rigorously proving the convergence of the algorithm under

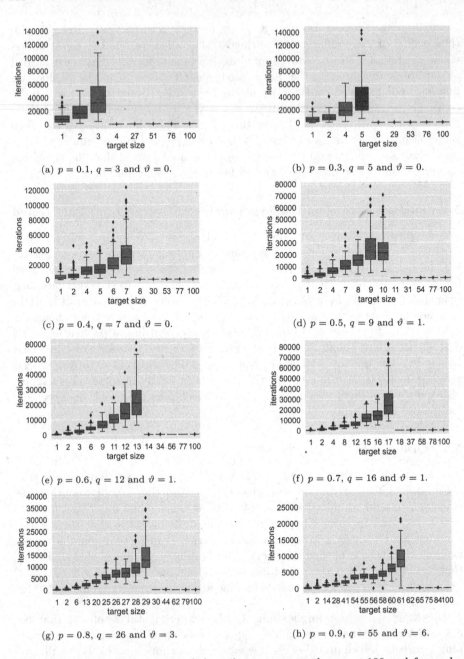

(a) $p = 0.1$, $q = 3$ and $\vartheta = 0$.

(b) $p = 0.3$, $q = 5$ and $\vartheta = 0$.

(c) $p = 0.4$, $q = 7$ and $\vartheta = 0$.

(d) $p = 0.5$, $q = 9$ and $\vartheta = 1$.

(e) $p = 0.6$, $q = 12$ and $\vartheta = 1$.

(f) $p = 0.7$, $q = 16$ and $\vartheta = 1$.

(g) $p = 0.8$, $q = 26$ and $\vartheta = 3$.

(h) $p = 0.9$, $q = 55$ and $\vartheta = 6$.

Fig. 2. Boxplots of iterations needed until convergence when $n = 100$ and for probabilities $p \in \{0.1, 0.3, 0.4, 0.5, 0.6, 0.7, 0.8, 0.9\}$. The x-axis corresponds to target sizes generated according to the sets S_a, S_b, and S_c that are presented in Sect. 5.1; these sizes depend on p as they depend on the parameters q and ϑ which ultimately depend on p. Furthermore, when $|c| > q + \vartheta$, the convergence is very fast and thus the deviation from the median of the iterations is insignificant.

Bernoulli $(p)^n$ distributions for values of $p \in (0,1)$ outside of the known proved regime, which is $(0, 1/3] \cup \{1/2\}$ based on [2]. Fourth, somehow surprisingly, the experimental results suggest that the convergence of the algorithm is actually *faster* in the unknown regime compared to the known one, when the target is short or medium (i.e., for target sizes that are expected to be difficult); e.g., compare the results between $p = 0.8$ and $p = 0.5$ in Table 2.

6 Conclusions

We studied the evolvability of monotone conjunctions under Bernoulli $(p)^n$ distributions using the standard mutation mechanism that appears in (1+1) EAs.. We extended the algorithm introduced in [2] by drawing inspiration from the convergence properties of the swapping algorithm under such distributions [1]. Our experiments indicate that the extension we proposed allows the formation of hypotheses that approximate well *any target function c* under *arbitrary* Bernoulli $(p)^n$ distributions since the computed solutions in our experiments were *stable* and more importantly *satisfied the goal of evolution required by (4) in every combination $(p, |c|)$ that we tested*. In the future, it would be interesting to prove rigorously this experimental result, as well as explore the convergence of this (1+1) EA-based mutation mechanism under distributions beyond Bernoulli $(p)^n$.

References

1. Diochnos, D.I.: On the evolution of monotone conjunctions: drilling for best approximations. In: Ortner, R., Simon, H.U., Zilles, S. (eds.) ALT 2016. LNCS (LNAI), vol. 9925, pp. 98–112. Springer, Cham (2016). https://doi.org/10.1007/978-3-319-46379-7_7

2. Diochnos, D.I.: On the evolvability of monotone conjunctions with an evolutionary mutation mechanism. J. Artif. Intell. Res. **70**, 891–921 (2021)

3. Diochnos, D.I., Turán, G.: On evolvability: the swapping algorithm, product distributions, and covariance. In: Watanabe, O., Zeugmann, T. (eds.) SAGA 2009. LNCS, vol. 5792, pp. 74–88. Springer, Heidelberg (2009). https://doi.org/10.1007/978-3-642-04944-6_7

4. Droste, S., Jansen, T., Wegener, I.: On the analysis of the (1+1) evolutionary algorithm. Theor. Comput. Sci. **276**(1–2), 51–81 (2002)

5. Feldman, V.: Evolvability from learning algorithms. In: STOC, pp. 619–628 (2008)

6. Kalkreuth, R., Droschinsky, A.: On the time complexity of simple cartesian genetic programming. In: IJCCI, pp. 172–179. ScitePress (2019)

7. Kanade, V.: Evolution with recombination. In: FOCS, pp. 837–846 (2011)

8. Koza, J.R.: Genetic Programming - On the Programming of Computers by Means of Natural Selection. Complex Adaptive Systems. MIT Press, Cambridge (1993)

9. Lissovoi, A., Oliveto, P.S.: On the time and space complexity of genetic programming for evolving Boolean conjunctions. J. Artif. Intell. Res. **66**, 655–689 (2019)

10. Mambrini, A., Oliveto, P.S.: On the analysis of simple genetic programming for evolving Boolean functions. In: Heywood, M.I., McDermott, J., Castelli, M., Costa, E., Sim, K. (eds.) EuroGP 2016. LNCS, vol. 9594, pp. 99–114. Springer, Cham (2016). https://doi.org/10.1007/978-3-319-30668-1_7

11. Pitt, L., Valiant, L.G.: Computational limitations on learning from examples. J. ACM **35**(4), 965–984 (1988)
12. Reyzin, L.: Statistical Queries and Statistical Algorithms: Foundations and Applications. CoRR abs/2004.00557 (2020)
13. Ros, J.P.: Learning Boolean functions with genetic algorithms: a PAC analysis. In: FOGA, pp. 257–275 (1992)
14. Snir, S., Yohay, B.: Prokaryotic evolutionary mechanisms accelerate learning. Discrete Appl. Math. **258**, 222–234 (2019)
15. Valiant, L.G.: A theory of the learnable. Commun. ACM **27**(11), 1134–1142 (1984)
16. Valiant, L.G.: Evolvability. J. ACM **56**(1), 3:1-3:21 (2009)

Accurate and Interpretable Representations of Environments with Anticipatory Learning Classifier Systems

Romain Orhand[1,2]([✉]), Anne Jeannin-Girardon[1,2], Pierre Parrend[1,3], and Pierre Collet[1,2]

[1] Icube Laboratory - UMR 7357, 300 bd Sébastien Brant, 67412 Illkirch, France
{rorhand,anne.jeannin,pierre.parrend,pierre.collet}@unistra.fr
[2] University of Strasbourg, 4 rue Blaise Pascal, 67081 Strasbourg, France
[3] EPITA, 14-16 Rue Voltaire, 94270 Le Kremlin-Bicêtre, France

Abstract. Anticipatory Learning Classifier Systems (ALCS) are rule-based machine learning algorithms that can simultaneously develop a complete representation of their environment and a decision policy based on this representation to solve their learning tasks. This paper introduces BEACS (Behavioral Enhanced Anticipatory Classifier System) in order to handle non-deterministic partially observable environments and to allow users to better understand the environmental representations issued by the system. BEACS is an ALCS that enhances and merges Probability-Enhanced Predictions and Behavioral Sequences approaches used in ALCS to handle such environments. The Probability-Enhanced Predictions consist in enabling the anticipation of several states, while the Behavioral Sequences permits the construction of sequences of actions. The capabilities of BEACS have been studied on a thorough benchmark of 23 mazes and the results show that BEACS can handle different kinds of non-determinism in partially observable environments, while describing completely and more accurately such environments. BEACS thus provides explanatory insights about created decision policies and environmental representations.

Keywords: Anticipatory Learning Classifier System · Machine learning · Explainability · Non-determinism · Building Knowledge

1 Introduction

Explainability has now become an important concern for automated decision making in domains such as healthcare, justice, employment or credit scoring, among others. Deep Learning models are widely used in these domains, because of their ability to extract relevant features from complex data. However, they are not intrinsically explainable and require the use of *post-hoc* models to shed light

E. Medvet et al. (Eds.): EuroGP 2022, LNCS 13223, pp. 245–261, 2022.
https://doi.org/10.1007/978-3-031-02056-8_16

on their decisions. Models exist that are, by design, more explainable, but at the cost of reduced performance in solving tasks: performance is thus balanced with explainability. The approach developed in this paper aims at enhancing the performance of such models *while* enabling them to provide more explanatory elements regarding their decisions.

We are interested in Reinforcement Learning models. Among intrinsically explainable Reinforcement Learning models, Anticipatory Learning Classifier Systems (ALCS) are rule-based machine learning algorithms that are based on the cognitive mechanism of Anticipatory Behavioral Control [19]. ALCS build their population of rules (called classifiers) by comparing successive perceptions of their environment in {conditions-actions-effects} tuples [11]: ALCS try to *anticipate* the consequences of an action according to their environmental situations. ALCS do not depend on a stochastic process to learn new tasks: Anticipatory Behavioral Control enables them to learn new tasks immediately, from the anticipation they built, giving insights to explain the use of the classifiers created by the system.

The work presented in this paper focuses on the ability of ALCS to *deal with non-deterministic environments* used in reinforcement learning problems, while making the classifiers of ALCS more explainable. Non-determinism can take different forms [16]: perceptual sensors can have irrelevant random attributes, be noisy or insufficient to determine the exact state of the environment (referred to as the *Perceptual Aliasing Issue*); the results of actions can be uncertain; rewards from the environment can be noisy. In particular, non-deterministic properties of the perceptual sensors or regarding the results of actions bring about *aliased states*, which are environmental states related to these forms of non-determinism. These aliased states prevent ALCS from achieving their task, if they cannot detect such states and build appropriate classifiers to deal with them.

This paper introduces BEACS (Behavioral Enhanced Anticipatory Classifier System) which aims to strengthen both the performance and the explainability of ALCS in non-deterministic, partially observable environments. The objective of BEACS is to build complete and accurate representations of its environment (*via* its population of classifiers), regardless of the non-deterministic properties of the environment, while being able to efficiently solve the task learned.

In Sect. 2, the main principles of Anticipatory Learning Classifier Systems are presented along with the mechanisms allowing them to handle non-determinism. After an analysis of these principles and mechanisms, BEACS is introduced in Sect. 3. Section 4 presents a study of the capabilities of BEACS through a thorough benchmarking on the different mazes used as test-beds in the literature. The results achieved by BEACS are discussed in Sect. 5, before concluding in Sect. 6.

2   Related Works

2.1   Principles of ALCS

As illustrated in Fig. 1, ALCS classifiers are mainly made of a $\{C, A, E\}$ tuple (consisting of a condition component C, an action component A and an effect

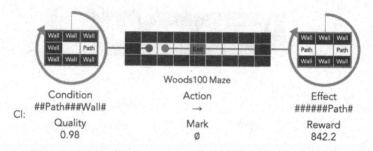

Fig. 1. Illustration of a classifier Cl of an ALCS in a maze environment, if the provided observations are the eight squares adjacent to each position starting from the North and clockwise. The hash is a wildcard that corresponds to all possible items in the condition and indicates there are no changes in the effect.

component E), a mark that specifies states for which the classifier has failed to anticipate, a measurement of the quality of anticipation q, and lastly, a prediction of the expected reward r [18].

Assessment of anticipation quality, and prediction of the expected rewards of classifiers are respectively done using the Anticipatory Learning Process and Reinforcement Learning.

Hence, the Anticipatory Learning Process is used to discover association patterns within the environment by means of the $\{C, A, E\}$ tuples. These tuples are built by comparing perceptions retrieved successively. ALCS classifiers are created or updated based on the differences between these perceptions. Reinforcement Learning is used to compute the expected rewards in order to fit the classifiers to the task being learned, and provide more adaptive capabilities to ALCS.

ALCS manage their population of classifiers by looping between perceiving new sensory inputs, evolving their population of classifiers thanks to both learning paradigms, and interacting with the environment by performing an action from the set of classifiers matching the current perception (for further details, refer to [6]).

ACS2 [6] is an enhanced version of Stolzmann's Anticipatory Classifier System (which was the first ALCS) [18]. It includes a genetic generalization mechanism to remove specialized attributes in the condition components of classifiers [2]. ACS2 also includes new action selection policies [3] to improve the evolution of the most general and accurate classifiers. Different exploration strategies of ACS2 were compared in [12] and an action planning mechanism was added to this model [21] in order to speed up the learning process. [13] replaced the reinforcement component of ACS2 by a mechanism that maximizes the averaged rewards, while [4] used a learning classifier system dedicated to approximating the optimal state values of the transitions learned between states of the environment. In parallel, two other ALCS were developed: YACS implements different heuristics from ACS2 to focus on the most relevant attributes in the condition and effect components of classifiers, as these attributes could be uncorrelated

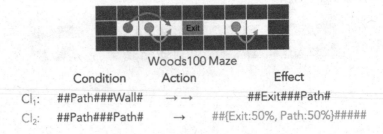

Woods100 Maze

	Condition	Action	Effect
Cl_1:	##Path###Wall#	→ →	##Exit###Path#
Cl_2:	##Path###Path#	→	##{Exit:50%, Path:50%}#####

Fig. 2. Illustration of a classifier Cl_1 having a Behavioral Sequence to bridge the aliased green state from a non-aliased blue state, as well as a classifier Cl_2 enhanced by PEP to represent the environmental transitions from the PAI state, according to the classifiers representation in Fig. 1.

[9]; MACS implements a new attribute in the effect component of its classifiers to enable the system to discover new patterns from its environment [8].

2.2 ALCS and Non-determinism

To allow ALCS to deal with non-deterministic environments, *Behavioral Sequences* (BSeq) [18] and *Probability-Enhanced Predictions* (PEP) [5] have been proposed, as depicted by Fig. 2. BSeq and PEP have both been integrated to ACS2 in [15] and [16]. They are triggered by classifiers that get both a correct anticipation and an incorrect anticipation in a unique state (*i.e.* in an aliased state).

BSeq enable the ALCS to bridge states that are related to the Perceptual Aliasing Issue using *sequences of actions*. However, BSeq do not enable the ALCS to build a complete and accurate representation of their environments as some states are skipped, and BSeq cannot promote the best decision policies because sub-optimal sequences of actions could be favored [17]. BSeq also imply a finer control of the population of classifiers by the ALCS, because the more these sequences are built, the more the population of classifiers will grow [15].

PEP were introduced in ALCS to deal with aliased states: PEP enable the *prediction of an ensemble of anticipations*, enabling the model to build a complete model of their environment. All items in the effect component of the $\{C, A, E\}$ tuple are replaced by PEP: they consist of an associative array in which keys are symbols related to the expected perceptive attributes, and values represent their probabilities to be anticipated by the classifier. The probabilities p, corresponding to the encountered aliased state, are updated in all the PEP as follows: $p = p + b_p * (1 - p)$, where b_p is an update rate, and all probabilities are then normalized. Nevertheless, both the probabilities computed in PEP and the sets of anticipated states they describe can be incoherent with the environmental settings of the ALCS: nonexistent states can be described by PEP (due to the combination of multiple associative arrays) and the computed probabilities are sensitive to their update parameter and the retrieved perceptions [17].

BEACS (Behavioral Enhanced Anticipatory Classifier System) is hereby introduced, with the goal of improving both the explainability of the system and its

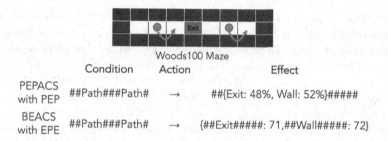

Woods100 Maze

	Condition	Action	Effect
PEPACS with PEP	##Path###Path#	→	##{Exit: 48%, Wall: 52%}#####
BEACS with EPE	##Path###Path#	→	{##Exit#####: 71,##Wall#####: 72}

Fig. 3. Illustration of PEPACS and BEACS classifiers enhanced by PEP and EPE in Woods100 to represent the environmental transitions from the PAI state, according to the representation depicted in the Fig. 1.

performance in non-deterministic partially observable environments. BEACS couples, for the first time, both Behavioral Sequences and PEP approaches to handle learning tasks in such environments, while each of these approaches is also improved. Because the Perceptual Aliasing Issue (PAI) is a type of aliasing that PEP manage, this coupling is based on the detection of PAI [17]. BEACS is therefore based on the state-of-the-art PEPACS that integrated PEP in ACS2 [16].

3 Behavioral Enhanced Anticipatory Classifier System

3.1 Enhancing PEP into EPE

PEP enhancements resulted in *Enhanced Predictions through Experience* (EPE). Both PEP and EPE have the same goal of allowing classifiers to anticipate several states, but they differ in the representations they employ. As depicted in Fig. 3, EPE consists in an associative array whose keys are the perceptions anticipated by the classifiers, and whose values are the number of occurrences when these perceptions have been anticipated. As a result, because each anticipated state is explicitly described and counted, EPE provides more detailed information than an effect component with multiple PEP. Moreover, this method does not require a dedicated learning rate to be set up, and the probabilities of each anticipated perceptive item can be retrieved.

BEACS triggers the construction of EPE classifiers (*i.e.* that uses EPE) by using the same aliased state detection mechanism as PEPACS. EPE classifiers are constructed similarly to PEP enhanced classifiers in PEPACS, with two exceptions: they are tagged with the aliased states that trigger their creation; their effect component is merged from those of their two parents, and the number of occurrences of each anticipation are summed. The number of occurrences of a given classifier is only updated when this classifier anticipates several states, otherwise a default value of 1 is set to the unique anticipation. Classifiers that cannot subsume each other and correspond to the same aliased state (due to their condition, mark, and aliased state tag) are used to avoid the generation of useless EPE classifiers.

The anticipation of several states can lead to over-generalization, where enhanced classifiers can be used in non aliased states because of the genetic generalization pressure. To prevent this issue, PEPACS completely replaces the enhanced effects of genetic generalization offspring with the anticipation of the current perception, at the cost of a knowledge loss and a reduced learning speed, as the system may have to gradually rebuild the enhanced effect. BEACS does not replace the enhanced effects. Instead, BEACS exploits the aliased state tag to control the evolution of EPE classifiers if they have been over-generalized: they are specialized from their aliased state tag instead of using the current perception; they can directly learn new anticipations from their aliased state tag only, by adding states they failed to anticipate to their EPE (the related counters are set to 1).

Finally, the mutation operator used in the genetic generalization mechanism was modified to consider the semantics of the wildcard used in ALCS: this wildcard corresponds to all possible perceptive attribute in the condition, and indicates the related attribute from the condition does not change in the effect (*e.g.* Fig. 1). Hence, a perceptive attribute can be generalized *via* mutation, only if the associated attribute of the effect does not predict both a change and an absence of change. This modification aims at preserving the coherence of BEACS classifiers by preventing the creation of such contradictory classifiers.

3.2   Coupling EPE with Behavioral Sequences

Allowing ALCS to distinguish PAI states (states related to the Perceptual Aliasing Issue) from other aliased states detected by the system is the first step towards coupling EPE and Behavioral Sequences. This differentiation is then used to condition the creation of behavioral classifiers (classifiers with a Behavioral Sequence). It enables BEACS to control more precisely when BSeq should be used and ultimately, the evolution of its population. The Perceptual Aliasing Issue occurs in partially observable environments when the system cannot differentiate states that are truly distinct. The goal is to focus on states reachable from a PAI (and different from it): these reachable states should be more numerous than the number of actions that lead to distinct states (when the same action lead to different states, only the most anticipated state is considered). Both the set of reachable states and the number of actions can be computed with the help of EPE classifiers.

To do so, the most experienced classifiers for each single action are retrieved from the set of classifiers that matches the current perceptive input (with respect to their marks and their aliased state tags), by computing the product of their experience and their cubic quality (this power is used to widen differences between classifier qualities). If these most experienced classifiers exist for all possible single actions and are experienced enough (according to a user defined threshold), the set of reachable states and the number of actions that are related to a perceptive change are computed using the $\{C, A, E\}$ tuple of these classifiers and the current perception.

While the detection of aliased states occurs at a classifier scale, the detection of PAI states should occurs at the scale of a *set* of classifiers. To avoid unneeded computational operations, BEACS does not attempt to detect the PAI states as soon as an aliased state is detected by a classifier: the PAI states detection occurs at the end of the anticipatory learning process. As BEACS also needs time to fit its classifiers to its environment in order to discover transitions between states, the occurrence of the detection of PAI states is similar to the way the genetic generalization takes place (as described by [6]): it depends on θ_{BSeq}, a user parameter representing the delay between two such consecutive detections, and an internal timestamp t_{BSeq} (added to each classifier) measuring the current delay. All states detected as PAI or no longer being PAI are registered in a list.

3.3   Enhancing the Behavioral Sequences

Once the use of Behavioral Sequences is triggered by the detection of PAI states, behavioral classifiers are built thanks to the penultimate classifier selected by BEACS in the state $s(t-1)$ and candidate classifiers in state $s(t)$ that successfully anticipated state $s(t+1)$. These candidate classifiers are temporarily stored by BEACS, until all the classifier anticipations have been considered in the Anticipatory Learning Process. Then, if state $s(t)$ has been registered as a PAI state, the $\{C, A, E\}$ tuples of the behavioral classifiers are made of: the condition component of the penultimate classifier, a fine-tuned effect component from the candidate classifiers and the penultimate classifier, and both action components in a sequence, while other internal parameters are set to default. The fine-tuned effect component is computed by replacing each anticipated change of the penultimate classifier and the candidate classifiers with the related perceptive attributes of state $s(t+1)$, and then by removing all effect attributes that match the condition component.

BEACS also stamps its behavioral classifiers with the PAI state that triggered their construction. If a state previously detected as PAI is no longer related to PAI, all behavioral classifiers related to this state are removed from the population of classifiers. This enables BEACS to adaptively build and delete behavioral classifiers as PAI states are detected, thus avoiding needless population growth.

As opposed to [14,15], BEACS no longer discriminates behavioral classifiers that lead to a loop between identical states: it is up to the reinforcement component of BEACS to fit the use of these classifiers, instead of decreasing their quality while their anticipations are correct. Thereby, the Anticipatory Learning Process used by BEACS is the same for all classifiers and the mechanism that prevent such loops has been removed.

BEACS genetic generalization mechanism was also extended to prevent the use of behavioral sequences in states unrelated to the Perceptual Aliasing Issue. To do so, behavioral classifiers are indirectly generalized through mutation by comparing the condition components of the offspring: if one perceptive attribute is generalized in one condition component and not in the other, the related perceptive attribute in the other can be generalized. This indirect generalization avoids building useless behavioral classifiers that would match states that do not lead to PAI states. Because behavioral classifiers can contain EPE, their mutation operator follows the modification introduced in Sect. 3.1 to preserve the meaning of the classifiers.

Finally, BEACS Reinforcement Learning component uses the concept of Double Q-Learning [10] to adapt the rewards predicted by the classifiers to the length of the action sequences in order to promote the usage of the shortest Behavioral Sequences. Each classifier Cl uses two estimators ($Cl.r_A$ and $Cl.r_B$) to compute its reward prediction $Cl.r$, by using the immediate reward ρ, the discounted maximum payoffs predicted in the next time-step $maxP_A$ and $maxP_B$, the discount factor γ, the reinforcement learning rate β, the number of actions in the Behavioral Sequence $\#act$, the maximal length of Behavioral Sequences B_{seq} and a configurable difference ϵ_r. Even if both estimators converged to the same value, ϵ_r allows BEACS to be biased in favor of the shortest sequences. The prediction reward of a classifier is scaled, so that the highest reward of one predictor is given when the sequence is made of a unique action, while the difference between the two estimators is used to decrease the prediction reward according to the length of the sequence of actions. Classifiers prediction rewards of an action set are updated as described by the Algorithm 1.

Algorithm 1. BEACS Reinforcement Learning Component

1: **function** UPDATEPREDREWARD(Cl, $maxP_A$, $maxP_B$, ρ, γ, β, $\#act$, B_{seq}, ϵ_r)
2:     **if** random() < 0.5: **then**
3:         $Cl.r_A \leftarrow Cl.r_A + \beta(\rho + \gamma maxP_B - Cl.r_A)$
4:     **else**
5:         $Cl.r_B \leftarrow Cl.r_B + \beta(\rho + \gamma maxP_A - Cl.r_B)$
6:     $max_r \leftarrow max(Cl.r_A, Cl.r_B)$
7:     $min_r \leftarrow min(Cl.r_A, Cl.r_B)$
8:     $Cl.r \leftarrow max_r - \frac{(max_r - min_r + \epsilon_r) *(\#act - 1)}{B_{seq}}$

BEACS was tested with a set of mazes, which are widely used as reinforcement learning benchmark [1]: the obtained results are presented in the following section.

4   Performance in Maze Environments

4.1   Experimental Protocol

Using the maze benchmark from [15], the experimental protocol is set in order to address the following questions:

- Can BEACS detect PAI states in order to efficiently build classifiers with Behavioral Sequences?
- Does the coupling of Behavioral Sequences with EPE in BEACS enable the system to build (a) complete representations of its environments, and (b) efficient decision policies?

- To what extent are the probabilities derived from PEP and EPE consistent with the non-deterministic properties of the environments?
- Can BEACS efficiently control the evolution of its populations of classifiers to alleviate the growth of its population due to the use of BSeq?

The benchmark is made up of 23 mazes of different complexities (due to the occurrence of PAI states for instance). To make the learning and the solving of the task more complex, the results of actions have a 25% chance of being uncertain, in which case the system performs a random action without knowing which one.

The goal of BEACS in these mazes is to construct a complete and accurate representation of its environment, by moving one grid-cell at a time, and in either eight adjacent positions, while attempting to reach the exit as fast as possible. Its perceptive capabilities are limited to the eight squares adjacent to each position. Its starting position in the mazes is random (but distinct from the exit).

BEACS is compared with BACS [15] and PEPACS [16] (control experiments) on the maze benchmark, as they are the state-of-the-art ALCS using Behavioral Sequences and PEP, respectively. For each maze of the benchmark, 30 runs were performed using each of these three ALCS. A run firstly consists of a succession of 5000 trials, that are constrained explorations until the exit or the maximal number of actions (100) are reached: ϵ is set to 0.8 for the ϵ-greedy policy used to select actions; the learning rate of the Anticipatory Learning Process and Reinforcement Learning, β, is set to 0.05; the PEP learning rate of PEPACS is set to 0.01; the maximal length of the Behavioral Sequences of BACS and BEACS is set to 3; θ_{BSeq} of BEACS is set to 1000 to manage the PAI states detection. Then, the ALCS are switched to pure exploitation (*i.e.* no Anticipatory Learning Process) and have 500 trials to bootstrap an efficient decision policy ($\epsilon = 0.2$, $\beta = 0.05$) and 500 more trials to stabilize the rewards ($\epsilon = 0$, $\beta = 0.05$), before recording the number of actions required by the ALCS to reach the exit for 500 more trials ($\epsilon = 0$, $\beta = 0.05$). Other ALCS-related parameters not described here are initialized to the default values provided in [6]. A detailed learning parameters analysis could be considered for future work to emphasise their role in the building of environmental representations and decision policies by ALCS.

4.2   Metrics

For each experiment, the following metrics were collected for the 3 ALCS: the size of populations of classifiers along with the ratio of reliable classifiers within the populations, the average number of steps required to reach the exit, the knowledge ratio, and the average EP-accumulated error (EP stands for Enhanced Predictions). The list of states considered as PAI states by BEACS was also collected.

The knowledge ratio is the ratio of correct transitions learned by at least one reliable classifier to all possible transitions. Only transitions that led to environmental changes are included.

The average EP-accumulated error is a new required metric because knowledge ratios only provide information about symbol occurrences in PEP, and not about the environmental fitness of the computed PEP probabilities: for each possible transitions in the maze using a unique action, theoretical probabilities associated with the reachable states are first computed given the non-deterministic properties of the maze. The difference between each PEP item of the effect component of the most experienced and reliable classifier (if one exist, otherwise the most experienced as defined in Sect. 3.2) and the corresponding theoretical probabilities are then computed. These differences are finally accumulated and averaged over the number of possible transitions, before being divided by the length of the effect component to get the average error by EP. In the case of EPE, a normalization of the counters associated to a perceptual attribute of interest can provide probabilities that are equivalent to those obtained by PEP.

All metrics were averaged over the 30 runs, for each environment. The obtained averages were compared with p-values computed by Welch t-test with (Welch-) Satterthwaite degrees of freedom (significance threshold 0.05) [7].

4.3   Performance

Can BEACS detect PAI states in order to efficiently build classifiers with Behavioral Sequences?

According to the environmental properties of the benchmark mazes, there were 1590 PAI states and 9810 non-PAI states throughout all experiments. BEACS has correctly identified 1490 of the 1590 PAI states, missed remaining 100 PAI states and incorrectly categorized 23 states as PAI. Thus, the balanced accuracy of the PAI state detection of BEACS is approximately 99.15%.

Does the coupling of Behavioral Sequences with EPE in BEACS enable the system to build (a) representations of its environments, and (b) efficient decision policies?

Figure 4 illustrates the knowledge ratios achieved by BEACS, BACS and PEPACS: BEACS and PEPACS were globally able to build complete representations of their environments, although PEPACS performed better than BEACS in 7 mazes, equally well as BEACS in 15 mazes (at least $p \geq 0.06$) and worse than BEACS in the remaining maze. BEACS did not achieve full knowledge of its environments in any of the experiments in two environments (MazeE1 and MiyazakiA) where it reached, at most, 97.84% and 99.31% respectively. PEPACS achieved full knowledge of its environments in every maze at least once.

Figure 5 shows the average number of steps required by the three ALCS to reach the exit. BEACS performed better than BACS in 20 mazes, equally well as BACS in the 3 remaining mazes ($p \geq 0.07$). BEACS performed better than PEPACS in 12 mazes, equally well as PEPACS in 3 mazes ($p \geq 0.24$) and worse than PEPACS in the 8 remaining mazes.

To what extent are the probabilities derived from PEP and EPE consistent with the non-deterministic properties of the environments?

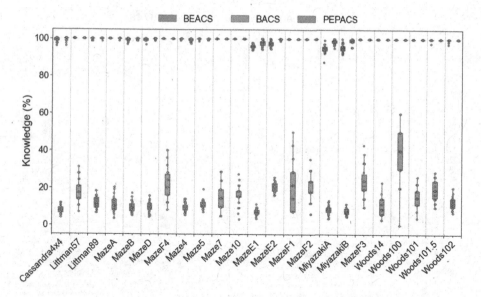

Fig. 4. Knowledge ratio achieved by BEACS, BACS and PEPACS. The higher the knowledge ratios, the better the performance. The use of PEP or EPE respectively permits PEPACS and BEACS to build complete representations of their environments.

The average EP-accumulated errors for each maze and ALCS are depicted in Fig. 6. BEACS has the lowest average EP-accumulated errors across all environments. BACS obtains, for 21 of the 23 environments, lower errors than PEPACS and larger errors than PEPACS for Cassandra4 × 4 and MazeE1. Therefore, the probabilities computed from the EPE of BEACS are the most consistent according to the non-deterministic properties of the environments.

Can BEACS efficiently control the evolution of its populations of classifiers to alleviate the growth of its population due to the use of BSeq?
Figure 7 shows the size of the populations of classifiers created by BEACS, BACS and PEPACS, as well as the ratios of reliable classifiers within these populations. In 21 environments, BEACS populations are smaller than BACS populations while in the remaining two mazes, BEACS populations are larger. BEACS populations are smaller than PEPACS populations in 15 environments and larger for the 8 remaining mazes. BEACS has the highest ratios of reliable classifiers in 19 mazes and shares the highest ratios with PEPACS in Woods101.5 ($p \geq 0.13$). PEPACS has the highest ratios of reliable classifiers in the remaining environments: MazeE1, MiyazakiA and Woods100.

5   Discussion

Some states related to the Perceptual Aliasing Issue are impossible to detect due to the aliasing detection mechanism.

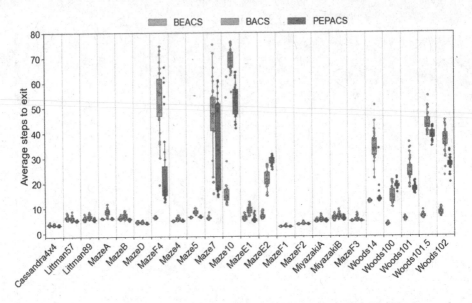

Fig. 5. Average steps to exit achieved by BEACS, BACS and PEPACS. The lower the average number of steps, the better the performance. BEACS is globally more efficient than BACS and PEPACS to reach the exit in non-deterministic mazes.

BEACS is the first ALCS to successfully detect when an aliasing state is related to the Perceptual Aliasing Issue. However, analyzing the 100 states that were not detected as PAI states revealed a limit: 90 of these states were not even detected as aliased. This is explained by the fact that truly distinct states in an environment can yield the same perceptions as well as the exact same environmental transitions to other PAI states. Because ALCS detect aliasing when several states are reachable for a state-action pair, such PAI states cannot currently be detected by BEACS or any ALCS.

BEACS Balances Performance and Explainability

Behavioral Sequences (BSeq) and Enhanced Predictions through Experience (EPE) are used together to improve both performance and explainability of ALCS. BEACS intends to generalize the results reported for both approaches in a range of environments with varying characteristics and non-deterministic properties that have never been tested in previous studies.

First of all, although the number of learning steps used in the experiments is not set up according to the complexity of the benchmark mazes (this complexity refers to, for instance, the size of the maze or its non-deterministic properties), BEACS outperforms BACS and is globally more efficient than PEPACS (as shown in Fig. 5). However, its performance suggest that its reinforcement component could be further improved to promote the use of the shortest sequences of actions, since BEACS used, at most, one extra step in the environments in which PEPACS performs better than BEACS. Correlating the achieved results

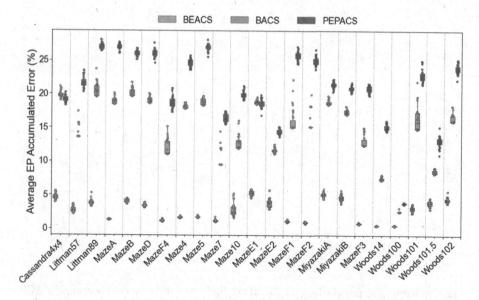

Fig. 6. Average EP-accumulated errors given the non-deterministic mazes, highlighting the gaps of the probabilities computed by PEPACS with the environmental settings. The lower the average EP-accumulated errors, the more accurate the environmental representations. The representations built by BEACS are more accurate than those of BACS and PEPACS.

of the ALCS with the intrinsic properties of each maze could be a direction for future research to improve their reinforcement component.

Then, even if BEACS performs slightly worse than PEPACS overall (up to about 4% worse on average over all environments), it is able to *create complete representations of its environments* (as seen in Fig. 4). The Behavioral Sequences are responsible for the observed discrepancies between PEPACS and BEACS. Indeed, their use implies that the system explores and fits these sequences to its environment at the expense of representation construction, which is thus slowed as Behavioral Sequences do not build reliable classifiers in PAI states.

However, the probabilities derived from the set of anticipations in BEACS classifiers are closer to the expected theoretical probabilities than those of BACS and PEPACS (as illustrated in Fig. 6): *BEACS environmental representations are thus much more accurate* than those of PEPACS and BACS. The probabilities computed by PEPACS are worse than those of BACS in 21 of 23 environments, even though PEPACS, as opposed to BACS, includes the PEP-mechanism to build accurate representations. In other words, BACS unreliable classifiers in aliased states may better describe the probability to anticipate next states than PEPACS reliable classifiers. This highlights the sensibility of the probabilities computed by PEPACS with regards to the experience of the system, when the system suffers from uncertainty in its action rather than relying on the experience of the system to make the probabilities converge, as BEACS does.

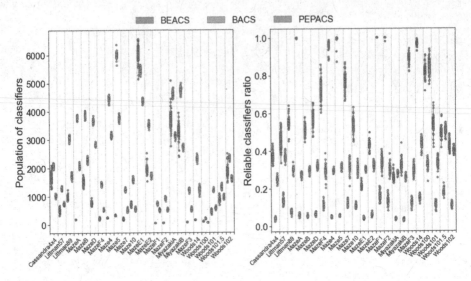

Fig. 7. Size of the populations of classifiers built by BEACS, BACS and PEPACS, along with the ratios of reliable classifiers within these populations. Small classifiers populations are easier to manipulate to extract knowledge. The higher these ratios, the more advanced the learning as the populations converge.

BEACS Explainability Assessment

BEACS computes its probabilities from EPE through experience, hence the larger the number of learning steps, the more accurate the probabilities. BEACS anticipations therefore provide new insights into classifier explainability by ensuring the reliability of the environmental representations: *BEACS classifiers can reliably be chained to trace the possible causes of a particular event.* However, as environments get more complex due to non-deterministic properties or perceptive inputs related to high-dimensional search spaces, populations of classifiers grow. The smaller the population of classifiers, the more BEACS is explainable. Thus, further works should focus on mechanisms efficiently reducing the populations of classifiers, such as compaction [20], by exploiting the knowledge acquired in BEACS population of classifiers.

Moreover, the representations used by BEACS to describe the classifier conditions and effects are kept unspoiled. This was possible thanks to the new mutation operator introduced in the genetic generalization mechanism, but at the expanse of the building of less general classifiers. Refining these representations to both highlight the changes in ALCS environments and build more general classifiers is a direction for future research.

6   Conclusion

This paper introduced BEACS (Behavioral Enhanced Anticipatory Classifier System) as an alternative machine learning model to solve reinforcement learning tasks, in an effort to increase both the *performance* and *explainability* of Anticipatory Learning Classifier Systems. BEACS couples *Behavioral Sequences* (BSeq) and *Enhanced Predictions through Experience* (EPE) to handle non-deterministic, partially observable environments, which are common in the real world. While Behavioral Sequences enable ALCS to bridge states which cannot be distinguished by perception alone (known as the Perceptual Aliasing Issue) using *sequences of actions*, Enhanced Predictions through Experience allow ALCS to build multiple anticipations in non-deterministic states (*i.e.* aliased states).

BEACS is the first ALCS integrating a mechanism to distinguish states related to the Perceptual Aliasing Issue from all other aliased states. This allows the system to know when Behavioral Sequences should and should not be used, as BSeq can be used to deal with PAI but not with other types of aliasing. The construction of classifiers using BSeq has been enhanced and now provides a better control of these classifiers. The length of sequences of actions is taken into account to fit these sequences more efficiently to the environment. BEACS uses the EPE mechanism to build more accurate and explainable representations of its environments. The EPE classifiers aim at describing precisely each states encountered by the system, according to the environmental properties. Finally, by adaptively deleting, generalizing, and specializing its classifiers, BEACS can better frame the expansion of its population.

The results of a thorough experimental protocol using maze environments show that BEACS (1) is the only ALCS that builds complete and accurate internal representations of its environment when faced with non-deterministic environmental properties such as the Perceptual Aliasing Issue or uncertain results of action, (2) describes more precisely the states anticipated by the classifiers along with their probabilities to be anticipated, (3) builds efficient decision policies to solve the learning tasks and (4) provides explanatory insights about created decision policies and environmental representations to its user.

Future works should focus on the management of classifiers populations, to ease the interpretation of these populations through compression, visualization or generalization, as well as the assessment of different Reinforcement Learning mechanisms that can be embedded within ALCS.

References

1. Bagnall, A.J., Zatuchna, Z.V.: On the classification of maze problems. In: Bull, L., Kovacs, T. (eds.) Foundations of Learning Classifier Systems. Studies in Fuzziness and Soft Computing, pp. 305–316. Springer, Heidelberg (2005). https://doi.org/10.1007/11319122_12
2. Butz, A.M.V., Goldberg, B.D.E., Stolzmann, C.W.: The anticipatory classifier system and genetic generalization. Nat. Comput. **1**, 427–467 (2002). https://doi.org/10.1023/A:1021330114221
3. Butz, M.V.: Biasing exploration in an anticipatory learning classifier system. In: Lanzi, P.L., Stolzmann, W., Wilson, S.W. (eds.) IWLCS 2001. LNCS (LNAI), vol. 2321, pp. 3–22. Springer, Heidelberg (2002). https://doi.org/10.1007/3-540-48104-4_1

4. Butz, M.V., Goldberg, D.E.: Generalized state values in an anticipatory learning classifier system. In: Butz, M.V., Sigaud, O., Gérard, P. (eds.) Anticipatory Behavior in Adaptive Learning Systems. LNCS (LNAI), vol. 2684, pp. 282–301. Springer, Heidelberg (2003). https://doi.org/10.1007/978-3-540-45002-3_16

5. Butz, M.V., Goldberg, D.E., Stolzmann, W.: Probability-enhanced predictions in the anticipatory classifier system. In: Luca Lanzi, P., Stolzmann, W., Wilson, S.W. (eds.) IWLCS 2000. LNCS (LNAI), vol. 1996, pp. 37–51. Springer, Heidelberg (2001). https://doi.org/10.1007/3-540-44640-0_4

6. Butz, M.V., Stolzmann, W.: An algorithmic description of ACS2. In: Lanzi, P.L., Stolzmann, W., Wilson, S.W. (eds.) IWLCS 2001. LNCS (LNAI), vol. 2321, pp. 211–229. Springer, Heidelberg (2002). https://doi.org/10.1007/3-540-48104-4_13

7. Fagerland, M.W., Sandvik, L.: Performance of five two-sample location tests for skewed distributions with unequal variances. Contemp. Clin. Trials 30, 490–496 (2009)

8. Gérard, P., Meyer, J.A., Sigaud, O.: Combining latent learning with dynamic programming in the modular anticipatory classifier system. Eur. J. Oper. Res. 160(3), 614–637 (2005)

9. Gerard, P., Stolzmann, W., Sigaud, O.: YACS: a new learning classifier system using anticipation. Soft Comput. 6, 216–228 (2002). https://doi.org/10.1007/s005000100117

10. Hasselt, H.: Double q-learning. In: Advances in neural information processing systems, pp. 2613–2621 (2010)

11. Hoffmann, J.: Anticipatory behavioral control. In: Butz, M.V., Sigaud, O., Gérard, P. (eds.) Anticipatory Behavior in Adaptive Learning Systems. LNCS (LNAI), vol. 2684, pp. 44–65. Springer, Heidelberg (2003). https://doi.org/10.1007/978-3-540-45002-3_4

12. Kozlowski, N., Unold, O.: Investigating exploration techniques for ACS in discretized real-valued environments. In: Proceedings of the 2020 Genetic and Evolutionary Computation Conference Companion, pp. 1765–1773 (2020)

13. Kozłowski, N., Unold, O.: Anticipatory classifier system with average reward criterion in discretized multi-step environments. Appl. Sci. 11(3), 1098 (2021)

14. Métivier, M., Lattaud, C.: Anticipatory classifier system using behavioral sequences in non-Markov environments. In: Lanzi, P.L., Stolzmann, W., Wilson, S.W. (eds.) IWLCS 2002. LNCS (LNAI), vol. 2661, pp. 143–162. Springer, Heidelberg (2003). https://doi.org/10.1007/978-3-540-40029-5_9

15. Orhand, R., Jeannin-Girardon, A., Parrend, P., Collet, P.: BACS: a thorough study of using behavioral sequences in ACS2. In: Bäck, T., et al. (eds.) PPSN 2020, Part I. LNCS, vol. 12269, pp. 524–538. Springer, Cham (2020). https://doi.org/10.1007/978-3-030-58112-1_36

16. Orhand, R., Jeannin-Girardon, A., Parrend, P., Collet, P.: PEPACS: integrating probability-enhanced predictions to ACS2. In: Proceedings of the 2020 Genetic and Evolutionary Computation Conference Companion, pp. 1774–1781 (2020)

17. Orhand, R., Jeannin-Girardon, A., Parrend, P., Collet, P.: Explainability and performance of anticipatory learning classifier systems in non-deterministic environments. In: Proceedings of the Genetic and Evolutionary Computation Conference Companion, pp. 163–164 (2021)

18. Stolzmann, W.: An introduction to anticipatory classifier systems. In: Lanzi, P.L., Stolzmann, W., Wilson, S.W. (eds.) IWLCS 1999. LNCS (LNAI), vol. 1813, pp. 175–194. Springer, Heidelberg (2000). https://doi.org/10.1007/3-540-45027-0_9

19. Stolzmann, W., Butz, M., Hoffmann, J., Goldberg, D.: First cognitive capabilities in the anticipatory classifier system, February 2000

20. Tan, J., Moore, J., Urbanowicz, R.: Rapid rule compaction strategies for global knowledge discovery in a supervised learning classifier system. In: Artificial Life Conference Proceedings, vol. 13, pp. 110–117 (2013)
21. Unold, O., Rogula, E., Kozłowski, N.: Introducing action planning to the anticipatory classifier system ACS2. In: Burduk, R., Kurzynski, M., Wozniak, M. (eds.) CORES 2019. AISC, vol. 977, pp. 264–275. Springer, Cham (2020). https://doi.org/10.1007/978-3-030-19738-4_27

Exploiting Knowledge from Code to Guide Program Search

Dirk Schweim[1]([⊠]) [iD], Erik Hemberg[2], Dominik Sobania[3] [iD],
and Una-May O'Reilly[2]

[1] Baden-Wuerttemberg Cooperative State University, Heidenheim, Germany
dirk.schweim@dhbw-heidenheim.de
[2] MIT CSAIL, Cambridge, MA, USA
{hembergerik,unamay}@csail.mit.edu
[3] Johannes Gutenberg University, Mainz, Germany
dsobania@uni-mainz.de

Abstract. Human code is different from code generated by program search. We investigate if properties from human-generated code can guide program search to improve the qualities of the generated programs, e.g., readability and performance. Here we focus on program search with grammatical evolution, which produces code that has different structure compared to human-generated code, e.g., loops and conditions are hardly used. We use a large code-corpus that was mined from the open software repository service GitHub and measure software metrics and properties describing the code-base. We use this knowledge to guide the search by incorporating a new selection scheme. Our new selection scheme favors programs that are structurally similar to the programs in the GitHub code-base. We find noticeable evidence that software metrics can help in guiding evolutionary search.

Keywords: Program Synthesis · Program Search · Software Search · Grammar Guided Genetic Programming · Genetic Programming · Grammatical Evolution · Mining Software Repositories

1 Introduction

A recent study [23] identified several problems in program search with grammatical evolution (GE, [18]). For example, conditionals or loops are often not effectively used since the fitness signal does not guide the search towards these complex structures [23]. Instead, small building blocks are combined and the search iteratively evolves very specialized programs. The authors come to the conclusion that "the current problem specification and especially the definition of the fitness

The authors thank Jordan Wick for sharing his expertise, the insightful discussions, and his help on our project. This work was supported by a fellowship within the IFI programme of the German Academic Exchange Service (DAAD).

E. Medvet et al. (Eds.): EuroGP 2022, LNCS 13223, pp. 262–277, 2022.
https://doi.org/10.1007/978-3-031-02056-8_17

functions do not allow guided search, as the resulting problem constitutes a needle-in-a-haystack problem" [23]. They state that a main challenge for future research in program search is to find new ways that help to guide the search.

In this article we focus on the question of how knowledge gained from human-generated code can be used as an additional bias to guide program search with GE. In most current GE approaches, general programming knowledge is only incorporated into the evolutionary search process via the BNF grammar. In effect, the evolved solutions are often unreadable as well as "bloated" [22] and therefore, hardly maintainable or testable. We extend the current approaches and investigate the possibility to use software metrics from an existing code-base to guide the search with GE for program search problems. Our work is a first step to evaluate the question how general programming knowledge can be used to guide an evolutionary search towards programs that are similar to human-generated programs.

Therefore, we mined a code-corpus, consisting of 211,060 real-world and high-quality Python functions. We use this human-generated code and measure the frequencies of software metrics that describe properties of the code in the code-base. Then, we propose multiple GE variants where the additional knowledge about code properties is used as an additional signal to guide the search. Our results show that additional information can help guide the program search. Furthermore, we gain valuable insight on how future approaches can be improved. For example, we learn that setting too many additional objectives is detrimental, because the conventional fitness signal is obfuscated.

In Sect. 2, we present related work. In Sect. 3, we describe how we mined the code-base from GitHub. Furthermore, we analyze the code-base and describe relevant software metrics. Section 4 describes our experiments and discusses the results. The article ends with concluding remarks (Sect. 5)

2 Related Work

Sobania and Rothlauf [23] state that a main challenge for future research in program search is to find better fitness signals and problem representations that help to guide the search. Petke [16] suggested to use existing code produced by software developers to develop new search operators. She discussed the idea that the knowledge gained from analysis of existing code-bases could be a form of template during mutation (similar to [17]). Hemberg et al. [9] proposed to add domain knowledge and novelty as an alternative fitness signal. The authors [9] extracted knowledge from program search problem definitions and used the gained knowledge to guide the search.

A larger number of studies investigate challenges in program search. For example, Dijkstra noted that the use of test cases does not allow to appropriately measure generalization [4]. For program search based on genetic programming, this is investigated in a recent paper [21]. Other challenges in program search have been collected by Krawiec [13]. He discusses the large search space, context-dependent behavior of functions, and multiple ways to describe desired functionality (see also multiple-attractor problem described in [1]). Forstenlech-ner et al. [7] found that some program search problems are easy, but others could not be solved at all by their approach. To study these differences in performance, Sobania and Rothlauf [23] empirically analyze GE search behavior on program search tasks. In their experiments, they find that GE is not able to solve program search tasks that use loops or conditions. Also, they note that mutations often lead to worse solutions and more complex code structures. In their experiments, they were not able to evolve code that was capable of solving moderately com-plex problems while being *structurally* similar to human-generated code. This means that not only the structure of evolved programs is complex in most cases but also that the functions are combined in ways that do not lead to functioning programs. They conclude that the search is often more similar to a needle-in-a-haystack problem and that GE searches in the wrong areas of the search space in these cases. Furthermore, [22] compared Python functions generated by differ-ent initialization methods for GE and GP with around 50,000 human generated functions mined from GitHub. They find large differences in the structure of abstract syntax trees (ASTs) as well as in how functions are combined between automatically and human-generated code. For example, software developers tend to use a limited set of language elements most of the time, whereas initialization approaches randomly combine the available functions and terminals, being only restricted by the rules defined (e.g., in the GE grammar). The authors suggest to evolve code that imitates human-generated code by incorporating perplexity pressure into the fitness function. The paper states that it is possible to evolve code that looks human-generated but the authors do not evaluate the generated code on real problems. Note that our code corpus subsumes this, and is more than four times larger, since we do not limit the number of function arguments.

3   GitHub Code Corpus

In our experiments we use human-generated code in the programming language Python that was mined from the software repository hosting service GitHub. Python is a widely used programming language and there are many open source projects freely available on GitHub. Furthermore, it is comparatively easy to parse Python source code.

On GitHub, users are able to rate software repositories. We only use reposito-ries with 150 or more positive user ratings ("stars"). We cloned a total of 10,723 repositories that met the aforementioned search criteria. Then, we iterated over every Python file in the repositories and extracted all functions. Next, comments and empty lines were removed from the extracted functions. Furthermore, we do not use class methods because they often perform very basic tasks (e.g., chang-ing class attributes). Overall, our code-corpus consists of 211,060 real-world and high-quality Python functions.

We use widely known software metrics to perform a descriptive analysis of the code-base, investigating the question if there are certain similarities in high-quality human-generated Python code that could be useful to help in guiding an evolutionary search. The software metrics are described in Sect. 3.1 and the results of the descriptive analysis are presented in Sect. 3.2.

3.1   Software Metrics

To investigate the properties of the source code, we use the following well known software metrics. We apply the metrics either directly on the source code representation or on its abstract tree representation, commonly referred to as the *abstract syntax tree* (AST) representation.

- **Lines of code (LOC)**: The number of lines of a given function (comments and empty lines are not taken into account).
- **Cyclomatic complexity**: The number of paths through the program (e.g., an if statement leads to two independent paths). The minimum cyclomatic complexity is 1 [14].
- **AST depth**: For an AST, this is the length of the longest non-backtracking path from the root of the tree to any tree node in the AST [12].
- **AST tree size**: The number of nodes in an AST.
- **Lexical diversity**: The ratio of the number of AST node types over the number of AST nodes [11] (i.e., number of different nodes in the AST tree divided by the size of the AST tree).

For more details and examples regarding the metrics please refer to [22].

We used the Python module radon[1] to calculate the LOC and the cyclomatic complexity. To get the AST depth, number of AST nodes, and lexical diversity, we first generated an AST object using astdump[2] for each of the functions in the code-corpus. Then, we recursively iterated over each of the AST objects to calculate the respective metrics.

3.2   Descriptive Analysis of the Code Corpus

We present and discuss the results of the descriptive analysis of the GitHub code-base. We calculate the different software metrics for each Python function in the code-base and count the respective frequencies. Lexical diversity is a continuous metric and therefore we use "bucketing". We count the frequencies of the lexical diversity in intervals with a size of 0.01: $\{x \in R | a < x \leq a + 0.01\} \forall a \in \{0, 0.01, ..., 0.99\}$. For example, the lexical diversity of a program in the code-base is 0.483, so the absolute frequency of programs with a lexical diversity $0.48 < x \leq 0.49$ is increased by one. LOC, cyclomatic complexity, AST depth, and number of AST nodes are discrete values and we count the respective frequencies without bucketing. Figures 1a–e plot the relative frequencies of the programs in the code-base over the respective values of a software metric.

Figure 1a presents the results for LOC. We can observe that the frequency of programs decreases with increasing LOC. The frequency of very small programs

---

[1] radon: https://pypi.org/project/radon/.
[2] astdump: https://pypi.org/project/astdump/.

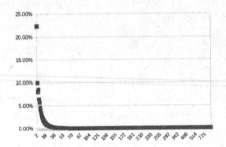

(a) Relative frequency of programs over the number of lines of code (LOC)

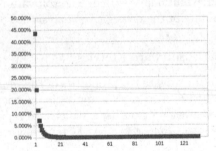

(b) Relative frequency of programs over the cycolmatic complexity

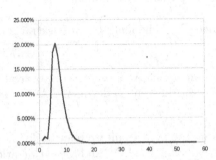

(c) Relative frequency of programs over the AST depth

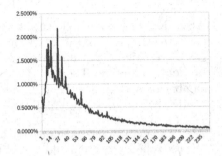

(d) Relative frequency of programs over the number of AST nodes

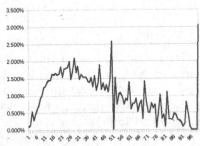

(e) Relative frequency of programs over the lexical diversity; lexical diversity is presented using numbered buckets with an interval size of 1 % (e.g., bucket 1 includes all programs with a lexical diversity $0 < x \leq 0.01$)

Fig. 1. Software metrics for the functions in the GitHub code-corpus

with only few LOC is very high—90% of the programs have between 2 and 21 LOC and the median number of LOC is 6.

Figure 1b shows the results for cyclomatic complexity. Similar to the results for LOC, we observe that the complexity is low in the majority of programs. 95% of the programs have a cycolmatic complexity between 1 and 10 and the median complexity is 2.

Results for AST tree depth are presented in Fig. 1c. The highest frequency can be observed for an AST tree depth of 5 and the median depth is 8. 95% of the programs have an AST tree depth between 2 and 12.

The number of AST nodes is presented in Fig. 1d and is more diverse compared to the previous metrics. 90% of the programs have between 2 and 215 AST nodes. The median number of AST nodes is 51.

Last, Fig. 1e presents the results for the lexical diversity. Buckets are numbered from 1 to 100. We can see several "spikes". For example, the relative frequency of programs with a lexical diversity between 0.5 and 0.51 (bucket 50) is about 2.58%, while the frequency between 0.51 and 0.52 (bucket 51) is only about 0.021%. These spikes can be explained by the small bucket size and, as a consequence, a high variance. Lexical diversity measures "vocabulary richness", meaning that a low lexical diversity indicates simplicity and repetition of the same concepts. The peak for the lexical diversity of 1. can be explained by trivial or very short programs (e.g., return input). The median lexical diversity is 0.37 and the figure shows that many programs have lexical diversities around this value. This indicates that human software developers rely on repeatedly using a limited set of language elements to solve a problem.

In summary, code that received positive ratings ("stars") by human programmers has several similarities in its structural properties. Often, it consists of short code with a low complexity where certain concepts are used repeatedly. These findings are in line with our expectations since it is common to reduce complexity of code by breaking down the code into several smaller functions. Please note that our brief descriptive analysis only investigates what a majority of GitHub users rate as "good and useful code". This does not mean that programmers should aspire to write such code—for example, it is an ongoing discussion if a lower number of LOC and a higher degree of modularization are desirable [2,6,20]. Furthermore, we want to point out that our evaluation does incorporate certain human biases—for example, people possibly avoid to use complex code or may not evaluate it positively. However, this is in line with the goal of this article: we seek to evolve simple, understandable code that looks like human-generated code. Therefore, it seems appropriate to use the metrics evaluated in this section to guide evolutionary search with the goal to improve the readability and maintainability of the generated code.

4   Experiments

It is an open question how additional information can be appropriately added to an evolutionary search to increase search performance. Furthermore, it is not clear what kind of information is helpful. In our experiments, we use the frequency distributions of the software metrics gained from the GitHub code-base and test multiple methods how this additional knowledge can be added to the search. We present our experimental setup (Sect. 4.1) and discuss the results (Sect. 4.2).

4.1   Experimental Setup

We first introduce a baseline algorithm referred to as *base*, a standard GE algorithm with widely used parameters. The parameters for *base* are presented in Table 1. Note that we use a large maximum tree depth of 30 which allows us to observe a relatively unconstrained search behavior. We do not allow wrapping during mapping and instead use a high initial genome length. Our algorithm uses tournament lexicase selection [24], where a subset of the population is compared sequentially on multiple test cases. If some programs have identical performance on all test cases, we randomly select one of these solutions.

Table 1. Baseline parameters

Parameter	Value
Generations	80
Initialization	Random initialization with valids and no duplicates [15]
Initial genome length	1,000
Population size	1,000
Variation operators	Subtree crossover (90%), subtree mutation (10%), crossover and mutation are only applied on valid individuals and limited to codons that are used during mapping from genotype to phenotype
Selection	Tournament lexicase selection (tournament size 10)
Elite size	5
Max. tree depth	30

We will also evaluate an alternative version of *base* denoted as $base\_d_{max}17$. In $base\_d_{max}17$, we set the maximum tree depth to 17 [12] to limit the size and complexity of the evolved code. Furthermore, we add parsimony pressure to the selection scheme—if there are multiple solutions with identical performance, we always select the smallest solution.

We compare the two aforementioned baseline approaches with four alternative variants, where the selection operator differs from the baseline approaches. The overall idea for the variants is to guide the search by conventional test case fitness in half of the cases and towards programs that have similar structures than the programs in the GitHub code-base in the remaining half of cases. Thus, in these variants, we use the conventional lexicase selection mechanism of *base* only in 50% of the cases. In the remaining 50%, we use an alternative selection scheme—a tournament lexicase selection where the conventional test case vector is replaced with a vector of the relative frequencies of software metrics. Therefore, we calculate the software metrics presented in Sect. 3.1 for each of the evolved programs and look up the relative frequencies of these software metrics measured in the GitHub code-base. As a result, we get a vector with relative frequencies for each evolved program. We use this vector within a lexicase selection scheme and select the programs with the highest relative frequencies. This means that programs with software metrics that are more frequent in the GitHub repository are favored over programs with less frequent metrics.

In *metrics50*, the vector of the relative frequencies of software metrics consists of lines of code, cyclomatic complexity, AST depth, AST tree size, and lexical diversity. The metrics used in *metrics50* describe the structure of the programs in the GitHub code-base. However, information about the type of instructions that are used in the GitHub code-base is not included into the search. Therefore, we introduce *metrics50+ngrams*. *metrics50+ngrams* is working like *metrics50*, except that frequencies of n-grams of ancestors are evaluated in the alternative selection scheme as well. An n-gram of ancestors in an AST tree is the sequence of a node i and its $n-1$ ancestor nodes (parent, grandparent, great-grandparent, etc.) on the same branch [10,19]. We evaluated n-grams of ancestors with $n = 2$ and $n = 3$ in the AST representations of the programs in the GitHub code-base. Every program can have multiple values (e.g., the programs AST has 5 different n-grams, some of them occur more than once). Thus, we count the 2- and 3-grams for each program; then, we normalize the frequencies over all 2- and 3-grams in the code-base to get overall n-gram frequencies. During evaluation, we count the 2- and 3-grams, add the relative frequencies and normalize over the number of 2- and 3-grams in the programs AST. Thus, two more values are added to the evaluation vector in this setup (one value for 2- or 3-grams, respectively).

The third option of using the knowledge of the GitHub code-base in an evolutionary search is a multi-objective search with NSGA-II [3]. In *NSGAII*, we use the vector with relative frequencies from *metrics50* and append the conventional fitness value to get the multi-objective vector. Furthermore, in *NSGAII+ngrams*, we add 2- and 3-gram frequencies to the multi-objective vector.

In Sect. 3.2 we saw that program metrics possibly could just guide the search towards simple and non-complex programs. To check this hypothesis, we introduce a last variant, *parsimony50*. In *parsimony50*, we use the selection mechanism of *base* with a probability of 50%. In the remaining 50%, we choose the program with the minimum number of AST nodes. Table 2 summarizes the variants of the baseline GE algorithm *base* that we compare in our experiments.

Note that the elite size is measured by the conventional fitness value in all variants, which prevents losing the best solutions found up to a certain point in the search. We evaluate all variants on three program search benchmark problems—count odds, smallest, and median [8] For our experiments, we used the PonyGE2 framework [5], including the respective grammars for program search problems.

Table 2. Overview of the variants of the baseline GE algorithm *base* that are compared in our experiments

Name	Description
$base\_d_{max}17$	Max. tree depth is set to 17 and parsimony pressure is added to the lexicase selection scheme
metrics50	An alternative selection scheme is used: 50% conventional lexicase selection, 50% lexicase selection where the test case vector is replaced with a vector of relative frequencies of software metrics
metrics50+ngrams	Same as *metrics50*, but in addition to the software metrics we also use 2- and 3-gram frequencies during selection
NSGAII	We use the vector with relative frequencies from *metrics50* and append the conventional fitness value to get the multi-objective vector, 6 objectives
NSGAII+ngrams	Same as *NSGAII* but the multi-objective vector is further extended with 2- and 3-gram frequencies, 8 objectives
parsimony50	An alternative selection scheme is used: 50% conventional lexicase selection, in the remaining 50%, we choose the program with the minimum number of AST nodes

Many more variants could be tested. In fact, we did various experiments with percentages of selection schemes different from 50. Furthermore, we did a number of experiments with a weighted lexicase selection scheme to account for different importance of the software metrics. However, the results did not show that some metrics were consistently more important than others over multiple benchmark problems. Due to space limitations, we limit our results to the seven carefully chosen variants presented above, which we think provide to the most interesting insights.

4.2 Results and Discussion

We investigate the possibility to use software metrics from an existing code-base to guide the search with GE for program search problems. We present and discuss our results.

Performance. First, we will evaluate the performance of the different search variants. Figures 2a–c show the percentage of solved test cases of the best solutions over the number of generations for three program search benchmark problems—count odds (Fig. 2a), smallest (Fig. 2b), and median (Fig. 2c) [8]. For each variant, we present the average result of 100 runs. Figure 2d shows the legend for Figs. 2a–c.

The two baseline algorithms *base* and $base\_d_{max}17$ evolve the best programs on all three problem instances. Programs evolved with *base* lead, on average, to slightly better results. Thus, limiting the depth to 17 and introducing the parsimony pressure to the selection scheme leads to a decreased performance.

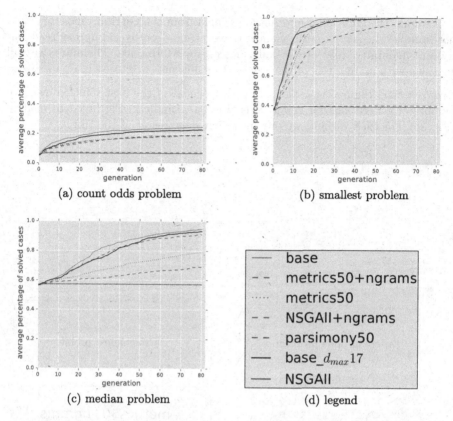

(a) count odds problem

(b) smallest problem

(c) median problem

(d) legend

Fig. 2. Percentage of solved test cases of the best solution in a generation over the number of generations for three benchmark problems; results are the average over 100 runs per variant

Results for *parsimony50* are worse, compared to the baseline variants. This is due to the strong parsimony pressure in this variant, where the smallest programs are selected in 50 % of the cases. As a consequence, the diversity is reduced.

The performance of *metrics50* and *metrics50+ngrams* are comparable on the count odds and the smallest problem instance. Both results are slightly worse than the results of *base* and *base_d_{max}17*. On the median problem instance, *metrics50* performs worse and *metrics50+ngrams* leads to results that are comparable to *base_d_{max}17*. The additional information of 2- and 3-grams in *metrics50+ngrams* helps guiding the search towards better solutions in this case.

NSGAII and *NSGAII+ngrams* led to the worst results on all three problem instances. Some possible reasons are that there are too many objectives, and that the conventional fitness signal is too weak and programs are often selected based on a software metric frequency. This clearly prevents the search from finding good solutions.

Overall, the additional information gained from the GitHub repository does not improve the search performance. However, our goal is to improve readability and maintainability of the code, not only performance. Therefore, we will continue with an analysis of the size of the solutions.

Program Size. Figures 3a–c plot the AST tree size of the best solution over the number of generations for count odds (Fig. 3a), smallest (Fig. 3b), and median (Fig. 3c). For each variant, we present the average result of 100 runs.

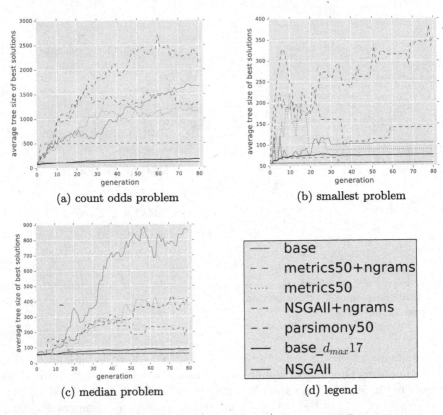

(a) count odds problem

(b) smallest problem

(c) median problem

(d) legend

Fig. 3. AST tree size of the best solution in a generation over the number of generations for three benchmark problems; results are the average over 100 runs per variant

We can see that the best programs found with *base* are very large compared to many other variants, especially on the median problem instance. The second baseline, *base_d_{max}17*, is able to find relatively small programs and only the programs found with *NSGAII* and *NSGAII+ngrams* are slightly smaller. Our experiments indicate that the multiobjective approaches with *NSGAII* and *NSGAII+ngrams* focus too much on program structure and this does not allow to find high-quality programs.

The size of the programs that are evolved with *metrics50+ngrams* and *metrics50* is large in many cases. Interestingly, the high parsimony pressure in *parsimony50* does also not effectively prevent bloat—the programs are much bigger than the programs that are evolved with *base_d$_{max}$17*. An explanation for this behavior is that, due to elitism, bloated solutions will always stay in the population when their performance is better compared to other programs that were optimized for their size. The search has to evolve small and highly fit solutions from time to time to effectively prevent bloat. This can be seen for *metrics50* and *metrics50+ngrams* on the smallest and for *metrics50+ngrams* on the median problems. From time to time the search finds small and favorable solutions and then the size of the best solution in the population decreases drastically. For *parsimony50*, we can only observe smaller changes—the code grows over multiple generations.

Program Content. In the last part of our analysis we want to focus on the AST node types that are used in the evolved programs. For better comparability we manually generated a solution. Listing 1.1 shows the hand-coded solution to the median problem. The code was written by following the rules of the grammar that is also used by the evolutionary algorithm variants. Lines 1–4 are predefined initializations that are also in all evolved programs. These lines were only included in the exemplary code for reasons of comparability to automatically evolved solutions. Only line 5 would have been evolved by an evolutionary algorithm.

Listing 1.1. Example of a small human solution to the median problem

```
1   def median(in0: int, in1: int, in2:int):
2       i0 = int(); i1 = int(); i2 = int()
3       b0 = bool(); b1 = bool(); b2 = bool()
4       res0 = int()
5       res0 = min(max(in2, min(in1, in0)),
6                  max(in1, min(in2, in0)))
```

We will compare the best programs evolved after 80 generations for the median problem with the hand-coded solution. We limit this part of the analysis on three variants—*base*, *base_d$_{max}$17*, and *metrics50+ngrams*. We selected *base* and *base_d$_{max}$17* because of the good performance on all three program search benchmarks (compared to the remaining variants). *metrics50+ngrams* was taken into account because it was the most successful approach that used the additional fitness signal and thus, is the most promising of our variants. Table 3 presents the number of AST nodes per node type used in the best solution after generation 80 on the median problem. Results are averaged over 100 evolutionary runs per variant. We highlighted the rows of the node types that we used in the small hand-coded solution.

Table 3. Used number of AST node types for the median problem for three different variants (*base*, *metrics50+ngrams*, and *base_d_{max}30*); results are the average over 100 runs per variant

Operator	Small human solution	base_d_{max}17	metrics50+ngrams	Base
Add	0	0.2	1.7	9.6
And	0	0.0	0.0	0.2
Assign	7	8.1	8.1	12.1
AugAssign	0	0.1	0.1	0.5
BinOp	0	0.5	5.2	28.3
BoolOp	0	0.0	0.0	0.6
Call	11	13.5	37.9	154.9
Compare	0	0.1	0.1	1.8
Eq	0	0.0	0.0	0.2
Gt	0	0.0	0.1	0.2
GtE	0	0.0	0.0	0.4
If	0	0.1	0.1	1.7
Load	17	20.7	59.4	255.6
Lt	0	0.0	0.0	0.4
LtE	0	0.0	0.0	0.3
Mult	0	0.2	1.8	9.1
Name	24	28.9	67.5	268.3
NameConstant	0	0.1	0.0	0.6
Not	0	0.0	0.0	0.7
NotEq	0	0.0	0.0	0.2
Num	0	0.3	5.3	28.1
Or	0	0.0	0.0	0.4
Store	7	8.2	8.2	12.7
Sub	0	0.2	1.8	10.1
UAdd	0	0.7	3.2	15.8
USub	0	0.3	2.8	13.4
UnaryOp	0	1.0	6.0	29.9
While	0	0.0	0.0	0.2
Total number of operations	**67.0**	**84.3**	**210.2**	**857.1**

It is very interesting to see that *base_d_{max}17* often evolves programs that use the same node types that are also used in the hand-coded program. Other node types are rarely used and bloat results from very few meaningless function calls, e.g., min(in0,in0). This is a good property if the search gets a clear fitness signal like in the median problem. On the other hand, it limits the possibility to find more complex solutions. For example, the grammars that we used would also allow more complex solutions where loops, conditionals, and comparisons are necessary. To find such a complex solution will be hard when following the conventional fitness signal.

On the contrary, bloat in *base* is due to various meaningless calls, e.g., a large amount of useless arithmetic operations. *metrics50+ngrams* is a promising approach that allows to evolve complexity but the amount of bloat is controlled.

In summary, if we take into account both, the performance and the size of the evolved programs, $base\_d_{max}17$ is the most favorable setting. In $base\_d_{max}17$, bloat is limited very effectively while the performance is comparable to *base*. However, the approach does not help to find complex programs. For example, our results indicate that more complex non-linear program structures like conditionals and loops are not effectively used by the current GE approaches (with "general grammars" that are not optimized for a problem instance)

In our experiments, we find evidence that software metrics and n-gram frequencies can help evolving good solutions, while helping to limit bloat and allowing for more complexity. Arguably, meta information such as the software metrics examined in this work may not be enough additional signal to be effectively exploited by evolutionary search. This is no big surprise, since it is also hard for humans to quantify code quality. Overall, our work is a first step towards the goal to effectively use additional input signals to guide the search towards meaningful complex programs.

5   Conclusion

Creating high-quality code is a complex task, even for humans. The goal of this paper was to discuss and evaluate the idea of how additional knowledge gained from a large amount of high-quality human-generated code can help in an evolutionary search. We find evidence that meta-information can help in guiding the search. However, the code metrics used in our experiments are rather simplistic, i.e., they do not capture the semantics or internal logic of the code.

Future work has to investigate how information from the existing code-base can be used more effectively to further improve the search performance. In future work, we will investigate:

- learn transition probabilities from code in code-base,
- use carefully chosen examples from a code repository to help guiding the search (or initializing it),
- use probabilistic models (e.g., deep learning approaches) to evaluate the code quality and incorporate this information into the search.

References

1. Altenberg, L.: Open problems in the spectral analysis of evolutionary dynamics. In: Menon, A. (ed.) Frontiers of Evolutionary Computation. Genetic Algorithms and Evolutionary Computation, vol. 11, pp. 73–102. Springer, Boston (2004). https://doi.org/10.1007/1-4020-7782-3_4

2. Basili, V.R., Perricone, B.T.: Software errors and complexity: an empirical investigation. Commun. ACM **27**(1), 42–52 (1984)

3. Deb, K., Pratap, A., Agarwal, S., Meyarivan, T.: A fast and elitist multiobjective genetic algorithm: NSGA-II. IEEE Trans. Evol. Comput. **6**(2), 182–197 (2002)

4. Dijkstra, E.W.: The humble programmer. Commun. ACM **15**(10), 859–866 (1972)

5. Fenton, M., McDermott, J., Fagan, D., Forstenlechner, S., Hemberg, E., O'Neill, M.: PonyGE2: grammatical evolution in python. In: Proceedings of the Genetic and Evolutionary Computation Conference Companion, pp. 1194–1201. ACM, Berlin (2017)

6. Fenton, N.E., Neil, M.: A critique of software defect prediction models. IEEE Trans. Softw. Eng. **25**(5), 675–689 (1999)

7. Forstenlechner, S., Fagan, D., Nicolau, M., O'Neill, M.: Towards understanding and refining the general program synthesis benchmark suite with genetic programming. In: 2018 IEEE Congress on Evolutionary Computation (CEC), pp. 1–6. IEEE (2018)

8. Helmuth, T., Spector, L.: General program synthesis benchmark suite. In: Proceedings of the 2015 Annual Conference on Genetic and Evolutionary Computation, pp. 1039–1046. ACM, New York (2015)

9. Hemberg, E., Kelly, J., O'Reilly, U.M.: On domain knowledge and novelty to improve program synthesis performance with grammatical evolution. In: Proceedings of the Genetic and Evolutionary Computation Conference, GECCO 2019, pp. 1039–1046. ACM, New York (2019)

10. Hemberg, E., Veeramachaneni, K., McDermott, J., Berzan, C., O'Reilly, U.M.: An investigation of local patterns for estimation of distribution genetic programming. In: Proceedings of the 14th Annual Conference on Genetic and Evolutionary Computation (GECCO 2012), pp. 767–774. ACM, New York (2012)

11. Johansson, V.: Lexical diversity and lexical density in speech and writing: a developmental perspective. In: Working Papers in Linguistics, vol. 53, pp. 61–79 (2009)

12. Koza, J.R.: Genetic Programming: On the Programming of Computers by Means of Natural Selection. MIT Press, Cambridge (1992)

13. Krawiec, K.: Behavioral Program Synthesis with Genetic Programming. Studies in Computational Intelligence, vol. 618. Springer, Cham (2016)

14. McCabe, T.J.: A complexity measure. IEEE Trans. Softw. Eng. **SE–2**(4), 308–320 (1976)

15. Nicolau, M.: Understanding grammatical evolution: initialisation. Genet. Program. Evolvable Mach. **18**(4), 467–507 (2017). https://doi.org/10.1007/s10710-017-9309-9D

16. Petke, J.: New operators for non-functional genetic improvement. In: Proceedings of the Genetic and Evolutionary Computation Conference Companion, pp. 1541–1542. ACM, New York (2017)

17. Petke, J., Harman, M., Langdon, W.B., Weimer, W.: Using genetic improvement and code transplants to specialise a C++ Program to a Problem class. In: Nicolau, M., et al. (eds.) EuroGP 2014. LNCS, vol. 8599, pp. 137–149. Springer, Heidelberg (2014). https://doi.org/10.1007/978-3-662-44303-3_12

18. Ryan, C., Collins, J.J., Neill, M.O.: Grammatical evolution: evolving programs for an arbitrary language. In: Banzhaf, W., Poli, R., Schoenauer, M., Fogarty, T.C. (eds.) EuroGP 1998. LNCS, vol. 1391, pp. 83–96. Springer, Heidelberg (1998). https://doi.org/10.1007/BFb0055930

19. Schweim, D., Wittenberg, D., Rothlauf, F.: On sampling error in genetic programming. Nat. Comput. (2021). https://doi.org/10.1007/s11047-020-09828-w

20. Selby, R.W., Basili, V.R.: Analyzing error-prone system structure. IEEE Trans. Softw. Eng. **17**(2), 141–152 (1991)

21. Sobania, D.: On the generalizability of programs synthesized by grammar-guided genetic programming. In: Hu, T., Lourenço, N., Medvet, E. (eds.) EuroGP 2021. LNCS, vol. 12691, pp. 130–145. Springer, Cham (2021). https://doi.org/10.1007/978-3-030-72812-0_9

22. Sobania, D., Rothlauf, F.: Teaching GP to program like a human software developer: using perplexity pressure to guide program synthesis approaches. In: Proceedings of the Genetic and Evolutionary Computation Conference (GECCO-2019), pp. 1065–1074. ACM, New York (2019)

23. Sobania, D., Rothlauf, F.: Challenges of program synthesis with grammatical evolution. In: Hu, T., Lourenço, N., Medvet, E., Divina, F. (eds.) EuroGP 2020. LNCS, vol. 12101, pp. 211–227. Springer, Cham (2020). https://doi.org/10.1007/978-3-030-44094-7_14

24. Spector, L.: Assessment of problem modality by differential performance of lexicase selection in genetic programming: a preliminary report. In: Proceedings of the 14th Annual Conference Companion on Genetic and Evolutionary Computation, GECCO 2012, pp. 401–408. Association for Computing Machinery, New York (2012)

Multi-objective Genetic Programming for Explainable Reinforcement Learning

Mathurin Videau[1]([✉]), Alessandro Leite[1], Olivier Teytaud[2], and Marc Schoenauer[1]

[1] TAU, Inria Saclay, LISN, Paris, France
mathurin.videau@dauphine.eu
[2] Meta AI Research, Paris, France

Abstract. Deep reinforcement learning has met noticeable successes recently for a wide range of control problems. However, this is typically based on thousands of weights and non-linearities, making solutions complex, not easily reproducible, uninterpretable and heavy. The present paper presents genetic programming approaches for building symbolic controllers. Results are competitive, in particular in the case of delayed rewards, and the solutions are lighter by orders of magnitude and much more understandable.

Keywords: Genetic Programming · Reinforcement Learning · Explainable Reinforcement Learning (XRL) · Genetic Programming Reinforcement Learning (GPRL)

1 Introduction

Interpretability plays an important role in the adoption and acceptance of machine learning (ML) models. A model is normally considered explainable if its users can understand the reasons for an output of a given input and if they can include it into their decision processes. When a model lacks understandability, its usefulness reduces since it may be hard to ensure correctness. While the literature has mostly focused on developing different techniques to explain supervised and unsupervised machine learning models and neural networks, reinforcement learning (RL) methods also require explanations to be adopted by a broad audience. In RL, an agent learns a particular behavior through repeated trial-and-error interactions with a specific environment. At each time step, the agent observes the state of the environment, chooses an action, and in return, receives a reward [23,51]. RL methods can be difficult to understand as they depend on the way the reward functions are defined, on how the states are encoded, and on the chosen policy. For this reason, different explainable artificial intelligence (XAI) methods have been proposed over the last years.

Explainable artificial intelligence (XAI) comprises a set of methods that aim to highlight the process that a machine learning model employed to output a

---

M. Videau—Now at Meta AI Research.

E. Medvet et al. (Eds.): EuroGP 2022, LNCS 13223, pp. 278–293, 2022.
https://doi.org/10.1007/978-3-031-02056-8_18

prediction using terms interpretable by humans [3,13]. Interpretability in this case means the degree to which humans understand the causes for a model output [36]. It contrasts with the concept of a black-box which cannot be understood by humans. Although, interpretability and explainability are usually used interchangeably, the former is an intrinsic property of a predictive model, whereas the latter is modeled as *post-hoc explanations* and thus, separated from the predictive model [18]. Genetic programming, linear regression, and decision trees up to a certain depth are examples of interpretable models, while neural networks and ensemble methods are considered black-boxes. *Post-hoc explanations* can be global or local. While *global explanations* describe the overall logic of a model independently of input queries, *local explanations* try to elucidate the reasons for an output produced for a specific input query. Post-hoc explainers can be agnostic or dependent of the underlying approach used by the black-box. *Feature importance* is an example of the former, and is hence used by many explanation methods to describe how crucially each feature contributes to a prediction, thus helping to understand the underlying process. In other words, they use the weights of each feature as a proxy for explicability. Examples include Local Interpretable Model-Agnostic Explanations (LIME) [41] and SHapley Additive exPlanations (SHAP) [32]. LIME explains a black-box by weighting the distance between the predictions made by an interpretable model and by the black-box for a given query instance. Then, it outputs the contribution of each feature for the prediction. SHAP, on the other hand, relying on cooperative game theory, describes how to distribute the total gains of the game to players according to their contributions, and similarly, it outputs the importance of each feature for the prediction. Other approaches include partial dependence plot (PDP) [7] and saliency map [47,48], for instance.

This paper focuses on *explainable reinforcement learning (XRL)*. We propose and analyze genetic programming (GP)-based RL (GPRL) policies for different control tasks (Sect. 3). The policies are programs representing symbolic expressions. In this work, the proxy used for interpretability is the size of the expression of the policy, and their terms (i.e., features). Experimental results (Sect. 4) show that GP-based RL policies can outperform state-of-the-art neural networks on various tasks, while being much more interpretable. Furthermore, they also demonstrate that traditional GP methods require additional support to solve motion tasks. Map-Elites [38] demonstrates to be a good option without deteriorating the interpretability of the policies, in contrast with imitation learning approaches. Source code is available at gitlab.inria.fr/trust-ai/xrl/gpxrl.

2   Related Work

Recent years have seen an increasing interest in explaining reinforcement learning policies. It is mainly due to the advancement of deep reinforcement learning (DRL) methods. On the one hand, many works have used decision trees [5,12,14,30,43] to try to understand how the state space is segmented into different actions: decision trees distill the behavior of the neural networks [5,12,30]. On the other hand, other studies rely on symbolic expressions to represent DRL policies either by program synthesis [22,52] or by symbolic regression methods [22,27,29,53,54]. The former uses neural networks to generate the programs while the latter relies mostly on genetic programming due to its historical performance when employed as a policy regularizer [22,27,53,54]. For example, Verma et al. [52] use the base *sketch* to generate programs that try to mimic a neural network using the mean squared error as proxy metric. Their results show that in addition to be interpretable, the policies can generalize better than the neural networks. Liventsev et al. [31] use the *Brainfuck* language to describe policies that are driven by both genetic programming and by a recurrent neural network (RNN). Their results show that although this combination lead to better program structure, they underperform deep reinforcement learning policies. Also, they might bring sparsity, but not really explainability. Recently, symbolic regression methods have been used to explain complex RL tasks. For instance, Wilson et al. [53] showed that GP-based policies can outperform neural networks in some specific Atari games tasks. However, their number of operations make them hard to understand. Also, on Atari games, Kelly et al. [24] used Tangled Program Graphs (TPG) to evolve a symbolic program that solves all the games. Much less complex than their deep neural network (DNN) challengers, their programs allow some explainability of their behavior, but remain difficult to understand globally. Hein et al. [22] demonstrated that similar performance can be observed on continuous control tasks, but their approach need sample trajectories to derive the GP policies. Kubalík et al. [27], on the other hand, got analytical expressions of the value function by framing the problem as a fixed point of the Bellman equation. Therefore, this approach demands knowledge about the transition function to enable learning. Landajuela et al. [29] showed that for continuous control tasks, symbolic regression methods helped by neural networks may outperform neural networks-only policies. In addition, in the cases where the dynamics of the tasks are known, the authors proved the stability of the symbolic policies. Nevertheless, for problems with multidimensional actions, this process requires pre-trained neural networks.

Table 1 summarizes the main existing works on GP-based RL policies. While literature has concentrated on evaluating the performance of RL policies for specific task environments, this work focuses on studying both the performance and interpretability of GP-based RL policies on various control tasks. Furthermore, we also investigate strategies to handle some identified limitations of traditional GP approaches when dealing with complex control tasks.

3   Explainable Reinforcement Learning Using GP

Reinforcement learning (RL) is usually formalized as a Markov decision process (MDP), i.e., a tuple (S, A, p, r), where S and A are the state and action spaces. At each discrete time step t, an agent observes the system state $s_t \in S$ and takes an action $a_t \in A$. The system state then changes to state s_{t+1} with probability $p(s_{t+1}|s_t, a_t)$ and the agent receives a reward $r(s_t, a_t, s_{t+1}) \in \mathbb{R}$, for a reward function $r : S \times A \times S \mapsto \mathbb{R}$. A *policy* is a function from S into A that associates to each state the action to be taken in that state (*only deterministic policies are considered in this work*).

Table 1. Summary of interpretable GP-based RL policies

Work	Approach	Environment	Objective(s)
[33]	MCTS	Mountain Car Acrobot	Cumulative mean reward + complexity
[52]	NN + Bayesian opt	TORCS	Cumulative reward
[29]	Deep Symbolic Regression	OpenAI Gym: Classical control, Box2D, Mujocco	Cumulative reward
[31]	RNN + GP	OpenAI Gym (4 envs)	Cumulative reward
[54]	NN + EFS	Acrobot Mountain Car Industrial Benchmark[21]	MSE
[53]	Mixed type Cartesian GP	Atari	Cumulative reward
[24]	Tangle Program Graphs	Atari	Cumulative reward
[27]	Multi-Gene GP	1-DOF, 2-DOF Magman	Bellman MSE
[22]	Tree GP	Montain Car, CartPole Industrial Benchmark [21]	Cumulative reward + complexity
This work	**Tree GP + Linear GP**	**OpenAI Gym: Classical control, Box2D, Mujoco**	**Cumulative reward + complexity**

The solution of an RL problem with time horizon $H \in [0, +\infty]$ and a discount factor $\gamma \in [0, 1]$ is a policy π^* that maximizes the expected discounted cumulative reward over all starting states $s_0 \in S$ and all realizations of the trajectory starting from s_0 according to the stochastic state transition p, hereafter called its *score*, and defined as follows.

$$\text{score}(\pi) = \mathbb{E}_{s_0} \left[\sum_{t=0}^{H-1} \gamma^t R(s_t, \pi(s_t)) \right] \tag{1}$$

The expectation in Eq. (1) above is estimated from several Monte-Carlo simulations of the policy at hand with random starting states (more below).

Explainability. Because there is no formal definition of explainability, a common practice is to use as a proxy the complexity of the obtained solutions [13,18]. *The size of an expression and the number of selected features in its formula determine the complexity of a policy.* Each operator and terminal is assigned a given elementary complexity (see Table 2), and the *global complexity is the sum over the whole formula of these elementary complexities* [22]. Furthermore, two ways are experimented with in this work to obtain simple solutions: two-objective optimization, with cumulated reward and complexity as objectives; biased operators that favor removal over additions of terms in the solution (details in Sect. 4.1).

Bandit-like Evaluation Strategy. GP policies have heterogeneous sizes and computational costs. In order to obtain an accurate estimate of their scores, we try to allocate our simulation budget as efficiently as possible, and in particular to run more Monte-Carlo simulations for promising individuals, using a multi-armed-bandit-like strategy as follows: a total budget T of simulations is allocated at each generation (details below). Each individual of the population (i.e., policy) is attributed an *upper confidence bound (UCB) value* defined by $\bar{x} + c\sqrt{\frac{\ln(n'+T)}{n}}$, where c is an exploration constant, $\bar{x}$ is the mean score of the policy and n' is an offset accounting for past simulations of this policy prior to this generation, and n the number of times this policy was simulated over all generations. Policies are chosen to be simulated based on this UCB score, by batches of k policies in parallel (i.e., the k ones with the highest UCB values are chosen). The policies with high UCB values are either the ones that have a high score, or the ones that have been simulated a small number of times. This process is repeated until the total budget T is exhausted. Individuals that have never been simulated, and hence have an infinite UCB value, are therefore simulated at least once. After each simulation, the UCB values of the simulated policies are updated: $\bar{x}$ takes into account the new score, and n is incremented by one. Note that in case of multi-objective optimization, this batch strategy is biased toward the best scoring individuals of the Pareto front – but these are the ones of main interest here.

Per Generation Simulation Budget. In conjunction with the bandit like strategy presented above, the global simulation budget per generation is gradually increased between generations. The reason is that the differences in scores between different policies are likely to decrease, and the variance of the scores needs to be decreased to improve the robustness of the ranking among policies when their differences become more and more subtle. The detailed parametrization of this scheduling is available in the code source (gitlab.inria.fr/trust-ai/xrl/gpxrl).

4   The Experiments

The first goal of the experiments is to quantify the score/interpretability trade-offs when using GP compared to the traditional direct policy search strategies usually embraced by RL approaches. Different benchmarks are used, with different levels of difficulty, and GP are compared with state-of-the-art algorithms, either pertaining to direct policy search, or to classical RL techniques. Furthermore, two different GP representations are considered in that respect, classical parse trees [26], and linear GP [8]. Likewise, as the literature lacks a recognized measure of interpretability, we will also deeply analyze and compare the results beyond complexity, regarding feature importance on the one hand, and exact analytical policies on the other hand.

4.1   GP Representations

We experimented with two GP representations, and implemented them in python using the DEAP library [16].

Tree-Based GP. The first representation is the standard parse tree [26], with *one point crossover*, and a *mutation operator* that either adds Gaussian noise to a random ephemeral constant with probability 0.3, or replaces a random subtree with a randomly generated one (with probability 0.7). We used non-dominated sorting genetic algorithm (NSGA)-II *non-dominated sorting tournament selection* based on the two objectives, score and complexity. But some RL tasks require multiple continuous actions as output, whereas trees only have one output. In such contexts, individuals are teams of trees, where each tree corresponds to one continuous action. All variation operators are performed on one of the trees of the team, and trees with same index are crossed-over. Unfortunately, this results in completely independent action policies, something rather inefficient.

Linear GP. We thus moved to linear GP [8], that can consider multiple continuous actions natively (as different registers). In such context, shared features can arise, improving both the score and the complexity of the policies. Standard *crossovers* for linear GP are used (i.e., exchange of a segment of instructions) and *mutation* is either an insertion or a deletion of a random instruction, or a random modification of an existing instruction. Tournament selection with tournament size of five is used. Furthermore, the probability of instruction removal is twice that of an insertion, creating a bias toward small programs (though NSGA-II would also be a viable alternative, not implemented at the moment).

Hyper-parameters. For both representations, evolution's parameters can be found in Table 3. The optimization ends after the fixed number of generations is reached. In both setups, it was experimentally assessed that high crossover rates did not improve the score of the resulting policies, while increasing their sizes: a low (or zero) crossover rate is hence used throughout this work.

Finally, the choice between (μ, λ) and $(\mu + \lambda)$ strategies was based on preliminary experiments. On the one hand, (μ, λ) tends to be more robust to noise but consistently forgets the best solution between generations, which produces high variance and non-monotonic convergence. On the other hand, $(\mu + \lambda)$ can find better solutions, but it is more subject to noise if individuals are not sufficiently simulated. Indeed, some solutions could have good fitness just because of a few lucky simulations. In our bandit like setup, this issue is less likely to occur since the individuals are continually tested throughout the evolution process. So, in the following experiments, we used the $(\mu + \lambda)$ schema. Also, these experiments showed us that the exploration constant c of the bandit doesn't have that much impact on the results, and it was set by default to $\sqrt{2}$.

4.2   Benchmarks and Evaluation

Open AI gym [9] was used to evaluate all policies here, on three different control environments: classical control, Mujoco, and Box2D. While classic control environment proposes easy tasks, Box2D and Mujoco offer more complex ones.

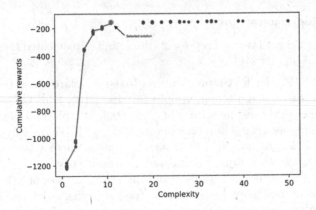

Fig. 1. A Pareto front found for the Pendulum, and the returned solution

Choosing the Solution. In the case of multi-objective optimization (for tree GP), the returned solution is manually chosen from the Pareto front as the one having the best complexity while being only slightly sub-optimal in terms of score. An example of such a selected solution can be seen in Fig. 1. For linear GP, the best individual according to the score, is returned. In all cases, the score of the returned solution is computed through 1000 independent simulations. Three runs have been performed for each setting (i.e., environment and hyper-parameters as in Table 3), and the best of the three is used in Table 2 and Fig. 2 (low variations between runs were observed). There is also a Colab Notebook showing the efficiency and portability of the symbolic policies presented in Table 2 at shortest.link/VHv.

4.3   Baselines

We compare the evolved GP-based policies with the ones obtained by neural network and Nested Monte-Carlo Search, two state-of-the-art approaches in RL and games. What is called the "neural network" policy below is in fact the best performing policy between Proximal Policy Optimization (PPO) [46], Soft Actor Critic (SAC) [19], or Advantage Actor Critic (A2C) [37] algorithms. PPO is an on-policy strategy that optimizes a first-order approximation of the expected reward while cautiously ensuring that it stays closed to the real value. SAC, on the other hand, is an off-policy algorithm that balances between the expected return and the entropy. Finally, A2C is an asynchronous gradient-based algorithm to turn agents' exploration process into a stationary one. These methods achieved impressive performance when used in different application domains. However, these baselines use a lot of information from the problem, including rewards at each time step. As this information is not necessarily available in all real-world settings, we add other methods which use only the total reward per episode, as the GP methods proposed in this work. These methods include Nested Monte-Carlo Search (NMCS) [10] and direct policy search (DPS) [28,34,45,49].

The "DPS" baseline below reports the best-performing DPS between CMA [20] or NGOpt [35], Population control [6], Differential Evolution [50], PSO [25], Meta-Models [4], or complex combinations that are proposed in Nevergrad [40], including NoisyRL, SpecialRL, and MixDeterministicRL, defined as follows. MixDeterministicRL runs PSO, GeneticDE and DiagonalCMA and keeps the best of the three for the second half of the budget. NoisyRL uses a chaining of a MixDeterministicRL plus a method for fine-tuning robustly to noise, and SpecialRL uses a chaining of MixDeterministicRL combined with population control for fine-tuning.

In order to reduce the complexity of DPS controllers, we tested (i) various architectures of neural networks as in [35, 40] (e.g., shallow, semi-deep, deep), (ii) different sizes of hidden layers, (iii) different optimization methods, and (iv) different initial step-sizes[1], keeping and plotting only the best result. In spite of being the most versatile tools with minimum constraints on the environment, we shall see that GP and DPS are competitive, while GP controllers have the lowest complexity.

5   Experimental Results

5.1   Quantitative Analysis

Table 2 shows the cumulative rewards of the policies in the various environments. GP-based policies outperform neural networks for simple and non-motion tasks. For the motion tasks, GP-based policies are obviously trapped in some local optimum. Indeed, they only manage to keep the agent in the upright position as much as possible. It is due to its high variance compared to the ones obtained by a neural network, as can be seen in Fig. 3.

We obtained good and relatively compact controllers by DPS, i.e., methods only using the total cumulated reward. In short, the scores are satisfying, competitive with PPO, SAC, and NMCS (sometimes better and sometimes worse). On the other hand, in spite of testing many architectures and optimization methods, DPS failed to compete with the GP-based approaches in terms of complexity, as shown in Fig. 2.

Beyond complexity, we evaluated the interpretability of GP-based policies through the number of features used in the symbolic expressions. As can be seen in Fig. 4, for each environment, GP-based policies does figure out the most important features to solve the tasks. Furthermore, they are sometimes easily explainable. For example, for the *LunarLander* environment, the behavior of the agent is Eq. (2): (1) stops the main engine after landing, (2) reduce rocket's speed as it moves close to the platform, (3) stabilize the rocket in its vertical axis and keep it in the center of the platform, and (4) reduce the speed of the rocket close to the center of the platform. We can even notice that the policy ignores the orientation of the rocket when deciding the action to execute, and decide

---

[1] This DPS benchmark has been merged in Nevergrad, and our experiments can be reproduced by «python −m nevergrad.benchmark gp −−num_workers = 60 −−plot».

Table 2. Scores (average cumulated rewards), after each policy was re-simulated 1000 times. DPS refers to the best result for moderate complexity of Direct Policy Search by Nevergrad, and NN to the best of PPO, SAC and A2C. For TreeGP and LinearGP we use the best training error of 3 runs and test it; we validated results by rerunning the whole process (including the best of 3) a second time and got similar results.

Environment	# in	# out	DPS	Tree GP	Linear GP	NN	NMCS
Control tasks							
Cartpole	4	2	500.0	500.0	500.0	500.0[†]	484.27
Acrobot	6	3	**-72.74**	-83.17	-80.99	−82.98[†]	-89.69
MountainCarC0	2	1	**99.4**	99.31[**]	88.16	94.56[‡]	97.89
Pendulum	3	1	**-141.9**	-154.36	-164.66	-154.69[‡]	-210.71
Mujoco							
InvDoublePend	9	1	**9360**	9092.17	9089.50	9304.32[‡]	–
InvPendSwingUp	5	1	893.3	**893.35**	887.08	891.45[‡]	–
Hopper	15	3	2094	999.19	949.27	**2604.91**[‡]	–
Box2D							
LunarLanderC0	8	2	282.5	**287.58**	262.42	269.31[†]	–
BipedalWalker	24	4	**310.1**	268.85	257.22	299.44[*]	–
BipedalWalkerHardcore	24	4	8.16	9.25	10.63	**246.79**[*]	–

[†]PPO [46], [‡]SAC[19] [*]A2C[37]

[**] Rely on operators' overflow protections, keeping only the best one for the non-linearity

to repair this "bug" in the policy. On the other hand, for abstract environments such as the *BipedalWalker* similar analysis is difficult. However, we can still observe that the actions strongly rely on their own articulations and not on the lidar (Eq. (4)).

$$\text{main engine:} a_0 = \underbrace{(y > 0)?}_{(1)} \underbrace{(-0.37y - \dot{y} + 0.1)}_{(2)} : 0 \tag{2}$$

$$\text{side engine: } a_1 = \underbrace{(4(\theta - x)}_{(3)} \underbrace{-\dot{x})4}_{(4)} \tag{3}$$

$$\text{hip1} : a_0 = \text{knee1}.\theta \tag{4} \qquad \text{hip2} : a_2 = \frac{\text{lidar}_7}{\text{knee1}.\dot{\theta}} - \text{hip2}.\theta + \text{hull}.\theta \tag{6}$$

$$\text{knee1} : a_1 = \frac{\text{knee1}.\dot{\theta}}{\text{lidar}_5} \tag{5} \qquad \text{knee2} : a_3 = \text{hull}.\theta - \text{knee2}.\theta \tag{7}$$

5.2 Dealing with the Local Minimum Trap

From these experiments, it seems that, on discontinuous search spaces, GP-based policies have a high risk of converging to some local minima. Indeed, since

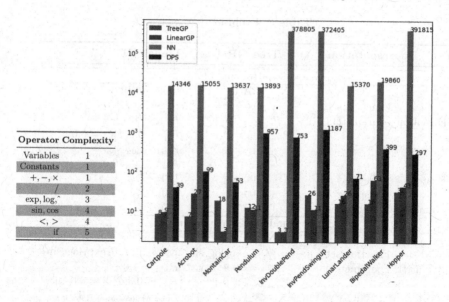

Fig. 2. Complexity of the policies based on expressions' size. Y-axis is in logarithmic scale

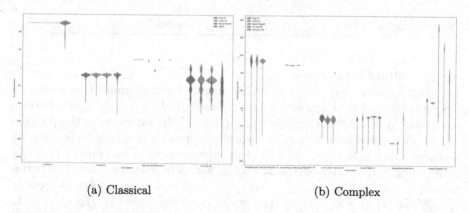

(a) Classical   (b) Complex

Fig. 3. Cumulative rewards of the solution policies with a more detailed view on the distributions over the post-evolution one thousand simulations. For graphic comprehension, inverse double pendulum and Hopper rewards were divided by ten and two respectively

changing a unique operation leads to important programs' changes, evolution has a hard time to transition from one local optimum to another. As a result, there is a lack of exploration for solving the task at hand. Next sections describe how imitation learning [1,2] and (QD) [39] could be used to tackle this issue and at the same time improve the score of symbolic RL policies – and how only QD succeeds.

Table 3. Evolution parameters

Representation	Tree GP	Linear GP
Classic control environments		
Strategy	NSGA-II	tournament
Function set	$\{+,-,\times,/,\text{if}\}$	$\{+,-,\times,/,\text{if}\}$
Evolution's parameters	$P_{\text{mut}} = 0.9$	$P_{\text{mut}} = 1.0$
	$P_{\text{crossover}} = 0.1$	$P_{\text{ins}} = 0.3, P_{\text{del}} = 0.6$
		$P_{\text{Instruction\_mut}} = 0.5$
		$P_{\text{crossover}} = 0.0$
Parents μ	100	100
Offspring λ	100	100
Number of generations	500	500
Mujoco and Box2D environments		
Strategy	NSGA-II	tournament
Function set	$\{+,-,\times,/,\text{if},\exp,\log,\sin\}$	$\{+,-,\times,/,\text{if},\exp,\log,\sin\}$
Evolution's parameters	$P_{\text{mut}} = 0.9$	$P_{\text{mut}} = 1.0$
	$P_{\text{crossover}} = 0.1$	$P_{\text{ins}} = 0.3, P_{\text{del}} = 0.6$
		$P_{\text{Instruction\_mut}} = 0.5$
		$P_{\text{crossover}} = 0.0$
Parents μ	500	500
Offspring λ	500	500
Number of generations	2000	2000

5.2.1 Imitation Learning

Imitation learning aims to accelerate learning by somehow mimicking successful demonstrations of solutions of the task at hand. In this case, the agent acquires knowledge by observing a teacher which performs the target task. The problem can be formulated as a supervised learning approach in which for a data set mapping states to actions, the goal of the agent results in minimizing the error of deviating from the demonstrated output. Formally, from a set of n demonstrations $\mathcal{D} = \{(s_0, a_0), \ldots, (s_n, a_n)\}$ with $s_i, a_i \in \mathcal{S} \times \mathcal{A}$, an agent learns a policy π such that $\pi(s_i) = a_i$, where $\pi(s_i)$ is the predicted action by the teacher. In this work, a pre-trained neural network played the role of a teacher π and a GP program (the learner) tries to imitate it by learning a policy $\hat{\pi}$ that minimizes a loss $\ell(\hat{\pi}(s_i), a_i)$, with ℓ being the mean square error for the continuous tasks and cross-entropy for the discrete ones. Results of two variants of this approach can be seen in Table 4. Behavioral cloning (BC) [44] comprises the basic imitation strategy that uses a static database of trajectories. DAGGER [42], on the other hand, uses a dynamic set of trajectories and runs additional simulations of the selected trajectories. None of these trials led to better result than the one presented in Sect. 4.1. Furthermore, these trials tend to produce more complex policies, reducing their interpretability (Fig. 4). This approach was hence abandoned.

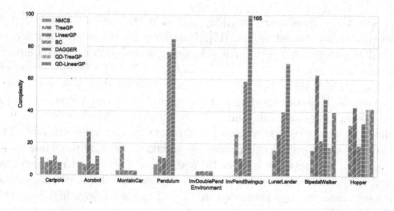

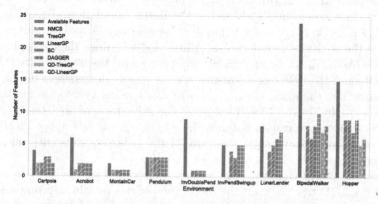

Fig. 4. Complexity of the GP-based policy based on both expression's size and selected features

Table 4. Mean cumulative rewards of policy obtained by Imitation Learning (left) and Map-Elites (right) on 1000 simulations

Environment	BC[44]	DAGGER[42]
Cartpole	500.0	500.0
Acrobot	-84.17	-81.302
MountainCar	94.06	94.46
Pendulum	-1032.09	-280.22
InvDoublePend	8523.78	8874.56
InvPendSwingUp	-104.01	427.92
LunarLander	247.28	272.62
BipedalWalker	-0.66	32.74
Hopper	59.87	713.78

Environment	QD-Tree GP	QD-Linear	NN
BipedalWalker	311.34	299.64	299.44*
Hopper	2152.19	1450.11	2604.91‡

* A2C [37] ‡ SAC [19]

5.2.2 Quality Diversity

Quality diversity is an optimization algorithm that aims to find a set of strong and maximally diverse solutions [39]. Diversity is measured in the behavioral space, considering that all the behaviors are equally important. In this work, in order to maintain and even maximize the diversity in the population, we rely on the Map-Elites algorithm [38] and in particular, a variant that takes into account noisy fitness values [15]. Based on its behavioral features, each individual is placed on a grid. All selections of individuals are independent, and proceed as follows: first, a cell is uniformly selected among the non-empty cells of the grid. If there are more than one individual in the cell, a random one is selected. To avoid too large grids, we use only two behavioral features, discretize them in ten intervals, and limit the number of individuals per cell to ten individuals by removing the worst individuals when new ones are placed there. These aspects, when put together, give a population size of at most one thousand individuals. To estimate the behavioral features and scores, at each generation, each new individual is simulated on three episodes. All the other parameters are the same from the one presented in Table 3 in the Mujoco and Box2D part. Once the Map-ELites algorithm round is finished, a subset of the grid is selected according to a score threshold, and is the initial population of the algorithm presented in Sect. 4.1, run for a hundred generations. This last part aims to fine-tune the solutions found by Map-Elites and to reduce their complexity by using NSGA-II. All these experiments were done with the QDpy library [11]. For *BipedalWalker*, the behavioral features are the mean amplitude of the hip1 and hip2 joints (i.e., the mean of $|s_4|, |s_9|$). For *Hopper*, the behavioral features are the mean amplitude of foot and leg joints (i.e., the mean of $|s_{13}|, |s_{11}|$).

Table 4 shows the results obtained by employing our QD approach. For the two locomotion environments, the score of the policies significantly increased. This improvement is clearly visible for the *Hopper* task. Indeed, in this environment, the policy changed from a static behavior (i.e., tree GP) to a walking one (i.e., QD-tree GP). Furthermore, the policies remain interpretable with respect to their degree of complexity and the number of features as can be observed in Fig. 4.

6   Conclusion and Further Work

In RL, a policy maps the state of an environment to the actions to be taken by an agent [51], and the agent must learn the action-state mapping that maximizes the cumulative rewards. Therefore, some states may be irrelevant or even inadequate for some policies. As a result, they may lead to policies that are hard to understand and explain. Nevertheless, the literature has mostly focused on using traditional machine learning methods and neural networks in order to explain reinforcement learning, whereas it is necessary to deeper understand its functioning and decisions. Likewise, the majority of works in explainable reinforcement learning has focused on specific task environments. In this paper, we investigated the use of GP-based RL policies considering both score and interpretability for several environments simultaneously. Our approach relied on parse trees [26] and linear GP [8] to represent the programs combined with a multi-arm bandit strategy to allocate the computational budget across the generations. Experimental results on three different types of control environments show that the GP-based RL policy can have score similar to state-of-the-art methods (e.g., neural networks), while still being explainable when considering the size of their expressions, and the selected features. Furthermore, we observed that standard GP methods need help to solve motion tasks correctly, as they stay stuck in local optima. Map-Elites [38] revealed to be an appropriate option without penalizing the interpretability of the policies. Nevertheless, the size of the grids determines the quality of the solutions and the convergence time. Consequently, it may be unsuitable for high-dimension problems. Bayesian optimization may handle convergence issue by selecting the grid to explore [17]. Another alternative comprises in incrementally increases the number of features to train a population to explore both the features and grids' size diversity. Further direction also includes the usage of Tangled Program Graphs (TPG) to enable code reuse. However, it still misses at the moment some native support for continuous actions.

Acknowledgements. This research was partially funded by the European Commission within the HORIZON program (TRUST-AI Project, Contract No. 952060).

References

1. Abbeel, P., Ng, A.Y.: Apprenticeship learning via inverse reinforcement learning. In: ICML, p. 1 (2004)
2. Argall, B.D., Chernova, S., Veloso, M., Browning, B.: A survey of robot learning from demonstration. Robot. Auton. Syst. **57**(5), 469–483 (2009)
3. Arrieta, A.B., et al.: Explainable artificial intelligence (XAI): concepts, taxonomies, opportunities and challenges toward responsible AI. IF **58**, 82–115 (2020)
4. Auger, A., Schoenauer, M., Teytaud, O.: Local and global order $3/2$ convergence of a surrogate evolutionary algorithm. In: GECCO, p. 8 (2005)
5. Bastani, O., Pu, Y., Solar-Lezama, A.: Verifiable reinforcement learning via policy extraction. arXiv:1805.08328 (2018)
6. Beyer, H.G., Hellwig, M.: Controlling population size and mutation strength by meta-ES under fitness noise. In: FOGA, pp. 11–24 (2013)
7. Biecek, P., Burzykowski, T.: Explanatory Model Analysis: Explore, Explain And Examine Predictive Models. CRC Press, Boca Raton (2021)
8. Brameier, M.F., Banzhaf, W.: Linear Genetic Programming. Springer, Cham (2007). https://doi.org/10.1007/978-0-387-31030-5
9. Brockman, G., et al.: OpenAI Gym. arXiv:1606.01540 (2016)
10. Cazenave, T.: Nested Monte-Carlo search. In: IJCAI (2009)
11. Cazenille, L.: QDpy: a python framework for quality-diversity (2018). bit.ly/3s0uyVv
12. Coppens, Y., Efthymiadis, K., Lenaerts, T., Nowé, A., Miller, T., Weber, R., Magazzeni, D.: Distilling deep reinforcement learning policies in soft decision trees. In: CEX Workshop, pp. 1–6 (2019)
13. Doshi-Velez, F., Kim, B.: Towards a rigorous science of interpretable machine learning. arXiv:1702.08608 (2017)
14. Ernst, D., Geurts, P., Wehenkel, L.: Tree-based batch mode reinforcement learning. JMLR **6**, 503–556 (2005)
15. Flageat, M., Cully, A.: Fast and stable map-elites in noisy domains using deep grids. In: ALIFE, pp. 273–282 (2020)

16. Fortin, F.A., De Rainville, F.M., Gardner, M.A., Parizeau, M., Gagné, C.: DEAP: evolutionary algorithms made easy. JMLR **13**, 2171–2175 (2012)

17. Gaier, A., Asteroth, A., Mouret, J.B.: Data-efficient exploration, optimization, and modeling of diverse designs through surrogate-assisted illumination. In: GECCO, pp. 99–106 (2017)

18. Gilpin, L., Bau, D., Yuan, B., Bajwa, A., Specter, M., Kagal, L.: Explaining explanations: an approach to evaluating interpretability of ML. arXiv:1806.00069 (2018)

19. Haarnoja, T., Zhou, A., Abbeel, P., Levine, S.: Soft actor-critic: off-policy maximum entropy deep reinforcement learning with a stochastic actor. In: ICML, pp. 1861–1870 (2018)

20. Hansen, N., Ostermeier, A.: Completely derandomized self-adaptation in evolution strategies. ECO **11**(1), 1–10 (2003)

21. Hein, D., et al.: A benchmark environment motivated by industrial control problems. In: IEEE SSCI, pp. 1–8 (2017)

22. Hein, D., Udluft, S., Runkler, T.A.: Interpretable policies for reinforcement learning by genetic programming. Eng. App. Artif. Intell. **76**, 158–169 (2018)

23. Kaelbling, L.P., Littman, M.L., Moore, A.W.: Reinforcement learning: a survey. JAIR **4**, 237–285 (1996)

24. Kelly, S., Heywood, M.I.: Multi-task learning in Atari video games with emergent tangled program graphs. In: GECCO, pp. 195–202 (2017)

25. Kennedy, J., Eberhart, R.C.: Particle swarm optimization. In: IJCNN, pp. 1942–1948 (1995)

26. Koza, J.R.: Genetic Programming: On the Programming of Computers by means of Natural Evolution. MIT Press, Massachusetts (1992)

27. Kubalík, J., Žegklitz, J., Derner, E., Babuška, R.: Symbolic regression methods for reinforcement learning. arXiv:1903.09688 (2019)

28. Kwee, I., Hutter, M., Schmidhuber, J.: Gradient-based reinforcement planning in policy-search methods. In: Wiering, M.A. (ed.) EWRL. vol. 27, pp. 27–29 (2001)

29. Landajuela, M., et al.: Discovering symbolic policies with deep reinforcement learning. In: ICML, pp. 5979–5989 (2021)

30. Liu, G., Schulte, O., Zhu, W., Li, Q.: Toward interpretable deep reinforcement learning with linear model u-trees. In: ECML PKDD, pp. 414–429 (2018)

31. Liventsev, V., Härmä, A., Petković, M.: Neurogenetic programming framework for explainable reinforcement learning. arXiv:2102.04231 (2021)

32. Lundberg, S.M., Lee, S.I.: A unified approach to interpreting model predictions. In: NeurIPS, pp. 4768–4777 (2017)

33. Maes, F., Fonteneau, R., Wehenkel, L., Ernst, D.: Policy search in a space of simple closed-form formulas: towards interpretability of reinforcement learning. In: ICDS, pp. 37–51 (2012)

34. Mania, H., Guy, A., Recht, B.: Simple random search provides a competitive approach to reinforcement learning. arXiv:1803.07055 (2018)

35. Meunier, L., et al.: Black-box optimization revisited: Improving algorithm selection wizards through massive benchmarking. In: IEEE TEVC (2021)

36. Miller, T.: Explanation in artificial intelligence: insights from the social sciences. Artif. Intell. **267**, 1–38 (2019)

37. Mnih, V., et al.: Asynchronous methods for deep reinforcement learning. In: ICML, pp. 1928–1937 (2016)

38. Mouret, J.B., Clune, J.: Illuminating search spaces by mapping elites. arXiv:1504.04909 (2015)

39. Pugh, J.K., Soros, L.B., Stanley, K.O.: Quality diversity: a new frontier for evolutionary computation. Front. Robot. AI **3**, 40 (2016)

40. Rapin, J., Teytaud, O.: Nevergrad - a gradient-free optimization platform (2018). bit.ly/3g8wghU
41. Ribeiro, M.T., Singh, S., Guestrin, C.: Why should I trust you? Explaining the predictions of any classifier. In: SIGKDD, pp. 1135–1144 (2016)
42. Ross, S., Gordon, G., Bagnell, D.: A reduction of imitation learning and structured prediction to no-regret online learning. In: AISTATS, pp. 627–635 (2011)
43. Roth, A.M., Topin, N., Jamshidi, P., Veloso, M.: Conservative q-improvement: reinforcement learning for an interpretable decision-tree policy. arXiv:1907.01180 (2019)
44. Russell, S.: Learning agents for uncertain environments. In: COLT, pp. 101–103 (1998)
45. Schoenauer, M., Ronald, E.: Neuro-genetic truck backer-upper controller. In: IEEE CEC, pp. 720–723 (1994)
46. Schulman, J., Wolski, F., Dhariwal, P., Radford, A., Klimov, O.: Proximal policy optimization algorithms. arXiv:1707.06347 (2017)
47. Selvaraju, R.R., et al.: Grad-CAM: Visual explanations from deep networks via gradient-based localization. In: ICCV, pp. 618–626 (2017)
48. Shrikumar, A., Greenside, P., Kundaje, A.: Learning important features through propagating activation differences. In: ICML, pp. 3145–3153 (2017)
49. Sigaud, O., Stulp, F.: Policy search in continuous action domains: an overview. arXiv:1803.04706 (2018)
50. Storn, R., Price, K.: Differential evolution - a simple and efficient heuristic for global optimization over continuous spaces. JGO 11(4), 341–359 (1997)
51. Sutton, R.S., Barto, A.G.: Reinforcement Learning: An Introduction, 2nd edn. MIT press, Cambridge (2018)
52. Verma, A., Murali, V., Singh, R., Kohli, P., Chaudhuri, S.: Programmatically interpretable reinforcement learning. In: ICML, pp. 5045–5054 (2018)
53. Wilson, D.G., Cussat-Blanc, S., Luga, H., Miller, J.F.: Evolving simple programs for playing Atari games. In: GECCO, pp. 229–236 (2018)
54. Zhang, H., Zhou, A., Lin, X.: Interpretable policy derivation for reinforcement learning based on evolutionary feature synthesis. Complex Intell. Syst. 6(3), 741–753 (2020). https://doi.org/10.1007/s40747-020-00175-y

Permutation-Invariant Representation of Neural Networks with Neuron Embeddings

Ryan Zhou[✉][iD], Christian Muise[iD], and Ting Hu[iD]

Queen's University, Kingston, ON K7L 2N8, Canada
{20rz11,christian.muise,ting.hu}@queensu.ca

Abstract. Neural networks are traditionally represented in terms of their weights. A key property of this representation is that there are multiple representations of a network which can be obtained by permuting the order of the neurons. These representations are generally not compatible between networks, making recombination a challenge for two arbitrary neural networks - an issue known as the "permutation problem" in neuroevolution. This paper proposes an indirect encoding in which a neural network is represented in terms of interactions between neurons rather than explicit weights, and which works for both fully connected and convolutional networks. In addition to reducing the number of free parameters, this encoding is agnostic to the ordering of neurons, bypassing a key problem for direct weight-based representation. This allows us to transplant individual neurons and layers into another network without accounting for the specific ordering of neurons. We show through experiments on the MNIST and CIFAR-10 datasets that this method is capable of representing networks which achieve comparable performance to direct weight representation, and that combining networks this way preserves a larger degree of performance than through direct weight transfer.

Keywords: Neuroevolution · Indirect Encoding · Neural Networks · Convolutional Neural Networks · Crossover · Permutation Invariance

1 Introduction

One of the main challenges in neuroevolution is developing an effective crossover operation. This is in large part due to what is known as the competing conventions or permutation problem [37]: given any particular neural network, an equivalent network can be obtained by permuting the order of the neurons along with the corresponding weights. In other words, functionally identical networks - that is, networks with the same computation graph - can have different representations simply because the units comprising them are defined in a different order. This implies two things: that the representation contains unnecessary information about the ordering of neurons, and that the internal representations for two networks are overwhelmingly likely to be incompatible. Crossover

© The Author(s), under exclusive license to Springer Nature Switzerland AG 2022
E. Medvet et al. (Eds.): EuroGP 2022, LNCS 13223, pp. 294–308, 2022.
https://doi.org/10.1007/978-3-031-02056-8_19

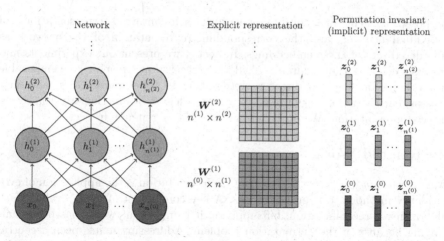

Fig. 1. A neural network (left) with $n^{(i)}$ hidden units per layer is traditionally represented by explicitly specifying the weights of the connections, usually as a matrix or tensor $W^{(i)}$ of dimension $n^{(i-1)} \times n^{(i)}$ (middle). We propose instead to view the network as sets of neurons (right), with a neuron j in layer i represented as a vector $z_j^{(i)}$. Weights are generated implicitly by calculating alignment coefficients between neurons. This representation is parameter efficient and there is no explicit ordering within each layer, rendering it permutation invariant.

between incompatible representations will generally be destructive to learned relationships.

Representing the network in a way that is agnostic to the neuron order, i.e., is permutation invariant with respect to the neurons, can reduce this problem of incompatible representations. In this paper, we propose neuron embeddings, an indirect encoding method for representing a neural network which views the network as unordered sets of neurons rather than ordered lists of weights (Fig. 1). This builds permutation invariance directly into the representation. The key to our approach is that the weights are not fixed, but are generated dynamically by individual neurons based on the other neurons present in the network. This allows neurons not only to be reordered but also moved between models in crossover operations. A neuron that is moved will adapt its weights to the new population it finds itself in. In addition, because direct weight representation implicitly contains information about neuron order, a permutation invariant indirect representation can be made smaller and more parameter efficient.

Our experiments with the proposed representation show that crossover using neuron embeddings significantly improves the performance of the resulting network compared to the same operation done using direct representation. We also propose and demonstrate a method by which this can be extended to convolutional neural networks, allowing the network to be permutation invariant with respect to the ordering of convolutional filters.

In the following section, Sect. 2, we will present some context and motivation and contrast our approach with existing ones. In Sect. 3, we introduce the proposed concept of neuron embeddings, self-contained representations of individual neurons, and the corresponding representation of the network as unordered sets of these embeddings. In Sect. 4 we present our experiments and results. We find that neuron embedding representation achieves comparable network performance to direct representation in fewer parameters, and that crossover with embeddings preserves a larger degree of functionality than with direct representation. We provide some concluding remarks in Sect. 5.

2   Related Work

Neuroevolution and Indirect Encoding. Neuroevolution is the application of evolutionary methods to neural networks. A key component of many evolutionary algorithms is recombination, but applying it to neural networks has been challenging because of the permutation problem. Addressing it has been a central focus of neuroevolution work [35]. Previous methods have approached this by looking for analogous structures in the network to limit the impact of permutation [37], or by sorting the neurons based on their connections [5]. However, these methods do not scale to the sizes of networks in modern deep learning. We propose that a more efficient solution is to build permutation invariance into the representation, thereby avoiding the problem.

A second challenge for large-scale neuroevolution is the large number of weights in a neural network, leading to impractically large genomes if direct encoding is used - that is, if each weight is coded for individually in the genome. Indirect encoding is an alternative approach which represents the network using a small number of parameters and uses rules to generate the weights [31,38]. This concept has proved successful at allowing larger networks to be trained with evolution [14,21,36]. Modern neural network architectures can also be viewed in this light; notably, convolution [11,23] and attention [42] generate large numbers of effective weights from small numbers of explicit parameters. We use indirect encoding in our method, generating weights based on a small number of vector representations.

Permutation Invariance in Neural Networks. Permutation invariance refers to the property that a function remains unchanged even when some aspect of it is permuted. Previous work has been done on introducing various forms of permutation invariance (PI) to neural networks, primarily focused on allowing neural networks to exhibit permutation invariance over the inputs. [9] and [45] introduce methods which use pooling operations to perform permutation-invariant operations for set inputs. [2] introduce permutation invariance into the features themselves by recombining pairs of features. Set Transformer [25] builds upon these by using self-attention to capture higher order interactions. Sensory neurons [39] use similar modular units to produce a PI policy. These methods address permutation invariance in the inputs rather than the network representation itself. We draw on these ideas in order to do the opposite - to represent an arbitrary neural network (which may or may not be permutation invariant with respect to the inputs) in a manner that is PI to shuffling of the neurons.

Neuron-Based Representation. Neuron-based representations have also previously been employed in the literature, often in the context of evolving individual neurons [12,26,32] or compact representations of networks [8,10,17,30]. Our work makes use of neuron-based representation to achieve permutation invariance, but is aimed at bridging the gap between these two applications. Our aim is not to train individual neurons in a population-based manner but instead to represent entire pretrained networks and discover structures which can be transferred between networks. Compared to previous work on full network representations, our approach not only represents single networks but also aims to improve cross-model compatibility between multiple networks by reducing networks down to transferable units. As such, the approach we propose is designed to make the individual neuron representations as self-contained as possible, without any interaction with network-specific structures such as hypernetworks.

Attention. Attention [42] is a highly successful mechanism which underpins many modern deep neural networks. The key strength of attention is its ability to generate a large number of attention scores using only a small number of parameters, and to do so dynamically, which can be seen as form of indirect encoding [40]. In addition, it does so in a permutation-invariant way, by only depending on the features of the two endpoints. Because of this key property, we base our model on the attention kernel with appropriate modifications. Attention as used in models such as Transformers [42] operates between the tokens given as inputs to the network; our method differs in that we use as endpoints the neurons themselves, generating a set of weights which are agnostic to the input.

Model Compression and Tensor Decomposition. Neural network compression refers to the general goal of reducing the size of a model in order to reduce the amount of storage or computation required without significantly impacting performance. One method of achieving this is through tensor decomposition. Because weights in neural networks may be represented with tensors, it is possible to express the full tensor as a product or sum of lower-rank or smaller tensors. Several methods for providing exact or approximate decompositions exist [1,20]; commonly used methods include CP [18], Tucker [41] and tensor train [27] decomposition. The method we describe in this paper can be viewed as a low-rank decomposition of the weight tensors, similar to the methods described in [16] and [44]. That is, for a weight matrix $W \in \mathbb{R}^{m \times n}$ with rank r, we approximate W with the product $W = XY$ with $X \in \mathbb{R}^{m \times r}$ and $Y \in \mathbb{R}^{r \times n}$. This reduces the number of parameters from mn to $r(m+n)$ [6]. There are two major points of contrast between our method and other tensor decompositions: first, our primary goal is to generate self-contained representations of neurons and so the embedding for each neuron is used twice - once to determine the incoming weights, and once to determine the outgoing weights. For this reason, our method imposes a symmetry constraint such that the two embeddings are identical in order to produce a single representation of the "role" of a neuron. Second, our method is only a decomposition in the case of the linear dot-product kernel; other attention kernels allow it to represent a broader class of functions.

3   Method

We will first describe how our method works for a simple feedforward network. Then, we will describe how convolutional neural networks can be represented as well. In short, we replace all weights in the network with a set of vector representations of the neurons present in the network. Weights are then generated in an attention-like way, with some modifications.

It is important that each neuron's representation contains all the information necessary to perform its function so that it can be moved between networks - thus, there is no equivalent to the query, key and value networks of attention which would need to be external to the neuron. This ensures a neuron's representation is fully self-contained, allowing it to be transplanted into a second neural network and generate new weights without requiring information from the original neural network.

Neuron Embedding. The core idea of our method is to introduce a learnable vector embedding $\mathbf{z}$ for each neuron (Fig. 1). This is simply a d-dimensional vector which represents the role of the neuron and can be trained via gradient descent. This is used to generate weight scores between it and all neurons in the previous layer using a kernel $K(\cdot, \cdot)$. We calculate the alignment score α_{ij} in a manner similar to attention by using a dot product kernel, and assign this score as the weight. That is, we take the dot product between the embedding $z_i^{(l)}$ of neuron i in layer l and the embedding $z_j^{(l+1)}$ of neuron j in layer $l + 1$ [42] with an optional nonlinearity σ:

$$\alpha_{ij} = K(z_i^{(l)}, z_j^{(l+1)}) = \sigma(z_i^{(l)} z_j^{(l+1)^{\top}}) \tag{1}$$

This is done efficiently as a matrix operation by packing the embeddings for both layers into the matrices $\mathbf{Z}^{(l)} \in \mathbb{R}^{n_l \times d}$ and $\mathbf{Z}^{(l+1)} \in \mathbb{R}^{n_{l+1} \times d}$, where n_i is the number of hidden units in the layer i. The activation vector $\mathbf{h}^{(l)}$ of layer l takes the place of the value function, giving us:

$$Attention(\mathbf{Z}^{(l)}, \mathbf{Z}^{(l+1)}, \mathbf{h}^{(l)}) = \sigma(\mathbf{Z}^{(l)} \mathbf{Z}^{(l+1)^{\top}}) \mathbf{h}^{(l)} \tag{2}$$

This can be implemented simply by assigning the matrix of attention scores to be the weight matrix $\mathbf{W}^{(l)}$. Note that unlike the Transformer formulation of attention, we use the unscaled dot product here. Scaling the dot product by $\frac{1}{\sqrt{d}}$ corrects the variance of the product to be 1 when the input embeddings have variance 1; however, we find in practice it is more effective to scale the initialization of the embeddings. Each component of the embedding is initialized to be normally distributed with standard deviation $\frac{1}{\sqrt{d}}$ or equivalently variance $\frac{1}{d}$, where d is the dimensionality of the embedding:

$$z_i \sim N(0, \frac{1}{d}) \tag{3}$$

This ensures the magnitude of the embedding vectors has a mean of 1, removing the need for scaling.

Bias. In addition to the embedding, each neuron contains a learnable bias b in order to match the overall function of a feedforward network. This bias has the same role as the bias in a feedforward layer, and is added after the weights are applied. Since each bias is specific to a single neuron, it can be considered part of the self-contained representation and moved to a different network.

Input Encoding. To generate the weights for the first layer, it is necessary to provide an embedding for each input to the network, which can be learned from the data [7]. A second possibility is to provide predefined embeddings; for example, through positional encodings [42]. We tested sinusoidal positional embeddings for one and two dimensions [42,43] as well as localized wavelets, but found that in practice, these fixed embeddings performed poorly. We allow a model to learn the input embeddings from the dataset, which can then be shared with subsequent models trained on the same dataset. This is important for cross-model transfer, as it provides the two models a common basis from which to work.

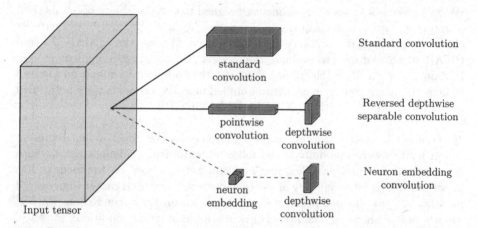

Fig. 2. Representation of a convolutional neuron. The standard representation explicitly specifies all the weights in the kernel. Depthwise separable convolutions provide an approximate replacement by splitting the kernel into a pointwise convolution, which mixes information across channels, and a depthwise convolution which applies one spatial kernel per channel. We replace the pointwise convolution with an implicit representation using neuron embeddings but keep the depthwise convolution, rendering the network permutation invariant to the ordering of filters but preserving spatial structure. Each neuron embedding and depthwise convolution pair represents a single output filter.

Encoding Convolutional Networks. Convolutional neural networks present a unique challenge. For a $k \times k$ filter with $n^{(i)}$ input channels, we have $k^2 \cdot n^{(i)}$ incoming weights. However, we only have $n^{(i)}$ embeddings in the layer below. In addition, we would like to do this in a way that can be encapsulated as a single neuron, allowing it to operate in a self-contained manner.

Our solution (Fig. 2) is to employ reversed order depthwise separable convolutions [3]. The standard order is to apply the $n^{(i)}$ depthwise convolutions first, followed by the pointwise convolution to expand the number of channels from $n^{(i)}$ to $n^{(i+1)}$. However, in order to produce self-contained representations, we would like to treat each pointwise-depthwise pair as a single neuron; for this, we need $n^{(i+1)}$ depthwise kernels. Thus, we reverse the order of operations, performing the pointwise convolution first to produce $n^{(i+1)}$ different channels in the output, and then assign each channel its own depthwise convolution. Since the pointwise convolution can be seen as a feedforward network along the channel dimension, we can represent this using neuron embeddings, with one embedding per output channel. Performing the steps in reverse order is also known as a blueprint separable convolution and exhibits improved training properties [13].

4   Experiments

We now present a series of experiments designed to test the ability of our method to represent equivalent networks to direct weight encoding, and to evaluate its ability to preserve performance under crossover. We use the MNIST [24] and CIFAR-10 [22] datasets to evaluate the models. All models were implemented in Python using the PyTorch library [29], and the code can be found on GitHub at https://github.com/ryanz8/neuron-embedding. Experiments were performed on a single computer with an NVIDIA RTX3090 GPU.

Hyperparameter Optimization. Hyperparameters for the direct weight representation models were manually tuned following empirical guidelines [28,33] with a small random search over learning rate and weight decay. As the focus of this paper is on the relative efficacy of the representation methods rather than overall performance, we did not perform heavy hyperparameter optimization. Rather, we attempt to showcase the models under similar starting conditions. As such, the hyperparameters of the neuron embedding representations were matched to those of the direct representations. This should favor the direct representation slightly; however, there is the possibility that the results will differ or the performance gap will be greater under different hyperparameters.

4.1   Training from Random Initialization

Our first experiment tests the ability of our method to achieve comparable performance to weight encoding when trained from random initialization. The intent is to test whether neuron embeddings can be trained the same way as direct weight representations without any special tuning. We compared two types of architectures: fully connected and convolutional, each using direct weight representation, against equivalents using neuron embedding representation. We chose training settings which yielded high performance after a short amount of training for the direct weight representations, and used the same settings without modification for the neuron embedding representations.

Table 1. Performance when trained from random initialization for fully connected (FC) models and convolutional (conv) models. "Direct" models use direct (explicit) weight representation. "Sep." models use reverse order depthwise separable convolutions (blueprint separable convolutions). "Emb." models (ours, bolded) use neuron embedding representation.

Dataset	Model	Parameters	Layers	Acc. (%)	CE Loss
MNIST	FC (direct)	318010	2 fc	98.05	0.0672
MNIST	**FC (emb.)**	**76416**	**2 fc**	**97.43**	**0.0999**
MNIST	FC (direct)	417640	5 fc	98.14	0.0710
MNIST	**FC (emb.)**	**97536**	**5 fc**	**97.44**	**0.1077**
MNIST	Conv. (direct)	160070	3 conv 2 fc	99.38	0.0294
MNIST	Conv. (sep.)	84750	3 conv 2 fc	99.27	0.03732
MNIST	**Conv. (emb.)**	**51598**	**3 conv 2 fc**	**99.00**	**0.0412**
CIFAR-10	ResNet9 (direct)	2438794	8 conv 1 fc	89.40	0.3962
CIFAR-10	ResNet9 (sep.)	287818	8 conv 1 fc	88.21	0.4312
CIFAR-10	**ResNet9 (emb.)**	**98298**	**8 conv 1 fc**	**86.90**	**0.4469**

All models unless otherwise specified were trained with cross-entropy loss [19], using the Adam optimizer on MNIST and SGD with momentum on CIFAR-10. Network widths are noted in brackets, with convolutional layers denoted with a superscript c. We test a 2-layer (400,10) and 5-layer (400,400,400,400,10) feedforward network and a 5-layer convolutional network $(16^c, 40^c, 1000, 100, 10)$ on MNIST, and a 9-layer ResNet $(64^c, 128^c, 128^c, 128^c, 256^c, 256^c, 256^c, 256^c, 10)$ [15] on CIFAR-10 designed based on the results of the DAWNBench benchmark [4,28]. For models using neuron embedding, we set the nonlinearity σ to be the identity for faster training. All models use ReLU activation for all layers except the output. Comparison was done using the best model found after 2000 steps of training as determined by cross-validation on a holdout set of 10000 data points. With Adam, we use a one-cycle learning rate schedule [34] and cosine annealing, with a learning rate of 0.01 and batch size of 1000 which has been shown to work well in combination with this schedule [33]. For stochastic gradient descent, we use linear annealing with a maximum learning rate of 2×10^{-4} obtained by hyperparameter search and a batch size of 512. The dimensionality of the neuron embeddings is set to 64 for fully connected models and 48 for convolutional models.

The results in Table 1 show that representation using neuron embeddings is able to achieve comparable performance to direct weight representation, when using standard training settings without modification. The slight difference in performance we attribute to the use of training settings optimized for direct weight representation; as we will show next, it is not due to the smaller number of parameters leading to a gap in expressiveness for this problem. We note that training time is also not impacted, and in some cases is actually reduced which we attribute to the smaller number of parameters.

Table 2. Results for training to a 2-layer reference network. An embedding dimension of 64 is sufficient to match the performance of this network within margin of error, while decreasing the embedding dimension degrades the performance. MSE refers to the mean squared deviation of the weights in the neuron embedding representation from the weights in the reference network. The mean-squared amplitude of the weights in the reference network is 0.0152.

Model	Free Parameters	Accuracy (%)	MSE
Reference	318010	97.48	-
Neuron embedding (64 dims)	76416	97.48	0.00036
Neuron embedding (32 dims)	38208	97.15	0.00053
Neuron embedding (16 dims)	19104	75.08	0.00095
Neuron embedding (8 dims)	9552	65.61	0.00177
Neuron embedding (4 dims)	4776	20.72	0.00414

4.2   Compression Ability

Our next experiment tests the ability of neuron embeddings to exactly reproduce the weights of a reference fully connected network. This tests the expressiveness of the neuron embeddings. We expect that if the network is able to reproduce the weights, then performance should match that of the reference network. We tested different values for d, the embedding dimension to show the effect of embedding expressiveness on the final accuracy.

To force the embeddings to replicate the weights, we train the embeddings by minimizing the mean squared loss over all the generated weights when compared to the reference network. This was chosen as it corresponds to minimizing the quantity

$$\sum_{i=1}^{N} \frac{1}{m_i n_i} \|\mathbf{W}_i - \mathbf{Z}_{i-1}\mathbf{Z}_i^T\|_F^2. \tag{4}$$

That is, it approximates the full-rank decomposition of the weight matrices normalized by the number of elements. Here $\mathbf{W}_i$ is the weight matrix for layer i, m_i and n_i are the dimensions of $\mathbf{W}_i$, $\mathbf{Z}_{i-1}$ and $\mathbf{Z}_i$ are the neuron embeddings for the layers $i-1$ and i, and $\|\cdot\|_F$ is the Frobenius norm. Models were trained using the Adam optimizer with a learning rate of 0.002 for 2000 steps.

Results are shown in Table 2. As can be seen, with sufficient d models are able to almost exactly match the performance of a directly encoded network. Insufficient expressiveness as a result of a too small d harms the performance of the network, but even with only 8 dimensions a significant fraction of the knowledge was still represented (with an accuracy of 65% versus the 10% of random chance). In all cases, the number of parameters of the neuron embedding model was smaller than that of the fully connected reference network, despite being able to match the weights.

4.3   Cross-model Compatibility

Our next experiment tests whether neuron-based representations enable better compatibility between different models. Our goal is to determine the degree to which the function of a neuron is preserved when moved to a different setting. This evaluates the potential of this representation for crossover operations and cross-model transfer learning.

We trained two models from random initialization, producing two different networks to act as a source network and a target network. We then trained two neuron embedding models to replicate the weights of each direct encoding parent. We use the same learned input encodings for both neuron embedding models, done by copying the learned input encodings from the target network to the source network before training. This did not affect the weights themselves and it was possible to replicate both the weights of the source and target network to high accuracy using the same embeddings for the inputs but different neuron embeddings for all subsequent layers.

We performed this process for both fully connected and convolutional models. The fully connected models contained 8 hidden layers with 400 neurons each and a 10 neuron output layer. The convolutional models consisted of three 3×3 reverse-order depthwise separable convolutional layers with 20, 40 and 80 neurons, followed by a 100 neuron fully connected hidden layer and the 10 neuron output layer.

Neuron Transplant. We tested compatibility for both pairs of models by transferring a variable number of neurons in the first hidden layer from the source network to the target network, which we refer to as a crossover operation. If the internal representations are compatible, we expect models to retain a greater degree of performance under this operation. Here, a crossover coefficient of 0.8 indicates that 80% of the neurons in that layer of the target network have been replaced and 20% of the neurons remain. A coefficient of 1.0 indicates that the entire layer has been replaced with the layer from the source network. Neurons are chosen in random order for this, and we repeat each experiment 10 times and report the mean and 95% confidence interval.

The results in Fig. 3 show that transplanting neurons in the hidden layer results in minor loss of performance for both models until roughly 1/3 of the neurons were replaced, after which performance deteriorates rapidly. When the entire layer was transferred, performance was close to chance for the direct encoding. This is as expected as the weights of the layer are adapted to their original setting and do not store information in a form usable by the new model. However, in the case of transfer through neuron embedding, we are able to preserve a larger fraction of the relationships even when the entire layer is transplanted to a new network.

We stress that the direct representation and the neuron embedding representation both encode the same networks with the same weights; thus, the greater information transfer is due entirely to the way in which the layers are encoded.

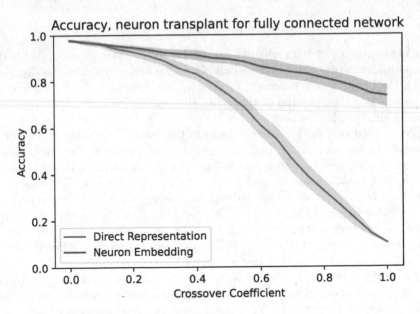

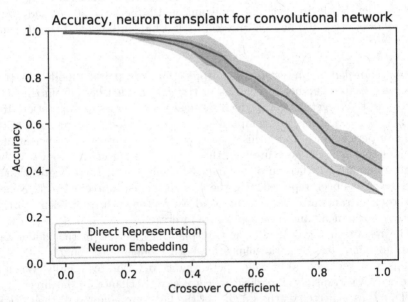

Fig. 3. Accuracy under neuron transplant for fully connected (top) and convolutional (bottom) models. Bold lines show the mean over 10 runs, and the shaded region indicates a 95% confidence interval for the mean. Crossover coefficient (horizontal axis) represents the fraction of neurons in the layer replaced by neurons from another model. We compare two identical networks encoded in two ways - direct encoding or neuron embedding. At 100% crossover, an entire layer from the source network is directly transplanted to the recipient network without any further training. We observe that the same network when encoded with neuron embedding maintains significantly more performance, and can function even when the entire layer is replaced.

Linear Interpolation. To investigate whether these results are an artifact of the neuron transplant method, we perform a second experiment, but rather than transferring single neurons we apply linear interpolation to every neuron in the layer simultaneously. For the direct representation, we linearly interpolate between the weights of the two models, and for the embedding representation we linearly interpolate between the corresponding embedding vectors of the neuron representation. Results of this operation are shown in Fig. 4. We observe similar results to the previous experiment for the fully connected model, suggesting that the representation itself is responsible for the results. However, we note slightly worse performance by both representations on the convolutional model. It is worth noting that the embedding vectors themselves are interpolated, producing entirely new embeddings; this suggests that it is possible to perform crossover on the neuron level, as well as on the network level.

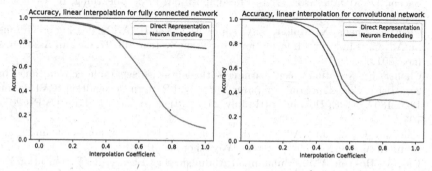

Fig. 4. Model accuracy under linear interpolation for fully connected model (left) and convolutional model (right). The weights and embedding vectors are directly interpolated by taking a weighted average, and all neurons in the layer are interpolated simultaneously. We observe similar results to the previous experiment on the fully connected network. Note that embedding vectors themselves are being changed; this suggests the possibility of neuron-level as well as network-level crossover.

5   Conclusion

In this paper we presented neuron embeddings, an indirect encoding method for representing a neural network in terms of unordered sets of individual neurons. This is a parameter-efficient representation which is also invariant to permutation of the neurons, allowing for better compatibility when performing crossover. Our method encapsulates the role of a neuron into a single self-contained representation which is used to generate the weights implicitly, allowing them to be transferred into a second neural network and still preserve some degree of function, even when the two networks are trained independently. This opens the door to new possibilities for neuroevolution, as this removes one important roadblock for crossover in neural networks, and can be used in conjunction with other methods such as those based on neuron alignment. In addition, the self-contained nature of the representations may prove useful for methods which evolve individual neurons, rather than complete networks. Of interest for future work is the extension of this method to larger hierarchical structures, which may also enable more efficient neural architecture search.

This work also has potential applications for cross-dataset knowledge transfer and transfer learning, which we intend to investigate in more depth moving forward. For example, it may be possible to transfer knowledge from multiple models or to improve upon existing methods of imitation learning. We also would like to further investigate whether neuron-based representation can aid in visualizing the patterns and knowledge contained in a neural network. If this is the case, this could lead to future applications for interpretability.

References

1. Bacciu, D., Mandic, D.P.: Tensor decompositions in deep learning. In: Computational Intelligence, p. 10 (2020)
2. Chen, X., Cheng, X., Mallat, S.: Unsupervised Deep HAAR Scattering on Graphs. In: Advances in Neural Information Processing System, vol. 27. Curran Associates, Inc. (2014)
3. Chollet, F.: Xception: deep learning with depthwise separable convolutions. In: 2017 IEEE Conference on Computer Vision and Pattern Recognition (CVPR), pp. 1800–1807. IEEE, Honolulu, HI, July 2017. https://doi.org/10.1109/CVPR.2017.195
4. Coleman, C., et al.: DAWNBench: an end-to-end deep learning benchmark and competition. In: NIPS ML Systems Workshop, p. 10 (2017)
5. Das, A., Hossain, M.S., Muhammad Abdullah, S., Ul Islam, R.: Permutation free encoding technique for evolving neural networks. In: Sun, F., Zhang, J., Tan, Y., Cao, J., Yu, W. (eds.) ISNN 2008. LNCS, vol. 5263, pp. 255–265. Springer, Heidelberg (2008). https://doi.org/10.1007/978-3-540-87732-5_29
6. Deng, L., Li, G., Han, S., Shi, L., Xie, Y.: Model compression and hardware acceleration for neural networks: a comprehensive survey. Proc. IEEE **108**(4), 485–532 (2020). https://doi.org/10.1109/JPROC.2020.2976475
7. Devlin, J., Chang, M.W., Lee, K., Toutanova, K.: BERT: pre-training of deep bidirectional transformers for language understanding. In: Proceedings of the 2019 Conference of the North American Chapter of the Association for Computational Linguistics: Human Language Technologies, vol. 1 (Long and Short Papers), pp. 4171–4186. Association for Computational Linguistics, Minneapolis, Minnesota, June 2019. https://doi.org/10.18653/v1/N19-1423, https://www.aclweb.org/anthology/N19-1423
8. Dürr, P., Mattiussi, C., Floreano, D.: Neuroevolution with analog genetic encoding. In: Runarsson, T.P., Beyer, H.-G., Burke, E., Merelo-Guervós, J.J., Whitley, L.D., Yao, X. (eds.) PPSN 2006. LNCS, vol. 4193, pp. 671–680. Springer, Heidelberg (2006). https://doi.org/10.1007/11844297_68
9. Edwards, H., Storkey, A.: Towards a neural statistician. In: 5th International Conference on Learning Representations (ICLR 2017), pp. 1–13 (2017)
10. Eliasmith, C., Anderson, C.H.: Neural Engineering: Computation, Representation, and Dynamics in Neurobiological Systems. Computational Neuroscience Series, A Bradford Book, Cambridge, MA, USA, October 2002

11. Fukushima, K., Miyake, S.: Neocognitron: a self-organizing neural network model for a mechanism of visual pattern recognition. In: Amari, S., Arbib, M.A. (eds.) Competition and Cooperation in Neural Nets, vol. 45, pp. 267–285. Springer, Berlin (1982). https://doi.org/10.1007/978-3-642-46466-9_18

12. Gomez, F.J.: Robust Non-Linear Control through Neuroevolution. Ph.D. thesis, University of Texas at Austin, August 2003

13. Haase, D., Amthor, M.: Rethinking depthwise separable convolutions: how intra-kernel correlations lead to improved mobilenets. In: 2020 IEEE/CVF Conference on Computer Vision and Pattern Recognition (CVPR), pp. 14588–14597. IEEE, Seattle, WA, USA, June 2020. https://doi.org/10.1109/CVPR42600.2020.01461

14. Hausknecht, M., Khandelwal, P., Miikkulainen, R., Stone, P.: HyperNEAT-GGP: a hyperNEAT-based Atari general game player. In: Proceedings of the 14th Annual Conference on Genetic and Evolutionary Computation, pp. 217–224 (2012)

15. He, K., Zhang, X., Ren, S., Sun, J.: Deep residual learning for image recognition. In: 2016 IEEE Conference on Computer Vision and Pattern Recognition (CVPR), pp. 770–778, June 2016. https://doi.org/10.1109/CVPR.2016.90

16. Jaderberg, M., Vedaldi, A., Zisserman, A.: Speeding up convolutional neural networks with low rank expansions. In: Proceedings of the British Machine Vision Conference 2014, pp. 88.1–88.13. British Machine Vision Association, Nottingham (2014). https://doi.org/10.5244/C.28.88

17. Karaletsos, T., Dayan, P., Ghahramani, Z.: Probabilistic meta-representations of neural networks. arXiv:1810.00555, October 2018

18. Kiers, H.: Towards a standardized notation and terminology in multiway analysis. J. Chemometrics **14**, 105–122 (2000). https://doi.org/10.1002/1099-128X(200005/06)14:33.0.CO;2-I

19. Kingma, D.P., Ba, J.: Adam: a method for stochastic optimization. In: Bengio, Y., LeCun, Y. (eds.) 3rd International Conference on Learning Representations, ICLR 2015, San Diego, CA, USA, 7–9 May 2015, Conference Track Proceedings (2015)

20. Kolda, T.G., Bader, B.W.: Tensor decompositions and applications. SIAM Rev. **51**(3), 455–500 (2009). https://doi.org/10.1137/07070111X

21. Koutník, J., Cuccu, G., Schmidhuber, J., Gomez, F.: Evolving large-scale neural networks for vision-based reinforcement learning. In: Proceedings of the 15th Annual Conference on Genetic and Evolutionary Computation, pp. 1061–1068 (2013)

22. Krizhevsky, A.: Learning Multiple Layers of Features from Tiny Images. Technical Report TR-2009 (2009)

23. LeCun, Y., et al.: Backpropagation applied to handwritten zip code recognition. Neural Comput. **1**(4), 541–551 (1989)

24. LeCun, Y., Cortes, C., Burges, C.: MNIST handwritten digit database. ATT Labs. **7**, 6 (2010). http://yann.lecun.com/exdb/mnist

25. Lee, J., Lee, Y., Kim, J., Kosiorek, A., Choi, S., Teh, Y.W.: Set transformer: a framework for attention-based permutation-invariant neural networks. In: International Conference on Machine Learning, pp. 3744–3753. PMLR, May 2019

26. Moriarty, D.E., Mikkulainen, R.: Efficient reinforcement learning through symbiotic evolution. Mach. Learn. **22**(1), 11–32 (1996). https://doi.org/10.1023/A:1018004120707

27. Oseledets, I.: Tensor-train decomposition. SIAM J. Sci. Comput. **33**, 2295–2317 (2011). https://doi.org/10.1137/090752286

28. Page, D.: How to Train Your ResNet, September 2018

29. Paszke, A., et al.: Pytorch: an imperative style, high-performance deep learning library. arXiv preprint arXiv:1912.01703 (2019)

30. Reisinger, J., Miikkulainen, R.: Acquiring evolvability through adaptive representations. In: Proceedings of the 9th Annual Conference on Genetic and Evolutionary Computation - GECCO 2007, p. 1045. ACM Press, London, England (2007). https://doi.org/10.1145/1276958.1277164
31. Schmidhuber, J.: Discovering neural nets with low Kolmogorov complexity and high generalization capability. Neural Netw. **10**(5), 857–873 (1997)
32. Schmidhuber, J., Wierstra, D., Gagliolo, M., Gomez, F.: Training recurrent networks by Evolino. Neural Comput. **19**(3), 757–779 (2007). https://doi.org/10.1162/neco.2007.19.3.757
33. Smith, L.N.: A disciplined approach to neural network hyper-parameters: part 1-learning rate, batch size, momentum, and weight decay. arXiv preprint arXiv:1803.09820 (2018)
34. Smith, L.N., Topin, N.: Super-convergence: very fast training of neural networks using large learning rates. In: Artificial Intelligence and Machine Learning for Multi-Domain Operations Applications, vol. 11006, p. 1100612. International Society for Optics and Photonics (2019)
35. Stanley, K.O., Clune, J., Lehman, J., Miikkulainen, R.: Designing neural networks through neuroevolution. Nat. Mach. Intell. **1**(1), 24–35 (2019)
36. Stanley, K.O., D'Ambrosio, D.B., Gauci, J.: A hypercube-based encoding for evolving large-scale neural networks. Artif. Life **15**(2), 185–212 (2009)
37. Stanley, K.O., Miikkulainen, R.: Evolving neural networks through augmenting topologies. Evol. Comput. **10**(2), 99–127 (2002)
38. Stanley, K.O., Miikkulainen, R.: A taxonomy for artificial embryogeny. Artif. Life **9**(2), 93–130 (2003)
39. Tang, Y., Ha, D.: The Sensory Neuron as a Transformer: Permutation-Invariant Neural Networks for Reinforcement Learning. arXiv:2109.02869, September 2021
40. Tang, Y., Nguyen, D., Ha, D.: Neuroevolution of self-interpretable agents. In: Proceedings of the 2020 Genetic and Evolutionary Computation Conference, pp. 414–424 (2020)
41. Tucker, L.R.: Some mathematical notes on three-mode factor analysis. Psychometrika **31**(3), 279–311 (1966). https://doi.org/10.1007/BF02289464
42. Vaswani, A., et al.: Attention is all you need. In: Proceedings of the 31st International Conference on Neural Information Processing Systems, NIPS 2017, pp. 6000–6010. Curran Associates Inc., Red Hook, NY, USA, December 2017
43. Wang, Z., Liu, J.C.: Translating math formula images to latex sequences using deep neural networks with sequence-level training (2019)
44. Yu, X., Liu, T., Wang, X., Tao, D.: On compressing deep models by low rank and sparse decomposition. In: 2017 IEEE Conference on Computer Vision and Pattern Recognition (CVPR), pp. 67–76. IEEE, Honolulu, HI, July 2017. https://doi.org/10.1109/CVPR.2017.15
45. Zaheer, M., Kottur, S., Ravanbakhsh, S., Poczos, B., Salakhutdinov, R.R., Smola, A.J.: Deep sets. In: Advances in Neural Information Processing Systems, vol. 30. Curran Associates, Inc. (2017)

Author Index

Printed in the United States
by Baker & Taylor Publisher Services